Praise for *The Politics of Social Protection in Eastern and Southern Africa*

'Based on outstanding multi-country research programmes at Cape Town, Manchester and UNU-WIDER, the contributions collected in this volume skilfully lay bare the politics of social assistance in sub-Saharan Africa, and the research toolbox required to do so. The volume makes a huge contribution to our understanding of emerging welfare institutions in the region and will be indispensable reading for researchers and policy makers worldwide.'

ARMANDO BARRIENTOS
Professor Emeritus in Poverty and Social Justice,
University of Manchester

'The recent creation or expansion of programmes of social protection all across East and Southern Africa raises intriguing and important issues for scholars of the region's politics. This book, with its admirable combination of empirical substance and analytic clarity, is a landmark contribution to this new field. It will be a key point of reference for our discussions and debates for many years to come.'

JAMES FERGUSON
Stanford University

'Economists devote a large share of their time to analyse the technical aspects of tax and social policies, and not enough time to analyse the political context in which these policies are to be adopted, often with less-than-desirable results. This excellent book helps to redress that imbalance. Through various case studies in Eastern and Southern Africa, it shows why an understanding of the political and institutional context in which policies are to be applied is as important for development results as are the technicalities of the policies themselves.'

SANTIAGO LEVY
Senior Fellow, Brookings Institution

'Social protection research has been preoccupied with operational questions. How to improve programme design? How to build efficient systems? Do cash transfers work? Today researchers ask more fundamental questions. Where did social protection come from? How did cash transfers spread through Africa so rapidly? Which institutions promoted social protection, and why? This engaging book provides fascinating insights and answers to these important questions, drawing on in-depth analysis of social protection policy processes in eight African countries. An indispensable read for everyone interested in social policy.'

STEPHEN DEVEREUX
Institute of Development Studies, Brighton, and University of the
Western Cape, Cape Town

'The expansion of social protection systems requires a fundamental reconsideration of our understanding of social development. This book takes on this challenge, providing rich theoretical and empirical analyses of the political, ideational, economic and transnational forces shaping these important policy shifts. It will become a significant landmark in the study of social welfare policy and will greatly influence the next generation of research on social welfare and inclusive development in the Global South.'

SARAH M. BROOKS
Ohio State University

The Politics of Social Protection in Eastern and Southern Africa

Edited by

SAM HICKEY, TOM LAVERS,
MIGUEL NIÑO-ZARAZÚA,
JEREMY SEEKINGS

A study prepared for the World Institute for Development Economics Research of the United Nations University (UNU-WIDER)

OXFORD
UNIVERSITY PRESS

OXFORD
UNIVERSITY PRESS

Great Clarendon Street, Oxford, OX2 6DP,
United Kingdom

Oxford University Press is a department of the University of Oxford.
It furthers the University's objective of excellence in research, scholarship,
and education by publishing worldwide. Oxford is a registered trade mark of
Oxford University Press in the UK and in certain other countries

First Edition published in 2020

Published in the United States of America by Oxford University Press
198 Madison Avenue, New York, NY 10016, United States of America

British Library Cataloguing in Publication Data
Data available

Library of Congress Control Number: 2019909011

ISBN 978–0–19–885034–2

DOI: 10.1093/oso/9780198850342.003.0001

Foreword

Since the mid-1990s there has been something of a quiet revolution in poverty reduction strategies with the proliferation and expansion of social assistance programmes that entail direct cash or in-kind transfers to the poor. While different studies define social assistance—and social protection more broadly—in different ways and use different data, generating different estimates of their coverage or reach, they concur that coverage has expanded dramatically across the global South. The beginning of this century has well witnessed a series of important political and political economy developments that have reshaped both state–society relations and the South's relationship with transnational actors and ideas.

To get a better understanding of this unfolding revolution with reforming government policy strategies, in early 2016 UNU-WIDER launched the research project The Political Economy of Social Protection in Developing Countries, using an innovative and integrated approach to the study of taxation and social protection systems in developing countries, with a strong focus on southern and eastern African countries. Taking a system-wide perspective allows for the exploration of the combined fiscal effect of tax and benefit reforms, in terms of resource mobilization, economic efficiency, and distributional impact. Social protection has emerged as a key policy strategy against poverty and vulnerability in many developing countries, and it has evolved into a wide number of different forms in terms of focus and targeting population, coverage, scope, and design features, with some programmes providing income transfers alone, while others combine income transfers with the utilization of social services and assets.

This book before the reader is the distillation of this research project. I am grateful to the book's authors for their scholarly contributions, and sincerely thank the editors for their analytical and editorial skills in bringing this wide and layered research work together for the essential reading of economists, policy makers, and development scholars.

UNU-WIDER gratefully acknowledges the support and financial contributions to its research programme by the governments of Finland, Sweden, in this case particularly the Swedish International Development Cooperation Agency—Sida, and the United Kingdom. Without this vital funding our research and policy advisory work would be impossible.

Kunal Sen
Director, UNU-WIDER
Helsinki, March 2019

Acknowledgements

This book is the outcome of collaborative work between three large research undertakings: the UNU-WIDER project The Economics and Politics of Taxation and Social Protection, the Cape Town-based programme Legislating and Implementing Welfare Policy Reforms (LIWPR), and the Manchester-based Politics of Social Protection project, which is part of the broader Effective States and Inclusive Development (ESID) Research Centre. We are grateful for the financial support from DFID (the UK's Department for International Development), the ESRC (Economic and Social Research Council), and UNU-WIDER. LIWPR was funded by DFID (UKAid) and the ESRC through their Joint Fund for Poverty Alleviation, award ES/J018058/1.

We owe our gratitude to many people who have been engaged through these individual research programmes, and at different stages, in developing and bringing this book to its successful conclusion. We would like to thank in particular Lorraine Telfer-Taivainen, UNU-WIDER's publications manager, for her outstanding editorial support that guided this book through to its successful completion.

A project meeting was held in Mexico City, on 8–10 February 2016. We are grateful to participants at the meeting (many of whom later contributed chapters to this book) for their ideas, comments, and suggestions on early drafts of papers. In particular, we want to thank Verónica Amarante, Camila Arza, Christine Awiti, Kaushik Basu, Juan Bogliaccini, Badru Bukenya, Carla Canelas, Lidia Ceriani, Blessing Chiripanhura, Silvio Daidone, Jason Davis, Marina Dodlova, Dragan Filipovich, Ira Gang, Selene Ghisolfi, Anna Giolbas, Björn Jahnke, Sanjay Jain, Petr Jansky, Takaaki Masaki, Hiroaki Matsuura, Paul Mosley, Christophe Muller, Mansoob Murshed, Kate Pruce, Thomas Roca, Nita Rudra, Belen Saenz de Miera Juarez, Yeasmin Sayeed, Nora Strecker, Victoria Tenenbaum, and Fredrick Wanyama.

The contributions from ESID were strongly informed by numerous engagements with academic and policy communities, including at successive Development Studies Association conferences and with many policy actors involved in promoting social protection. Particular thanks are due to Armando Barrientos for his inspiration and critical guidance, to many ESID colleagues and associates for their support and encouragement, particularly Kunal Sen,

David Hulme, and Anna McCord, and to the numerous colleagues beyond ESID who provided peer reviews of earlier versions of what are now this book's chapters. We are also grateful to Julia Brunt, Kat Bethell, Julie Rafferty, and Clare Degenhardt for their expert organizational guidance in seeing the project through to conclusion.

Adam Swallow at Oxford University Press gave us very useful advice in shaping and organizing the book for publication. The constructive suggestions of OUP's anonymous peer reviewers also helped improve the book in several ways.

Our contributing authors dealt with our demands and numerous editorial requests with great patience and have provided us with excellent co-operation throughout the editorial process. Together they have contributed with their very diverse source of wisdom, experience, and insight. We have been very fortunate to have been able to collaborate with such an outstanding team and we thank them most sincerely for their hard work, commitment to this project, and assistance in bringing this collection to publication.

Last but not least, we thank our families, and in particular Ixchel Niño-Piiparinen, Michael, Jesse, and Noah Hickey, Shea McClanahan, and Alice and Arthur Lavers, for their support, encouragement, and patience during many days of absence, and often working late hours that were required to bring this book to successful completion.

Sam Hickey, Tom Lavers, Miguel Niño-Zarazúa, and Jeremy Seekings
March 2019

Contents

List of Figures

List of Tables

List of Abbreviations

ABC	All Basotho Convention
ADLI	Agricultural Development-Led Industrialization
AFORD	Alliance for Democracy
AISP	Agricultural Input Subsidy Programme
ANC	African National Congress
AUSPF	African Union Social Policy Framework
BCP	Basutoland Congress Party
BDP	Botswana Democratic Party
BNF	Botswana National Front
BPP	Botswana People's Party
CB-CCT	community-based conditional cash transfer
CBHI	Community-Based Health Insurance
CCM	Chama Cha Mapinduzi
CCT	conditional cash transfer
CDF	Common Development Fund
CGP	child grant programme
CIDA	Canadian International Development Agency
CSO	civil society organization
DAC	Development Assistance Committee
DFID	Department for International Development
DPP	Democratic Progressive Party
DRC	Democratic Republic of Congo
EDPRS	Economic Development and Poverty Reduction Strategy
EICV	Integrated Household Survey on Living Conditions (Enquête Intégrale sur les Conditions de Vie des ménages)
EPRDF	Ethiopian Peoples' Revolutionary Democratic Front
EPRI	Economic Policy Research Institute
EPRP	Ethiopian People's Revolutionary Party
ESID	Effective States and Inclusive Development
ESP	Expanding Social Protection
ESRC	Economic and Social Research Council
FAO	Food and Agriculture Organization
FARG	Genocide Survivors Support and Assistance Fund (Fond d'Assistance aux Rescapes du Genocide)
FISP	Farmer Input Support Programme (Zambia)
FISP	Farm Input Subsidy Programme (Malawi)

FRA	Food Reserve Agency
FSP	Food Security Programme
FYDP	Five-Year Development Plan
GDP	gross domestic product
GNI	gross national income
GNU	Government of National Unity
GoL	Government of Lesotho
GTP	Growth and Transformation Plan
GTZ	German Development Agency (Gesellschaft für Technische Zusammenarbeit)
IFI	international financial institution
ILO	International Labour Organization
IMF	International Monetary Fund
PDL-HIMO	Labour-Intensive Local Development Programme (Programme de Développement Local à Haute Intensité de Main d'Œuvre)
LCD	Lesotho Congress for Democracy
LIWPR	Legislating and Implementing Welfare Policy Reforms
LODA	Local Administrative Entities Development Agency
MASAF	Malawi Social Action Fund
MCDMCH	Ministry of Community Development, Mother and Child Health
MCP	Malawi Congress Party
MFPED	Ministry of Finance, Planning and Economic Development
MGLSD	Ministry of Gender, Labour and Social Development
MHSDMU	Medicines and Health Services Delivery Monitoring Unit
MINADEF	Ministry of Defence
MINALOC	Ministry of Local Government
MINECOFIN	Ministry of Finance and Economic Planning
MININFRA	Ministry of Infrastructure
MMD	Movement for Multiparty Democracy
MMP	mixed member proportional
MoH	Ministry of Health
MSEs	Micro and Small Enterprises
MTEF	Medium-Term Expenditure Framework
MTT	*Mudzi* (Village) Transformation Trust
MWSCA	Maseru Women's Senior Citizens Association
NDP	national development plan
NGO	non-governmental organization
NHIS	national health insurance scheme
NIP	National Independence Party
NISSA	National Information System for Social Assistance
NPO	non-profit organization
NRM	National Resistance Movement
NSPP	National Social Protection Policy

NSPS	National Social Protection Strategy
NSSF	National Social Security Fund
OAP	old-age pension
OCP	Orphan Care Programme
ODA	official development assistance
OECD	Organisation for Economic Co-operation and Development
OVC	orphans and vulnerable children
P4H	Providing for Health
PASDEP	Plan for Accelerated and Sustained Development to End Poverty
PF	Patriotic Front
PIPaHR	Presidential Initiative on Poverty and Hunger Reduction
POVNET	Network on Poverty Reduction
PP	People's Party
PPP	purchasing power parity
PRSP	Poverty Reduction Strategy Paper
PSNP	Productive Safety Net Programme
PSSN	Productive Social Safety Net
PWAS	Public Welfare Assistance Scheme
RANU	Rwandese Alliance for National Unity
RCT	randomized controlled trial
RDRC	Rwanda Demobilization and Reintegration Commission
REPOA	Research on Poverty Alleviation
REPSSI	Regional Psychosocial Support Initiative
REST	Relief Society of Tigray
RLDSF	Rwandan Local Development Support Fund
RPF	Rwanda Patriotic Front
RtVP	Reaching the Very Poorest
SACU	Southern African Customs Union
SADC	South African Development Community
SAGE	Social Assistance Grants for Empowerment
SAPI	Social Assistance, Politics and Institutions
SCG	senior citizen's grant
SCT	social cash transfer
SHI	social health insurance
SIDA	Swedish International Development Agency
SSA	sub-Saharan Africa
SSRA	Social Security Regulatory Authority
TASAF	Tanzania Social Action Fund
TGE	Transitional Government of Ethiopia
TPLF	Tigrayan People's Liberation Front
UDF	United Democratic Front
UNDP	United Nations Development Programme
UNIP	United National Independence Party

UNRISD	United Nations Research Institute for Social Development
UNU-WIDER	UNU World Institute for Development Economics Research
UPND	United Party for National Development
USAID	United States Agency for International Development
VUP	Vision 2020 Umurenge Programme
WB	World Bank
WFP	World Food Programme

Notes on Contributors

Badru Bukenya is a Uganda-based academic, policy analyst, and development practitioner. He is currently a lecturer in the Department of Social Work and Social Administration, Makerere University, Kampala. His research focuses on development more broadly and specifically on the politics of social protection, health service delivery, public sector reforms, children and youth, and state–civil society engagement. He is the co-editor of *The Politics of Inclusive Development* (OUP, 2015) and his work has been published in leading development studies journals.

Maria Granvik Saminathen is a doctoral candidate in public health at the Centre for Health Equity Studies, Department of Public Health Sciences, Stockholm University. She holds a master's degree in development studies from the University of Cape Town. The Lesotho study was conducted while employed at the Centre for Social Science Research at the University of Cape Town. Her current research is focused on the effect of the school context and sociodemographic school segregation on adolescents' psychological wellbeing.

Sam Hamer has degrees from Yale (2014) and the University of Cape Town (2016).

Sam Hickey is a professor of politics and development in the Global Development Institute, University of Manchester, and Research Director of the Effective States and Inclusive Development Research Centre. His work on the politics of development has been published in *African Affairs*, *Journal of Development Studies*, and *World Development*. He has edited eight collections, most recently *The Politics of Inclusive Development* (OUP 2015, with Kunal Sen and Badru Bukenya), *The Politics of Negotiating Gender Equity in the Global South* (Routledge 2019, with Sohela Nazneen and Eleni Sifaki), and *The Politics of Education in Developing Countries* (OUP 2019, with Naomi Hossain).

Tom Lavers is a senior lecturer at the Global Development Institute at the University of Manchester. His research focuses on the political economy of development with a focus on land, agrarian transformation, employment, and social policy. He has published in leading journals in agrarian studies, development studies, and African studies.

Miguel Niño-Zarazúa is a development economist and former research fellow at UNU-WIDER where he led the research programme on fiscal policy and social protection in developing countries. His research is in the microeconomics and political economy of welfare benefit systems and anti-poverty programmes in developing countries. Miguel has published extensively in development economics and development studies journals and edited several special issues in leading academic journals.

Miguel is Associate Editor and Member of the Editorial Advisory Board of the *Journal of International Development*.

Kate Pruce is a PhD candidate at the University of Manchester's Global Development Institute and a researcher with the Effective States and Inclusive Development research centre. Kate's research is on the politics of global policy transfer, examining the case of social cash transfers in Zambia. Her research interests also include the comparative political economy of social protection adoption, expansion, and implementation in low- and middle-income countries.

Jeremy Seekings is a professor of political studies and sociology at the University of Cape Town, and visiting professor at Yale. He led a research programme on Legislating and Implementing Welfare Policy Reforms at the University of Cape Town. His most recent books (both co-authored with Nicoli Nattrass) were *Policy, Politics and Poverty in South Africa* (2015) and *Inclusive Dualism: Labour-Intensive Development, Decent Work, and Surplus Labour in Southern Africa* (2019).

Marianne S. Ulriksen works at the Danish Centre for Welfare Studies (DaWS), Department of Political Science, University of Southern Denmark, and is associated with the Centre for Social Development in Africa (CSDA), University of Johannesburg. Her research areas include comparative politics, political economy of welfare policy development, social protection, social justice, poverty and inequality, and resource mobilization and taxation. Her research work focuses primarily on southern and eastern Africa.

1

The Negotiated Politics of Social Protection in East and Southern Africa

Sam Hickey, Tom Lavers, Miguel Niño-Zarazúa, and Jeremy Seekings

1. Introduction

Since the mid-1990s there has been something of a 'quiet revolution' in poverty reduction strategies with the proliferation and expansion of social assistance programmes that entail direct cash or in-kind transfers to the poor (Hanlon et al. 2010). While different studies define social assistance (and social protection more broadly) in different ways and use different data, generating different estimates of their coverage or reach, they concur that coverage or reach have expanded dramatically across the global South, including in sub-Saharan Africa (SSA). These past two decades have also been characterized by a series of important political and political economy developments that have reshaped both state–society relations within SSA and its relationship with transnational actors and ideas. In this introductory chapter we argue that the (uneven) expansion of social assistance has to be seen in this context rather than as read off from general indicators of economic or political development. These developments include highly contested processes of democratization, often involving a (re)assertion of clientelistic and sometimes authoritarian forms of governance, and processes of deagrarianization that continue to transform rural livelihoods in particular.

The nature of Africa's engagement with external forces has in some cases been transformed by the declining influence of traditional aid actors vis-à-vis 'rising powers', new natural resource finds, and the changing nature of international debt. In the evidence and analysis offered in this book, we show how the process through which social protection has been promoted, contested,

Sam Hickey, Tom Lavers, Miguel Niño-Zarazúa, and Jeremy Seekings, *The Negotiated Politics of Social Protection in Eastern and Southern Africa* In: *The Politics of Social Protection in Eastern and Southern Africa*. Edited by: Sam Hickey, Tom Lavers, Miguel Niño-Zarazúa, and Jeremy Seekings, Oxford University Press (2020).

DOI: 10.1093/oso/9780198850342.003.0001

and rolled out closely reflects the *negotiated* character of statehood in Africa (Hagmann and Péclard 2011), both in terms of the heavily transnationalized nature of governance in SSA and also as part of a bargaining process between rulers and ruled, whereby concerns with electoral success, legitimacy, and popular pressures are increasingly influential over budgetary allocations and welfare provision.

We argue that African political agency has played a powerful role in the contested expansion of social protection, with the countries that reveal the highest levels of commitment to social protection driven more by domestic political imperatives than by external pressure. Importantly, this process has been strongly informed not only by global influences and elite-level machinations but also by the historical character of welfare regimes in the region, particularly in terms of long-standing ideas around deservingness and the role of the state in the context of ongoing processes of deagrarianization (Lavers 2013; Seekings forthcoming).

1.1. Tracking the rise of social assistance in east and southern Africa

Definitional debates abound regarding the scope and appropriateness of related but distinct terms such as social assistance, social protection, and social safety nets. While acknowledging the importance of these debates and associated terminology, our primary focus here is on state social assistance programmes that provide support in cash or in-kind to households and/or individuals as a means of addressing poverty, vulnerability, or food insecurity. Such schemes are commonly financed through a combination of taxes and development assistance, rather than direct financial contributions from programme participants. As such, our cases include examples of programmes such as old-age pensions and family allowances that provide income support to vulnerable groups to smooth consumption and mitigate the effects of shocks; programmes such as conditional cash transfers that provide income support to households together with incentives for the utilization of health and education services; and workfare (or public works programmes), especially where such programmes provide something close to an employment guarantee. Social assistance, as defined here, is one component of the broader concept of social protection, which, according to most definitions, also includes social insurance and labour market regulation. In contemporary Africa, it is social assistance that predominates within broader debates over social protection (Niño-Zarazúa et al. 2012; World Bank 2018; Seekings forthcoming).

The widespread agreement that social assistance has expanded rapidly across the global South can be demonstrated with data from various sources, including the International Labour Organization (ILO 2017), World Bank (2017b), and also the most recent Social Assistance, Politics and Institutions (SAPI) database (UNU-WIDER 2018).[1] To illustrate, SAPI suggests that, globally, nearly 900 million people currently benefit, directly or indirectly, from social assistance (UNU-WIDER 2018). African countries lag behind other parts of the global South. The SAPI database counts more than 60 million people—about 15 per cent of the population living in extreme poverty[2]—currently receiving a cash transfer through a total of eighty-six programmes in thirty-seven countries (see Table 1.A1 in the Appendix).[3] The number of countries with social assistance programmes has risen, largely driven by a growing number of public works and family allowances, but also old-age pensions, and cash transfers for human development (see Figure 1.1), although the combined reach of these programmes has risen more modestly. 'Coverage' rates and public expenditure might be lower in Africa than in some other parts of the global South (ILO 2017; World Bank 2017b), at least by some definitions of social assistance, but social assistance is very clearly on the agenda of many African countries.

Africa is far from homogeneous. There is considerable variation in how and the extent to which social assistance (and social protection more generally) has evolved in SSA. Africa has the highest effective coverage (as measured by the ILO) at 48 per cent of the population (ILO 2017: table B.3), with its system of social assistance costing close to 4 per cent of gross domestic product (GDP). In stark contrast, other countries have small and less generous programmes targeted at the extremely poor. Few countries have coverage rates (as measured by the ILO) above 10 per cent, and expenditure on social assistance is often less than 0.5 per cent of GDP (ILO 2017). It is unlikely, however, that any country has no programme. Even in countries across the Sahel and Horn of Africa, with weak or failed states, non-governmental organizations (NGOs) and quasi-state

[1] The SAPI database provides a synthesis of longitudinal and comparable information on: (i) social assistance programmes, (ii) country-level information on economic and social performance, and (iii) political institutions in developing countries; see UNU-WIDER (2018).

[2] Calculations based on the share of the population living on less than US$1.90 a day at 2011 purchasing power parity, as defined by the World Bank (2017a).

[3] Estimates based on a typology described in Barrientos and Niño-Zarazúa (2010).

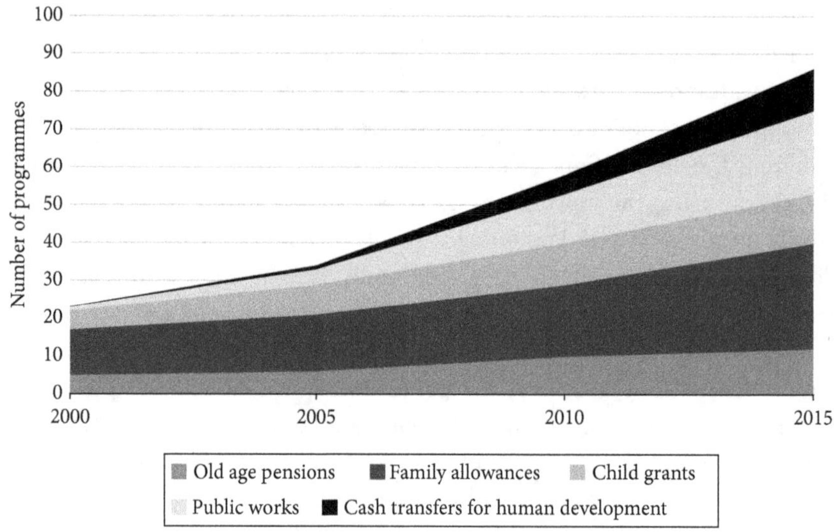

Fig. 1.1. The recent evolution of social assistance in sub-Saharan Africa by type of programme.

Source: Authors' illustration based on UNU-WIDER's (2018) Social Assistance Politics and Institutions database (SAPI).

institutions operate feeding and food or cash-for-work programmes (see Osofisan 2011). According to one recent review (ODI 2016), forty of the forty-eight countries in SSA now have at least one social assistance programme, a doubling since 2010.

The chapters in this book examine how and why social assistance programmes have expanded, at different paces and to different extents, across a set of countries in east and southern Africa. The case studies are based on research conducted as part of two research programmes based at the Universities of Cape Town and Manchester. Both the Cape Town-based programme on 'Legislating and Implementing Welfare Policy Reforms' (LIWPR) and the Manchester-based 'Politics of Social Protection' project, which is part of the broader Effective States and Inclusive Development (ESID) research centre, were funded by the British Department for International Development (DFID), the former jointly through the UK's Economic and Social Research Council. The UNU-WIDER project on 'The Economics and Politics of Taxation and Social Protection' helped bring the two projects together, including through a symposium held in Mexico City in February 2016, providing the impetus and resourcing for this book.[4]

[4] For more on these three research initiatives, see IDCPPA (n.d.), ESID (www.effective-states.org), and UNU-WIDER (n.d.).

These initiatives shared a concern that SSA remains largely 'off the map' of the growing global literature on social protection and welfare state-building, and that African cases do not fit well into existing global typologies or explanations. The vast majority of research on social protection in Africa, mostly commissioned by aid donors, has had an overwhelmingly technical focus, concerned with issues such as measuring the welfare impacts of particular programmes, examining how best to design targeting and delivery systems, and assessing the degree of fiscal space for policy reform. In contrast, the studies conducted for the ESID and LIWPR programmes, some of which are included in this book, focused on the politics of policy reform (and non-reform). The research teams used process-tracing methods to identify the key drivers of government decisions either to reject proposed reforms or to adopt or expand social assistance programmes (George and Bennett 2004; Collier 2011). Documents from states and international organizations provided an important frame, but the most important sources were key interviews with actors involved in negotiating social assistance within country contexts. The resulting case studies offer detailed accounts of how contested processes of policy reform played out over time in relation to wider political and political economy developments. The chapters focus on eight cases, with a ninth chapter focusing on one of the major international organizations immersed in reforms in many of these cases.

The eight countries—Botswana, Ethiopia, Lesotho, Malawi, Rwanda, Tanzania, Uganda, and Zambia—vary in most general economic and political dimensions (see Table 1.1) as well as in the particulars of their social assistance systems (see Table 1.A1 in the Appendix). While none are in west Africa, and all are broadly anglophone, they encompass much of the diversity of cases across SSA. They include a country with high GDP per capita, very little official development assistance (ODA), little agricultural employment, and low absolute poverty (Botswana) as well as low-income countries with massive ODA, considerable agricultural employment, and high poverty rates (especially Malawi). Some of the countries have small populations (especially Botswana and Lesotho); one has a very large population (Ethiopia). Some (Botswana, Lesotho, Zambia, and Malawi) were credibly democratic as of 2015, whilst others remained far from being so (Rwanda, Ethiopia, Uganda).

Our eight case studies also encompass much of the variation that exists across SSA in terms of social assistance programmes. They include countries with widespread pension and other cash transfer programmes (Botswana, Lesotho), countries that have been slowly expanding pilot programmes (Malawi, Uganda, Zambia), and countries with a stronger emphasis on

Table 1.1 Economic and political conditions in the country case studies

Country	GDP per capita (US$, 2016)	Population (millions, 2016)	Poverty rate (%, year)[1]	Agricultural work (%, 2016)[2]	Net ODA as % of government expenditure[3]	Quality of democracy (2016)[4]
Botswana	6,924	2	18 (2009)	26	2	8
Ethiopia	707	102	34 (2010)	71	96	−2
Lesotho	1,040	2	60 (2010)	40	32	8
Malawi	300	18	71 (2010)	70	88	6
Rwanda	703	12	60 (2013)	75	76	−3
Tanzania	879	56	49 (2011)	67	27	3
Uganda	580	41	35 (2012)	72	47	−1
Zambia	1,270	17	58 (2015)	55	33	7

Note: [1] Poverty rate measured as share of population with incomes below US$1.90 per person per day at 2011 prices, purchasing power parity (PPP).
[2] Employment in agriculture as % of total employment.
[3] Net official development assistance received by countries as % of central government expenditure.
[4] Polity IV scale from -10 for fully authoritarian to +10 for fully democratic.
Source: Authors' compilation based on World Development Indicators (World Bank 2017a) and the Polity IV database (Center for Systemic Peace 2016).

workfare (Ethiopia, Rwanda, Tanzania). The case studies do not include, however, the former settler states of South Africa and Namibia, or the Indian Ocean island-state of Mauritius. The welfare states of South Africa (and hence its former quasi-colony, Namibia) and Mauritius long predate those of other countries across SSA (Seekings 2007, 2011; Ulriksen 2012). South African and Mauritian cash transfer programmes influenced the design of programmes elsewhere in Africa (directly in the case of Mauritius and Zanzibar (Seekings 2016b); more indirectly in the case of South Africa and its neighbours, as the case studies of Lesotho and Botswana below indicate). Nor does the book consider the countries of west or north Africa.

While our focus is on the politics of whether and how social assistance programmes become adopted, this cannot be understood independently of the broader character of the economy and public policy, or what has been called the 'distributional regime' (Seekings and Nattrass 2005). In countries across Africa, 'who gets what' depends on both the 'market' distribution and the pattern of redistribution effected (directly and indirectly) through public policy. Across most of SSA, policy makers face choices not only between what interests to promote but also what policies to prioritize. Crucially, even those policy makers committed to improving the welfare of the poor must choose how to allocate scarce resources between subsidizing aspects of peasant production (through, for example, fertilizer subsidies or free seed) and social assistance to poor households. In many countries, including (most clearly)

Botswana and Ethiopia, current social assistance measures have their origins in 'emergency' drought relief. Protecting citizens against the risk of drought led to workfare and feeding programmes, and later other cash transfers. In these countries, social assistance expanded as the limits to agrarian strategies became clearer. In other cases, however, the agrarian option remains credible and politically appealing. In both Malawi and Zambia, social assistance has been sidelined by governments' preference for fertilizer subsidies. Social assistance has become important in Africa when and where the prior agrarian distributional regime has broken down.

2. The Changing Literature on Welfare State-Building and African Cases

The global study of the drivers of social protection—or welfare state-building—has gone through at least four phases, applied primarily to the advanced capitalist economies of the global North (Hicks and Esping-Andersen 2005; Castles et al. 2010). Welfare state-building was first viewed as driven by economic modernization, which drove political and demographic change (Wilensky 1975). From the 1980s this approach was superseded by one focusing on 'power resources', i.e. the distributional struggles between competing interest groups. This approach focused on the political power wielded by the major classes and the ensuing class conflicts and compromises characteristic of capitalist democracies (especially Korpi 1983; Esping-Andersen 1990, 1999; Huber and Stephens 2001). Esping-Andersen's (1990) seminal contribution revolved around his insight that welfare regimes varied in form separately to their level of commitment. Scholars of the USA criticized this approach for its neglect of political institutions (e.g. Amenta et al. 2001). By the mid-2000s, a concern with the role of ideas and norms had expanded from historical case studies to a more general engagement with cross-national variation (e.g. Béland 2005; van Oorschot et al. 2008) and transnational diffusion (e.g. Obinger et al. 2013).

The more recent study of countries across the global South has been influenced strongly by the power resources approach focused on the political economy. Haggard and Kaufman (2008) show in their comparative study of Latin America, East Asia, and Central and Eastern Europe that strong regional differences persist even when controlling, in regression models, for various measures of economic modernization or development. They explain inter-regional variation in terms of differences in periods of critical realignment—'the composition of the political elite and in the political and legal status of labor and peasant organizations and mass political parties' (Haggard and Kaufman 2008: 45). Similar arguments have been made with respect to Latin America, in both comparative studies of this one region (Pribble 2011; Huber and Stephens 2012) and case studies of individual countries within it (e.g. Dion 2010), and East Asia (e.g. Yang 2017). Recently, a similar political economy approach has been used to explain variation between Indian states (e.g. Tillin et al. 2015).

The literature has little to say about Africa. Indeed, one early study emphasized the supposed absence of welfare states in Africa (Bevan 2004). Recent reviews have pointed to key and distinctive features of African cases: a historically rooted emphasis on social assistance for a predominantly rural population rather than social insurance for formally employed public sector and industrial workers; the importance of rural and agrarian rather than urban and industrial risks, and of the challenges of deagrarianization; and the important role played by transnational actors in combination with domestic actors (Hickey 2008; Niño-Zarazúa et al. 2012; Lavers 2013; Seekings 2013, forthcoming; Lavers and Hickey 2016). Until now there have been few detailed studies of individual countries that allow for analysis of either specific policy outcomes or overall variation within Africa. The case studies presented in this book provide a rich and novel base for analysing variation within Africa, as well as the distinctiveness of Africa in relation to other regions across the global South.

In explaining varied policy outcomes, the case studies conducted at ESID and LIWPR have employed slightly different approaches. The ESID studies have been influenced strongly by the literature on 'political settlements' in the global South, an approach with marked parallels with the 'power constellations' approaches to explaining variation between welfare states in the global North (Lavers and Hickey 2016). The LIWPR studies have attached more importance to the political institutions—especially political parties and elections—that characterize much of Africa since (re)democratization in the 1990s. The two approaches reflect in part the selection of cases in each research programme. The ESID research covered three distinctly undemocratic or only weakly democratic countries (Ethiopia, Rwanda, and Uganda) as well as two more competitive democracies (Zambia and Kenya).[5] The LIWPR research also covered the minimally democratic case of Uganda, but focused

[5] ESID has more recently conducted studies of social assistance in Ghana, Mozambique, Senegal, Sierra Leone, and Tanzania.

primarily on more competitive democracies (including, in addition to Zambia, Ghana, and Kenya, the cases of Botswana, Zimbabwe, Malawi, Tanzania (and Zanzibar), Lesotho, South Africa, and Mauritius). In practice, the two research programmes broadly converged, paying attention to both political economic and more specifically political factors, including a strong focus on the role of ideas, even if they arrived there from somewhat different starting points.

'Political settlements' can be defined as 'a combination of power and institutions that is mutually compatible, and also sustainable in terms of economic and political viability' (Khan 2010: 4). The analytical focus of political settlement theory is on the power relations between political, economic, and social elites; between these elites and non-elite groups; and how this distribution of power both shapes and is shaped by the formal and informal institutions that distribute resources and political power. From this perspective, social protection is a resource whose distribution is subject to competition and negotiation and which is shaped by the survival strategies of political elites. The power resources literature in the global North focused on class struggles and coalition building in the context of relatively developed capitalist markets and functioning representative democracies. Countries across the global South tend to have much less developed capitalist markets and weak or no democratic political institutions. The political settlements approach has thus considered other forms of political incorporation and mobilization, including along ethnic and regional lines or through patron–client relationships, and highlights the importance of informal as well as formal political institutions.

Studies by ESID have gone beyond Khan (2010, 2017), however, in emphasizing, first, that political settlements do not merely reflect the balance of power between interest groups but are also held together by common ideas that provide a shared understanding between the factions party to a political settlement (Lavers and Hickey 2016). These ideas can take many different forms such as nationalism, developmentalism, socialism, or opposition to communism (Hickey et al. 2015; Lavers 2018). It is useful here to distinguish between three types of idea: *policy ideas* that provide potential solutions to predefined social problems; *problem definitions* that provide ways of framing particular social issues, favouring certain types of policy solution over others; and *paradigms* or political philosophies that serve as overarching road maps (Béland 2005: 8; Schmidt 2008). Second, in a context in which donors continue to finance a significant portion of central government expenditure, although with significant variation across countries (see Figure 1.1), the domestic focus of political settlements theory must be complemented by an acknowledgement of the transnationalized nature of governance in contemporary Africa (Hagmann and Péclard 2011; Hickey et al. 2015). Foreign donors operate as a distinct faction (or factions) within political settlements whose power and influence do not simply follow from the importance of the resources they provide and the ideas they promote but, vitally, depend on the evolution of aid relations over years and the strategies African governments have derived to manage these donors (Whitfield 2009; Lavers and Hickey 2016). Third, the term 'political settlement' unfortunately and misleadingly implies that politics remains settled or static following a 'settlement'. While political settlements imply a degree of institutional stability over the short to medium term, they are inherently dynamic (Behuria et al. 2017), transformed not only through economic growth and financial or other shocks, but also as a result of political challenges posed by groups previously excluded from political power. The ensuing processes of change can be either slow and gradual, or rapid and transformative.

There are a number of ways in which the political settlement may shape the evolution of social protection. The resources provided through social protection can be an important part of the distributive bargain that underpins stability of the political settlement itself. In South Africa, relatively generous social transfers to a broad section of the population have become an integral part of the post-apartheid distributive bargain, compensating the mostly unskilled, unemployed, and poor population for an economic growth path that is capital- and skill-intensive (Seekings and Nattrass 2005, 2015). Even where social protection does not yet constitute a sufficiently large resource to be considered a central component of the political settlement itself, social protection policy-making is still likely to be shaped by the incentives generated by the settlement and the dominant ideas of ruling elites.

In country after country across SSA, over a single generation, one-party states, life presidents, and authoritarian regimes have given way to term limits, multi-party elections, and the ousting of presidents and parties through electoral defeat (Carbone 2013; Cheeseman 2015). In the eight countries studied, four have experienced government turnovers following electoral defeat (thrice in Lesotho, twice in each of Zambia and Malawi, and once in Kenya). In a fifth case (Botswana), the incumbent party has won several elections by narrow margins (as is the case in Zanzibar, part of Tanzania). Even in Uganda, elections have prompted an authoritarian president to adopt popular reforms (e.g. Stasavage 2005).

Competitive elections shift the incentives facing political elites, who can choose to use social protection policy as a material or ideological resource to win or retain electoral support. Political elites may be unable to retain power solely through the distribution of rents within the elite, and instead must reach out to voters through promises to distribute resources (van de Walle 2007, 2014). In SSA, as in Latin America previously, there has been some 'democratisation of clientelism' (Gay 1998). Recent research suggests that democracy has been a key factor in public health and education reforms (Carbone 2012; Kudamatsu 2012; Harding and Stasavage 2013; Carbone and Pellegata 2017).

The quality of democracy in contemporary Africa remains very uneven, however. Not only do incumbents often ensure that the 'democratic' playing field is not level, but political parties in SSA tend to be vehicles for patronage politics rather than programmatic reform. Few parties have a strong organizational base. Some have no clear ideological position. Many political parties have remained the highly personalized vehicles for the career advancement of individual politicians, while politics becomes a competition to build sufficiently broad ethnic or regional coalitions to secure electoral majorities (van de Walle 2014; Cheeseman 2015). Patronage and clientelism remain the dominant political practices in many parts of SSA (Cheeseman 2016). The flaws are evident even in the sample of eight countries examined in the book, which cover the full range of possibilities along the democracy–authoritarian continuum (see Table 1.1) (Levitsky and Way 2010; Bogaards and Elischer 2016).

The case studies in this book examine the interactions between different actors over policy reforms while locating these in a broader analysis of the underlying character of politics—i.e. the political settlement—in each country. The case studies examine how the efforts of transnational actors to promote particular forms of social assistance through a combination of ideational influence and financial leverage intersect with domestic political processes in particular national contexts. Here, the degree to which donor policy ideas fit with the incentives provided by particular political settlements and democratic competition is a vital consideration. Likewise, the ability of social protection advocates to forge coherent coalitions of transnational actors, politicians, bureaucrats, and civil society representatives, and, vitally, how these relate to influential figures within the settlement, have an important bearing on social protection policy-making.

3. Transnational Actors and Policy Diffusion

Perhaps the most immediately striking aspect of the policy-making process in SSA is the prominence of transnational actors, international finance organizations, national aid donor agencies, and international NGOs. As previous studies have emphasized, transnational actors have been highly influential in policy reform across much of Africa (Devereux 2010; Cherrier 2014). All major international agencies involved in development have now adopted a commitment to social protection, and social protection is explicitly included in the Sustainable Development Goals, as Hickey and Seekings discuss in Chapter 10.

Transnational actors have diverse approaches. The World Bank, for example, has promoted the Latin American model of 'conditional' cash transfers primarily for families with poor children into SSA, together with workfare programmes (Peck and Theodore 2015). The ILO has promoted both the expansion of social insurance and social assistance. HelpAge International has promoted universal social pensions, while the UK's DFID has tended to promote means-tested but otherwise social assistance. The World Food Programme has promoted workfare programmes as a substitute for direct feeding schemes.

Transnational actors have employed a wide array of tactics in their promotion of reform. Within Africa, multiple agencies have invested heavily in policy advocacy, with DFID in particular 'working politically' to secure their objectives. They have typically invited political leaders and senior bureaucrats to seminars and on study tours; they commissioned and distributed research on the benefits, design, and costs of programmes, and provided technical assistance to government departments; they initiated (and subsequently monitored and evaluated) experimental/pilot programmes; and often played a major role in drafting bold national statements about social protection policy. Donors have funded significant parts of or even entire programmes.

The embrace and advocacy of social assistance by transnational actors has not consistently led to a similar embrace by national governments, however. Across much of east and southern Africa, governments have resisted the reforms endorsed and promoted by transnational actors. While aid donors and international agencies are often perceived to have considerable power, our case studies suggest that their power has been often limited to putting the idea of policy reforms on the agenda, falling short of ensuring that governments actually adopt and implement reforms. This ideational power is far from insignificant. It is not a coincidence that social assistance programmes have been introduced in most African countries during the particular historical period within which social assistance has risen to prominence as a global social policy (Hickey and Seekings, Chapter 10). But donors and agencies have often failed to persuade national governments either to extend (or 'scale up') experimental programmes across the whole country or to accept full financial responsibility for the programmes.

In the extreme case of Zambia, Pruce and Hickey show in Chapter 7 that pilot programmes operated for ten years before the national government began to expand them, despite the use of reformist discourse in planning documents. In Lesotho, Granvik Saminathen argues in Chapter 6 that donors were important in the partial introduction of a child grant, but not in the earlier and more fulsome introduction of old-age pensions. In Tanzania, Ulriksen in Chapter 5 shows that the government of Tanzania has steadfastly resisted assuming any responsibility for World Bank-initiated cash transfer programmes. Seekings also shows in Chapter 2 that international organizations played no part in the introduction of old-age pensions in Botswana, and the government of Botswana subsequently resisted proposals that it introduce a general child or family grant. Meanwhile, Lavers shows in Chapter 3 that the government of Ethiopia resisted donor pressure to reform the emergency relief system for years, only introducing the Productive Safety Net Programme (PSNP) when domestic political crises forced a rethink in policy. These cases point to the fact that donor power is easily overestimated.

The bounded power of international organizations reflects in part the shifting financial position of most African countries. In the 1980s and 1990s, highly indebted African countries were susceptible to external pressure. Debt relief in the early 2000s reduced the power of international organizations. Some national governments remain heavily dependent on foreign aid, as Table 1.1 shows. Overseas development aid to Ethiopia is valued at almost 100 per cent of central government expenditure. Malawi (at 88 per cent) and Rwanda (at 76 per cent) are not far behind. But many other countries—including low-income countries such as Tanzania and Zambia—are much less dependent, and middle-income countries such as Botswana receive very little aid. Unsurprisingly, international organizations exert very little influence in Botswana. Even in aid-dependent countries, however, ODA buys less influence over social assistance reforms than might be expected, as revealed in Lavers' chapters on Ethiopia and Rwanda.

Almost no country in SSA spends as much on social assistance as the major international organizations recommend. Both the ILO and World Bank have advocated the introduction of social assistance programmes costing several percentages of GDP, but almost no national governments have approved expenditures of more than 0.5 per cent of GDP, and most governments balk at even smaller expenditures (Seekings 2017a). This is partly because governments in many low- and lower middle-income countries in SSA lack the fiscal capacity to implement social protection systems to scale (Barrientos and Niño-Zarazúa 2011). The precarious level of institutionalization and financing that remains characteristic of most transfer programmes in the region (see Table 1.A1 in the Appendix) reflects continuing economic fragility, partly due to the systemic effects from the Great Recession of the late 2000s and early 2010s, but also due to the structure of these economies (IMF 2017).[6]

The case studies in this book argue that whether or not national governments introduce or expand social assistance programmes depends primarily on the nature of politics within each country. Bilateral donors and international organizations are certainly players on the national stage, but they have rarely acted as a united force (frequently on account of their divergent approaches and organizational dynamics) and individually have played subordinate roles. In Uganda, as Bukenya and Hickey show in this volume, the initial failure of transnational actors to persuade the government to introduce social cash tranfers was in part due to divisions between them; their subsequent success followed agreement that one organization (DFID) would take the lead. Similarly in Ethiopia, as Lavers shows in Chapter 3 and in a forthcoming study (2019), a rare moment of coordination between donors during the 2003 food crisis forced the government to engage in the discussions that led to the PSNP, while the subsequent donor fragmentation over the design of the programme enabled the government to dictate key aspects of the design. Donor coordination around a shared agenda also helped give impetus to social assistance reforms adopted in Zambia, as described in Chapter 7.

Some of the international organizations have themselves recognized that successful reform requires that national states take 'ownership' of reforms and have made efforts to align their advocacy with political incentives and ideas (Hickey and Seekings, this volume). If external actors overplay their hand, they undermine the likelihood of local ownership of the process. This is evident in the contrast between Tanzania and Zanzibar. In Tanzania, as Ulriksen shows in her chapter, the World Bank has poured considerable resources into social assistance, funding the roll-out of the Productive Social Safety Net through the Tanzania Social Action Fund. The national government has declined to pay for any programmes itself. In Zanzibar—a largely autonomous territory within Tanzania—the idea of a universal pension was

[6] For a detailed discussion on the role of taxation and revenue mobilization in state-building and economic development, see Addison et al. (2018) and the accompanied articles in the same issue.

also placed on the agenda and then promoted for five years by external actors, especially HelpAge International. The reform was effected only when the Zanzibari state saw it as their initiative with external actors providing assistance (Seekings 2016b).

International organizations have often been most effective when they have facilitated policy transfer (and adaptation) from one country to another. Ethiopia's PSNP provided an important inspiration for Rwanda's Vision 2020 Umurenge Programme (as Lavers has shown in his chapter). However, the attraction of Ethiopia's PSNP was in part because Rwanda shared the Ethiopian government's developmental vision and paradigmatic worldview, including the importance of self-reliance. Meanwhile, global and even regional initiatives and 'agreements' on social protection have had little direct influence on national-level policy-making. African governments were party to the UN-wide Social Protection Floors Initiative and the ILO's Recommendation 202 on national Social Protection Floors. The African Union adopted a Social Policy Framework in 2008. The process-tracing conducted for the case studies failed to uncover evidence that these external agreements did more than legitimate—to some extent—the possibility of social protection. The experience of international organizations in SSA points to the limits to their power and influence. When they do influence national policy-making, their preferred approach is more often translated rather than simply applied or replicated.

4. State and Society

While transnational actors have exercised some influence on the expansion of social assistance within SSA, the case studies here emphasize that the timing of scheme adoption, the types of programmes adopted or rejected, and the degree of programme expansion are all fundamentally driven by domestic political dynamics. Cases as diverse as Ethiopia, Malawi, and Uganda all highlight how donor pressure for policy reform and the expansion of social assistance has been resisted over extended periods, only resulting in programme adoption and expansion when domestic political factors shift or where donors realign their advocacy efforts to fit with dominant ideas and incentives within national-level politics. Here we focus on how these political dynamics, particularly in terms of political settlements, ideas, and electoral politics, have shaped the adoption and expansion of cash transfer programmes in our eight case study countries.

4.1. Social assistance and the politics of elite survival in east and southern Africa

In stark contrast to research on the politics of welfare states and social protection in Latin America, and also in the South Asian context, the case studies in this book suggest that popular political mobilization has played a minimal role in the expansion of social assistance in east and southern Africa. Instead, the driving force for reform has been where social assistance is incorporated as an element of the political survival strategies employed by domestic political elites to build regime legitimacy, secure political allegiance, or win over electoral support. These survival strategies differ according to both the nature of the political settlement within each country, with reference to the balance of power relations among elites and between elites and subjects, and the dynamics that flow from these shifting power relations. Of the case studies that employ the political settlements framework, a clear divergence exists between those countries where political power is concentrated among a handful of political elites within a dominant ruling party (Ethiopia and Rwanda) and those in which power is more dispersed among elite groups (Uganda and Zambia). In the former, electoral politics are a mere façade, offering little to no possibility of regime change. In contrast, in the latter some degree of dispersal of political power in Uganda and Zambia requires that politicians prioritize building broad political coalitions through alliances and the distribution of rents in order to win elections.

There are strong similarities between the Ethiopia and Rwanda cases in terms of how this basic political settlement translates into commitment to particular forms of social assistance. In each case, the ruling elite secured political power through military means, and this narrow elite is commonly associated with a minority ethnic group, which would stand little chance of maintaining power through the distribution of rents and coalition-building strategies common in Uganda and Zambia. Instead, both regimes have adopted a developmental orientation as a foundational element of their political settlements, seeking to build regime legitimacy through the delivery of rapid and broad-based socioeconomic development, alongside the suppression of political voice outside the ruling party. These clear developmental visions initially excluded social assistance—quite explicitly in the case of Ethiopia (Lavers, this volume)—while prioritizing ideas of self-reliance and the importance of maximizing resources for broad-based economic development. It was only in the context of perceived threats to the political settlement—including a major food crisis in 2002/3 following a series of

'Armageddons' facing the leadership in Ethiopia and rising inequality that threatened to undermine the post-ethnic national building strategy in Rwanda—that social assistance schemes have been integrated into existing development strategies as a means of enhancing regime legitimacy and neutralizing potential political threats (see Chapter 4 on Rwanda). In doing so, very particular forms of social assistance have been adopted and rapidly rolled out, with a strong focus on productive programme designs through an emphasis on the development of community infrastructure through labour-intensive public works and links between receipt of transfers and credit and livelihoods schemes to promote self-reliance and graduation.

A very different process unfolded in Uganda and Zambia, as shown in the respective chapters (8 and 7). While ruling parties in these countries periodically express a desire to pursue developmental or social democratic agendas, these have been inconsistently applied in practice, not least as a result of the necessity of elite coalition building and rent distribution that undermines developmental impulses. As such, ruling party ideology has provided little in the way of support for the expansion of social assistance, while concerns about the dangers of welfare dependency resulted in significant opposition, particularly from finance ministries in both cases. Rather, the original strategy for social assistance in Uganda and Zambia came from donors who lobbied extensively to secure approval for pilot cash transfer schemes. These pilots were then the focus of further advocacy efforts focused on building the evidence base for programme efficacy (particularly in Zambia) and organizing visits for influential politicians and bureaucrats to demonstrate the programmes in action. However, the moderate levels of political support that have ultimately been secured in each case, particularly in Uganda, only materialized as a result of domestic political shifts and attempts by donors to align their advocacy efforts with the interests and ideas of ruling elites (see also Grebe and Mubiru (2014) and Grebe (2014) on Uganda; and Kabandula and Seekings (2016) and Siachiwena (2016) on Zambia).

However, it is not just the type of political settlement that matters, but also the way in which the shifting nature of power relations that underpin them can generate perceived threats to the legitimacy and stability of the ruling coalition. The willingness and urgency of elites to extend social assistance can be linked directly to the level of threat that they perceived themselves to be under. The response has been weakest where the political threat to ruling elites was weak, as in Zambia and Uganda, and highest where the threat was perceived to be high (Ethiopia and Rwanda). During the mid-2000s when donors started to promote social assistance in Uganda and Zambia, the respective political elites did not face a significant crisis that threatened their legitimacy or hold on power. The main motivation for political elites in these contexts was to secure local-level political support in the context of certain lower-level shifts within the political settlement, rather than cope with threats to the deal itself. For example, in Zambia, the direct trigger for increasing expenditure on social assistance was a crisis in the agricultural subsidy system which had constituted the primary mode of rent distribution used by elites to maintain legitimacy and political support in rural areas (see Mason et al. 2013).

In contrast, the strongest cases of elite commitment to social assistance derive from perceived threats—even existential threats—to the political settlement to which social assistance is seen as a potential solution. Here, elites have been motivated by broad concerns about political legitimacy, as well as mitigating specific threats to the ruling coalition that originate in distributional crises.[7] In addition to the 'Armageddons' that political elites in Ethiopia perceived themselves to be threatened by, Rwanda's ruling elite was catalysed by the failure to translate economic growth into a reduction of poverty or inequality, thereby threatening the coalition's claims to promote inclusive development and build a post-ethnic society. The case of Botswana suggests that these findings hold across time. The chapter by Seekings shows how the prolonged drought that the country experienced in the 1960s helped instigate a response that would set in place a process of building the welfare regime apparent today. This crisis coincided with a critical political moment within the process of state formation in Botswana, with the new ruling coalition keen to establish its developmentalist and nation-building credentials, in part to assuage concerns that a certain element of the Tswana elite would seek to govern in sectional rather than national interests. In Botswana, as in South Africa, the welfare state became a major pillar of the legitimacy not only of democratically elected government but also of the democratic institutions themselves.

The chapters on Lesotho and Tanzania also incorporate aspects of the adapted political settlements framework to explain the social assistance policy process. In both cases, dominant party settings provided sufficient stability and long-term horizons to enable coherent decision-making on social assistance. In Tanzania, in a dominant party setting the adoption of a clear productivist developmental vision and an emphasis on self-reliance has favoured productivist forms of social assistance, requiring labour supply

[7] In line with past research that highlighted the importance of crises in the adoption of social protection policies (Hickey 2009).

from households and other conditions, rather than pure income transfers. Meanwhile in Lesotho, the transition from an extended period of highly unstable competitive politics to a more stable dominant party system following reform to the electoral system provided the ruling elite with an opportunity to introduce a social pension.

4.2. Electoral politics

If political settlements underpin enduring patterns of politics, elections provide opportunities for change. The case studies in this book provide a rather mixed picture regarding the influence of electoral competition on policy reform. There are certainly examples in which the general trend from dominant leaders and parties to increasingly competitive, multi-party elections during the 1990s and 2000s has spurred campaign promises to expand the reach and generosity of social assistance. In some cases, candidates have sought to brand or distinguish themselves in terms of social protection. More often, social assistance has been a valence issue, with competing political parties outlining similar views, whether in favour of or sceptical towards social protection. The chapter on Botswana shows that the ruling Botswana Democratic Party (BDP) had long branded itself as the party of drought relief. Faced with stronger challenges from urban-based opposition parties that themselves advocated increased expanded public provision, the BDP moved to introduce old-age pensions and to expand its feeding and workfare programmes. Likewise, Granvik Saminathen argues in her Lesotho chapter that the social pension was introduced in a period of political dominance and stability, although the pension payment rates subsequently became a focus for competition between political parties promising voters ever higher rates. In Zambia, Hickey and Pruce show that the expansion of the social cash transfer programme followed the change of government in 2011, although this had not been an issue in the election itself. Furthermore, the chapter on Uganda shows that the addition of a fifteenth district in the original pilot was linked to the ruling party's political strategy for building support in the opposition-leaning north of the country, while the subsequent roll-out of the scheme was intended to provide visible state transfers in the lead-up to presidential elections in 2016. The case of Malawi, however, provides a somewhat cautionary tale regarding the potential of social protection as an electoral strategy. Hamer and Seekings argue that in a context in which competing candidates had already staked out the pro-growth and pro-peasant political brands, President Banda resorted to a pro-poor and pro-women social assistance brand as part of her electoral strategy. Though her resounding defeat had multiple causes, the results suggest that the political appeal of social assistance has its limits.

The other case studies do not identify electoral politics as a major driver of social assistance. In Tanzania, the adoption of a new social pension was announced prior to the 2015 elections, but, as Ulriksen argues, this has not been matched with budgetary allocations and it is unclear whether there is any real commitment to meeting those electoral promises. Finally, and unsurprisingly, there is little evidence that electoral competition had any real effect on the adoption of social assistance programmes in the highly dominant party regimes in Ethiopia and Rwanda. Despite common claims in the literature regarding the influence of the 2005 elections on the adoption of the PSNP earlier that year, Chapter 3 shows that the drivers of the programme lay in earlier distributional crises and revision of the government's development strategy. The political protests and violence following the highly contested 2005 elections in Ethiopia did, however, influence the recent adoption of the urban PSNP. Here localized electoral losses in urban areas, as well as the large-scale opposition protests held in 2005, provided a spur for a renewed political strategy that combined both repression and closing of political space, alongside more populist initiatives to win back support including food subsidies, employment schemes, and, latterly, the urban PSNP.

4.3. The role of ideas

Variation between countries, and between governments in a country, also reflects ideological differences. Governments and other actors make choices when they are aware of alternative models or possibilities, and in light of their ideologies and beliefs as well as their calculation of interests. While political elites across much of Africa are generally resistant to the idea of 'handouts', they often also recognize collective responsibilities for certain categories of deserving poor, including even working-age adults and their dependants in times of drought. Within what might be considered a general conservative liberalism there are important variations. In Botswana, for instance, the political leaders—beginning with the founding President Seretse Khama and continuing under his successors from the BDP—developed a benignly conservative welfare doctrine that justified public support along conservative lines

(Seekings 2016a). A similarly conservative view of welfare and deservingness seems to hold in Uganda, also, where donors' initial advocacy efforts were unsuccessful until they were re-framed within a politically acceptable discourse regarding the need to preserve the dignity of vulnerable and deserving groups such as the elderly, rather than 'the poor' in general (see Chapter 8). Conservatism also seems to have underpinned the widespread anxiety over 'dependency', i.e. citizens (especially poor citizens) becoming dependent on government 'handouts' undermining their self-reliance and work ethic; see Seekings (2017b). Political leaders seem to embrace policy reform when incentives (rooted in political crisis or competition) combine with a sense of responsibility to overshadow any anxiety over dependency.

Paradigmatic ideas regarding the importance of rapid and relatively inclusive socioeconomic development have been strong influences on social assistance policy in Ethiopia and Rwanda. In each case, regimes associated with minority ethnic groups have sought to build regime legitimacy and promote political stability through rapid development, requiring all policy, including social assistance, to contribute to these productive objectives. Despite the strong Marxist–Leninist roots in Ethiopia, in both countries the resulting approach to social protection is in stark opposition to social democratic ideas, with a strong resistance to perceived western-style welfare dependency (see Chapter 3). In Ethiopia, at least, developmentalism has also been specifically framed in opposition to a caricatured neoliberalism. Nonetheless, government ideas on social protection in Ethiopia and Rwanda have actually resonated most strongly with the neoliberal, or what has more generously been described as 'inclusive neoliberal', views of the post-Washington Consensus World Bank at points. The resulting social assistance programmes have been narrowly targeted on the poorest and most food insecure, with a strong emphasis on work requirements for anyone receiving support, and links to livelihood programmes aimed at making recipients productive and thereby enabling them to graduate from support.

Efforts to frame social assistance as a policy solution to a particular set of social problems were also influential at times, although only extensively so where they also fitted well with the types of paradigmatic ideas discussed above (Schmidt 2010). For example, new evidence that the rate of poverty reduction was declining helped convince some bureaucrats and politicians in countries like Rwanda and Zambia that new policy solutions were required. Chapter 7 informs us how in Zambia bureaucrats who had been co-opted into transnational policy coalitions in support of social assistance were able to point to evaluation evidence from randomized controlled trials that revealed the social cash transfer scheme to be more effective and efficient than other government interventions.

Our work on these normative and ideological dimensions of public policy help to fill a conspicuous gap in the existing literatures on African politics, namely the politics that animates negotiations between elites and state-citizens, and between politicians and bureaucrats, which is informed by the ideas as well as the material incentives of the actors involved. In showing how the ideas and discursive strategies of key players within politics and international development can help explain the 'politics of change' around social assistance in Africa, we reflect the growing sense that political elite behaviour is not shaped solely by material self-interest (Hall 1993; Blyth 2002; Schmidt 2010). This is consistent with the constructivist turn in political studies (Hay 2011: 65–82), and Hagmann and Péclard's (2011) insistence that the negotiation of statehood in Africa involves a significant discursive element.

5. Conclusion

The process through which social assistance has been promoted, contested, and rolled out thus closely reflects the *negotiated* character of statehood in east and southern Africa (Hagmann and Péclard 2011), both in terms of the heavily transnationalized nature of governance, which continues to offer an influential role for external actors and ideas, and also the terms of the bargain between rulers and ruled, whereby concerns with electoral success, legitimacy, and popular pressures are increasingly influential over budgetary allocations and welfare provision. Our evidence suggests that political agency in the region has played a powerful role in this process, with the countries that reveal the highest levels of commitment to social assistance driven more by domestic political imperatives, and in some cases 'neighbourhood' effects, than by external pressure. Importantly, this process has been strongly informed not only by global imperatives and elite-level machinations but also by the particular historical character of welfare regimes in SSA, particularly in terms of long-standing ideas around deservingness and the role of the state, and the related effort to manage ongoing processes of deagrarianization.

It is worth pointing out some tensions arising between different elements in our analysis. On the one hand, and contrary to the Latin American experience, we find evidence that dominant and authoritarian regimes can be equally, and even more, committed to and capable of delivering social assistance than their more democratic counterparts. On the other hand, we also find that multi-party elections—and other aspects of democracy, including the media—can play a positive role in driving up a focus on social assistance. This could lead us to re-open long-standing debates regarding the relative strengths and weaknesses of democratic as opposed to authoritarian regimes. However, we would argue that such debates tend to shed more heat than light (Kelsall 2014). What matters is the specific nature of state–society relationships in different contexts, how these are being reconfigured in different ways, and what this means for elite power, citizenship, and broader issues of legitimate and accountable rule. Contrasting democracy with authoritarianism is also unhelpful when it comes to discussing the strategic implications of the findings discussed here in practical terms. It is of little use to tell politicians and civil servants in Zambia and Ghana that Rwanda and Ethiopia are doing better than they are at delivering social assistance because they have dominant political settlements.

Understanding social assistance as forming part of the processes through which negotiated processes of statehood are currently taking place in east and southern Africa offers a good deal of analytical power and helps reveal the possibility that social assistance may more readily form part of the politics of patronage in SSA than a politics of 'rightful claims' (see Ferguson (2015)), initially at least. This is not to deny that democratization can have a positive effect on extending social assistance; indeed, some of our cases are broadly consistent with van de Walle's (2014: 231) claim that democratization is likely to provide incentives to make clientelism more redistributive by extending services and benefits to larger sections of the population. Social assistance within east and southern Africa, then, is both flowing from and helping to embed very different political forms, not all of which are well aligned with contemporary hopes for a new politics of citizenship and social contracts on the continent.

Appendix

Table 1.A1 Coverage of social assistance in sub-Saharan Africa

Country	Programme	Type of programme[1]	Level of institutionalization[2]	Start year	Coverage (direct and indirect beneficiaries)				Agencies involved
					2015	2010	2005	2000	
Angola	Cartão Kikuia	Pure income transfer	Precarious institutionalization	2013	250,000	n.e.	n.e.	n.e.	Ministry of Commerce
Botswana	Old-Age Pension	Pure income transfer	Institutionalized	1996	493,570	450,000	400,000	350,000	Department of Social Protection, Ministry of Local Government and Rural Development
Botswana	Ipelegeng—Public Works	Income transfers + community assets	Institutionalized	2008	55,000	n.a.	n.e.	n.e.	Department of Social Protection, Ministry of Local Government and Rural Development
Botswana	Destitute Persons' Allowance	Pure income transfer	Institutionalized	2003	33,730	30,518	n.a.	n.e.	Department of Social Protection, Ministry of Local Government and Rural Development
Botswana	National Orphan Care Programme	Pure income transfer	Institutionalized	1999	175,380	n.a.	52,537	n.a.	Department of Social Protection, Ministry of Local Government and Rural Development and UNICEF
Burkina Faso	Orphans and Vulnerable Children	Pure income transfer	Pilot	2008	16,250	n.e.	n.e.	n.e.	Ministry of Social Welfare, Ministry of Education and Ministry of Health, Plan International, the International HIV/AIDS Alliance and UNICEF
Cameroon	Cameroon Social Safety Nets Project	Income transfers + community assets	Pilot	2014	200,000	n.e.	n.e.	n.e.	Government of Cameroon, with support from International Development Association and the World Bank

Cape Verde	Pensão de Solidariedade Social	Pure income transfer	Precarious institutionalization	2006	105,000	100,000	n.e.	n.e.	Ministry of Youth, Employment and Human Resources Development of Cape Verde and the National Centre of Social Pensions
Congo, Republic of	LISUNGI Safety Nets Project	Income transfers + human capital investment	Pilot	2014	18,704	n.e.	n.e.	n.e.	Ministry of Social Affairs, World Bank, French Development Agency, UNICEF
Djibouti	Programme National de Solidarité Famille	Pure income transfer	Precarious institutionalization	2015	32,685	n.e.	n.e.	n.e.	State Secretariat for National Solidarity
Djibouti	Social Safety Net Programme	Income transfers + community assets	Pilot	2010	7,500	7,500	n.e.	n.e.	Djibouti Social Development Agency and the World Bank
Ethiopia	Meket Livelihoods Development Project	Income transfers + community assets	Pilot	2003	46,600	45,000	n.a.	n.e.	Government of Ethiopia
Ethiopia	Productive Safety Net Programme	Income transfers + community assets	Institutionalized	2005	7,640,000	7,000,000	5,000,000	n.e.	Government of Ethiopia with financial support of a consortium of donors (Canadian International Development Agency (CIDA), DFID, European Commission, USAID, and the World Bank)
Gambia	Family Strengthening Programme	Income transfers + human capital investment	Precarious institutionalization	2011	650	n.e.	n.e.	n.e.	Department of Social Welfare

(*continued*)

Table 1.A1 Continued

Country	Programme	Type of programme[1]	Level of institutionalization[2]	Start year	Coverage (direct and indirect beneficiaries)				Agencies involved
					2015	2010	2005	2000	
Ghana	Livelihood Empowerment Against Poverty programme	Income transfers + human capital investment	Precarious institutionalization	2008	725,000	177,500	n.e.	n.e.	Ministry of Gender, Children and Social Protection and Ministry of Employment and Social Welfare with financial support of a consortium of donor (UNICEF, DFID, and the World Bank)
Guinea	Productive Social Safety Net Programme—Pilot Cash Transfer Programme	Income transfers + community assets	Pilot	2012	200,000	n.e.	n.e.	n.e.	Government of Guinea and the World Bank
Guinea	Cash Transfer for Health, Nutrition and Education	Income transfers + human capital investment	Pilot	2013	10,000	n.e.	n.e.	n.e.	Government of Guinea and the World Bank
Guinea-Bissau	Protecção Social	Pure income transfer	Precarious institutionalization	2013	2,000	n.e.	n.e.	n.e.	Instituto Nacional de Seguranca Social
Ivory Coast	Temporary Employment Opportunities for Youth	Income transfers + community assets	Pilot	2011	12,693	n.e.	n.e.	n.e.	Government of Ivory Coast, French Government, and the World Bank
Kenya	Cash Transfer for Orphans and Vulnerable Children	Pure income transfer	Pilot	2004	1,300,000	400,000	n.a.	n.e.	Ministry of Home Affairs Children's Department, DFID, UNICEF, Swedish International Development Agency (SIDA)
Kenya	Older Persons Cash Transfer	Pure income transfer	Precarious institutionalization	2006	295,000	165,000	n.e.	n.e.	The Ministry of Gender, Children and Social Development with financial support of a consortium of donors (the World Bank, DFID, UNICEF, WFP, OXFAM, and HelpAge International)

Kenya	The Hunger Safety Net Programme	Pure income transfer	Pilot	2009	400,000	n.a.	n.e.	n.e.	Ministry for the Development of Northern Kenya, DFID, and Australian Department for Foreign Affairs and Trade
Kenya	Persons with Severe Disabilities Cash Transfer Programme	Pure income transfer	Precarious institutionalization	2012	45,505	n.e.	n.e.	n.e.	The Ministry of Gender, Children and Social Development with financial support of a consortium of donors (the World Bank, DFID, UNICEF, WFP)
Lesotho	Lesotho Old-Age Pension	Pure income transfer	Institutionalized	2004	425,435	415,000	345,230	n.e.	Department of Pensions, Ministry of Finance and Development Planning
Lesotho	Child Grants Programme	Pure income transfer	Precarious institutionalization	2007	122,500	n.a.	n.e.	n.e.	Ministry of Social Development with financial support from the European Commission
Liberia	Social Cash Transfer Programme	Pure income transfer	Pilot	2009	10,000	9,500	n.e.	n.e.	National Social Cash Transfer Secretariat, Ministry of Planning and Economic Affairs, and the National Social Protection Steering Committee, with support from UNICEF and European Commission
Madagascar	Le Transfert Monétaire Conditionnel	Income transfers + human capital investment	Precarious institutionalization	2014	1,000	n.e.	n.e.	n.e.	Ministry of National Education, National Office of Nutrition and Ministry of Public Health
Malawi	Social Cash Transfer Programme	Pure income transfer	Pilot	2006	1,522,670	400,000	n.e.	n.e.	Government of Malawi, UNICEF, Global Fund to Fight AIDS, Tuberculosis and Malaria, Kreditanstalt für Wiederaufbau (KfW), Irish Aid, the European Union, and World Bank
Malawi	Zomba Cash Transfer Program	Income transfers + community assets	Pilot	2008	4,000	n.a.	n.e.	n.e.	World Bank

(continued)

Table 1.A1 Continued

Country	Programme	Type of programme[1]	Level of institutionalization[2]	Start year	Coverage (direct and indirect beneficiaries)				Agencies involved
					2015	2010	2005	2000	
Malawi	Improved Livelihoods Through Public Works	Income transfers + community assets	Precarious institutionalization	1995	434,000	n.a.	n.a.	n.a.	Government of Malawi, World Bank
Malawi	The Irrigation, Rural Livelihoods and Development Project		Pilot	2005	677,502	n.a.	n.a.	n.e.	World Bank
Malawi	LDF/MASAF/WB Public Works programme		Pilot	2005	521,000	n.a.	n.a.	n.e.	Local Development Fund, Malawi Social Action Fund, and World Bank
Malawi	Rural Infrastructure Development Programme		Pilot	2012	26,201	n.a.	n.e.	n.e.	European Union
Malawi	Food-for-Assets programme		Pilot	2008	85,000	53,260	n.e.	n.e.	WFP
Mali	Bourses Maman	Income transfers + human capital investment	Pilot	2002	2,500	2,500	n.a.	n.e.	Government of Mali and UNICEF
Mali	Jigisemejiri—Tree of Hope	Income transfers + human capital investment	Pilot	2013	218,025	n.e.	n.e.	n.e.	Government of Mali and World Bank

Mauritius	Old-Age Pension	Pure income transfer	Institutionalized	1958	737,948	447,540	483,208	447,540	Ministry of Social Security, National Solidarity and Senior Citizens Welfare and Reform Institutions/Ministry of Finance and Economic Development
Mauritius	Basic Widows' Pension	Pure income transfer	Institutionalized	1950	20,302	21,815	22,672	21,323	Ministry of Social Security, National Solidarity and Senior Citizens Welfare and Reform Institutions
Mauritius	Basic Invalids' Pension	Pure income transfer	Institutionalized	1950	30,715	27,679	25,646	19,958	Ministry of Social Security, National Solidarity and Senior Citizens Welfare and Reform Institutions
Mauritius	Basic Orphans' Pension	Pure income transfer	Institutionalized	1950	400	369	n.a.	n.a.	Ministry of Social Security, National Solidarity and Senior Citizens Welfare and Reform Institutions
Mauritius	Child Allowance	Pure income transfer	Institutionalized	1960	16,311	18,556	18,367	n.a.	Ministry of Social Security, National Solidarity and Senior Citizens Welfare and Reform Institutions
Mozambique	Programa Subsídio Social Básico	Pure income transfer	Precarious institutionalization	1997	359,859	217,000	69,095	n.a.	Government of Mozambique, DFID, Government of the Netherlands, UNICEF, ILO, IMF, the World Bank, European Union, Irish AID, SIDA, WFP, and USAID
Mozambique	Programa De Acção Social Produtiva		Precarious institutionalization	2012	288,267	n.e.	n.e.	n.e.	Government of Mozambique and the World Bank
Namibia	Old-Age Pension	Pure income transfer	Institutionalized	1949	750,000	754,275	n.a.	483,800	Ministry of Health and Social Services
Namibia	Disability Grant	Pure income transfer	Institutionalized	1995	26,346	n.a.	n.a.	n.a.	Ministry of Labour and Social Welfare
Namibia	Child Maintenance Grant	Pure income transfer	Institutionalized	1977	117,663	86,086	34,707	20,000	Ministry of Gender Equality and Child Welfare
Namibia	Foster Parent	Pure income transfer	Institutionalized	1960	17,825	n.a.	n.a.	n.a.	Ministry of Gender Equality and Child Welfare

(continued)

Table 1.A1 Continued

Country	Programme	Type of programme[1]	Level of institutionalization[2]	Start year	Coverage (direct and indirect beneficiaries)				Agencies involved
					2015	2010	2005	2000	
Namibia	Special Maintenance Grant and Safety Allowance	Pure income transfer	Institutionalized	1960	114,512	n.a.	n.a.	n.a.	Ministry of Gender Equality and Child Welfare
Niger	Cash Transfers for Food Security and Cash for Work	Income transfers + community assets	Pilot	2011	85,988	n.e.	n.e.	n.e.	Government of Niger; World Bank, UNICEF
Nigeria	In Care of the Poor	Income transfers + human capital investment	Precarious institutionalization	2007	110,000	93,750	n.e.	n.e.	National Poverty Eradication Programme and Office of the Senior Special Assistant to the President
Nigeria	Ekiti State Social Security Scheme	Pure income transfer	Precarious institutionalization	2011	20,000	n.e.	n.e.	n.e.	Ekiti state government
Nigeria	Osun Elderly Persons Scheme	Pure income transfer	Precarious institutionalization	2012	8,460	n.e.	n.e.	n.e.	Osun state local government
Rwanda	Vision 2020 Umerenge Programme	Income transfers + community assets	Institutionalized	2008	643,193	27,200	n.e.	n.e.	Ministry of Local Government
Rwanda	Rwanda Demobilization and Reintegration Programme	Pure income transfer	Institutionalized	1997	36,000	n.a.	n.a.	n.a.	Rwanda Demobilization and Reintegration Commission and Ministry of Finance and Economic Planning
Rwanda	Genocide Survivors Support and Assistance Fund	Pure income transfer	Institutionalized	1998	21,039	n.a.	n.a.	n.a.	Ministry of Local Government

Sao Tome and Principe	Maes Carenciadas	Income transfers + human capital investment	Pilot	2014	30,600	n.e.	n.e.	n.e.	Government of Sao Tome and Principe/ UNICEF
Sao Tome and Principe	Bolsa Escola	Income transfers + human capital investment	Pilot	2015	2,000	n.e.	n.e.	n.e.	Government of Sao Tome and Principe
Senegal	Rapid response Child-focused social transfer	Pure income transfer	Precarious institutionalization	2009	710,000	n.a.	n.e.	n.e.	Cellule de Lutte Contre la Malnutrition, Government of Senegal
Senegal	Programme National de Bourses de Sécurité Familiale	Income transfers + human capital investment	Precarious institutionalization	2013	1,000,000	n.e.	n.e.	n.e.	Government of Senegal
Senegal	Conditional Cash Transfer for Orphans and Vulnerable Children	Income transfers + human capital investment	Pilot	2008	5,000	5,000	n.e.	n.e.	Ministry of Education and National Committee against AIDS with support from USAID, World Bank, UNICEF
Seychelles	Old-Age Pension	Pure income transfer	Institutionalized	1979	45,205	n.a.	n.a.	n.a.	Seychelles Pension Fund
Sierra Leone	Unconditional Cash Transfer for the Old and Needy/Social Safety Net programme	Pure income transfer	Precarious institutionalization	2007	13,547	16,000	n.e.	n.e.	Ministry of Employment and Social Security and Ministry of Health

(*continued*)

Table 1.A1 Continued

Country	Programme	Type of programme[1]	Level of institutionalization[2]	Start year	Coverage (direct and indirect beneficiaries)				Agencies involved
					2015	2010	2005	2000	
Sierra Leone	Cash for Work	Income transfers + community assets	Precarious institutionalization	2010	45,993	n.a.	n.e.	n.e.	Ministry of Finance and Economic Development, the World Bank, and National Commission for Social Action
South Africa	Older Persons' Grant	Pure income transfer	Institutionalized	1928	15,761,310	13,118,595	10,720,585	9,387,690	South Africa's Social Security Agency
South Africa	Child Support Grant	Pure income transfer	Institutionalized	1998	11,953,974	10,047,986	5,661,500	974,724	South Africa's Social Security Agency
South Africa	Care Dependency Grant	Pure income transfer	Institutionalized	2004	140,645	110,304	88,889	n.e.	South Africa's Social Security Agency
South Africa	Foster Child Grant	Pure income transfer	Institutionalized	2004	539,791	479,283	252,106	n.e.	South Africa's Social Security Agency
South Africa	Expanded Public Works Programme	Income transfers + community assets	Institutionalized	2004	1,240,000	210,000	1,700	n.e.	Department of Public Works
South Africa	Disability Grant	Pure income transfer	Institutionalized	1946	1,098,018	1,224,294	1,307,551	608,761	South Africa's Social Security Agency
South Africa	Grant-in-Aid	Pure income transfer	Institutionalized	2004	119,541	n.a.	n.a.	n.e.	South Africa's Social Security Agency
South Sudan	Capacity Building Institutional and Human Resource Development Project	Income transfers + community assets	Precarious institutionalization	2007	2,000	2,000	n.e.	n.e.	Government of South Sudan

Swaziland	Old-Age Grant	Pure income transfer	Institutionalized	2005	325,000	300,000	140,000	n.e.	Department of Social Welfare
Swaziland	Public Assistance Grant	Pure income transfer	Institutionalized	1985	5,075	5,000	n.a.	n.a.	Department of Social Welfare
Tanzania	Tanzania Community-Based Conditional Cash Transfer	Income transfers + human capital investment	Pilot	2008	13,000	6,000	n.e.	n.e.	Government of Tanzania; International Development Association, DFID, USAID, UNICEF, World Bank, and WFP
Tanzania	Tanzania Social Action Fund/ Productive Social Safety Net Programme	Income transfers + community assets	Precarious institutionalization	2000	6,000,000	5,000	n.a.	n.a.	Government of Tanzania, IDA, DFID, SIDA, USAID, UNICEF, UNDP, ILO, World Bank, and UNFPA
Togo	Cash Transfer Programme for Vulnerable Children in Northern Togo	Pure income transfer	Pilot	2013	14,828	n.e.	n.e.	n.e.	Government of Togo, World Bank, UNICEF
Togo	Travaux à Haute Intensité de Main d'OEuvre	Public Works	Pilot	2012	12,590	n.e.	n.e.	n.e.	Ministry of Community Development, World Bank
Uganda	Social Assistance Grants for Empowerment	Pure income transfer	Pilot	2007	105,836	45,000	n.e.		Ministry of Gender, Labour and Social Development, DFID, Irish AID, UNICEF
Uganda	Direct Income Support under the Expanding Social Protection Programme	Pure income transfer	Precarious institutionalization	2010	123,153	n.e.	n.e.	n.e.	Ministry of Gender, Labour and Social Development, DFID, Irish AID, UNICEF

(continued)

Table 1.A1 Continued

Country	Programme	Type of programme[1]	Level of institutionalization[2]	Start year	Coverage (direct and indirect beneficiaries)				Agencies involved
					2015	2010	2005	2000	
Uganda	Second Northern Uganda Social Action Fund Project (NUSAF 2)	Income transfers + community assets	Precarious institutionalization	2009	77,000	n.a.	n.e.	n.e.	Government of Uganda, World Bank, and DFID
Zambia	Child Grant Programme	Pure income transfer	Precarious institutionalization	2010	20,000	n.e.	n.e.	n.e.	Ministry of Community Development, Mother and Child Health
Zambia	Social Pension	Pure income transfer	Precarious institutionalization	2014	300,000	n.e.	n.e.	n.e.	Ministry of Community Development, Mother and Child Health
Zambia	Public Welfare Assistance Scheme	Pure income transfer	Precarious institutionalization	1950	25,859	n.a.	n.a.	n.a.	Ministry of Community Development and Social Services, Ministry of Health, Ministry of Education, World Vision, and Germany's Deutsche Gesellschaft für Internationale Zusammenarbeit (GIZ)
Zambia	Social Cash Transfer Programme	Pure income transfer	Pilot	2004	900,000	20,000	5,900	n.e.	Government of Zambia, UNICEF, DFID, Irish Aid, Government of Finland, SIDA, WFP, ILO
Zimbabwe	Public Assistance Monthly Maintenance Allowance Programme	Pure income transfer	Precarious institutionalization	1998	33,440	29,719	25,997	20,562	Department of Social Services

Zimbabwe	Harmonized Social Cash Transfer Programme	Pure income transfer	Pilot	2011	236,013	n.e.	n.e.	n.e.	Government of Zimbabwe, UNICEF
Total coverage in sub-Saharan Africa					60,419,346	36,574,229	24,655,690	12,334,358	
Coverage as % of regional poverty headcount index[3]					14.6%	9.1%	6.4%	3.2%	

Notes: [1] We follow Niño-Zarazúa et al. (2012) and Barrientos and Niño-Zarazúa (2010) and adopt a typology that distinguishes social assistance programmes by objectives and core design features: first, *pure income transfers* such as old-age pensions and family allowances are designed to smooth consumption and protect vulnerable groups, including children, the elderly, and people with disabilities, from extreme deprivation. Second, *income transfers + community assets* provide income support to households with members of working age in exchange for labour supply and take a 'productivist' approach in their design to mitigate idiosyncratic risks and the effect of variations in economic conditions. Finally, *income transfers + human capital investment* are programmes that provide income support to households in poverty as well as preferential access to, and incentives for the utilization of, health or education services. These programmes adopt a 'human development' approach with the explicit objective of reducing present and future poverty.

[2] 'Institutionalized' indicates a leading role of central governments in the implementation and coordination of programmes. In such cases, programmes usually have national coverage, and are well integrated into legislation and the governments' budgets, even when supported by donors. 'Precarious institutionalization' reflects the leading role of central governments in programme implementation, although financial and administrative considerations remain major challenges. 'Pilot' indicates a leading role of donors in the implementation of programmes and therefore their future institutionalization remains uncertain.

[3] Estimates from the World Bank (2017), based on population and poverty rates measured by the share of the population living on less than US$1.90 a day at 2011 purchasing power parity.

'n.e.' stands for non-existent by the reference year. 'n.a.' stands for no available data.

Source: Authors' compilation based on UNU-WIDER (2018) Social Assistance, Politics and Institutions (SAPI) database.

Acknowledgement

The authors gratefully acknowledge support from the UK's Department for International Development, ESRC, and UNU-WIDER. Naturally, any errors are ours.

References

Addison, T., M. Niño-Zarazúa, and J. Pirttilä (2018). Fiscal policy, state building and economic development. *Journal of International Development*, 30(2), 1–8.

Amenta, E., C. Bonastia, and N. Caren (2001). US social policy in comparative and historical perspective. *Annual Review of Sociology*, 27, 213–34.

Barrientos, A. and M. Niño-Zarazúa (2010). Effects of non-contributory social transfers in developing countries. In International Labour Office (Ed.), *Extending Social Security to All*. Geneva: ILO.

Barrientos, A. and M. Niño-Zarazúa (2011). Financing social protection for children in crisis contexts. *Development Policy Review*, 29(5), 603–20.

Behuria, P., L. Buur, and H. Gray (2017). Studying political settlements in Africa. *African Affairs*, 116(464), 508–25.

Béland, D. (2005). Ideas and social policy. *Social Policy and Administration*, 39(1), 1–18.

Bevan, P. (2004). Conceptualising in/security regimes. In I. Gough and G. Wood (Eds.), *Insecurity and Welfare Regimes in Asia, Africa and Latin America*. Cambridge: Cambridge University Press.

Blyth, M. (2002). *Great Transformations*. Cambridge: Cambridge University Press.

Bogaards, M. and S. Elischer (2016). Competitive authoritarianism in Africa revisited. *Zeitschrift für Vergleichende Politikwissenschaft*, 10(1), 5–18.

Carbone, G. (2012). Do new democracies deliver social welfare?. *Democratization*, 19(2), 157–83.

Carbone, G. (2013). Leadership turnovers in sub-Saharan Africa. ISPI Analysis 192. Milan: Italian Institute for International Political Studies.

Carbone, G. and A. Pellegata (2017). To elect or not to elect. *Journal of Development Studies*, 53(12), 2017.

Castles, F.G., S. Leibfried, J. Lewis, H. Obinger, and C. Pierson (Eds.) (2010). *The Oxford Handbook of the Welfare State*. Oxford: Oxford University Press.

Center for Systemic Peace (2016). The Polity IV Project Database. Center for Systemic Peace.

Cheeseman, N. (2015). *Democracy in Africa*. Cambridge: Cambridge University Press.

Cheeseman, N. (2016). Patrons, parties, political linkage, and the birth of competitive-authoritarianism in Africa. *African Studies Review*, 59(3), 181–200.

Cherrier, C. (2014). The politics of revenue mobilisation for social transfers in sub-Saharan Africa. Paper presented at the 14th EADI General Conference on Responsible Development in a Polycentric World. Bonn.

Collier, D. (2011). Understanding process tracing. *PS: Political Science and Politics*, 44(4), 823–30.

Devereux, S. (2010). Building social protection systems in southern Africa. Paper prepared in the framework of the European Report on Development, European Union and European University Institute (accessed 15 November 2017).

Dion, M. (2010). *Workers and Welfare*. Pittsburgh, PA: University of Pittsburgh Press.

Esping-Andersen, G. (1990). *The Three Worlds of Welfare Capitalism*. Cambridge: Cambridge University Press.

Esping-Andersen, G. (1999). *Social Foundations of Postindustrial Economies*. Oxford: Oxford University Press.

Ferguson, J. (2015). *Give a Man a Fish*. Durham, NC: Duke University Press.

Gay, R. (1998). Rethinking clientelism: demands, discourses and practices in contemporary Brazil. *Revista Europea de Estudios Latinoamericanos y del Caribe/European Review of Latin American and Caribbean Studies*, 65, 7–24.

George, A.L. and A. Bennett (2004). *Case Studies and Theory Development in the Social Sciences*. Cambridge, MA: MIT.

Grebe, E. (2014). Donor agenda-setting, bureaucratic advocacy and cash transfers in Uganda, 2002–13. CSSR Working Paper 354. Cape Town: University of Cape Town.

Grebe, E. and J.B. Mubiru (2014). The politics of welfare policy-making and cash transfers in Uganda. CSSR Working Paper 353. Cape Town: University of Cape Town.

Haggard, S. and R.R. Kaufman (2008). *Development, Democracy, and Welfare States*. Princeton, NJ: Princeton University Press.

Hagmann, T. and D. Péclard (2011). *Negotiating Statehood*. Oxford: Wiley-Blackwell.

Hall, P.A. (1993). Policy paradigms, social learning, and the state. *Comparative Politics*, 25(3), 275–96.

Hanlon, J., A. Barrientos, and D. Hulme (2010). *Just Give Money to the Poor*. London: Kumarian Press.

Harding, R. and D. Stasavage (2013). What democracy does (and doesn't do) for basic services. *Journal of Politics*, 76(1), 229–45.

Hay, C. (2011). Ideas and the construction of interests. In D. Béland and R.H. Cox (Eds.), *Ideas and Politics in Social Science Research*. Oxford: Oxford University Press.

Hickey, S. (2008). Conceptualising the politics of social protection in Africa. In A. Barrientos and D. Hulme (Eds.), *Social Protection for the Poor and Poorest*. London: Palgrave Macmillan.

Hickey, S. (2009). The politics of protecting the poorest. *Political Geography*, 28, 473–83.

Hickey, S., K. Sen, and B. Bukenya (Eds.) (2015). *The Politics of Inclusive Development*. Oxford and New York: Oxford University Press.

Hicks, A. and G. Esping-Andersen (2005). Comparative and historical studies of public policy and the welfare state. In T. Janoski, R. Alford, A. Hicks, and M. Schwartz (Eds.), *Handbook of Political Sociology*. New York: Cambridge University Press.

Huber, E. and J.D. Stephens (2001). *Development and Crisis of the Welfare State: Parties and Policies in Global Markets*. Chicago, IL: University of Chicago Press.

Huber, E. and J.D. Stephens (2012). *Democracy and the Left*. Chicago, IL: University of Chicago Press.

IDCPPA (Institute for Democracy, Citizenship and Public Policy in Africa) (n.d.). Legislating and implementing welfare policy reforms. Available at http://www.idcppa.uct.ac.za/LIWPR; www.effective-states.org (accessed 15 November 2017).

ILO (2017). *World Social Protection Report, 2017–2019*. Geneva: International Labour Organisation.

IMF (2017). *Regional Economic Outlook: Sub-Saharan Africa*. World Economic and Financial Surveys. Washington DC: International Monetary Fund.

Kabandula, A. and J. Seekings (2016). Donor influence, the Minister of Finance and Welfare Policy Reform in Zambia, 2003–11. CSSR Working Paper 395. Cape Town: University of Cape Town.

Kelsall, T. (2014). Authoritarianism, democracy and development. DLP State of the Art Paper 3. Birmingham: Development Leadership Programme.

Khan, M. (2010). *Political Settlements and the Governance of Growth-Enhancing Institutions*. Miemo. London: SOAS.

Korpi, W. (1983). *The Democratic Class Struggle*. London: Routledge.

Kudamatsu, M. (2012). Has democratization reduced infant mortality in sub-Saharan Africa? *Journal of the European Economic Association*, 10, 1294–317.

Lavers, T. (2013). The political economy of social policy and agrarian transformation in Ethiopia. PhD Thesis. Bath: University of Bath.

Lavers, T. (2018). Taking ideas seriously within political settlements analysis. ESID Working Paper. Manchester: Effective States and Inclusive Development Research Centre, the University of Manchester.

Lavers, T. (2019). Social protection in an aspiring 'developmental state': the political drivers of Ethiopia's PSNP. *African Affairs*, advance access online.

Lavers, T. and S. Hickey (2016). Conceptualising the politics of social protection expansion in low-income countries. *International Journal of Social Welfare*, 25(4), 388–98.

Levitsky, S. and L.A. Way (2010). *Competitive Authoritarianism*. Cambridge: Cambridge University Press.

Mason, N., T.S. Jayne, and N. van de Walle (2013). Fertilizer subsidies and voting patterns: political economy dimensions of input subsidy programs. Selected Paper prepared for presentation at the AAEA and CAES Joint Annual Meeting, Washington, DC, 4–6 August.

Niño-Zarazúa, M, A. Barrientos, S. Hickey, and D. Hulme (2012). Social protection in sub-Saharan Africa. *World Development*, 40(1), 163–76.

Obinger, H., C. Schmitt, and P. Starke (2013). Policy diffusion and policy transfer in comparative welfare state research. *Social Policy & Administration*, 47(1), 111–29.

ODI (2016). *Cash Transfers: What Does the Evidence Say?* London: ODI.

Osofisan, W. (2011). *Pension Watch: Social Protection in Old Age*. London: HelpAge International.

Peck, J. and N. Theodore (2015). *Fast Policy: Experimental Statecraft at the Thresholds of Neoliberalism*. Minneapolis, MN: University of Minnesota Press.

Pribble, J. (2011). Worlds apart: social policy regimes in Latin America. *Studies in Comparative International Development*, 46(2), 191–216.

Schmidt, V.A. (2008). Discursive institutionalism. *Annual Review of Political Science*, 11(1), 303–26.

Schmidt, V.A. (2010). Taking ideas and discourse seriously. *European Political Science Review*, 2(1), 1–25.

Seekings, J. (2007). Not a single white person should be allowed to go under. *Journal of African History*, 48(3), 375–94.

Seekings, J. (2011). British colonial policy, local politics and the origins of the Mauritian welfare state, 1936–1950. *Journal of African History*, 52(2), 157–77.

Seekings, J. (2013). The politics of social policy in Africa. In N. Cheeseman, D. Anderson, and A. Scheibler (Eds.), *Routledge Handbook of African Politics*. London: Routledge.

Seekings, J. (2016a). A lean cow cannot climb out of the mud, but a good cattleman does not leave it to perish. CSSR Working Paper 387. Cape Town: University of Cape Town.

Seekings, J. (2016b). The introduction of old-age pensions in Zanzibar. CSSR Working Paper 393. Cape Town: University of Cape Town.

Seekings, J. (2017a). Affordability and the political economy of social protection in contemporary Africa. WIDER Working Paper 2017/43. Helsinki: UNU-WIDER.

Seekings, J. (2017b). The discourse of dependency and the agrarian roots of welfare doctrines in Africa. *SozialPolitik*, 2. Available at https://www.sozialpolitik.ch/fileadmin/user_upload/2017_2_Article_Seekings.pdf.

Seekings, J. (forthcoming). Are African welfare states different? Welfare state-building in (anglophone) Africa in comparative perspective. CSSR Working Paper. Cape Town: University of Cape Town.

Seekings, J. and N. Nattrass (2005). *Class, Race, and Inequality in South Africa*. London: Yale University Press.

Seekings, J. and N. Nattrass (2015). *Policy, Politics and Poverty in South Africa*. London: Palgrave.

Siachiwena, H. (2016). Social protection policy reform in Zambia during the Sata presidency, 2011–2014. CSSR Working Paper 377. Cape Town: Centre for Social Science Research, University of Cape Town.

Stasavage, D. (2005). The role of democracy in Uganda's move to universal primary education. *Journal of Modern African Studies*, 43(1), 53–73.

Tillin, L., R. Deshpande, and K.K. Kailash (Eds.) (2015). *Politics of Welfare*. Delhi: Oxford University Press.

Ulriksen, M.S. (2012). Welfare policy expansion in Botswana and Mauritius. *Comparative Political Studies*, 45(12), 1483–509.

UNU-WIDER (2018). Social Assistance, Politics, and Institutions (SAPI) database [online]. Helsinki: United Nations University World Institute for Development Economics Research (UNU-WIDER). Available at https://www.wider.unu.edu/project/sapi-social-assistance-politics-and-institutions-database (accessed 15 January 2018).

UNU-WIDER (n.d.). The economics and politics of taxation and social protection. Available at https://www.wider.unu.edu/project/economics-and-politics-taxation-and-social-protection (accessed 15 June 2017).

van de Walle, N. (2007). Meet the boss, same as the old boss? In H. Kitschelt and S. Wilkinson (Eds.), *Patrons, Clients and Policies: Patterns of Democratic Accountability and Political Competition*. Cambridge: Cambridge University Press.

van de Walle, N. (2014). The democratization of clientelism in sub-Saharan Africa. In D. Abente Brun and L. Diamond (Eds.), *Clientelism, Social Policy and the Quality of Democracy*. Baltimore, MD: Johns Hopkins University Press.

van Oorschot, W., M. Opielka, and B. Pfau-Effinger (Eds.) (2008). *Culture and Welfare State*. Cheltenham: Edward Elgar.

Whitfield, L. (Ed.) (2009). *The Politics of Aid*. Oxford: Oxford University Press.

Wilensky, H.L. (1975). *The Welfare State and Equality*. Berkeley, CA: University of California Press.

World Bank (2017a). World development indicators. DataBank. Available at http://databank.worldbank.org/data/reports.aspx?source=world-development-indicators (accessed 15 January 2018).

World Bank (2017b). ASPIRE: The atlas of social protection—indicators of resilience and equity. Available at http://datatopics.worldbank.org/aspire/indicator/social-assistance (accessed 20 November 2017).

World Bank (2018). *Realising the Full Potential of Safety Nets in Africa.* Washington DC: World Bank.

Yang, J-J. (2017). *The Political Economy of the Small Welfare State in South Korea.* Cambridge: Cambridge University Press.

2

Building a Conservative Welfare State in Botswana

Jeremy Seekings

1. Botswana as a Distinctively African Welfare State

Overviews of welfare regimes in Africa distinguish typically between the middle-income countries of southern Africa (including Botswana) and the lower-income countries elsewhere on the continent (Garcia and Moore 2012; Niño-Zarazúa et al. 2012). The more expansive welfare states in the southern African countries are said to have been 'driven by settler elites' prior to the mid-1990s, and by a mix of newly democratic politics and 'sub-regional demonstration effects' thereafter (Niño-Zarazúa et al. 2012: 165–6). South Africa's welfare state did indeed originate in the racist politics of the early twentieth century (Seekings 2007), and Namibia's welfare state reflects its history as a de facto colony of South Africa (Devereux 2007). Settler politics do not explain the origins of the welfare states in either Mauritius or Botswana, however. The Mauritian welfare state resulted from the distinctive political economy of Mauritius, with a large agricultural Indo-Mauritian working class on sugar plantations and a growing Indo-Mauritian middle class (Seekings 2011; Ulriksen 2012). Botswana had neither a significant population of settlers or immigrants nor the class structure of either South Africa or Mauritius, yet it too built a substantial welfare state in the late twentieth century—to the point that the extent of the welfare state generated widespread anxiety among the country's elite.

Botswana's route to welfare state-building proceeded through the programmes, institutions, and ideology developed in a hitherto agrarian society in response to drought. In this, the case of Botswana prefigures a more general process underlying welfare state-building across much of Africa. Most African welfare states have their origins in the social risks facing peasants as a result of drought together with related changes in agrarian society that undermined the willingness or ability of kin to support the poor. Most African welfare states

Jeremy Seekings, *Building a Conservative Welfare State in Botswana* In: *The Politics of Social Protection in Eastern and Southern Africa*. Edited by: Sam Hickey, Tom Lavers, Miguel Niño-Zarazúa, and Jeremy Seekings, Oxford University Press (2020).
DOI: 10.1093/oso/9780198850342.003.0002

were *not* a response to the risks facing workers as a result of industrialization and urbanization—as had been the case in the more industrialized countries of Europe (e.g. Esping-Andersen 1990), Latin America (e.g. Huber and Stephens 2012), and even East Asia (e.g. Yang 2017).

Its agrarian origins explain why previous studies have provided sharply conflicting assessments of Botswana's welfare state. One set of scholars has focused on Botswana's enduring failure to include all of its citizens in the benefits of growth. Bar-On (2001) emphasized the parsimony of the country's welfare policies and concluded that 'Botswana's social assistance scheme fails many of the very poor completely, and those who do benefit from it are receiving steadily less of the nation's increasing prosperity' (2001: 264). Ulriksen (2011, 2012) contrasted Botswana with Mauritius. Both were multi-party democracies with open, middle-income economies and competent state institutions. Both invested heavily in public education, as well as public health and housing. But Botswana spent much less on social protection and had no national social security legislation. Hickey (2011) similarly contrasted Botswana unfavourably with South Africa. In contrast, World Bank studies have described Botswana's social protection system as 'one of the most extensive…in the region' in terms of both the range and coverage of programmes (Garcia and Moore 2012: 227), and as 'mature and complex' (BIDPA and World Bank 2013: x). Devereux also assessed that 'By African standards, Botswana implements an unusually comprehensive set of social welfare programmes for its poor and vulnerable citizens' (2007: 554).

Botswana's social assistance programmes reach a large proportion of the population. As much as one half of the population receives food and about 10 per cent of the population receives other social assistance benefits even in non-drought years, with the proportions rising sharply in drought years. Seleka et al. (2007: 33) calculate that government transfers reduced the poverty headcount rate in 2002/3 by 10 percentage points, from about 40 per cent to about 30 per cent. Whilst coverage is widespread, total expenditure is modest. This is primarily because most benefits are set at parsimonious levels. 'Minimum assistance' is provided to 'genuine destitute persons', as the government itself puts it (Botswana 2002: 2). The old-age pension introduced in 1996 was set at just one quarter of the value of its equivalent in neighbouring South Africa, and workfare 'wages' are similarly low. As a result, poverty might be reduced but is certainly not eliminated. The conservative character of the welfare state is evident also in the preference for workfare and for the provision of benefits in kind (and more recently food coupons). Furthermore, programmes assume and respect the centrality of the family: workfare is designed to enable a working-age adult breadwinner to support his or her familial dependents; a 'destitutes' programme is intended to support households where there is no able-bodied, working-age adult; pensions and orphan support became necessary when individuals fell outside families, in the case of the elderly because of shrinkage in the 'extended' family. None of the social assistance programmes are statutory, i.e. none are based in legislation, and there is no dedicated ministry for social welfare.

The governing party also developed a distinctively conservative welfare doctrine to justify its interventions. The state sought to strengthen the social order built around the family and the community, and to limit interventions in markets. Botswana's welfare state was not built on universalist, egalitarian, or highly redistributive principles. It thus resembled the conservative welfare regimes of continental Europe, which perpetuated stratification of households by class and status as well as gendered inequalities within households, rather than the social democratic welfare states in the Nordic countries (van Kersbergen 2003).[1]

Botswana was an early example of a distinctively African welfare state, characterized by a distinctively conservative approach to precisely who is decommodified, how, to what extent, and with what legitimating ideology. The value of examining the history of welfare state-building in Botswana in the late twentieth century is precisely because it prefigured subsequent processes and patterns of welfare state-building elsewhere in east and central Africa. This chapter examines how and why a conservative welfare state was built in Botswana. Sections 2 and 3 examine the origins of welfare programmes in drought relief in the 1960s and 1970s and their institutionalization and consolidation in the 1980s and 1990s. Section 4 focuses on how the particular form of the welfare state in Botswana was shaped by social, economic, and cultural factors, whilst section 5 examines the impetus to reform provided by political competition. Whilst spectacular economic growth from the 1970s facilitated the construction of a welfare state in Botswana, political dynamics explain the incentives facing the Botswana Democratic Party (BDP). The conclusion reflects further on how the case of Botswana fits into the broader landscape of welfare state-building.

2. Drought and the Foundations of the Welfare State

Welfare policies in Botswana have long revolved around three major components: food or cash-for-work, i.e. workfare, for able-bodied adults; 'supplementary'

[1] This comparison was suggested by Tlou, Parsons, and Henderson (1995).

feeding programmes for designated 'vulnerable groups', i.e. children, pregnant women, and lactating mothers; and additional support for selected categories of people, initially along the lines of poor relief for 'destitutes' who could not support themselves and were not being supported adequately by kin, and later through universal old-age pensions and support for orphans. In contrast to neighbouring South Africa, Botswana has never introduced a general child support grant paying benefits to poor mothers or other caregivers.

All three major components of public welfare provision date back to independence (from colonial rule) in the mid-1960s. At the time Botswana was a sparsely populated, arid country with a small population of about half a million. It was one of the poorest countries in the world, with GDP per capita about one half of its northern neighbour Zambia and one tenth of its southern neighbour South Africa. The new country had little infrastructure and few public services. Whilst the country had never had many settlers, it was highly stratified, with a wealthy cattle-owning Tswana elite, a large population of small Tswana farmers with few or no cattle, and a non-Tswana underclass. The country was chronically vulnerable to drought.

Independence coincided with terrible drought and famine. The government negotiated with the newly established World Food Programme (WFP) over food aid for, at one point, more than half of the population, as well as stock feed for cattle. Massive support from the WFP and elsewhere—with an estimated value of at least 2 per cent of GDP—averted starvation (although one third of the country's cattle died). When it became clear that famine would continue beyond the scope of a WFP 'emergency operation', the BDP government and the WFP together designed a suite of 'developmental' programmes. First, feeding programmes provided directly for pre-school and primary school children, and pregnant and lactating mothers (and, later, tuberculosis patients also). Second, food-for-work programmes provided rations to working-age adults working on 'self-help' projects, building school facilities, roads, etc.; the rations were intended to support entire households. In addition, assistance was expanded for other 'destitutes' who were unable to work on grounds of age or infirmity (Seekings 2016a).

The drought of the mid- and late 1960s also shaped the development, within the government and BDP, of a conservative welfare doctrine (Seekings 2016b). The drought added to the pressure on the BDP government to articulate the relationships between and respective responsibilities of citizens and state. Crucially, the state assumed responsibilities supposedly undertaken hitherto by the chiefs (Makgala 2012). It also adapted existing understandings of chiefly authority and responsibility to accommodate the new state institutions. The result was a doctrine that represented the state as benign, with clear responsibilities to the poor, but at the same time emphasized the responsibilities of the poor themselves to contribute to their own welfare.

The 1970s were years of relatively good rains and harvests. The country's cattle herds grew rapidly. Drought did not disappear, however, and the government began to institutionalize its relief and recovery programmes. The regular feeding programmes expanded steadily. Food-for-work programmes stopped and started until 1978, when a decision was made to operate continuously, i.e. in non-drought as well as drought years. The government also sought to formalize its support for 'destitutes' who were unable to work, and who needed support in good years as well as bad. In 1974 the responsible Minister asked his cabinet colleagues to decide 'whether the nation has reached that stage of economic and social advancement at which it can afford to begin succouring at the end of their lives the very poorest people of all'. Although he believed 'that the time has come to take a major step towards implementing a genuine long-term programme of relief for the chronically destitute', opposition from the Ministry of Finance and Development Planning (headed by the Vice-President, Quett Masire) stalled the proposed reforms.[2]

The government expected that economic growth would end poverty. The government focused initially on the cattle industry, to the benefit of many BDP leaders and bureaucrats who had acquired large cattle ranches. In the 1970s, the government's focus shifted to mining. Rapid economic growth led, however, to growing inequality. The incomes of the rich and even the formally employed working class grew sharply, with only modest benefits trickling down to the poor.

When drought recurred in 1978–9, the government and WFP together provided drought relief for about 80 per cent of the population. The government formalized its public works programme (as the Labour-Intensive Public Works Programme) and introduced a new National Policy on Destitute Persons. The latter provided for minimal benefits in kind for any individual 'who is rendered helpless due to natural disaster or temporary hardship', and had neither assets (with a limit of four cows) nor close kin to support them (Gooch and Macdonald 1981; Botswana 2002).

[2] Botswana National Archives (BNA), OP 28/6: 'Social Welfare: "Chronic" Destitutes', Draft Cabinet Memorandum drafted by Ministry of Local Government and Lands, 7 February 1974, signed by the Minister, K.P. Morake, and subsequent correspondence.

An even more severe drought recurred between 1981 and 1986. Arable production fell by two thirds. Three hundred thousand cattle had died by 1984. The government responded by expanding its drought relief and recovery programmes: feeding programmes were extended to provide meals for school children over weekends and during school holidays; the public employment programme was expanded, and also introduced cash payments alongside food rations; and more generous food parcels were distributed to much larger numbers of 'destitutes'. Once again, more than half of the population benefited from one or other feeding programme (Botswana 1991: 452). As in the late 1980s, drought relief was followed by drought recovery efforts. Drought relief and recovery programmes were run through existing, largely bureaucratic structures, not by politicians. They were widely acclaimed as a great success, and a good example of the general dictum that democracies do not permit drought to lead to deaths on a large scale (e.g. Dreze and Sen 1989; Teklu 1995; De Waal 1997).

In 1985, concluding their study of the drought relief programmes, Holm and Morgan had assessed that:

> Drought relief is coming to assume a role in Botswana politics comparable to education and welfare in the industrialised countries. Indeed, it is already so popular that the leaders of the BDP have resisted pressures for cuts from bureaucrats. It will be difficult for the Ministry of Finance and Development Planning, which quite naturally concerns itself with balancing the budget, to find a politically acceptable way of reducing the various relief programmes, once the drought is over. (Holm and Morgan 1985: 476)

Holm and Morgan were soon proved correct as the government not only prepared for further droughts but also moved to address more fully the challenge of chronic poverty.

3. The Consolidation of Welfare Programmes in the 1990s

The combination of drought and economic growth pushed the government to consolidate its welfare programmes in the 1990s. In 1990, consultants completed a study for the government of its drought relief programmes since 1981. This informed, first, the government's seventh *National Development Plan* (NDP) (Botswana 1991). Poverty persisted even in years of good rain, indicating 'a structural poverty problem' (ibid.: 17). Social justice and the decline of extended family support required government action: 'Government food aid, its drought relief and recovery programmes, and other aid measures targeted for the destitute are intended to supplement the incomes of the very poor in order to ensure that their disposable incomes, both cash and in kind, provide them with a minimum standard of living' (ibid.: 33). But rising costs (and declining foreign aid) meant that programmes needed to be rationalized. The government envisaged that 'existing assistance measures' would 'be consolidated into a simple, single-channel "safety net", based on strict eligibility criteria, for disadvantaged households', which could easily 'be expanded during drought to protect basic needs and the productive assets of vulnerable households' (ibid.: 89). In 1992, a Government Paper proposed various reforms, which were discussed further at a major conference on 'drought management' in late 1993. These reforms included reduced benefits for workfare, to allow broader coverage without commensurate expense, and to ensure more precise (self-) targeting on the very poor. Workfare would, however, be paid in cash, not in kind. Feeding programmes would also be more narrowly targeted (Botswana 1993).

Policy reform was driven also by the threatened (and finally effected) withdrawal of the WFP from Botswana, which was itself due to Botswana's economic growth, which raised GDP per capita above the threshold at which the country ceased to be eligible for free WFP food aid. The WFP had raised with the Government of Botswana the issue of the transfer of financial responsibility as early as the late 1970s, but enduring drought meant that this was repeatedly postponed. In anticipation of the transfer of financial responsibility for drought relief and related welfare programmes, the Government of Botswana budgeted for drought relief and related programmes in its 1991 *National Development Plan*. A drought in 1992–3 was the last for which Botswana received WFP emergency food aid, although the WFP's phased withdrawal from school and other feeding programmes was finally completed only in 1997.

As the transfer of responsibility of feeding programmes from the WFP to the government's own budget became more imminent, the government was compelled to think more carefully about the design of its programmes. On the one hand, it was concerned not to perpetuate 'dependency', which might entail more precise targeting of some programmes. On the other, it was forced to consider which citizens were 'deserving', and especially which chronically poor citizens were deserving of support in non-drought as well as drought years. The dilemma was set out explicitly in the seventh *National Development Plan*: 'The major challenges Government faces is to ensure that the temporary reliance of vulnerable groups on drought relief does not become a permanent dependency' (Botswana 1991: 389). Across most of Africa, post-colonial governments were wary of encouraging laziness and 'dependency' by providing overly generous assistance ('handouts') to households with able-bodied, working-age adults. Botswana was unusual in that drought had led to programmes with unusually broad coverage, whilst economic growth had led to the WFP's withdrawal. Questions of 'dependency' were therefore addressed earlier in Botswana than elsewhere.

Feeding programmes for children and other 'vulnerable' groups were least controversial, although there was some discussion over the scope of the programmes and especially whether they needed to be better targeted on the poor. The government took over full financial responsibility for these from the WFP in 1997. Provision for 'destitutes', on the other hand, had always been more controversial. The government did nudge up the value of the benefit in 1990 (ibid.: 389) and resolved to restrict eligibility to people who were unfit for work (Botswana 1993). The big question, however, was whether there were specific groups of people for whom the destitutes policy was no longer adequate.

The most pressing group of chronically destitute were the elderly. Hitherto, Botswana's safety nets were based on the assumptions that most elderly people either supported themselves or were supported by their kin and the small number of exceptions was covered adequately by provision for 'destitutes'. Social and economic change made both assumptions doubtful. In April 1988, after years of drought, Members of Parliament from both the BDP and opposition parties called for the introduction of old-age pensions.[3] The government's response was to commission research (through the Ministry of Health), resulting in a workshop in Gaborone in 1993 (see Bruun, Mugabe, and Coombes 1994). The research confirmed that many elderly people—especially widows—were impoverished, without sufficient support from children or destitute relief. Elderly people told researchers that 'our children do not seem to care much about us; we are forced to sit back and wait for any form of relief, hoping that the Government has also not forgotten us'. But the government apparently also 'does not know that old people exist' (Ngome 1994: 105–6). Following the 1993 workshop, an inter-ministerial working group was reportedly set up to continue discussions over ministerial responsibilities to address the challenge of poverty among the elderly. The BDP's 1994 election manifesto included the promise at least to 'study the feasibility

[3] *Hansard*, 8 April 1988, pp. 971–8.

and the affordability of an old age pension scheme' (BDP 1994: 19, para 13.3). Drought recurred again in 1995. Early in 1996, the Minister of Finance and Development Planning (and Vice-President), Festus Mogae, announced that non-contributory old-age pensions would be introduced. In his memoirs, published a decade later, Masire wrote that the BDP was aware that 'traditional' support systems were withering, especially in the towns, and poverty was growing among the elderly. 'We discussed the idea of an old age pension scheme for many years', he wrote; 'by 1996, we felt that we had enough revenue coming from diamonds, and those funds belonged to all Batswana. So we discussed it and decided to go ahead' (Masire 2006: 234).

The old-age pension programme and the assumption of responsibility for feeding programmes cost close to 1 per cent of GDP. This level of recurrent expenditure would have been a massive outlay for many African countries, but for Botswana it was less than the government was spending on drought relief and recovery much of the time. Moreover, at the time public finances seemed buoyant. Former Deputy-Minister of Finance and long-time cabinet member David Magang later accused Masire of profligacy as minister, throwing money away (2008: 475). The eighth NDP (1997/8–2002/3) forecast budget surpluses, with rising revenues outpacing the rising expenditure (Botswana 1997a: 69–71). In 1998/9, however, the country incurred its first budget deficit since 1982/3, of more than 6 per cent of GDP. Deficits recurred also in 2001/2 and 2002/3 (Botswana 2003: 35–9). Whilst the deficit was driven primarily by the public sector wage bill, increased domestic funding of welfare programmes also contributed.

Orphans comprised a second category inadequately covered by destitute relief. The Ministry of Local Government was tasked with keeping a register of orphans and providing them—and their foster families—with necessary food and other benefits in kind (such as school uniforms). As the number of orphans grew, due primarily to AIDS, the Ministry was unable to cope. By 1998 it was thought that less than one half of all orphans were registered. In 1999, the government approved a Short-Term Plan of Action for Orphans, which provided for the appointment of dedicated child welfare officers and committees, and initiated a new Orphan Care Programme (OCP) to take orphans off general destitute relief. Through the 2000s there were about 50,000 orphans being supported under this programme. Although there were fewer beneficiaries than there were old-age pensioners, the cost of the food basket for orphans (and their foster families) was much higher than the value of an old-age pension, which meant that the total cost of the OCP was about the same as the total cost of the old-age pension scheme (Chinyoka 2019).

Finally, in 2002, the government reformed its 'destitutes policy'. The new policy defined more clearly 'permanent' destitutes (comprising primarily the disabled) and 'temporary' destitutes (resulting from drought or the death of or desertion by a breadwinner). Special provision was made for 'needy children' (other than orphans, who were covered by the OCP). The 'Revised Policy' raised the value of the food basket and introduced for the first time a modest cash benefit on the grounds that destitutes needed cash (for items such as toothpaste and paraffin) as well as food rations. The 2002 Revised Policy was more generous but it remained highly moralistic, based on an understanding of destitution that encompassed a failure to take advantage of opportunities to improve one's life. The Policy identified the 'responsibilities' of destitutes and specified appropriate actions to be taken if they 'flouted' these responsibilities (Botswana 2002: 11–12).

By the early 2000s drought relief programmes funded heavily from abroad had been extended and consolidated into a permanent welfare state funded from domestic revenues. There are no good data on precisely what proportion of the population benefited from the various government programmes. Seleka et al. (2007) report that one in three households was receiving support from one or other programme as of 2002/3, but this figure seems to have excluded school feeding programmes. By 2009/10, the proportion had risen further. Although only about 10 per cent of the population benefited directly from cash (or 'near-cash') programmes, many of these supported large households, so the proportion of *indirect* beneficiaries was much larger. An even larger number of individuals benefited from feeding programmes: Given some overlap between programmes, it is likely that approximately one quarter of the total population benefited from school meals, and a similar proportion directly from other programmes. It is probably true that a large majority of households benefited from one or other government welfare programme. Cash benefits remained parsimonious, however, especially in comparison with neighbouring South Africa.

In the 2000s, when new social assistance programmes were being introduced across much of Africa, Botswana's government focused rather on containing costs. The finance minister warned in 2010 that the number of people receiving assistance was 'economically unsustainable'.[4] The government rejected proposals for a broader child grant, first in 2010, and then again in 2013 (when the proposals were made by the World Bank). Expenditure on

[4] 2010 budget speech (presented by O.K. Matambo, Monday 8 February 2010, *Hansard*, vol. 163, part I.

programmes for children in Botswana remained at about 0.7 per cent of GDP, i.e. about one half of the level in neighbouring South Africa. Botswana's various social assistance programmes cost a total of about 1.9 per cent of GDP (BIDPA and World Bank 2013: 42), which was substantially less than in South Africa but more than in most African countries. One programme that did see significant reform—or at least repackaging—was workfare. Another review of Destitute Policy, in August 2008, recommended (again) that able-bodied 'destitutes' should be enrolled in workfare instead.[5] This required that the workfare programme be extended to all parts of the country where there were able-bodied destitutes. The former Labour-Intensive Public Works Programme was renamed the *Ipelegeng* programme, becoming permanent rather than intermittent and poverty- rather than drought-focused, from 2008/9 (Hamer 2016).

4. Economic, Social, and Cultural Change

The expansion and consolidation of a welfare state in Botswana—much earlier than in most of Africa (excepting South Africa)—reflected the availability of resources as well as the perceived need. Economic growth was exceptional, with GDP per capita in 2008 fourteen times higher in real terms than it had been at independence. This ensured rising public revenues. At the same time, the welfare state was 'necessary' to ensure that the benefits of growth were shared across the whole population. Economic growth did not eliminate poverty. Even with an expanding welfare state, 19 per cent of the population fell below the national poverty line in 2009/10, and the poverty gap remained large in relation to the resources spent on safety net programmes. Whilst the population was urbanizing rapidly, poverty remained highest in rural areas. A rising proportion of rural households had no cattle, little or no land, and weak or no kin or other networks through which they could claim support. Poverty was the result of deagrarianization in rural areas rather than urbanization.

As early as 1977/8, a year of reasonable rain and production, one survey found that only 7 per cent of households were able to meet their food needs through their own production. Almost all households were dependent on other sources of food, especially income from waged work, whether as migrants in neighbouring South Africa (in the mid-twentieth century) or

[5] Ibid.

within Botswana itself (in the later part of the century) (Vierich and Sheppard 1980: 50). The simplest measure of deagrarianization in Botswana is the declining proportion of households, including of households in rural areas only, who had access to cattle, whether through ownership or some kind of lease arrangement (including *mafisa*, i.e. the traditional system of loaned cattle). In the 'traditional' agricultural sector, i.e. excluding about 500 large commercial farms, 32 per cent of farming households had no cattle in 1981. By 1995, this proportion had risen to 49 per cent (Botswana 1997a: 227–8).

A social aspect of deagrarianization was the shrinkage of kinship obligations. The official narrative of Tswana culture emphasizes the extended family. In 1970, for example, then Vice-President Masire praised the 'African extended family... with its built-in system of social security' as 'an invaluable institution'. He warned that, 'if the extended family system were to disintegrate we would all be the losers'. He continued to laud 'the traditional system of sharing natural resources of water and grazing, and land generally' for providing 'a sound basis on which to build a just and egalitarian society' (quoted in Kooijman 1978: 212). Contemporary ethnographic studies reported, however, that the extended family system was threatened by the rise in individualism and decline in perceived obligations towards kin, including even parents. Kooijman, who conducted research in the early 1970s, reported a decline in the former practice of young men ploughing for their parents. She illustrates this with a discussion of one poor family, whose kin were not prepared to support them except in return for work. A wealthy kinsman told Kooijman that 'I cannot give him food without him or his family working for us. My wife could never agree to a free gift of corn. She would ask me what I am doing by giving food to "lazy" people'. Perhaps in part in consequence, poor people were often ashamed to ask for help (ibid.: 234–5). In the early 1990s, government officials repeatedly recognized that the extended family system was disintegrating (e.g. Botswana 1991: 18; Bruun et al. 1994). In the parliamentary debate on the old-age pension in 1996, an opposition MP recalled that 'before independence, the sense of communal obligation was very strong as the care of the aged, orphans and the disabled was voluntarily undertaken by relatives under the system of extended family. Now, today, as you are all aware, that sense has now died. What remains is the sense of everybody for himself and God for us all'.[6]

The BDP government's response to the persistence of poverty amidst social change was shaped by its understanding of Tswana culture and its paternalistic

[6] BNF MP for Kanye, Mr S. Gabathswane. *Hansard*, Thursday 15 February 1996, p. 95.

but conservative ideology. From the mid-1960s, the BDP sought to appropriate traditions of responsibility. The official narrative of Tswana culture places a very heavy emphasis on tradition, more explicitly than most other national cultures in east and southern Africa. According to this narrative, chiefs had clear responsibilities for the poor. In the case of the Batswana, when the chief (*kgosi*) was installed, he was told:

> *Morafe wa gago ke oo*
> *O babalele*
> *Ke wena ramasiela, ke wena rabahumanegi*
> *Kgosi ke kgosi ka batho.*

Translated: There is our nation, care for it, you are the father of the orphans and the poor, the king is the king by the grace of the people (Tlou 1998). The BDP was led by a traditional leader (Seretse Khama, who had effectively been deposed as chief of the BaNgwato after marrying a British woman), but was nonetheless a 'grand coalition' of the modernizing, educated 'new men' who became commercial cattle farmers, embraced liberal democracy, and removed many of the powers of chiefs (Gillett 1973; Parson 1984; Tlou et al. 1995; Samatar 1999; Sebudubudu with Molutsi 2009). The BDP was not a broad-based nationalist movement nor was it led by a natural ideologue (such as Nyerere, in Tanzania).

Formed to negotiate independence and having won an overwhelming majority in the pre-independence elections, the BDP had to define an ideology setting out the relationships between the new (BDP-run) state and its citizens. In the late 1960s and early 1970s, Khama, Masire, and the BDP, with the assistance of their mostly expatriate scriptwriters, crafted conservative doctrines of government, growth, and welfare. These doctrines were shaped profoundly by the drought and ensuing destitution and poverty that accompanied independence and the government's determination to transfer powers from the chiefs to the new state. With respect to welfare specifically, the result was a doctrine with four key elements. First, it idealized rural society and demonized urban life. Second, it emphasized 'self-help' and was hostile to 'dependency' on the charity of the state. Third, it aspired to social harmony, despite inequality. Finally, it proposed a sharing of responsibility between individuals and the state. The overarching concept was *kagisano*, which was usually translated as 'unity, peace, harmony and a sense of community' (Gulbrandsen 2012; Seekings 2016b).

BDP leaders were liberal in their preference for markets over the state, and were conservative on many social issues (including both the family and sex), but saw the state and society as having responsibilities for the poor. These responsibilities were shared with the poor themselves: The poor had a responsibility to work hard and take advantage of whatever opportunities were open to them; they should not rely on government 'handouts'. Improved productivity was always to be preferred to welfare. Khama and Masire were insistent that their ideology was not socialist (see Seekings 2016b). At the end of Masire's presidency, the BDP's ideology was rearticulated in *Vision 2016*. *Vision 2016* invoked the Tswana concept of '*botho*': 'This refers to one of the tenets of African culture—the concept of a person who has a well-rounded character, who is well-mannered, courteous and disciplined, and realises his or her potential both as an individual and as a part of the community to which he or she belongs' (Botswana 1997b: 2). *Vision 2016* set out a clear, implicit commitment to social justice. Botswana would become 'a compassionate and caring society, offering support and opportunity to those who are poor, and including *all* people in the benefits of growth' (ibid.: 8, emphasis in original). *Vision 2016* envisaged that poverty would be halved by 2007, and absolute poverty would be eliminated by 2016. This would be achieved primarily through economic growth and the provision of opportunities, but 'there will be a social safety net for those who find themselves in poverty for any reason' (ibid.: 9). At the same time, Botswana should worry about the 'deterioration of national values'. In a section on the '"give me" attitude', *Vision 2016* insisted on the importance of avoiding 'a culture of dependency' (ibid.: 25).

Festus Mogae, who was Masire's Vice-President and Minister of Finance and Development Planning before succeeding Masire as President in 1998, emphasized even more strongly the need for balance between public and individual responsibilities. He affirmed repeatedly his commitment to tackling the challenges of poverty and unemployment but saw this in terms of 'mutual social responsibility'. 'National development', he explained in his budget speech in 1993, was 'a cooperative endeavour, and we must all play our part.' Mutual self-responsibility meant 'that self-reliance takes precedence over appeals to Government for assistance'.[7] In the first BDP election manifesto under his leadership, Mogae called for 'self-reliance as opposed to a dependency syndrome' (Mogae 1999).

BDP leaders' anxiety over dependency (on 'handouts') reflected the reach of the programmes that they had implemented since independence. References

[7] *Hansard*, vol. 110, part 1, Monday 8 February 1993, p. 4. See also the BDP's 1994 election manifesto.

to 'dependency' proliferated in the mid-1980s, as programmes were expanded in response to chronic drought (Seekings 2017). As anthropologists noted, rural villagers came to see the new state 'as a generous patron':

> Many villagers see 'the government', often personified by the President, the local member of parliament or other local representatives of the state, as *motswadintle*—as 'he from whom good things come'... The general attitude is that 'the government' or the 'BDP' will deliver the goods, so that villagers can live their village lives... [I]n 1990, when a number of programmes relating to an eight-year-long drought had just been brought to an end, the general attitude among villagers was that the state's behaviour was *maswe* (bad). Two years later the government (no doubt thanks to the impending election) reintroduced many of these programmes and the general attitude shifted in a more positive direction.
>
> (Helle-Valle 2002: 195–6; see also Gulbrandsen 2012)

At the same time, as Helle-Valle notes, the government bureaucrats on the front line of the new state treated villagers with disdain.

5. Political Competition

The combination of drought and economic growth underlay both the need and possibility of expanding public provision for—and decommodification of—the poor. But the actual impetus to reform was political. BDP leaders were pushed to reform by two forms of political competition. First, at and soon after independence, the BDP leadership sought to provide the new state with some legitimacy through assuming responsibilities previously attached to chiefs. Later, including especially in the early 1990s, the BDP faced serious electoral challenges from rival political parties. Social assistance programmes may have led to distasteful dependency, in the view of BDP leaders, but they also underpinned the legitimacy of the new state and continuing electoral support for the governing party.

At independence, the BDP under Seretse Khama sought to build the institutions of a 'modern' state, to assume most of the functions performed hitherto by chiefs. In Botswana, to a greater extent than elsewhere, chiefs had been integral to colonial governance. The Chieftainship Act of 1966, subsequent Amendment Acts, and other legislation transferred most of the chiefs' legislative and executive roles to new institutions, including especially popularly elected district councils and related bureaucrats (Gillett 1973; Vengroff 1977). Khama himself was the rightful chief of the Bangwato but he threw his lot in with other educated cattle owners in the BDP. For him, as well as for Masire, chiefly authority was both an obstacle to economic growth and change and a source of continuing tribal division. Drought relief provided a vehicle for reconstituting relations between state and citizenry, i.e. for a new social contract. Prior to independence, colonial District Commissioners had worked through chiefs and headmen to address drought. From independence, drought relief was administered by District and Village Development Committees. Ideologically, also, the BDP could wrap the new state in the flag of paternalist responsibility (Seekings 2016b).

By the mid-1970s the new state had established its hegemony. Thereafter, the primary challenge to the BDP came from other political parties. The distinctive expansion of the welfare state in Botswana in the decades following independence reflected in part the country's unusually democratic political system. Almost uniquely in Africa, Botswana held multi-party elections regularly, although the country has never experienced any turnover in government. The BDP won more than half of the vote in every election from the pre-independence election of 1965 through to 2009. The BDP had a comfortable parliamentary majority throughout this period, even when its share of the vote was only just over 50 per cent, because of the Westminster-style first-past-the-post constituency system. In 2014, for the first time, it failed to win a majority of the vote but nonetheless retained a majority of seats in parliament. The BDP is arguably the most successful party in Africa in terms of its success in remaining in office for fifty years (and counting). The limits to democracy in Botswana have been well documented (Nthomang 2007; Good 1996, 2016). Nonetheless, the BDP has faced electoral challenges, and these have pushed it into more extensive policy reform that it might have undertaken in the absence of electoral competition. The election of 1994, when the BDP's share of the vote fell dramatically to 53 per cent, was a particularly powerful shock.

The BDP has always faced vocal criticism from opposition parties, including initially the Botswana People's Party (BPP) and later the Botswana National Front (BNF). The BDP restricted the BPP and BNF to a small number of seats until 1994, when the BNF won thirteen seats (to the BDP's twenty-seven), with support concentrated in urban areas. Whilst both the governing BDP and opposition parties (and trade unions) were rhetorically pro-poor, their rhetoric differed. The BDP espoused a paternalist, conservative doctrine, whilst the opposition presented a more orthodox social democratic discourse (with occasional Marxist flourishes).

The BDP has used public expenditure to bolster its electoral support, especially in rural areas. Faced with competition from the new BNF in the 1969 elections, Khama's government secured continued support from the WFP for drought recovery programmes (and other rural development programmes). In 1979, MPs from the BDP reportedly pressed the government to declare a drought so that drought relief programmes could pour money into their constituencies in the run-up to that year's elections (Munemo 2012: 132–3). Press reports from the 1979 election campaign indicate that the distribution of food aid was an important campaign issue (ibid.: 147). 'Young Turks' in the BDP criticized the party's leaders for neglecting inequality whilst pursuing economic growth (Pickard 1987: 170). The 1984 elections have been described as being 'critical in bringing BDP to see the political value of drought relief' (Holm and Cohen 1988: 36). The Cabinet reportedly overruled the Ministry of Finance and expanded massively the drought relief budget in order to maintain the BDP's support in rural areas (ibid.).

In 1994, the BNF criticized the BDP for 'dividing the nation into the haves and the have-nots', and promised that a BNF government would 'create more jobs' and 'provide social welfare for the most needy', including free education, contributory and non-contributory old-age pensions, dependents' and orphans' benefits, unemployment benefits, and pre-school facilities for working parents (BNF 1994: 3–8). Following its narrow victory in the 1994 elections, and looking forward to the next elections in 1999 (Nthomang 2007: 212), the BDP government moved to introduce old-age pensions and orphans' benefits, and to assume financial responsibility for feeding programmes, despite the considerable cost of these at a time when the budget was beginning to take strain. Later, in the 2009 and 2014 elections, BDP leader and president Ian Khama (the son of Seretse Khama) sought to brand himself as pro-poor through, inter alia, expanding the *Ipelegeng* workfare programme (Hamer 2016).

Scholars who have conducted ethnographic research in rural areas suggest that the BDP's expansion of state provision (on top of governing during very rapid economic growth) was crucial to it sustaining its electoral support in its rural strongholds. Until the late 1980s, 'the ruling party and the government it dominated exercised its hegemony so forcefully . . . that it was no simple matter for the opposition to establish a convincing political alternative'. When the government provided schools and clinics, roads and water supplies, and feeding programmes, all that the opposition could criticize was that this was not enough (Gulbrandsen 2012: 249). The BDP insisted that its leaders—and government officials—participated in popular meetings (*kgotla*), where they were exposed to (controlled) criticisms of the government's performance with respect to development. Holm and Morgan noted in 1985 that the BDP—from the president down to local councillors—had come to view drought relief as 'a very effective means of reinforcing its rural support' (1985: 476). A survey showed that 'the single most important reason given by respondents...for being a member of the BDP was the Drought Relief Programme' (Molutsi 1989: 128). In the face of widespread allegations of elite corruption, pro-poor welfare programmes were crucial to sustaining the BDP's electoral support.

Electoral competition helps to explain both the expansion of public provision and its pronounced rural bias. Munemo (2012) argues, perversely, that the BDP implemented cash-for-work programmes rather than food aid in the 1980s because of its strength, as the incumbent party, *not* because of its electoral vulnerability. His overarching hypothesis, applied to several countries, is that electorally vulnerable government prefer food aid which politicians can manipulate to consolidate their support, whilst more secure parties are happy to shift from discretionary expenditures to programmes administered by bureaucrats. Contra Munemo's hypothesis, Botswana was a case of a governing party introducing more and more programmatic reforms as its share of the vote declined.

The case of Botswana extends our understanding of the role of partisan politics in policy reform. Centre-left parties, with strong bases among the urban and industrial working class, have often been the primary drivers of expanding social programmes, including in India, Mexico, Korea, and Brazil (Dion 2010; Huber and Stephens 2012; Seekings 2012; Yang 2017). In a number of countries, however, centre-right parties have embraced and even expanded social programmes. In cases such as Mexico and Chile, they did this in reaction to centre-left initiatives (Fairfield and Garay 2017). In Botswana, the BDP acted *pre-emptively*, initially to usurp the roles of chiefs, and later to shore up its rural support base in the face of rising challenges from urban-based opposition parties.

6. Conclusion

Botswana was one of the pioneers in welfare state-building in Africa. By the time of Seretse Khama's death, in mid-1980, the state was already massively involved in the decommodification of its citizens through providing a safety net that was wide (and very wide during times of extreme drought). This was a welfare state that insured its citizens against the risk (of drought) that was most pressing in a still largely rural society. This was not a welfare state that insured its citizens primarily against the risks associated with urbanization and industrialization. Drought intermittently pushed into poverty households that were headed by working-age, able-bodied adults. Food-for-work programmes providing rations for a single adult per household were intended to strengthen families, not compensate for family breakdown. At the same time, the state accepted responsibility for children and mothers and for 'destitute' people who were unable to work, but at minimal levels. The long drought of the 1980s pushed the government to expand and entrench relief and recovery programmes. In the 1990s, faced with the withdrawal of the WFP and enduring poverty, the BDP consolidated its welfare programmes. As Ulriksen (2011, 2012) and Hickey (2011) emphasize, Botswana's welfare state was modest in comparison with the more generous welfare states of Mauritius and South Africa. By comparison with the rest of Africa, however, it was extensive in terms of both coverage and expense (costing close to 2 per cent of GDP).

The predominant approach to explaining variation between welfare states (or regimes) focuses on the political power of the classes produced by capitalist industrialization. Where working classes were organized, united, and willing to forge alliances with family farmers or sections of the middle class, then social democracy became hegemonic, and universal, egalitarian welfare states were built. This was the case across much of northern Europe (e.g. Esping-Andersen 1990; Baldwin 1990; Huber and Stephens 2001) and, from the late 1990s, East Asia (Yang 2017). In Germany, in contrast, labour-intensive agriculture predominated in the early twentieth century, and farmers were recruited into a conservative coalition that sought to repress trade unions and left-wing parties whilst co-opting some workers (especially civil servants) into corporatist institutions. After the Second World War, the German middle classes supported conservative reforms because they wished to preserve occupationally segregated social insurance programmes (and ensuing status differentials) and remained loyal to the Christian Democrats. The experiences of the early industrializers in Latin America—Argentina, Chile, and Brazil—were more similar to the German model, in that large parts of the formally employed working class were co-opted into corporatist institutions that preserved a status hierarchy (and excluded most of the urban as well as rural poor) (Huber and Stephens 2012). The risks facing people varied more between classes within societies than they did across national boundaries, but politics played out very differently in different national settings.

The choices made by political parties, informed by their ideologies, were consequential in terms of the kind and extent of welfare state that was built. Germany's history of absolutism (rather than liberal democracy) and Catholicism (with its commitment to preserving the traditional family) shaped its welfare state (Esping-Andersen 1990: 26–33, 133–5). Even after the Second World War, the Christian Democratic understanding of social citizenship emphasized 'duties rather than rights, the family and the social group rather than the individual, society rather than the state, and distributional justice rather than social justice' (Van Kersbergen 2003: 178), with distributional justice understood in terms of classes or status groups receiving their fair but unequal shares.

Citizens of Botswana faced very different risks to their counterparts in more industrialized and urbanized societies. From the 1960s through the 1980s, and even into the 1990s, the primary risk was drought. In a society that remained largely agrarian—notwithstanding the dependence of the 'peasantariat' (or semi-proletarianized peasantry) also on the remittances of migrant workers, especially on South African mines (Parson 1984)—drought pushed most households into poverty and destitution. Even the rich were affected, through the decimation of their herds of cattle, which were the source of both wealth and status. In the mid- and late 1960s, again at the end of the 1970s, and then through most of the 1980s, the newly independent state faced immense pressure to address the challenges of drought and famine. The scope for public provision was expanded by the tax revenues generated by rapid economic growth and the existence of a broadly Weberian bureaucracy, facilitating a programmatic response to poverty rather than the deployment of discretionary patronage.

How the state responded, however, was shaped by politics. As Ulriksen (2012) emphasizes, the absence of an independent middle class meant that the political elite faced little political pressure to implement the more 'social democratic' programmes introduced in Mauritius. Successive governments have been reluctant to increase either direct or indirect taxation (Ulriksen 2017). Nonetheless, the leadership of the BDP, drawn from the educated, cattle-owning elite, was under pressure to legitimate the new state, which entailed taking over responsibilities from chiefs, and to consolidate electoral support for the BDP in the face of competition from opposition parties. The BDP's core support lay in rural areas, and the party consolidated its support through massive drought relief, then drought recovery, and then continuing welfare programmes.

The conservative welfare regime in Botswana had some features in common with the conservative regimes of continental Europe: The state sought to co-opt public sector workers, in part through social security (spending 1.2 per cent of GDP on this, compared to just under 2 per cent on all 'safety nets'); and the BDP and state were strongly committed to both the status hierarchy and the family. But the welfare regime was far less statist than in countries such as Germany, leaving protection against risks to the market as well as kin. Botswana's welfare state was more residual than the conservative one in Europe, providing means-tested benefits for the poor (including through workfare), whilst universal programmes (such as the old-age pensions and school feeding programmes) provided modest benefits. Social insurance remained very limited.[8] Moreover, Botswana's welfare state was hardly corporatist. In these respects, the welfare regime in Botswana was more akin to a conservative, familialist version of the liberal variant of welfare regimes that Esping-Andersen identified in Europe. The BDP adhered to a conservative ideology, but not one with roots in Catholicism. It was an ideology of modernization, but one concerned more with the challenges of deagrarianization than those of urbanization and industrialization.

Botswana's route to building a welfare state was very different to the routes followed by either Mauritius or South Africa. Both Mauritius and South Africa recognized in the mid-twentieth century that welfare programmes were required because deagrarianization had resulted in a large population that was vulnerable to poverty but was unable to support itself through subsistence agriculture. Across most of Africa, colonial and post-colonial states imagined that poverty could be addressed through interventions to strengthen peasant agriculture. These agrarian welfare regimes remained vulnerable to drought, and hence required drought relief programmes. Botswana's experience with drought between the 1960s and 1980s pushed its governing party to the recognition that relief programmes were needed on a permanent, not temporary, basis.

This agrarian route to welfare state-building has been followed by other African countries also. Across much of east and southern Africa drought and social change pushed governments—usually with help from the WFP and elsewhere—into welfare programmes. The impetus has almost always been

[8] Botswana provided pensions for white-collar public sector employees. These were privatized in 2001, requiring massive capital transfers during 2002–3. There is no mandatory social insurance (although this was debated in parliament in 2008), and manual workers in the public sector are not covered by the public sector scheme. Most workers rely on gratuities or severance payments (including through provident funds)—see Selolwane (2012): 112–15, 120–2.

rural rather than urban. In this volume, Lavers documents the shift from emergency drought relief programmes to permanent social assistance in Ethiopia, where severe drought was common and disastrous. In Ethiopia, the governing party sought first to sustain peasant agriculture through an agrarian welfare regime. In the 2000s it became apparent that 'emergency' programmes were needed all of the time. The result was the Productive Safety Net Programme (PSNP), from 2005, which combined workfare with cash transfers and feeding schemes for individuals or households unable to work.

In Botswana, the form of reform was shaped by the ideology of the governing party, but the impetus came from political considerations: first, ensuring the legitimacy of the post-colonial state and, later, sustaining support for the governing party among voters. Across much of Africa, redemocratization in the 1990s provided strong electoral incentives to political parties to appear to be addressing the challenges of poverty. In societies where peasant agriculture remains viable—and there are opportunities for raising productivity—many voters, parties, and governments prefer that public funds are allocated to farm input subsidies, i.e. to sustain an agrarian welfare regime. Across much of Africa, however, it is evident that more and more people slip through the cracks of an agrarian welfare regime and require programmatic support. In many countries, individual leaders, factions, or whole parties have championed the expansion of social protection (as is evident in the chapters in this volume on Malawi and Zambia). Ethiopia and Rwanda followed a slightly different path, in which electoral politics played little or no role, although the governing parties in both countries were very concerned with their legitimacy. In both its responsiveness to voters' concerns and its ensuing, cautious support for welfare programmes (at the same time as it was concerned over 'dependency'), the BDP in Botswana in the late twentieth century prefigured the shifting policy positions of many governments in both semi-democratic and largely authoritarian contexts elsewhere in Africa in the 2000s.

Acknowledgements

The background research for this study was funded by an award from the UK Department for International Development through the UK Economic and Social Research Council for the project on 'Legislating and Implementing Welfare Policy Reforms' and through UNU-WIDER's project on 'The Economics and Politics of Taxation and Social Protection'. I gratefully acknowledge the support. I am also very grateful to Luca Mancurti and Daniela Demel of the World Food Programme Library and Research Centre in Rome for help on the WFP's operations in Botswana.

References

Baldwin, Peter (1990). *The Politics of Social Solidarity: Class Bases of the European Welfare State, 1875–1975*. Cambridge: Cambridge University Press.

Bar-On, Arnon (2001). Providing so little for so few: Botswana's Social Assistance Scheme. In Francis Wilson, Nazneen Kanji, and Einar Braathen (Eds.), *Poverty Reduction: What Role for the State in Today's Globalized Economy?* London: Zed, with CROP, 246–68.

BDP (1994). *Election Manifesto 1994*. Gaborone: Botswana Democratic Party.

BIDPA and World Bank (2013). *Botswana Social Protection Assessment*. Gaborone: Botswana Institute for Development Policy Analysis and Washington DC: World Bank.

BNF (1994). *Manifesto for the General Elections 1994*. Gaborone: Botswana National Front.

Botswana (1991). *National Development Plan 7, 1991–1997*. Gaborone: Ministry of Finance and Development Planning.

Botswana (1993). *Report on the National Conference on Drought Management*. Gaborone: Ministry of Finance and Development Planning.

Botswana (1997a). *National Development Plan 8, 1997/98–2002/03*. Gaborone: Ministry of Finance and Development Planning.

Botswana (1997b). *Vision 2016*. Gaborone: Ministry of Finance and Development Planning.

Botswana (2002). *Revised National Policy on Destitute Persons*. Gaborone: Ministry of Local Government and Rural Development.

Botswana (2003). *National Development Plan 9, 2003/04–2008/09*. Gaborone: Ministry of Finance and Development Planning.

Bruun, Frank Jarle, Mbulawa Mugabe, and Yolande Coombes (Eds.) (1994). *The Situation of the Elderly in Botswana: Proceedings from an International Workshop*. Universities of Botswana and Oslo.

Chinyoka, Isaac (2019). *Familial Child Welfare Regimes: The Case of Botswana, 1966–2017*. CSSR Working Paper 430. Cape Town: Centre for Social Science Research, University of Cape Town.

Devereux, Stephen (2007). Social pensions in Southern Africa in the twentieth century. *Journal of Southern African Studies*, 33(3), 539–60.

De Waal, Alex (1997). *Famine Crimes: Politics and the Disaster Relief Industry in Africa*. Oxford: James Currey/IA.

Dion, Michelle (2010). *Workers and Welfare*. Pittsburgh, PA: Pittsburgh University Press.

Drèze, Jean and Amartya Sen (1989). *Hunger and Public Action*. Oxford: Clarendon Press.

Esping-Andersen, Gøsta (1990). *The Three Worlds of Welfare Capitalism*. Oxford: Oxford University Press.

Garcia, Marito and Charity M.T. Moore (2012). *The Cash Dividend: The Rise of Cash Transfer Programs in Sub-Saharan Africa*. Washington DC: World Bank.

Gillett, Simon (1973). The survival of chieftaincy in Botswana. *African Affairs*, 72(187), 179–85.

Gooch, Toby and John Macdonald (1981). *Evaluation of 1979/80 Drought Relief Programme*. Gaborone: Ministry of Finance and Development Planning.

Good, Kenneth (1996). Authoritarian liberalism: defining characteristic of Botswana. *Journal of Contemporary African Politics*, 14, 1.

Good, Kenneth (2016). Democracy and development in Botswana. *Journal of Contemporary African Studies*, 35, 113–28.

Gulbrandsen, Ørnulf (2012). *The State and the Social: State Formation in Botswana and its Precolonial and Colonial Genealogies*. New York: Berghahn.

Hamer, Sam (2016). *"Our Father's Programmes": Political Branding around Social Protection in Botswana, 2008–2014*. CSSR Working Paper 370. Cape Town: Centre for Social Science Research, University of Cape Town.

Helle-Valle, Jo (2002). Seen from below: conceptions of politics and the state in a Botswana village. *Africa*, 72(2), 179–202.

Hickey, Sam (2011). The politics of social protection: what do we get from a 'social contract' approach? *Canadian Journal of Development Studies/Revue canadienne d'études du développement*, 32(4), 426–38.

Holm, John and Mark Cohen (1988). Enhancing equity in the midst of drought: the Botswana approach. *Journal of Social Development in Africa*, 3(1), 31–8.

Holm, John and Richard G. Morgan (1985). Coping with drought in Botswana: an African success. *Journal of Modern African Studies*, 23(3), 463–82.

Huber, Evelyne and John Stephens (2001). *Development and Crisis of the Welfare State: Parties and Policies in Global Markets*. Chicago, IL: University of Chicago Press.

Huber, Evelyne and John Stephens (2012). *Democracy and the Left: Social Policy and Inequality in Latin America*. Chicago, IL: University of Chicago Press.

Kooijman, K.F.M. (1978). *Social and Economic Change in a Tswana Village*. Leiden: African Studies Centre, University of Leiden.

Magang, Davi (2008). *The Magic of Perseverance: The Autobiography of David Magang*. Cape Town: Centre for Advanced Studies of African Society.

Makgala, Christian John (2012). Provision of local services by tribal administrations in Bechuanaland Protectorate, 1900–1966. *South African Historical Journal*, 64(4), 787–806.

Masire, Quett (2006). *Very Brave or Very Foolish?* Gaborone: Macmillan Botswana.

Mogae, Festus (1999). *'Foreword' to BDP Election Manifesto 1999*. Gaborone: Botswana Democratic Party.

Molutsi, Patrick (1989). Whose interests do Botswana's politicians represent? In John Holm and Patrick Molutsi (Eds.), *Democracy in Botswana*. Gaborone: Macmillan, 120–32.

Munemo, Ngonidzashe (2012). *Domestic Politics and Drought Relief in Africa*. Boulder, CO: Lynne Rienner.

Ngome, Eric (1994). A rapid assessment of the perception of the elderly on the problem of ageing in Botswana. In Frank Jarle Bruun, Mbulawa Mugabe, and Yolande Coombes (Eds.), *The Situation of the Elderly in Botswana: Proceedings from an International Workshop*. Universities of Botswana and Oslo, 103–8.

Niño-Zarazúa, Miguel, Armando Barrientos, Samuel Hickey, and David Hulme (2012). Social protection in sub-Saharan Africa: getting the politics right. *World Development*, 40(1), 163–76.

Nthomang, Keitseope (2007). Democracy and social policy in Botswana. In Yusuf Bangura (Ed.), *Democracy and Social Policy*. London: Palgrave Macmillan, for UNRISD, 189–218.

Parson, Jack (1984). *Botswana: Liberal Democracy and the Labor Reserve in Southern Africa*. Boulder, CO: Westview.

Pickard, Louis (1987). *The Politics of Development in Botswana*. Boulder, CO: Lynne Rienner.

Samatar, A.I. (1999). *An African Miracle: State and Class Leadership and Colonial Legacy in Botswana Developmen*t. Portsmouth, NH: Heinemann.

Sebudubudu, David with Patrick Molutsi (2009). Leaders, elites and coalitions in the development of Botswana. DLP Research Paper 2 (Developmental Leadership Programme).

Seekings, Jeremy (2007). "Not a single white person should be allowed to go under": Swartgevaar and the origins of South Africa's Welfare State, 1924–1929. *Journal of African History*, 48(3), 375–94.

Seekings, Jeremy (2011). British colonial policy, local politics and the origins of the Mauritian welfare state, 1936–1950. *Journal of African History*, 52, 157–77.

Seekings, Jeremy (2012). Pathways to redistribution. *Journal für Entwicklungspolitik (Austrian Journal of Development Studies)*, 28(1), 14–34.

Seekings, Jeremy (2016a). *Drought Relief and the Origins of a Conservative Welfare State in Botswana, 1965–1980*. CSSR Working Paper 378. Cape Town: Centre for Social Science Research, University of Cape Town.

Seekings, Jeremy (2016b). *"A Lean Cow Cannot Climb Out of the Mud, But a Good Cattleman Does Not Leave It to Perish": The Origins of a Conservative Welfare Doctrine in Botswana Under Seretse Khama, 1966–1980*. CSSR Working Paper 387. Cape Town: Centre for Social Science Research, University of Cape Town.

Seekings, Jeremy (2017). The discourse of dependency and the agrarian origins of welfare doctrines in Africa: the case of Botswana. *Sozialpolitik.ch*. 2. Available at https://www.sozialpolitik.ch/fileadmin/user_upload/2017_2_Article_Seekings.pdf.

Seleka, Tebogo B., Happy Siphambe, Dolly Ntseane, Nomtuse Mbere, Charity Kerapeletswe, and Chris Sharp (2007). *Social Safety Nets in Botswana: Administration, Targeting and Sustainability*. Gaborone: Botswana Institute for Development Policy Analysis.

Selolwane, Onalenna (2012). Welfare, social protection and policy reduction. In Selolwane (Ed.), *Poverty Reduction and Changing Policy Regimes in Botswana*. London: Palgrave Macmillan with UNRISD, 102–38.

Teklu, Tesfaye (1995). Labour-intensive public works in Botswana and Tanzania. In Joachim von Braun (Ed.), *Employment for Poverty Reduction and Food Security*. Washington DC: International Food Policy Research Institute, 144–73.

Tlou, Thomas (1998). The nature of Batawana states: towards a theory of Batawana traditional government—the Batawana case. In Wayne Edge and Mogopodi Lekorwe (Eds.), *Botswana: Politics and Society*. Pretoria: van Schaik, 11–31.

Tlou, Thomas, Neil Parsons, and W. Henderson (1995). *Seretse Khama 1921–1980*. Gaborone: Botswana Society.

Ulriksen, Marianne S. (2011). Social policy development and global financial crisis in the open economies of Botswana and Mauritius. *Global Social Policy*, 11(2–3), 194–213.

Ulriksen, Marianne S. (2012). Welfare policy expansion in Botswana and Mauritius: explaining the causes of different welfare regime paths. *Comparative Political Studies*, 45(12), 1483–509.

Ulriksen, Marianne S. (2017). Mineral wealth and limited redistribution: social transfers and taxation in Botswana. *Journal of Contemporary African Studies*, 35(1), 73–92.

Van Kersbergen, Kees (2003). *Social Capitalism*. London: Routledge.

Vengroff, Richard (1977). *Botswana: Rural Development in the Shadow of Apartheid*. Cranbury, NJ: Associated University Presses.

Vierich, Helga and Christopher Sheppard (1980). *Drought in Rural Botswana: Socio-Economic Impact and Government Policy*. Gaborone: Ministry of Agriculture, January.

Yang, Jae-jin (2017). *The Political Economy of the Small Welfare State in South Korea*. Cambridge: Cambridge University Press.

3

Distributional Concerns, the 'Developmental State', and the Agrarian Origins of Social Assistance in Ethiopia

Tom Lavers

1. Introduction

The existing literature emphasizes the innovation of recent social assistance initiatives—particularly cash transfers (Hanlon et al. 2010). However, a narrow focus on the recent expansion of cash transfers obscures from view a broader range of policies that African states have long used to support rural populations (Seekings 2012), as well as skewing emphasis towards proximate drivers of programme adoption and expansion. Notably, the literature has emphasized the role of donors as part of an epistemic community spreading social assistance ideas around the world (Von Gliszczynski 2015; Cherrier 2016). This work risks neglecting deeper continuities between social assistance and longstanding mechanisms by which states distribute resources within society, as well as the broader political economic context against which the social assistance agenda has taken shape in specific national contexts. This chapter examines Ethiopia, home to one of the largest social assistance programmes in Africa—the Productive Safety Net Programme (PSNP)—as well as a range of other noteworthy programmes brought together under a new National Social Protection Policy. The analysis highlights the deep roots of social assistance within the state's distributional strategies, particularly with respect to the rural population, land access, and the challenge of food insecurity.

A growing literature analyses the important role for the state in the Ethiopian Peoples' Revolutionary Democratic Front's (EPRDF's) development strategy (Lavers 2012a; Oqubay 2015; Clapham 2018). To date a major consideration has been the successes and limitations of Ethiopia's proclaimed 'double digit growth' (Hagmann and Abbink 2011), with much less discussion

Tom Lavers, *Distributional Concerns, the 'Developmental State', and the Agrarian Origins of Social Assistance in Ethiopia* In: *The Politics of Social Protection in Eastern and Southern Africa*. Edited by: Sam Hickey, Tom Lavers, Miguel Niño-Zarazúa, and Jeremy Seekings, Oxford University Press (2020).
DOI: 10.1093/oso/9780198850342.003.0003

of the distribution of these economic gains. Yet the distributional implications of development have been at the forefront of the EPRDF's thinking since it came to power in 1991 and even beforehand during the Tigrayan People's Liberation Front's (TPLF's) administration of Tigray during the 1980s. Existing work is quite correct to highlight the great emphasis that the EPRDF places on delivering rapid economic development. However, this chapter shows that the EPRDF never pursued growth at all costs, instead seeking to manage economic transformation in the interests of social and political stability. To this end, the ruling party pays close attention to distributional concerns as a means of limiting social and political instability.

This chapter traces the evolution of this distributional strategy, showing how change and continuity reflect the interplay between evolving ideas and political interests among the EPRDF leadership. From the early days of the TPLF, rapid and *broad-based* socioeconomic progress has been seen as a key means of securing popular support. While this basic orientation is evident from the 1970s, the means by which this is pursued has changed over time. First, there has been a shift in EPRDF ideology from the socialism that influenced the TPLF during the struggle to the present focus on 'developmentalism'. Second, there has also been an evolution in the EPRDF's social policy approach, from what can be described as an 'agrarian' distributional regime—which sought to provide welfare through access to land and other resources required for agricultural livelihoods—to a 'productivist-pauperist' model—which targets social assistance narrowly to specific groups, yet seeks to ensure that protective policies also have productive impacts. These changes were motivated primarily by a series of political and distributional crises in the early to mid-2000s.

At the time of writing, Ethiopian politics is in the midst of highly uncertain political changes resulting from mass anti-government protests in Oromiya, the appointment of Abiy Ahmed as Prime Minister in April 2018, and the political reforms he has undertaken. While the chapter highlights some of the many causes of the protests and key political challenges that the new government faces, given the uncertainty at the present time, the chapter limits its analytical focus to the period prior to Abiy taking office. The chapter draws on research conducted over ten years on politics, social policy, and agrarian transformation in Ethiopia. This involved primary research in Ethiopia in 2009–10 and on regular visits during 2014–18. More than seventy key informant interviews were conducted with senior political figures, bureaucrats, donor representatives, and consultants. This primary material was supplemented by government policies and strategies, as well as published interviews and speeches by the former Prime Minister, Meles Zenawi.

Section 2 sets out the chapter's analytical framework. The chapter then applies this framework to the EPRDF's policy initiatives under three distinct eras: first, the policies pursued in liberated areas of Tigray; the initial development strategy pursued as a national government from 1991 to the early 2000s; and then the 'developmental state' project since the mid-2000s. Section 6 concludes.

2. A Framework for Analysing the Politics of Distribution in Developing Countries

Among the most prominent analyses of distribution in advanced economies is Esping-Andersen's (1990) book, *The Three Worlds of Welfare Capitalism*. While his much-cited regime typology is of little relevance for the analysis of a low-income economy, there are useful insights from his work for analysing the politics of distribution in developing countries. The first is that a regime refers to the 'systematically interwoven' nature of social structure, employment, and social policies (Esping-Andersen 1990: 2). Social and economic policy are in essence two sides of the same coin and so need to be analysed together (Polanyi 2001; Mkandawire 2004). As such, policy makers make social policy choices in response to and/or in anticipation of broader distributional concerns rather than in isolation from other policy areas (Huber and Stephens 2001; Seekings and Nattrass 2005). The second is that a regime comprises not just social policies but a complementary set of institutions and interests that reproduces itself over time, leading to distinct patterns of welfare and distribution of resources between countries.

There have been several attempts to translate the insights from Esping-Andersen's work to the very different contexts of developing countries. Gough and Wood (2004) extend Esping-Andersen's focus on the balance of provision between state and market to include other actors involved in the production of welfare and insecurity in developing countries such as the community, family, and transnational actors. While their approach offers many benefits, highlighting the different forms and levels of provision to different societal groups, their work intentionally downplays the role of the state. Given that the purpose of this chapter is to analyse the drivers of state social assistance, Jeremy Seekings' work is more relevant in that it seeks to identify the dominant form of state provision within particular national settings. Seekings develops the concept of a 'distributional regime', which combines interlocking 'welfare, labor market and "growth-path" policies' (Seekings 2008: 24). Seekings proposes three ideal regime types, though acknowledging that more than one regime often co-exists within a country. The first is a 'labourist regime' prevalent, for example, in Latin America, in which the state provides support for formal sector workers through subsidised social insurance and labour regulation. The second is the 'pauperist regimes' where states recognize that some section of the population requires support independent of their status as workers, with provision provided through narrowly targeted social assistance schemes. The third variety, of particular relevance to sub-Saharan Africa, is the agrarian regimes, which support the peasantry through land reform and a range of agricultural services to smallholder farmers, including agricultural extension and irrigation.

A further distinction made in the regimes literature concerns welfare policies in East Asian developmental states. Seekings (2008) argues that since welfare supported workers through employer-based social insurance, these countries are best classified as labourist regimes. Yet, this only partially captures the rationale underlying provision in these countries. Rather, the core motivation was to use social policy to promote economic development and, as such, 'social policy is not conceived as an autonomous sphere of policy concerned to de-commodify and extend social rights. Rather it is part of an economic and developmental strategy to secure high growth rates and to transform national development' (Gough 2004: 182). While the regime was 'labourist' in relying significantly on social insurance, it was at its core distinctively 'productivist' in using social protection as a means of enforcing savings rates and generating resources for state-led investment (White and Goodman 1998; Holliday 2000).

This chapter's aim is not to add to the often pedantic debates about whether one or another country fits a particular 'regime type'. Rather the intention is to use Seekings' typology as a heuristic device to highlight the changing nature of the EPRDF's distributional policies and as an entry point to explain the political drivers of this shift. A common thread of the welfare state literature views social policy as the outcome of a distributional struggle between contending interest groups in the context of institutional constraints (Huber and Stephens 2001). Great emphasis is placed on political mobilization of the working class through unions and leftist political parties to demand redistribution. In the context of a developing country such as Ethiopia, while the basic insight that social policy is the result of a distributional struggle is useful, this approach must be adapted (Lavers 2013a; Lavers and Hickey 2016). First, where democratic institutions cannot be taken for granted, political mobilization may be constrained. While interest groups may have limited ability to mobilize and express demands, political elites nonetheless make policy decisions based on their perceptions of the threat posed by different social groups. Second, politics in such contexts tends to be more weakly institutionalized, while informal political institutions may actually dominate the formal 'rules of the game'.

While these interest-based explanations have provided important insights into the development of welfare systems (Huber and Stephens 2001), they are based on a limited understanding of human motivation and, as such, have been subject to growing critique. Actors promoting policy reform are 'motivated as much by ideological commitments as by strict material interests' (Brady 2009: 103). Ideas therefore provide an important complement to interest-based explanations of social policy development. Such ideas include overarching ideologies such as socialism, neoliberalism, or developmentalism, which shape individuals' perception of their own interests and provide a roadmap as to how to proceed, as well as social norms regarding the expected impacts such policies have on individual behaviour and incentives (Schmidt 2008).

The analysis that follows explores the changing nature of the distributional regime under the EPRDF as a result of changing ideas and interests within the ruling party. The analysis therefore focuses on the political survival strategies (Migdal 2001) employed by the EPRDF, including vitally how the Front has negotiated periods of cohesion and fragmentation within the ruling coalition, as well as class and ethnic divisions within society, and how this is reflected in evolving distributional strategies. To provide political context for the reforms undertaken since the EPRDF came to power in 1991, the chapter begins with an overview of the TPLF's liberation struggle. Given the constraints imposed by the conflict, it would be an overstatement to describe this as a distinct distributional regime. However, the period establishes basic continuities in the TPLF/EPRDF approach to distribution.

3. Distribution and Mobilization in Liberated Tigray

The TPLF originated in the socialist-inspired student movement at Haile Selassie I University in the early 1970s. Although the military Derg regime that came to power in 1974, displacing Emperor Haile Selassie, adopted a radical Marxist-Leninist agenda, the Derg and different factions within the student movement were divided by ideological questions related to class and nationalities (Berhe 2008). Like many student activists, the TPLF left the cities during the Red Terror of the late 1970s and returned to the western lowlands of their native Tigray to start armed opposition.

The TPLF employed an ethno-nationalist message, fomenting resentment at the marginalization of Tigray within Ethiopia, as a means of mobilizing the peasantry (Young 1997). However, the 'TPLF leadership understood that success depended on its ability to maintain the unwavering commitment of the peasants' and, as a result, they quickly adopted a Maoist approach to organization and warfare (Young 1997: 172; Berhe 2008). This involved 'delivery, and control, of socio-economic advantage' in areas liberated by the TPLF through 'health, education and agricultural services, and relief and rehabilitation support' (Vaughan 2011: 625). Common features of the TPLF approach to service delivery were emphases on community mobilization, self-reliance, and ensuring that services also made a productive contribution.

Land reform was one of the principal means by which the TPLF sought to achieve these goals, redistributing land to promote equality, while banning land sales in order to protect farmers from displacement (Young 1997). Land reform was explicitly framed in class terms and aimed to turn the peasantry into 'a "homogeneous mass" with common needs, interests and outlook' (Vaughan and Tronvoll 2003: 117). In part, this focus can be attributed to the socialist ideologies that influenced the TPLF, which shared the 'land to the tiller' slogan with other revolutionary groups. However, as one TPLF founding member describes, land reform was a low priority until competing organizations, including the Derg and the Ethiopian People's Revolutionary Party (EPRP)—a rival Marxist group fighting the Derg—started to conduct their own land redistributions (Berhe 2008). While land reform aimed to promote equality, it was adopted in part to secure the support of rural Tigrayans and urban merchants, while punishing opponents (Berhe 2008).

The TPLF also founded the Relief Society of Tigray (REST) in 1978 as a dedicated relief and development organization, channelling support from western NGOs to Tigray. While much of the burden for coping with food insecurity remained with households and communities, REST assumed importance as the Derg restricted humanitarian assistance to TPLF-controlled areas, as a means of undermining the TPLF (De Waal 1997; Milas and Latif 2000). REST—technically autonomous, but in reality an arm of the TPLF (Young 1997)—distributed food aid during the 1984/5 famine, using food aid as a productive resource, and engaging recipients in agricultural and environmental rehabilitation programmes through public works projects (Salih 2013).

While TPLF social provisioning was constrained by the ongoing conflict, the activities undertaken were based on common principles: first, that socioeconomic progress is a means of building support and enhancing legitimacy. This emphasis might well be attributed to the interests of the TPLF, which had few options other than to win the support of the peasantry as a means of pursuing its struggle. However, the second is ideological—the idea that people are expected to contribute whatever resources they have in exchange for support they receive and that welfare provision should not merely be protective, but also make a productive contribution. While the overarching ideology of the TPLF—which drew on Maoism, Marxism-Leninism, and, latterly, the model of Albania under Enver Hoxha (Berhe 2008)—has evolved subsequently, these features of welfare provisioning remain consistent.

4. Agricultural Development-Led Industrialization and the Pursuit of an Agrarian Distributional Regime

The TPLF removed the Derg from Tigray and seized national power in 1991. The new government faced significant challenges internally and externally. The TPLF had spent almost the entire conflict in Tigray mobilizing the Tigrayan population—just 6 per cent of Ethiopia's total—based on an ethno-nationalist message. While the TPLF was militarily dominant post-1991, it lacked national legitimacy, with large sections of the population viewing the new government with suspicion. The TPLF's response was to extend the successful approach from Tigray, namely a combination of ethno-nationalism and the delivery of socioeconomic progress. As the TPLF's ambitions grew from controlling Tigray to governing Ethiopia, it formed the EPRDF, a coalition of ethno-nationalist parties intended to represent Ethiopia's ethnic groups, and introduced a federal system to provide for ethnic self-determination (Vaughan and Tronvoll 2003). The government also formulated a new development strategy—Agricultural Development-Led Industrialization (ADLI)—to provide the broad-based socioeconomic development to win popular support.

Second, the EPRDF came to power shortly after the collapse of the Soviet Union at a time when socialism had been discredited. After years of civil war the new government desperately needed external resources to support reconstruction and development, and the main aid sources were the multilateral and western bilateral donors at the peak of the Washington Consensus. It is hardly surprising that the EPRDF abandoned its adherence to Albanian socialism. The transformation was swift, with the EPRDF ditching its Marxist terminology—in public, if not in internal debates—and adopting a discourse of market-based development and democratization. The EPRDF agreed structural adjustment programmes with the World Bank and IMF, and framed ADLI in terms of the establishment of a 'free market economy' (MoFED 2003: 13).

4.1. Agricultural development-led industrialization

ADLI was first outlined by the Transitional Government in 1993/4 (TGE 1994). However, little progress was made in its implementation until the early 2000s because of the challenges of post-conflict reconstruction, resource shortages, the 1998–2000 Eritrean war, and, as Prime Minister Meles later argued, disagreements among the leadership (Zenawi 2006). The 2001 split in the TPLF leadership, initially over the Eritrean war (Tadesse and Young 2003; Vaughan and Tronvoll 2003), resulted in a fundamental realignment of the EPRDF, with the expulsion of senior TPLF figures among the party's 'left wing' (Lefort 2012: 682), ending the system of leadership through consensus and leaving Meles in 'a position of unchallenged supremacy' (Tadesse and Young 2003: 397).

ADLI served multiple objectives: a long-term development strategy; a distributional strategy that integrated social and economic policies; and a political strategy for managing the instability inherent to periods of rapid transformation. ADLI may have been framed as a means of creating a 'free market economy', but in reality it is nothing of the sort. While economic reforms did remove price controls and privatize some state enterprises, instead of the Washington Consensus, Meles looked for policy inspiration in the experiences of South Korea and Taiwan (MoFED 2003; Zenawi 2006). Unsurprisingly, then, given the state-led model pursued by these 'developmental states', it is the state, not the market, that is the centrepiece of ADLI.

The premise of ADLI is that as a labour-rich and capital-poor country, to make the best use of Ethiopia's resources, labour-intensive, non-mechanized agriculture should be implemented alongside technologies such as irrigation, fertilizer, and improved seeds, which improve yields but do not replace labour (TGE 1994; MoFED 2003). Increased agricultural productivity is expected to lead to national food security and stimulate labour-intensive industry through forward production linkages—the supply of wage foods and industrial inputs—and backward linkages—with increasingly affluent smallholder farmers providing demand for domestic production of fertilizer, farm implements, and consumption goods. Agriculture will also be a source of export commodities providing the foreign exchange with which to import capital goods required for industrialization. Consequently, in this agriculture-first strategy, '[a] griculture is ... believed to be a potential source to generate primary surplus to fuel the growth of other sectors of the economy (industry)', leading to labour-intensive industrialization (MoFED 2002: 41; MoI 2002).

Throughout the 1990s and early 2000s, donors pushed the government to carry out further reforms, including the privatization of land, banking, and telecommunications, all to no avail (Feyissa 2011). Meanwhile, the donor response to ADLI's state-led development model in the early 2000s was 'ridicule'.[1] The idea of Ethiopia modelling itself on Korea and Taiwan seemed preposterous. Moreover, the emphasis on the state clashed with the more limited role envisaged by the Washington Consensus and post-Washington Consensus. The latter included the social protection agenda that was just emerging among the main donor agencies in the early 2000s (see Hickey and Seekings, this volume).

4.2. The central role of state land ownership in ADLI

The Derg nationalized land in 1975, and state land ownership was maintained under the EPRDF. State land ownership is central to ADLI's economic, social, and political objectives and the distributional regime that it entails. Policy statements identify three main socioeconomic objectives of the land policy, each with important distributional implications. First, state land ownership—including a prohibition on land sales and rental restrictions—protects the peasantry from displacement.[2] Meles even claimed that state land ownership provides a form of 'social security' to peasants by guaranteeing access to land and therefore an agricultural livelihood (cited in Marcus 1995). In stark contrast to neo-classical economics, for which clearly defined private property rights are vital, for the EPRDF, '[t]he question of access to land should ... be addressed from the point of view of both output growth and the welfare of the people' (MoFED 2002: 53). ADLI presents market forces as damaging to peasant security, necessitating state intervention.

[1] Interviews with former DFID and World Bank officials by Skype, 9 and 23 July 2015, respectively.

[2] ADLI was much less concerned with protection for those engaged in pastoralism and shifting cultivation in predominately lowland regions. 'Settlement' was considered the best means of addressing these supposedly unsustainable livelihoods, bringing them in line with the main thrust of ADLI (MoFED 2003: 58).

A second role of the land policy, like the socialist rationales used to justify Derg and TPLF land reforms, is to promote equality and prevent class differentiation. The EPRDF regularly voiced fears that land privatization would lead to the re-emergence of wealthy landowners and exploitative feudal or capitalist labour relations, playing on smallholders' concerns about displacement:

> By fully privatizing land ownership, one starts the process of differentiation. The creative, vigorous peasant farmer gets to own larger pieces of land and the less effective get to be left to live in doubt... We do not believe this is the right approach in our country... It is simply assumed that those who would buy land would be the very ones who would use it best. We do not know of any logic or evidence to prove that. (Meles cited in The Reporter 2000)

In contrast, by retaining land in the hands of the smallholder masses, the economic surplus resulting from agricultural productivity increases accrues to those same farmers, resulting in an inherently egalitarian development model (MoFED 2003).

Finally, the land policy has a productive role, enabling the state to allocate factors of production—labour, capital, and land (MoFED 2002: 53; MoFED 2003). Specifically, state land ownership ensures that land remains in the hands of smallholders, who will employ labour-intensive agricultural production techniques, in contrast to market-based land allocation, which would lead to land concentration and capital-intensive production, wasting Ethiopia's main resource, its labour force.

> If we pursue a development strategy that does not make much use of labor and land resources in economic activity, the contribution of such factors of production to Ethiopia's development will be forestalled, thereby causing a pace of development that is well below potential. If, on the other hand, we rely too heavily on capital as a basis of our development effort, then our efforts will be curtailed by the limited availability of this resource. Our development strategy that is centered on agriculture and rural development promotes a judicious use of factors of production. (MoFED 2003: 10)

The result is a development model that integrates concerns with growth and distribution, economic, and social policy. In effect this is a state-led attempt—in Polanyian (2001) terms—to 'embed' economic development within an agrarian distributional regime in which state welfare is provided not through social assistance or social insurance, but rather the allocation of land and agricultural extension services.

4.3. ADLI as a political strategy

ADLI was also a political strategy, fundamentally concerned with building political support and managing economic transformation. ADLI is a broad-based approach that aims to improve the living standards for the smallholder majority, in line with the TPLF's strategy in Tigray. The control of land has long been a central means of securing and maintaining political power in Ethiopia (Hoben 1973; Rahmato 2009), as elsewhere. The EPRDF—following on from the TPLF experience—continued to see the peasantry as its core political base and state ownership was a means of securing the support of the peasantry and preventing the re-emergence of a landholding class that might threaten the EPRDF (Rahmato 2009). However, it is actually population growth that was considered the 'single over-riding challenge' facing the country (TGE 1994: 8), resulting in rural land shortages, food insecurity, and 'the persistent onslaught of rural to urban migration' (Office of the Prime Minister 1993). Uncontrolled urban and inter-ethnic migration are considered the source of 'economic, political and social instabilities' (MoFED 2002: 56), contributing to the growth of a politically dangerous class of under- and unemployed urban migrants (MoFED 2003).

While ADLI is ultimately expected to lead to industrial development and the expansion of urban employment opportunities (MoFED 2003: 26), for the time being, 'in the absence of better employment opportunities' the land policy encourages 'farmers to remain on their land, thereby avoiding unproductive and potentially harmful labor mobility' that 'may even be detrimental to peace and stability' (MoFED 2003: 27). What ADLI proposes therefore is state-managed structural transformation, with the land policy limiting urban migration in the interests of political stability until such time as ADLI has created sufficient industrial employment to remove restrictions.

> We do not believe that the long-term future and destiny of our peasant farmers is to be stuck in the mud, so to speak. We feel that ultimately there has to be industrialization, ultimately these people have to find to get [sic] employment outside agriculture. (Meles cited in The Reporter 2000)

4.4. The food security problem that would not go away

ADLI assumes that agricultural productivity increases would benefit all farmers, addressing food insecurity and removing the need for targeted support (MoFED 2003). This approach was based not only on the merits of ADLI but also deep ideological concerns about the dangers of handouts that would undermine work incentives and lead to dependency (Lavers 2019). In reality, though, the humanitarian system that originated in the 1984/5 famine expanded with the World Food Programme, USAID, and others providing annual assistance to some 5–6 million food-insecure people throughout the 1990s. As was the case in Botswana (Seekings, this volume), in Ethiopia subsequent social assistance programmes built on this humanitarian machinery. While donors and international NGOs played a major role in this humanitarian system, the government shaped the delivery mechanisms in line with its ideological commitments and built on REST's relief model (Salih 2013).[3] The Transitional Government of Ethiopia (TGE) attempted to mobilize emergency relief for developmental objectives, requiring all relief to able-bodied people to be provided through employment generation schemes.

4.5. Changing ideological reference points and political interests

After 1991, the EPRDF ditched its socialist rhetoric, gradually adopting the role models of Korea and Taiwan in place of Albania. Despite this apparent ideological sea change, what is perhaps most notable in this discussion are the continuities between the approach employed by the TPLF in Tigray and the EPRDF as the national government. First, ethnic self-determination and broad-based socioeconomic progress were seen as the solution to the limited ruling party legitimacy. To that end, the government outlined ADLI, an integrated distributional strategy combining economic, social, and political objectives for managing structural transformation and securing popular support. State land ownership played a central role in all these objectives and, as such, it was hardly surprising that donors who attempted to pressure the government into privatizing land were given short shrift, with Meles famously declaring that land privatization would only happen 'over the EPRDF's dead body'. Second, where targeted food aid was provided with donor support, this

[3] Interview, former USAID official, by Skype, 15 July 2015.

was shaped by the EPRDF's ideological commitments to ensuring recipients worked for support received and that this provision also made a productive economic contribution.

As such, ADLI sought to consolidate an agrarian distributional regime in which state provision was through the distribution of land and agricultural inputs, rather than social assistance. To that end, there was a massive push to train agricultural extension workers, expand the system of cooperatives, and increase use of improved agricultural inputs. However, as discussed in section 5, while the core principles of building support through socioeconomic progress and ensuring that welfare is productive remain important influences to the present day, this agrarian regime has gradually been deconstructed since the mid-2000s with social protection programmes increasingly taking its place.

5. Ethiopia's 'Developmental State' and an Emerging Pauperist-Productivist Regime

Since the mid-2000s, the EPRDF's development strategy has progressed from the original articulation of ADLI to a self-proclaimed 'developmental state' model. There is clear continuity between ADLI and the 'developmental state' in terms of the focus on industrialization, the promotion of economic linkages between agriculture and emerging industry, and the export of processed products rather than primary commodities. As such, the argument that the EPRDF's development strategy has moved on from ADLI is not to say that ADLI has been abandoned. That said, the developmental state involves significant policy shifts from the original ADLI, particularly from a distributional perspective. As discussed below, the 'developmental state' model entails a change in agricultural strategy, moving away from ADLI's broad-based focus that sought to raise the productivity of *all* smallholders, to a dual strategy that supports, on one hand, the better-off smallholders in a position to take advantage of new technologies and, on the other, agricultural investors employing capital-intensive production techniques. Ethiopia's 'developmental state' also involves a more active industrial policy, in contrast to ADLI's agriculture-first approach. This shift in economic strategy has resulted in the gradual erosion of the agrarian distributional regime that ADLI had sought to construct, and a complementary shift towards a 'productivist-pauperist' model.

The change in strategy was an evolutionary process rather than a one-off reform, beginning with the 2005 Plan for Accelerated and Sustained Development to End Poverty (PASDEP) and gathering pace during the 2010 and

2015 Growth and Transformation Plans (GTP 1 and 2). The catalyst for these changes were a series of existential political crises or what became known in the EPRDF leadership as 'Armageddons'.[4]

The first Armageddon was the 2001 TPLF split. While the initial response was to re-affirm commitment to ADLI, the split had broader ramifications for the EPRDF's ideological approach that shaped the evolution of the strategy over time. The principal cause of the split was the handling of the Eritrean war and a power struggle between Meles and a dissident group in the TPLF (Tadesse and Young 2003; Vaughan and Tronvoll 2003). However, Meles subsequently claimed that,

> ...the full articulation of the paradigm [developmentalism] with all its policy implications was one of the key causes of the most serious split in the history of the ruling party that took place in 2000–2001. (Zenawi 2006)

Vitally, the split resulted in the decision taken to reject socialism and to embrace capitalist development. This entailed expanding the party's ranks beyond the peasantry, to include key interests vital to economic growth: the national bourgeoisie, diaspora capital, and the wealthiest farmers (Tadesse and Young 2003; Lefort 2010; Simon 2011). As a Marxist group, the TPLF had historically been sceptical of both capitalists and wealthy farmers (Young 1997; Berhe 2008). But from the mid-2000s, domestic, foreign, and diaspora investors who fit with government priorities were actively courted (Lavers 2012a) and wealthier farmers were made a central focus of the development strategy, enrolled en masse as 'model farmers' and EPRDF members (Lefort 2010).

Subsequent Armageddons challenged the assumptions underpinning ADLI. During the 2002/3 food crisis some 14 million people required emergency support from donor agencies in order to survive (Lavers 2019). This crisis highlighted that achieving food security through their own production—the objective of ADLI—was implausible for many households. Population growth in the context of land shortages was resulting in the division of land into economically unviable plots (Rahmato 2003), while the limited adoption of improved inputs constrained agricultural productivity (Dercon and Vargas Hill 2009). This situation closely resembled what Meles had previously described as the 'nightmare scenario': population growth in the absence of

[4] As noted in an interview with former Deputy Prime Minister, Addisu Legesse, Addis Ababa, 7 October 2015; and former Minister of Communications, Bereket Simon, in his book (Simon 2011).

agricultural productivity growth and off-farm job creation leading to growing food insecurity in rural areas and politically problematic urban migration and unemployment (Meles cited in The Reporter 2000).

Finally, the 2005 elections exposed political problems resulting from the comparative neglect of urban areas and growing urban migration. The EPRDF lost every seat in Addis Ababa and many others in urban centres around the country, while urban protests met the EPRDF's declaration of overall victory. According to the deputy Prime Minister, these events constituted 'another Armageddon',[5] reinforcing longstanding concerns about the dangers of urban unemployment and highlighting the need for urgent action rather than waiting for agriculture-led growth to generate urban employment, as described in ADLI (Simon 2011).

The remainder of this section outlines the revisions to the development strategy—first the 'developmental state' model and then the emerging distributional regime. This distributional regime entails new forms of social assistance that respond to ADLI's failings and the 'disembedding' effects of the 'developmental state'. However, it is worth noting that while the development model was revised, the EPRDF's longstanding strategy of securing support through socioeconomic progress continued. EPRDF leadership remained convinced that 'economic development is the answer to any discontent' (Simon 2011). Since the mid-2000s, the EPRDF has sought legitimacy through the delivery of 'double digit growth' (Zenawi 2010) and reaching 'the level of a middle-income economy as of 2020–23' (MoFED 2010: 21).

5.1. Beyond ADLI: the developmental state model

ADLI was based on the assumption of the inverse relationship—that small-scale, labour-intensive agriculture is more productive and efficient than large-scale production (MoFED 2003). ADLI did not differentiate between smallholders, assuming that agricultural inputs would be scale-neutral, with all farmers benefiting. Policy since the mid-2000s has taken a very different approach, focusing on the wealthiest smallholders—enrolled as 'model farmers'—with greater potential for technology adoption and commercial production, effectively excluding many poor farmers (Lefort 2010, 2012; Lavers 2013a). Lefort (2012: 682) cites EPRDF party documents pointing to

[5] Interview, Addisu Legesse, former deputy Prime Minister and Minister of Agriculture and Rural Development, Addis Ababa, Ethiopia, 7 October 2015.

the failings of the previous 'pro-poor strategy' that had 'prevented "the farmer from escaping a hand-to-mouth and scattered way of life", because the Front's goal was "to detach the farmers from commercialization" instead of "focusing on market economy as the centre of rural activities"'. Agricultural policy now aimed to capture farmers' 'private initiative' to commercialize smallholder production, focusing on high-value crops and high-potential areas (MoFED 2005: 46).

Complementary reforms were undertaken in land tenure. This included massive land registration programmes since the mid-2000s to improve tenure security and investment incentives, and to prevent the further division of land into unviable plots (Lavers 2017).[6] In Amhara, the regional government removed all rental restrictions to allow wealthier farmers to rent land from poor farmers, leading to increased productivity and differentiation.[7] Further initiatives undertaken as part of the Agricultural Growth Programme and Agricultural Transformation Agency have similarly focused on high-potential areas and high-potential farmers.

The government has also actively promoted capital-intensive agricultural investments (Lavers 2012a), again marking a departure from ADLI. ADLI had noted the potential for large-scale, capital-intensive agricultural investments in sparsely populated lowlands, but this was very much a secondary focus to the smallholder emphasis described above (TGE 1994; MoFED 2003) and such capital-intensive investments remained an unrealized ambition. However, since the late 2000s and the onset of the 'global land rush', the government leased large tracts of supposedly 'uncultivated' land to investors and, in doing so, dismissed the land claims of politically marginal populations involved in pastoralism and shifting cultivation (Lavers 2012b).

In an inversion of ADLI's smallholder focus, moreover, the government has promoted small-scale but capital-intensive investments in densely populated highland areas particularly for horticulture and floriculture projects. Here smallholders are displaced where the government believes there is the potential for increased agricultural productivity and the shift to high-value crops (Lavers 2012b). In line with the government's longstanding concern about the dangers of displacement and urban migration, the government favours capital *and* labour-intensive projects that require large numbers of workers, such as

[6] Interview with the head of land administration in the Ministry of Agriculture and Rural Development (MoARD), Addis Ababa, 17 January 2009.

[7] Interview with a senior expert in the Amhara Bureau of Environment, Planning and Land Administration and Use (BoEPLAU), Bahir Dar, 18 March 2010.

flower farms, or projects that combine investor capital with family farms through outgrower schemes (Lavers 2012b).

Finally, and by no means least, in contrast to ADLI's *agriculture-first* approach, the 'developmental state' simultaneously promotes *agricultural and industrial* development. Rather than waiting for agricultural productivity growth to stimulate industry, as previously, from the 2005 PASDEP onwards there was a shift, with the prioritization of a handful of high-potential, export-oriented sectors, namely: meat, leather, and leather products; textiles and garments; and horticulture and floriculture (Oqubay 2015). Under the 2010 GTP, the emphasis further expanded from export industry to import substituting industry, including: sugar, cement, chemicals, steel, pharmaceuticals, and engineering; and the creation of industrial parks throughout the country to attract major transnational firms. A key part of this industrial policy has been massive state investment in infrastructure to improve the investment environment. This includes expansion of the transport network, including roads, railways, and airports, as well as a series of major dams to support irrigated agricultural plantations and provide reliable electricity for growing industry and export to neighbouring countries (Verhoeven 2013).

5.2. From an agrarian towards a productivist-pauperist distributional regime

The 'developmental state' implies a fundamental shift in the distributional regime and the deconstruction of the agrarian model based on access to land and agricultural livelihoods. Rapid population growth, land shortages, and the prioritization of new forms of agricultural, industrial, and infrastructural development have rendered the guarantee to land all but meaningless for a significant proportion of the population. In its place, social protection programmes initiated since 2005 have plugged the gaps—compensating for a shortage of land and employment opportunities while still seeking to promote productive activity. As these are gradually institutionalized, they resemble a productivist-pauperist distributional regime.

The 'developmental state' offers certain groups significant economic opportunities through investment opportunities and employment with state organizations or private firms. These include foreign and diaspora investors, domestic capitalists, some of those with the required education (secondary and above) and skills to find employment, and model farmers with sufficient land, labour, finance, and political connections to take advantage of new technologies and market opportunities. These are exactly the groups that the EPRDF embraced post-2001. What is less clear is how this new growth path will benefit the EPRDF's original core constituency—the masses of smallholder farmers—for which ADLI, however ineffectively, had sought to cater. Less well-off smallholders have progressively limited access to agricultural extension services and improved inputs and therefore limited potential to raise agricultural productivity. Meanwhile, a whole generation of young adults in rural areas have no land access given severe land shortages, land registration, and the moratorium on future land redistributions.[8] In effect, the 'developmental state' has dismantled the agrarian distributional regime that ADLI had sought to create, resulting in an increasingly inegalitarian growth path.

In many respects the industrial strategy is impressive and has rightly attracted media and academic attention. Yet industrialization alone cannot absorb the huge amounts of surplus labour resulting from land shortages and high rates of population growth. The recently opened industrial park in Awassa is expected to create 100,000 jobs when fully operational, with a further 20,000 each in Kombolcha and Mekele (Addis Fortune 2017). Government targets include construction of a total of seven industrial parks by 2020 and the creation of two million manufacturing jobs by 2025. In turn these industrial jobs would no doubt support additional service sector jobs. While this level of job creation would be a major achievement, in a country whose population is estimated at approximately 105 million, it pales in comparison to the millions of young adults who have limited opportunities in agriculture and need employment. Data are not good, but to give an indication, the last census in 2007 found that there were approximately 40 million people under the age of twenty at the time, many of whom will now be in or entering into the labour force with varying levels of educational attainment. While some may have the opportunity to pursue an agricultural livelihood, vast numbers will not as a result of the severe land shortages. Indeed, a 2011 survey found that unemployment in urban areas was 18 per cent, while 48 per cent of respondents reported being underemployed (Broussar and Gebrekidan Tekleselassie 2012: 13). Meanwhile the majority of young people who fail to complete secondary education have no access to new manufacturing jobs, which require such qualifications.

Rural landlessness and urban unemployment are two symptoms of the same underlying challenge: despite its considerable successes, the developmental state

[8] There has been no further land redistribution since the EPRDF came to power in 1991, with the exception of Amhara in 1997.

model has been unable to create sufficient livelihood opportunities—rural or urban—leading to serious distributional failings. In response to the erosion of the agrarian distributional regime and the distributional failings of the growth path, the government has introduced and expanded social assistance to those with limited economic opportunities who might otherwise present a political threat to the ruling party. While this agenda has been promoted by some of Ethiopia's foreign donors—in line with the global trends described in Hickey and Seekings (this volume)—the government's motivations are shaped by longstanding domestic political concerns. First, the delivery of tangible benefits continues to be seen as the best way of securing political support with targeted programmes introduced in response to specific political crises. Second, social programmes that provide protection to vulnerable people are also expected to make productive impacts, while anyone receiving support should contribute labour in return.[9] Third, deep concerns about the political dangers of urban migration and the need for mass employment opportunities continue to shape the design and objectives of particular policies. The result is an emerging productivist-pauperist distributional regime to replace the agrarian model envisaged under ADLI.

The PSNP is the largest such programme and was established in 2005 to support chronically food-insecure households through public works for able-bodied participants and unconditional direct support for those unable to work. From 2015, the PSNP provided support to up to 10 million people per year. The PSNP was a direct response to the 2002/3 food crisis, which highlighted ADLI's inability to resolve food insecurity (Lavers 2019). While Ethiopia's foreign donors have provided the vast majority of the finance and promoted many of the ideas included in the PSNP, government ideas and objectives fundamentally shaped the programme (Lavers 2019). First, the PSNP's public works focus builds on longstanding ideas regarding the importance of productive contributions and concerns about welfare dependency going back to the TPLF era. As in Botswana, this commitment to public works reflects a congruence of ideas between national political elites and transnational actors—the World Bank, USAID, and World Food Programme (WFP) in Ethiopia and WFP in Botswana (Seekings 2016; Seekings, this volume; Lavers 2019). Second, from its inception, the PSNP was linked to livelihoods

[9] In addition to social assistance, the same ideas regarding self-reliance and the need to mobilize resources for development have underpinned social insurance expansion with a mandatory formal sector pension scheme introduced in 2010, legislation for mandatory social health insurance, and a community-based health insurance scheme for the informal sector that is rapidly expanding to cover some 11 million people by 2017 (Lavers 2019).

programmes providing credit and extension services to increase household production and work towards 'graduation' from support.

Under ADLI, state land ownership was intended to guarantee an agricultural livelihood for the peasant majority. The 2002/3 food crisis highlighted the inability of the land policy to fulfil this mission and, as such, the PSNP compensated for the limitations of the land policy, ensuring the viability of rural livelihoods in food-insecure areas (Lavers 2013b). The EPRDF initially intended the PSNP as a short-term stop-gap with the ultimate solution to food insecurity lying in economic transformation and the creation of non-agricultural employment (Lavers 2019).[10] Yet, with the failure to reduce the PSNP caseload over the last fourteen years, there has been a gradual acceptance that the PSNP is not going anywhere. Under donor pressure, the government has taken on an increasing role in financing the PSNP (Lavers 2019).

Protests against the 2005 elections further reinforced government concerns about urban unemployment. In addition to repression of political opposition, the government introduced several social programmes. Once again, these initiatives follow EPRDF ideology, requiring labour contributions in return for support and aiming to make both productive and protective contributions. The 2006 Youth Development Package promoted Micro and Small Enterprises (MSEs) to provide unemployed urban youth with economic opportunities. As with model farmers, government assistance was expected to secure youth political support by enrolling participants as party members (Di Nunzio 2014; Gebremariam 2018). Furthermore, in 2006 the government launched the Integrated Housing Development Programme which built 245,000 housing units by 2015 in cities across the country, including 175,000 in Addis (Keller and Mukudi-Omwami 2017). The programme is intended to placate urban populations by providing housing for poor and middle-income households, while creating employment for unskilled labourers.

Another response to 2005 and inflation in food prices since 2008 has been the adoption of an urban PSNP from 2016–17 that will expand to cover some 600,000 people over the coming years (Lavers 2019). This UPSNP operates in the country's major cities and adopts a similar design to the rural programme. Government respondents acknowledge that the UPSNP is the direct result of the failure of the development strategy to provide rural livelihoods, with the UPSNP intended to limit political instability.[11] While the UPSNP has started

[10] Interview with an expert in the Food Security Coordination Directorate, Addis Ababa, 1 and 7 October 2015.

[11] Interview with the Programme Head, Urban Food Security and Job Creation Agency, Addis Ababa, 29 January 2016.

relatively small, widespread anti-government protests across Oromiya in 2014–16, which took place in small towns and cities across the region, have prompted the Ministry of Urban Development to propose the UPSNP's expansion over ten years to cover some 4.7 million people in 972 towns and cities with a population greater than 2,000. The threat of urban migration to political stability is again at the forefront of the ministry's thinking, with the UPSNP intended to limit migration to major cities.[12]

5.3. Rapid growth and growing distributional concerns

Meles once argued that guaranteed land access constituted 'the only social security the peasants have' (Meles Zenawi, cited in Marcus 1995), with state land ownership forming the basis of an agrarian distributional regime. The political and economic crises of the early to mid-2000s revealed the limitations of this distributional model, while the construction of a 'developmental state' and rapid population growth have gradually eroded the protections that it provided. Since 2005 the government has expanded social assistance to compensate to some degree for these failings. As such, while undeniably important, the EPRDF's focus is not just on growth and industrialization, but rather a *politically managed process* of structural transformation that minimizes the social and political instability arising from rapid change. New social assistance programmes build on longstanding productivist principles—requiring labour contributions in exchange for basic protection while mobilizing resources for productive objectives. As such, government policy is moving in the direction of a productivist-pauperist distributional regime. Ethiopia provides a useful contrast with Botswana, as described by Seekings (this volume). As in Ethiopia, the origins of social assistance in Botswana lie in longstanding drought relief programmes. In Ethiopia the transition from emergency relief towards longer-term social assistance was the result of a dominant party responding to distributional crises. Meanwhile, in Botswana, a comparable transition was motivated by severe droughts, but also growing electoral competition during the 2000s.

6. Conclusions

This chapter has situated the expansion of social assistance in Ethiopia within the context of changing economic models and political dynamics. The chapter

[12] Interview with the Programme Head, Urban Food Security and Job Creation Agency, Addis Ababa, 29 January 2016.

argues that the emergence of social assistance not only derives from donor advocacy, but also flows directly from the erosion of the previous agrarian distributional regime and the need to address fundamental political and distributional challenges. While this shift in distributional regime involves significant changes, there are nonetheless continuities in the ruling party's approach. First, the delivery of broad-based socioeconomic progress has been a mainstay of TPLF/EPRDF's political strategy since the 1970s. Second, while the central objective since coming to power in 1991 has been to achieve industrialization, there is also a fundamental concern with the distributional challenges of such a process, leading to major concerns about urban migration, unemployment, and landlessness. Third, social assistance initiatives, subordinated to the necessity of promoting development, have taken a 'productivist' form throughout, with all programmes also expected to promote self-reliance and productive economic contributions.

Theoretically, the chapter suggests that the common tendency in the literature to focus on short-term drivers of policy change risks obscuring programmes' deeper roots in longstanding mechanisms by which states project authority and provide support to rural areas. In Ethiopia, as elsewhere, the state has sought to support rural populations through access to land and agricultural inputs. In this sense, the PSNP, though employing a new policy model, represents considerable continuity with past initiatives. Furthermore, social assistance is an integral part of the political economic strategy employed by the ruling party to promote national development and retain political power. As such, in Ethiopia, where a dominant and cohesive ruling coalition has been pursuing a strong state-led development project, social assistance is not merely a donor initiative, as suggested in some parts. Instead, social assistance is integrated into domestic political economy and used to promote political stability.

Finally, it should be noted that—alongside debates about the implementation of ethnic federalism, concerns about TPLF dominance within the EPRDF, and the brutality of police and military—the distributional challenges noted in this chapter were among the main drivers of widespread anti-government protests since 2015. In particular the shortage of land and employment opportunities and the displacement of smallholders to make way for investors emerged as important flashpoints in the protests. From 2018 under new Prime Minister Abiy Ahmed the EPRDF will continue to face the central distributional challenge identified here regarding how economic and social policy can combine to provide sufficient protection and economic opportunities for Ethiopia's rapidly growing population. New industrial parks—though impressive—can only address part of this challenge. This seems likely to leave an important political space for the further consolidation of this productivist-pauperist model in the coming years.

Acknowledgements

This chapter draws on PhD research at the University of Bath, funded by the Economic and Social Research Council (ESRC) (2008–13), a Visiting Research Fellowship at the United Nations Research Institute for Social Development (UNRISD) in 2013–14, and research on the politics of social protection for the Effective States and Inclusive Development (ESID) Research Centre at the University of Manchester. The support of all these organizations is gratefully acknowledged. Past iterations of this work have benefited from comments by Pip Bevan, Graham Brown, Joe Devine, Catherine Dom, Sam Hickey, Shea McClanahan, Thandika Mkandawire, Guy Standing, and Sarah Vaughan.

References

Addis Fortune (2017). More industrial parks, fewer investors [online]. Available at https://addisfortune.net/articles/more-industrial-parks-fewer-investors [Accessed 9 February 2018].

Berhe, A. (2008). A political history of the Tigray People's Liberation Front (1975–1991): revolt, ideology and mobilisation in Ethiopia. PhD thesis. Vrije Universiteit, Amsterdam.

Brady, D. (2009). *Rich Democracies, Poor People: How Politics Explain Poverty.* Oxford and New York: Oxford University Press.

Broussar, N.H. and Gebrekidan Tekleselassie, T. (2012). Youth employment: Ethiopia country study. *IGC working paper*, 12 (0592).

Cherrier, C. (2016). The expansion of basic social protection in low-income countries: an analysis of foreign aid actors' role in the emergence of social transfers in sub-Saharan Africa. PhD thesis. Maastricht University, Maastricht.

Clapham, C., 2018. The Ethiopian developmental state. *Third World Quarterly*, 39(6), 1151–65.

Dercon, S. and R. Vargas Hill (2009). Growth from agriculture in Ethiopia: identifying key constraints. Presented at the Ethiopian Strategy Support Programme (ESSP) II policy conference 'Accelerating Agricultural Development, Economic Growth and Poverty Reduction in Ethiopia', 22–4 October 2009, Hilton Hotel, Addis Ababa: IFPRI.

De Waal, A. (1997). *Famine Crimes: Politics and the Disaster Relief Industry in Africa.* London: African Rights & the International African Institute.

Di Nunzio, M. (2014). Thugs, spies and vigilantes: community policing and street politics in inner city Addis Ababa. *Africa*, 84(3), 444–65.

Esping-Andersen, G. (1990). *The Three Worlds of Welfare Capitalism*. Cambridge: Cambridge University Press.

Feyissa, D. (2011). Aid negotiation: the uneasy 'partnership' between EPRDF and the donors. *Journal of Eastern African Studies*, 5(4), 788–817.

Gebremariam, E.B. (2018). The politics of developmentalism, citizenship and urban youth in Addis Ababa, Ethiopia. PhD thesis. University of Manchester, Manchester.

Gough, I. (2004). East Asia: the limits of productivist regimes. In: I. Gough and G. Wood (Eds.), *Insecurity and Welfare Regimes in Asia, Africa and Latin America: Social Policy in Development Contexts*. Cambridge: Cambridge University Press, 169–201.

Gough, I. and G. Wood (Eds.) (2004). *Insecurity and Welfare Regimes in Asia, Africa and Latin America: Social Policy in Development Contexts*. Cambridge: Cambridge University Press.

Hagmann, T. and J. Abbink (2011). Twenty years of revolutionary democratic Ethiopia, 1991 to 2011. *Journal of Eastern African Studies*, 5(4), 579–95.

Hanlon, J., D., Hulme and A. Barrientos (2010). *Just Give Money to the Poor: The Development Revolution from the Global South*. Sterling, VA: Kumarian Press.

Hoben, A. (1973). *Land Tenure Among the Amhara of Ethiopia: The Dynamics of Cognatic Descent*. Chicago, IL: University of Chicago Press.

Holliday, I. (2000). Productivist welfare capitalism: social policy in East Asia. *Political Studies*, 48(4), 706–23.

Huber, E. and J.D. Stephens (2001). *Development and Crisis of the Welfare State: Parties and Policies in Global Markets*. Chicago, IL: University of Chicago Press.

Keller, E.J. and E. Mukudi-Omwami (2017). Rapid urban expansion and the challenge of pro-poor housing in Addis Ababa, Ethiopia. *Africa Review*, 9(2), 173–85.

Lavers, T. (2012a). 'Land grab' as development strategy? The political economy of agricultural investment in Ethiopia. *The Journal of Peasant Studies*, 39(1), 105–32.

Lavers, T. (2012b). Patterns of agrarian transformation in Ethiopia: state-mediated commercialisation and the 'land grab'. *The Journal of Peasant Studies*, 39(3–4), 795–822.

Lavers, T. (2013a). The political economy of social policy and agrarian transformation in Ethiopia. PhD thesis. University of Bath, Bath.

Lavers, T. (2013b). Food security and social protection in highland Ethiopia: linking the Productive Safety Net to the land question. *The Journal of Modern African Studies*, 51(3), 459–85.

Lavers, T. (2017). Land registration and gender equality in Ethiopia: how state–society relations influence the enforcement of institutional change. *Journal of Agrarian Change*, 17(1), 188–207.

Lavers, T. (2019). Social protection in an aspiring 'developmental state': the political drivers of Community-Based Health Insurance in Ethiopia. *ESID Working Paper*, 71.

Lavers, T. (2019). Social protection in an aspiring 'developmental state': the political drivers of Ethiopia's PSNP. *African Affairs*, Advance access online.

Lavers, T. and S. Hickey (2016). Conceptualising the politics of social protection expansion in low income countries: the intersection of transnational ideas and domestic politics. *International Journal of Social Welfare*, 25(4), 388–98.

Lefort, R. (2010). Powers–mengist–and peasants in rural Ethiopia: the post-2005 interlude. *The Journal of Modern African Studies*, 48(3), 435–60.

Lefort, R. (2012). Free market economy, 'developmental state' and party-state hegemony in Ethiopia: the case of the 'model farmers'. *The Journal of Modern African Studies*, 50(4), 681–706.

Marcus, H.G. (1995). A breakfast meeting with Prime Minister Meles [online]. Available at http://www.hartford-hwp.com/archives/33/008.html [Accessed 15 July 2009].

Migdal, J.S. (2001). *State in Society: Studying How States and Societies Transform and Constitute One Another*. Cambridge: Cambridge University Press.

Milas, S. and Latif, J.A. (2000). The political economy of complex emergency and recovery in northern Ethiopia. *Disasters*, 24(4), 363–79.

Mkandawire, T. (Ed.) (2004). *Social Policy in a Development Context*. Basingstoke: Palgrave Macmillan/UNRISD.

MoFED (2002). *Ethiopia: Sustainable Development and Poverty Reduction Program*. Addis Ababa: Ministry of Finance and Economic Development (MoFED): Federal Democratic Republic of Ethiopia.

MoFED (2003). *Rural Development Policy and Strategies*. Addis Ababa: Ministry of Finance and Economic Development (MoFED).

MoFED (2005). *Ethiopia: Building on Progress. A Plan for Accelerated and Sustained Development to End Poverty (PASDEP)*. Addis Ababa: Ministry of Finance and Economic Development (MoFED): Federal Democratic Republic of Ethiopia.

MoFED (2010). *Growth and Transformation Plan (GTP)*. Addis Ababa: Ministry of Finance and Economic Development (MoFED): Federal Democratic Republic of Ethiopia.

MoI (2002). *Industry Development Strategy of Ethiopia*. Addis Ababa: Ministry of Industry (MoI).

Office of the Prime Minister (1993). *National Population Policy of Ethiopia*. Addis Ababa: Office of the Prime Minister.

Oqubay, A. (2015). *Made in Africa: Industrial Policy in Ethiopia*. New York: Oxford University Press.

Polanyi, K. (2001). *The Great Transformation: The Political and Economic Origins of Our Time*. Second edition. Boston, MA: Beacon Press.

Rahmato, D. (2003). Poverty and agricultural involution. In: D. Rahmato (Ed.), *Some Aspects of Poverty in Ethiopia*. Addis Ababa: Forum for Social Studies, 1–15.

Rahmato, D. (2009). *The Peasant and the State: Studies in Agrarian Change in Ethiopia 1950s—2000s*. Addis Ababa: Addis Ababa University Press.

Salih, M. (2013). REST: post-war reconstruction and environmental rehabilitation. In: M. Salih (Ed.), *Environmental Politics and Liberation in Contemporary Africa*. New York: Springer Science & Business Media, 119–34.

Schmidt, V.A. (2008). Discursive institutionalism: the explanatory power of ideas and discourse. *Annual Review of Political Science*, 11(1), 303–26.

Seekings, J. (2008). Welfare regimes and redistribution in the South. In: I. Shapiro, P.A. Swenson, and D. Donno (Eds.), *Divide and Deal: The Politics of Distribution in Democracies*. New York and London: New York University Press, 19–42.

Seekings, J. (2012). Pathways to redistribution: the emerging politics of social assistance across the global 'South'. *Journal für Entwicklungspolitik*, XXXVIII (I–2012), S.14–34.

Seekings, J. (2016). 'A lean cow cannot climb out of the mud, but a good cattleman does not leave it to perish': The origins of a conservative welfare doctrine in Botswana under Seretse Khama, 1966–1980. *CSSR Working Paper No.*, 387.

Seekings, J. and N. Nattrass (2005). *Class, Race, and Inequality in South Africa*. London: Yale University Press.

Simon, B. (2011). *A Tale of Two Elections: A National Endeavour to Put a Stop to an Avalanche (In Amharic: Ye-hulet Merchawoch Weg: Nadan Yegeta Hagerawi Rucha)*. Addis Ababa.

Tadesse, M. and J. Young (2003). TPLF: reform or decline? *Review of African Political Economy*, 30(97), 389–403.

TGE (1994). *An Economic Development Strategy for Ethiopia*. Addis Ababa: Transitional Government of Ethiopia.

The Reporter (2000). 'I have never heard of any convincing reason as to why we should privatize land' [online]. *The Reporter (Addis Ababa)*. Available at http://www.hartford-hwp.com/archives/33/053.html [Accessed 8 July 2009].

Vaughan, S. (2011). Revolutionary democratic state-building: party, state and people in the EPRDF's Ethiopia. *Journal of Eastern African Studies*, 5(4), 619–40.

Vaughan, S. and K. Tronvoll (2003). *The Culture of Power in Contemporary Ethiopian Political Life*. Stockholm: Swedish International Development Cooperation Agency.

Verhoeven, H. (2013). The politics of African energy development: Ethiopia's hydro-agricultural state-building strategy and clashing paradigms of water security. *Philosophical Transactions of the Royal Society A: Mathematical, Physical and Engineering Sciences*, 371(2002), https://doi.org/10.1098/rsta.2012.0411.

Von Gliszczynski, M. (2015). *Cash Transfers and Basic Social Protection: Towards a Development Revolution?* New York: Springer.

White, G. and R. Goodman (1998). Welfare orientalism and the search for an East Asian welfare model. In: R. Goodman, H.-J. Kwon, and G. White (Eds.), *The East Asian Welfare Model: Welfare Orientalism and the State*. London: Routledge, 3–24.

Young, J. (1997). *Peasant Revolution in Ethiopia: The Tigray People's Liberation Front, 1975–1991*. Cambridge: Cambridge University Press.

Zenawi, M. (2006). Speech by HE Meles Zenawi, Prime Minister of the Federal Democratic Republic of Ethiopia for the Africa Task Force, Brooks World Poverty Institute, Manchester University, UK, 3–4 August 2006 [online]. Available at http://www.ethioembassy.org.uk/Archive/Prime%20Minister%20Meles%20Africa%20Task%20Force%20speech.htm [Accessed 24 July 2011].

Zenawi, M. (2010). Keynote address by H.E. Mr Meles Zenawi, Prime Minister of the Federal Democratic Republic of Ethiopia. Presented at the 5th International Conference on Federalism, 13 December 2010, Addis Ababa, Ethiopia.

4

Understanding Elite Commitment to Social Protection

Rwanda's Vision 2020 Umurenge Programme

Tom Lavers

1. Introduction

The Rwandan government introduced the Vision 2020 Umurenge Programme (VUP) with donor support in 2008. The VUP comprises: public works; unconditional direct support for those unable to work; and a financial services component that promotes financial literacy and provides credit. The programme was gradually rolled out from an initial thirty pilot sectors.[1] By June 2014 public works were operating in 180 of 416 sectors and providing support to 104,310 households, while direct support reached 61,948 households in 330 sectors. At this point, total programme coverage was roughly 6 per cent of the population and the equivalent of 13 per cent of those below the national poverty line.[2]

This chapter analyses the political economy dynamics influencing the adoption and evolution of the VUP, employing the 'adapted political settlements framework' described in Chapter 1 of this volume and in Lavers and Hickey (2016). This framework focuses on the interaction between the political settlement, the distributional regime, and particular policy domains. In this framework, the political settlement comprises not just competing interest groups and a compatible set of formal and informal institutions as in Khan's original work (2010), but also a set of paradigmatic ideas that provide a shared understanding between these interest groups. The *distributional regime* meanwhile encompasses the existing mechanisms for distributing resources within

[1] Administratively Rwanda is divided into (from largest to smallest): districts, sectors (s. *umurenge*/ pl. *imirenge*), cells, and villages.

[2] Author's calculations based on the average household size in the latest Rwandan census.

Tom Lavers, *Understanding Elite Commitment to Social Protection: Rwanda's Vision 2020 Umurenge Programme*
In: *The Politics of Social Protection in Eastern and Southern Africa.* Edited by: Sam Hickey, Tom Lavers, Miguel Niño-Zarazúa, and Jeremy Seekings, Oxford University Press (2020).
DOI: 10.1093/oso/9780198850342.003.0004

society, including but by no means limited to social protection. Finally, the policy domain is shaped by the ideas and incentives that flow from the overarching political settlement, but also contestation and negotiation between domestic and transnational actors within the policy domain involving the formation of *policy coalitions* advocating particular problem framings and policy ideas. This framework suggests that commitment to social protection will be influenced by: the incentives flowing from the political settlement; the degree of ideational fit between particular problem frames and policy models advocated by social protection proponents with the paradigmatic ideas that underpin the settlement; and the potential for social protection to address politically important failings of the prevailing distributional regime.

The chapter employs a process tracing methodology (George and Bennett 2004) to reconstruct the policy-making process based on semi-structured, key informant interviews with senior politicians and technical staff within government (eleven interviews), representatives of donors and international organizations (nine interviews), and foreign consultants (seven interviews). These respondents are detailed at the end of the chapter and constitute the majority of key actors, past and present, involved in design and programme administration. These interviews were conducted during fieldwork in Rwanda in May 2015 and before and afterwards by Skype with key people who had subsequently left the country. The analysis links this policy-making process to underlying political settlement dynamics and policy context. For this purpose the chapter draws on the existing academic literature on Rwandan politics, official policy documents, and statistics.

The chapter finds that specific characteristics of the political settlement shape strong elite commitment to the VUP. The VUP is a direct response to distributional problems—high rates of poverty and inequality—perceived in government to pose a threat to the political settlement. While the VUP's objectives and framing have shifted over time, the VUP has never been solely a social transfer programme, but an integral part of the government's development strategy. Within this context, the government has actively sought to learn from outside expertise, including the social protection ideas promoted by development partners. However, these transnational ideas are purposely re-interpreted and adapted by government to fit existing policy ideas and framings with a view to meeting its overall developmental and political goals.

The chapter begins by analysing Rwanda's political settlement and the broader distributional regime within which the VUP operates (sections 2 and 3). The analysis then turns to the VUP itself, focusing on the adoption of the programme and its evolution over time (section 4). Section 5 concludes.

2. The Political Settlement Under the RPF

Rwanda's current political settlement originates in the Rwanda Patriotic Front's (RPF's) military victory in 1994 that ended the genocide and civil war. Following a period of post-conflict reconstruction, around 2000 there was a series of departures from the ruling coalition that led to a high degree of cohesion within the ruling coalition, strong control of political elites over lower-level factions, and little to no elite opposition in the country.

2.1. From post-conflict reconstruction to the current political settlement

The RPF was the dominant force in the Government of National Unity (GNU, 1994–2000); however, there were clear attempts to present an image of power-sharing between political parties, as well as ethnic balance, with the new president, Pasteur Bizimungu, being a Hutu from the RPF. Nonetheless, the RPF could not count on widespread support across Rwanda. The new government was ruling over a majority Hutu population that had been subject to extensive propaganda demonizing the RPF (Prunier 1998; Uvin 1998), while a significant proportion of the population had taken part in massacres of Tutsis during the genocide. Furthermore, with government structures and infrastructure all but destroyed during the conflict, and opposition troops making regular incursions into Rwanda from the Democratic Republic of Congo (DRC), a direct threat to the ruling coalition remained. As such, the government relied heavily on military and security forces to quickly restore social order and re-build state capacity (Golooba-Mutebi 2008; Reyntjens 2013).

The current political settlement was forged in the period between the late 1990s and the 2003 Constitution. At this time there was a wave of resignations, expulsions, and defections from the ruling coalition, including the prime minister, president, and speaker of the National Assembly, while the Mouvement Démocratique Républicain, the second largest party, was banned for promoting sectarianism. Although the government continued to rule as a coalition, these changes strengthened the RPF's position. Meanwhile, Paul Kagame—previously vice-president—became president in 2000, comfortably winning subsequent elections.

As with so much in Rwandan politics, these events are subject to wildly diverging interpretations. For critics, the expulsions and defections constituted the centralization of power by the RPF and President Kagame (Reyntjens 2013).

In contrast, more favourable analysts argue that these expulsions can be explained by a lack of commitment by certain individuals and factions to core ideas of the ruling coalition (discussed in section 2.2) (Golooba-Mutebi and Booth 2013). Either way, the result is that there is no significant elite competition to the RPF-led coalition within Rwanda, with opponents limited to vocal Rwandan diaspora and remnants of opposition forces in the DRC.

President Kagame is widely acknowledged to be enormously powerful and central to all key government decisions. This power derives in part from his strong support both within the RPF and in the military. Indeed, the military remains key to state power in Rwanda (Booth and Golooba-Mutebi 2011; Jowell 2014). Beyond the Ministry of Defence (MINADEF), probably the two most important ministries are the Ministry of Finance and Economic Planning (MINECOFIN) and the Ministry of Local Government (MINALOC). MINALOC's prominent position results from the radical decentralization reforms undertaken since 2000, with all sectoral activities coordinated through MINALOC. Analyses of Rwanda's political settlement have also pointed to the prominent position of state, party, and military-owned business conglomerates and the important role they play in financing the party, reducing the need to finance politics through corruption (Booth and Golooba-Mutebi 2011; Behuria 2015).

The RPF coalition received relatively little donor support immediately after the genocide. Since the late 1990s, however, the UK Department for International Development (DFID), the US, the World Bank, and the European Union have provided as much as 50 per cent of the government budget in 2010, though declining to approximately 30 per cent by 2014 (IMF 2015: 17). As such, foreign donors are a key component of the political settlement, providing resources to sustain the ruling coalition. Nevertheless, the government views donors as unreliable because of the failure of foreign governments to stop the genocide, the limited support afterwards, and repeated conflicts with donors over human rights (Hayman 2009). Indeed, donors play a dual role within the political settlement, supporting the ruling coalition with resources, but also periodically challenging it.

Not only is Rwanda's political settlement characterized by elite cohesion and centralization of power around the president, but the political elite has also dominated lower-level factions. Ostensibly a means of enhancing local participation, the ambitious political, administrative, and financial decentralization implemented since 2000 is frequently noted as having enhanced central control over local administrations (Chemouni 2014; Ingelaere 2011; Purdeková 2011). *Imihigo*—a form of performance contract—detail specific targets to be met in the coming year by government officials. In principle, *imihigo* combine national priorities and community objectives. In practice, however, research concludes that national priorities dominate and that *imihigo* enhance accountability of local government officials upwards to the national government (Chemouni 2014; Ingelaere 2011). *Imihigo* provide strong incentives for officials to deliver on their targets as a result of the formal signing ceremonies held with the president and their use as the basis for promotion and dismissal.

2.2. Developmental ambitions and the role of ideas in the political settlement

Analyses have pointed to the RPF's 'systemic vulnerability'[3] as an explanation for its developmental outlook (Chemouni 2014; Mann and Berry 2016). From this perspective the need to broaden the ruling coalition—which continues to be associated with a Tutsi minority (Ansoms 2009)—alongside resource constraints and ongoing security threats provide the ruling elite with little option but to establish a 'developmental state'. However, the interests of the ruling elite cannot be neatly separated from the paradigmatic ideas regarding Rwandan society and the role of the state that are the subject of consensus within the ruling coalition and that form the basis of a strategy to maintain the coalition going forward. The changes in the ruling coalition around 2000 helped forge this consensus on a set of key paradigmatic ideas. These ideas can be traced directly to the 1998 Urugwiro process—a series of discussions on the future of Rwanda—and more broadly to the RPF's Eight Point Programme first outlined in 1987, although the exact articulation of these ideas emerged only incrementally (Reyntjens 2016). These ideas are core to the political settlement in that there is no space either within or outside the ruling coalition to contest them (Desrosiers and Thomson 2011; Golooba-Mutebi and Booth 2013; Reyntjens 2013).

The first paradigmatic idea is the need to move beyond the ethnic and regional divisions that dominated colonial and post-colonial administrations. According to the RPF, ethnicity is a colonial construction that introduced previously non-existent divisions into Rwandan society (Desrosiers and Thomson 2011; Pottier 2002; Reyntjens 2016). The RPF's aim—going back to the Rwandese Alliance for National Unity (RANU), the predecessor of the

[3] Drawing on Doner et al.'s (2005) concept, used to explain East Asian developmental states.

RPF (Prunier 1998)—is to promote a unified national identity in place of ethnic and regional self-identification and thereby to return to the supposed harmony of the pre-colonial era. This rationale translates into the rejection of ethnicity or region as the basis for policy choices (Golooba-Mutebi and Booth 2013); the promotion of re-vitalized 'customary' institutions from this harmonious era; and intolerance for ethno-political mobilization or even ethnic identification (Reyntjens 2016).

The second idea concerns the need to deliver rapid and inclusive socio-economic development that gives all sections of the population a stake in the political settlement (Golooba-Mutebi and Booth 2013). The reference point for all government strategies since 2000 and an expression of the political settlement forged at that time is Vision 2020, which aims to make Rwanda a middle-income country and to eliminate extreme poverty. These targets reflect an acknowledgement that poverty, land shortages, and population pressure were among the causes of the genocide (Pottier 2002) and, consequently, that resolving these problems is key to ensuring it never happens again. As aptly summed up by former Minister of Local Government, Protais Musoni,

> The thinking in Vision 2020 and back to 1997 was that we believe we need a unified nation to achieve development and provide services to people. But singing about unity is not enough, we still need the cement that is an equitable distribution for everybody in order to cement the sense and pride of a nation . . . With poverty, people can say 'we have a nation that is unified, but what is in it for me?' (int. respondent RG2)

The government's concern is that the persistence of poverty and inequality could provide the motivation for those who lose out to return to divisionism and conflict. As such, poverty and inequality are seen by the government to pose a direct threat to its post-ethnic vision and, by implication, the ruling coalition.

The third paradigmatic idea is the importance of self-reliance of Rwanda, but also of individuals. The focus on self-reliance can be traced back to the years of guerrilla warfare of many RPF members (Clark 2014; Reyntjens 2016). More broadly, the need for independence is linked to a distrust of the outside world from the colonial era and during the genocide (Chemouni 2016; Hayman 2009). As such, the government is frequently vocal about the need to move beyond aid dependence in the long-term, and to protect its policy autonomy in the short-term (Hayman 2009). The importance of national self-reliance is also mirrored in the focus on individual self-reliance. No one should receive services for free for fear of creating a culture of dependency (Chemouni 2018), while the work ethic of individuals is essential to national development. As President Kagame stated at his inauguration in 2000,

> If we can utilize the resources that God has given to us to good effect, we can eradicate poverty... We would like to urgently appeal to the Rwandese people to work. As the Bible says, 'he who does not work should not eat'.
>
> (cited in Ansoms 2009: 297)

The fourth foundational idea is the need to avoid political clientelism, which threatens to undermine developmental efforts and could lead to resurgent ethno-political mobilization (Chemouni 2014; Golooba-Mutebi and Booth 2013). From this perspective, electoral competition provides incentives for government officials to resort to clientelism and corruption as means of securing elected office. Consequently, party competition in local government elections is prohibited and during the last twenty years the RPF has pursued a zero-tolerance approach to corruption that has limited patronage politics.

Based on these ideas, the post-ethnic, developmental vision of the ruling coalition and its political legitimacy are closely intertwined. The possibility of resurgent sectarian divisions constitutes an existential threat for a regime that continues to be associated with an ethnic minority, while rapid development and poverty reduction, alongside the suppression of ethnicity, regionalism, and clientelism, are seen as the means to transcend these divisions.

While these paradigmatic ideas certainly have their merits, they nonetheless leave the regime open to criticism (Desrosiers and Thomson 2011; Reyntjens 2016), at least some of it justifiable. For example, critics argue that developmental progress conceals political repression and merely papers over the divisions that contributed to the genocide, avoiding real reconciliation (Straus and Waldorf 2011). Meanwhile, others claim that the promotion of national unity has been used to maintain authoritarian rule and to cover up the domination of a minority ethnic group (Ansoms 2009; Pottier 2002; Reyntjens 2013).

3. Vision 2020 Umurenge Within the Distributional Regime

State social protection in Rwanda dates back to the colonial introduction of a pension scheme in 1962. However, social insurance only reached employees in the small formal sector. Under previous governments, support for the rural population took the form of agricultural subsidies, as well as health and educational provision rather than social assistance. The GNU introduced programmes, including elements of social protection, to respond to specific issues arising from the post-conflict context, including: the Rwanda Demobilization and Reintegration Commission (RDRC) in 1997 to reintegrate demobilized soldiers, including through short-term cash transfers; and the Genocide Survivors Support and Assistance Fund (Fond d'Assistance aux Rescapes du Genocide, FARG) in 1998 to provide financial support and advocacy for genocide survivors.

One of the most politically important challenges facing the ruling coalition in the 1990s was how to accommodate large numbers of return migrants to Rwanda. For the RPF, the right of return for those displaced in 1959 was the key motivation for the civil war, while accommodation of those displaced during the civil war was central to claims of promoting national unity. A programme of *umudugudu* or villagization was conducted to relocate scattered dwellings into consolidated settlements to make more efficient use of scarce land. However, the government's ambitions soon expanded from re-integrating migrants to relocating the entire rural population into planned settlements (Hilhorst and Leeuwen 2000).

3.1. Beyond reconstruction: Vision 2020

Vision 2020 outlined the overarching objectives guiding subsequent policies and strategies. However, the document is short on clear policy prescriptions. The first strategy to act on this Vision was the 2002 Poverty Reduction Strategy Paper (PRSP), which focused on the need to raise agricultural productivity and invest in infrastructure. The PRSP noted plans to develop a social protection policy, while in the early 2000s government ministries launched a range of uncoordinated initiatives related to social protection, although many were not originally framed as such.

From 1999, the health ministry piloted and then rolled out the Mutuelles de Santé, a community-based health insurance scheme that achieved unprecedented coverage in rural and informal sectors (Chemouni 2018), as well as formal sector health insurance schemes. Then, *Ubudehe* was launched as part of the 2002 PRSP and is one of several programmes that seek to revitalize 'customary' practices to address contemporary problems. *Ubudehe* provides grants of €1,000 to communities to encourage cooperation in the identification and achievement of community goals. As part of this process, *Ubudehe* classifies households throughout the country into six wealth categories. The programme has subsequently been framed as a form of social protection.

In 2003, MINALOC initiated the Labour-Intensive Local Development Programme (Programme de Développement Local à Haute Intensité de Main d'Œuvre, PDL-HIMO), building on public works projects going back to 1978. Although not initially framed as social protection, PDL-HIMO constitutes a direct precursor to the VUP and a programme with significant overlap given its objective of combining employment creation with infrastructure development. Despite enormous ambitions, the programme suffered from insufficient donor funding and a lack of technical expertise. Labour-intensive public works have, nonetheless, been taken up by other ministries.

In 2005, MINALOC produced the National Social Protection Policy (NSPP). This policy was advocated by the World Bank (int. respondent RG2) and closely followed its Social Risk Management framework. However, the policy was weak on details and, though it listed *Ubudehe*, PDL-HIMO, and health insurance as part of social protection, it was not well integrated with other government policies. According to former Minister Protais Musoni, MINALOC lacked expertise in social protection at the time and, by 2007, 'we were struggling with the ideas and the VUP came and took over' (int. respondent RG2). The VUP can therefore be seen as the latest in a series of social protection initiatives—notably FARG, *Ubudehe*, and the mutuelles—that have been politically prioritized over the past twenty years.

3.2. Stalled progress and renewed efforts to meet Vision 2020

Following the devastation of the genocide, economic growth was strong in the 1990s and steady in the first half of the 2000s. However, it became increasingly evident that growth was leading to rising inequality and making little contribution to poverty reduction. Comparison of the first two rounds of the Integrated Household Survey on Living Conditions (Enquête Intégrale sur les Conditions de Vie, EICV) showed that despite average growth of 6.4 per cent per year between 2000/1 and 2005/6 (MINECOFIN 2007: 5), the poverty rate decreased by just 3.5 per cent (NISR 2007). Furthermore, because of population growth, the poverty headcount actually increased, while inequality increased from an already high Gini coefficient of 0.47 in 2000/1 to 0.51 in 2005/6 (NISR 2007). EICV results also highlighted regional inequalities, with a significant reduction in poverty in the eastern province, but an increase in the poverty headcount in the south.

The result of these discussions was the Economic Development and Poverty Reduction Strategy (EDPRS) (2008–13), which introduced the VUP. Evaluation of the EDPRS was in stark contrast to the first PRSP. The government hailed the achievement of a 'perfect developmental "hat trick" of sustained economic growth (8% average), poverty reduction (12% points) and a reduction in income inequality' (MINECOFIN 2013: ix). These results appear to constitute a remarkable success, although inequality remained extremely high. Rapid poverty reduction is attributed to growth in agricultural productivity, diversification into off-farm activities, and reduced fertility, though the impact of the VUP itself is unclear (World Bank 2015). These apparent successes led to renewed optimism in government and even more ambitious targets. A revised Vision 2020 in 2012 set targets of 11.5 per cent growth per year and a reduction of extreme poverty from 24 to less than 10 per cent during the EDPRS2 period (2013–18). Initial EICV4 results for 2010/11–2013/14 show continued progress, with strong economic growth, and further reductions in poverty and inequality (NISR 2015).[4]

4. The Adoption and Evolution of the VUP

The VUP policy process can be loosely disaggregated into three phases, addressed in sections 4.1 to 4.4: the drafting of the original programme document during 2007; the detailed design phase and piloting in 2008; and the programme's evolution during roll-out and discussions on the National Social Protection Strategy (NSPS) from 2009.

4.1. The initial policy development

The VUP originated in the annual government leadership retreat in February 2007. The Minister of Finance, James Musoni, presented results of the EICV2 to assess progress and plan for EDPRS1. Slow rates of poverty reduction and rising inequality clearly demonstrated a failing of the government strategy. The leadership decided that something needed to be done, with several observers pointing specifically to President Kagame himself, who demanded swift action (int. respondents RG1, RG3).

[4] The EICV4 has, however, provoked controversy, with claims that calculation of the poverty line was manipulated to give a false impression of progress (Reyntjens 2015). If correct, this would raise questions about the accuracy of official statistics more broadly.

Government respondents denied that the VUP was a response to specific demands made by interest groups or electoral pressures, and, unlike the situation prevailing in most other countries covered in this volume, interviews suggest there was no concerted donor push to promote social assistance in Rwanda before 2007.[5] Instead, persistent high poverty rates and high and rising rates of inequality represented an emerging political problem that threatened the government's narrative of building national unity through socioeconomic progress—a key feature of the political settlement. Continuing Protais Musoni's earlier analogy, the lack of progress threatened to erode the 'cement' that held together the government's strategy and, by implication, the political settlement itself. The outcome of the retreat was the formation of a committee comprising members of MINALOC and MINECOFIN, with the Minister of Local Government, Protais Musoni, given responsibility for developing a programme within six months. Despite having no policy proposals at that stage, the president launched the initiative at the Millennium Villages Project in March 2007 (int. respondent RG1). From the very beginning, the programme was conceived as one of three core pillars of the EDPRS, with the goal of ensuring 'that economic growth rapidly translates into poverty reduction' (MINECOFIN 2007: 75). The leadership retreat therefore generated strong commitment to addressing the problem, but without any clear policy direction. As such, Protais Musoni was under considerable pressure to deliver an ambitious programme in a very short timeframe (int. respondent RG11).

In the following months, Protais Musoni held discussions with a MINECOFIN advisor, representatives of the World Bank and DFID, and MINALOC staff. While the original impulse for the VUP was an emerging threat to the political settlement and the paradigmatic ideas that underpin it, it was through discussions within this policy coalition that the VUP took shape. The World Bank and DFID proposed looking at Ethiopia's Productive Safety Net Programme (PSNP) and paid for state ministers for the economy and local government to undertake a study tour during 2007 (int. respondents RG1, RG2, RD4). The state minister for local government also visited Zambia's Kalomo cash transfer pilot (see Pruce and Hickey, Chapter 7 of this volume) with donor support, and the MINALOC team reviewed literature on other programmes. However, the PSNP and the Food Security Programme (FSP) of

[5] The reasons are not entirely clear, but appear to be linked to turnover of social development advisors in DFID Rwanda and the absence of senior, in-country social protection staff at the World Bank.

which it is a part was the main foreign policy model that influenced the Rwandan government (int. respondents RG2, RG9).[6]

The economic advisor seconded to MINALOC drafted the VUP programme document in close discussion with Protais Musoni, drawing heavily on the PSNP/FSP model. Ethiopia's FSP at that time comprised: the PSNP, including public works for households with an able-bodied adult and direct support for households without; a credit and extension programme; and a resettlement programme. The VUP has three main components; public works, direct support, and financial services, which includes credit for programme participants. The VUP was also originally intended to implement large-scale villagization.

Among the reasons why the PSNP/FSP appealed to the Rwandan government was that it enabled them to build on existing policies and ideas. The state minister who took part in the study tour highlighted that Ethiopia, like Rwanda, had already launched far-reaching decentralization (int. respondent RG11), and the VUP was seen as a means of deepening the decentralization started in 2000, also under Protais Musoni. The Vision 2020 Umurenge Programme, as the name suggests, was intended to build the administrative and implementation capacities of each *umurenge* (sector). Furthermore, public works built on MINALOC's experience with PDL-HIMO. As Protais Musoni put it, 'the VUP was not starting from nowhere, we knew exactly how to do HIMO' (int. respondent RG2). Likewise, the VUP adopted *Ubudehe*'s wealth classification to target VUP participants[7] and built on the experience of *Ubudehe* community transfers, in which Minister Protais saw a precedent for direct support (int. respondents RG2, RG10).

Furthermore, many of the paradigmatic ideas that influenced the Ethiopian government regarding the PSNP resonated strongly with the paradigmatic ideas within Rwanda's ruling coalition. Principally, both governments worry about creating 'welfare dependency' among the poor (int. respondent RG11; Lavers 2019, Chapter 3 of this volume). In Rwanda, this concern relates to paradigmatic ideas within the ruling coalition regarding the need for rapid development and self-reliance. The result is the VUP's emphasis on ensuring that all recipients who are able to work should do so rather than being given

[6] Respondents pointed to donor facilitation of this policy transfer. However, ruling parties in Rwanda and Ethiopia have close links and direct inter-governmental links may also have been influential.

[7] Increasingly government support—including the VUP, health insurance subsidies, and school bursaries—has been allocated to the poorest *Ubudehe* categories, transforming the classification from a community-based poverty mapping tool into a mechanism for resource allocation (Gaynor 2014; Sabates-Wheeler et al. 2015).

'handouts' and a need to provide clear paths to 'graduation' for programme participants.

Despite donor framing of the VUP as a social protection programme, for Protais Musoni and his team the VUP was never seen merely in those terms. Instead, for the government the VUP was an integrated 'Local Development Program' that aimed at agrarian and societal transformation in line with the prioritization of rapid socioeconomic development. The original programme document reserved the phrase *social protection* for direct support for 'the neediest people who are landless and unable to work', excluding public works which was instead intended to 'revive' the underfunded PDL-HIMO (GoR 2007: 22). As such, right from the start the VUP was expected not just to reduce poverty, but also to contribute to another key EDPRS priority: rural infrastructure. In doing so, the programme design raises important definitional questions regarding public works as social protection and as an infrastructure development programme (McCord 2008).

The VUP, as originally conceived, was to contribute to 'umudugudu-ization' or villagization (GoR 2007). Protais Musoni's visit to the Millennium Villages project several years earlier had been influential, but he had remained unsure as to how to scale up the approach (int. respondent RG2). The influence of the Millennium Villages is evident in the VUP programme document that envisages using public works to construct planned 'model umudugudu' with improved access to services (GoR 2007). Attempting to learn from problems with earlier villagization, which tended towards coercive implementation and faced local resistance (Hilhorst and Leeuwen 2000), the VUP pursued an 'incentive-based' villagization, creating infrastructure and services first to encourage people to relocate (int. respondent RG5; GoR 2007).

The importance political elites placed on the VUP, based on the perceived threat to the political settlement, translated into strong pressure on the design team regarding the pace of the roll-out and expected impact of the programme. VUP targets were derived from the gap between Vision 2020 targets and the slow progress by 2007 (GoR 2007: 6), rather than a realistic assessment of the programme's potential. The plan involved an exponential expansion from thirty pilot sectors to nationwide coverage within five years. The expectation was that after just six months in the programme all participants would be ready for graduation (int. respondents RD1, RC2, RC4). These objectives underscore the lack of technical capacity within government at the time and the political rather than technical drivers of the design process.

The VUP is also notable for relative consensus between the World Bank and DFID rather than the advocacy of competing social protection models, as in some other countries. This may reflect individual organizational representatives. One donor respondent explicitly noted that she had tried to learn from past experiences in other countries where donors had been in competition (int. respondent RD1). It is also clear that with strong government ownership of the policy agenda, space for donor influence is limited in Rwanda (int. respondents RD2, RD6). However, it may also be that the PSNP/FSP model aided consensus. The World Bank and DFID are among the main PSNP donors and the model already constituted a hard-fought compromise (Lavers 2019). Furthermore, there is a clear contrast between donor support for the VUP and indifference regarding PDL-HIMO, despite the strong similarities between the two programmes. The VUP's success reflects changing donor fashions and the rise of social protection on the global development agenda (int. respondent RG2). The framing of the VUP fit a specific moment, in contrast to the limited funding available for public employment programmes.

In summary, a failure of the distributional regime—namely, persistent high rates of poverty and inequality—was perceived by political elites as a threat to the political settlement and the paradigmatic ideas that underpin it. This threat generated a high level of elite commitment, and strong pressure to take quick action, but no clear policy approach. The policy coalition of Rwandan politicians and technocrats and foreign donors rushed to deliver a programme design in a short space of time. This political pressure contributed to an initial programme document that was enormously ambitious and technically weak, and that oversold the potential of a programme with which there was little experience within government. In spite, or perhaps because, of this over-ambition, the cabinet approved the VUP in August 2007.

4.2. From huge ambitions to designing a social protection programme

A programme coordinator was hired following cabinet approval and the VUP was placed within MINALOC's Common Development Fund (CDF), used to finance community infrastructure projects. At that stage it was necessary to translate the huge ambitions and sweeping assumptions in the programme document into an implementable plan. Given its lack of technical expertise, MINALOC sought assistance from the World Bank and DFID. Donor representatives from that time acknowledge that the programme document had 'severe limitations' from a social protection perspective (int. respondent RD1), and in early 2008, they hired a team of foreign consultants, including several social protection experts, to produce programme guidelines.

In selecting consultants the donors turned, in the words of one of the team, to 'their PSNP stalwarts' (int. respondent RC6), deliberately selecting several people who had worked on the PSNP (int. respondents RD4, RC3, RG9). The VUP coordinator described how he sat down with these consultants to examine in detail the activities conducted by Ethiopia's regional, *wereda* (district), and *kebele* (sub-district) governments and how these responsibilities might be distributed across Rwanda's decentralized governance system (int. respondent RG9). At this stage discussions were focused on technical details. Nevertheless, one of the consultants was told repeatedly by Protais Musoni that he was in regular communication with 'the boss'—President Kagame—about the design (int. respondent RC5), again highlighting the VUP's strong political importance.

During the design and early stages of implementation, relations between donors and some government officials appear to have become somewhat strained, especially regarding the original coordinator. DFID, in particular, placed great importance on direct support for the poorest and most vulnerable. In return, the programme coordinator repeatedly criticized the negative effects of European welfare systems on work incentives, while arguing that some donors were bringing European experiences that were irrelevant to Africa (int. respondents RG9, RC4, RD1). This perspective clearly fits with key paradigmatic ideas regarding dependency and self-reliance, discussed in section 2.2. Nevertheless, certain government concessions were achieved including an acknowledgement, absent from the programme document, that the most vulnerable households 'will never graduate and will continue to require a level of direct financial support' (MINALOC 2009).

Public works design also has important implications for the VUP's contribution to poverty reduction. In Ethiopia, several donors insisted on an agreement regarding the 'primacy of transfers': that participants are entitled to payment for a certain number of workdays regardless of government capacity to organize public works (Lavers 2019). No such agreement exists for the VUP, with the result that, like PDL-HIMO, the number of workdays and, consequently, the transfer of resources to the poor depend on the government's capacity to organize projects. By design, therefore, the programme is driven by infrastructure priorities, not just social protection.

MINALOC introduced public works in May 2008, direct support in January 2009, and financial services in January 2010. This roll-out reflected CDF's experience in public works, as well as the management of participant expectations, avoiding the perception of the programme as a government handout (int. respondent RG9). In the first year thirty sectors were selected, the poorest in each district across the country, with another two or three sectors per district to be added in each of the following years (int. respondent RG2). In hindsight, roll-out plans were entirely unrealistic given resource and capacity constraints (int. respondents RG2, RC2). The roll-out plan was adapted to add one sector per district each year—still a significant challenge—that implied a very long-term process. This selection also set aside clear evidence at the time that poverty, though present throughout the country, was concentrated in the southern province. As argued above, an important element of the political settlement is a commitment to transcend past divisions, both ethnic and regional, through inclusive development. This translated into a rejection of regional criteria as the basis for policy-making, preventing the prioritization of the poorest province (int. respondents RD1, RD4, RG10).

The original VUP coordinator left after seven months and the PDL-HIMO coordinator took over in late 2008. At the end of 2008, DFID also funded three foreign technical assistants, including a social protection specialist, to help administer the programme, given the shortage of technical capacity. Several donor representatives and consultants argued that the original coordinator did not understand social protection, as the donors saw it, and that bringing in new management who 'got it' was a key step (int. respondents RC5, RD1). It was therefore during 2008 through the design phase carried out within a policy coalition of government and donor technocrats—but with strong oversight from key political figures within the ruling coalition—that the VUP began to resemble a social protection programme, as understood within the development industry. World Bank decentralization funds were used to hire programme staff, and CDF's own funds used to finance public works in the initial thirty sectors. DFID started contributing in 2009 and the EU, Swedish International Development Agency (SIDA), and UNICEF joined subsequently. However, government funding remained a large proportion of programme expenditure throughout, averaging 69 per cent over the first three and a half years (OAG 2012).

Several respondents argued that MINECOFIN and, in particular, Minister James Musoni were sceptical about the VUP early on (int. respondents RC2, RC4, RC5, RD1, RD4). That said, there are no suggestions that MINECOFIN sought to block funding altogether. While some efforts were made to limit financial exposure, there was commitment to funding the programme. It is unclear to what extent this was the result of the president's strong support in the face of resistance from MINECOFIN or of a basic level of cautious support from MINECOFIN.

The adoption of the VUP therefore created space for a transnationalized policy coalition to form and discuss policy options. Lack of government technical capacity enabled donors to shape the problem definition and policy design, strengthening the VUP's social protection credentials. However, the proposals considered within the policy coalition were constrained by the perceived interests and ideas flowing from the political settlement, strongly influencing, for example, the productive focus and the emphasis on self-reliance. As such, the VUP policy coalition differs in important respects from those in some of the other cases in this volume. The VUP policy coalition was not bound by a shared set of ideas or the goal of advocating any particular policy. Rather, the coalition operated as a technical working group, examining policy proposals and their fit with the incentives and ideas flowing from the political settlement.

4.3. Reform and continuity within the social protection strategy

At the end of 2009, a cabinet reshuffle replaced Protais Musoni with James Musoni as Minister of Local Government. Whatever James Musoni's earlier concerns about the VUP, he became a strong supporter at MINALOC (int. respondents RC2, RD4), overseeing the expansion of the VUP and the drafting of the NSPS.

By 2008 the 2005 NSPP was already seen as out of date and surpassed by the VUP. As such, there was a need to bring together the VUP, as the new centrepiece of the NSPS, with FARG, RDRC, *Ubudehe*, and social insurance into one integrated approach (int. respondent RG6). A consultation process was held involving different levels of government, development partners, and other interest groups. This NSPS process followed ratification of the 2008 African Union Social Policy Framework (AUSPF). While the AUSPF is noted in the NSPS, however, it was not discussed at all during Rwandan policy discussions (int. respondent RG6) and was not mentioned by any respondents as an influence. Instead, the NSPS was solely attributed to the need for domestic policy coherence.

The consultation process contrasted with the earlier donor consensus. The government's decision to invite discussion and their apparent uncertainty opened up space for advocacy. UNICEF, Save the Children, and HelpAge advocated a lifecycle approach, drawing on the Social Protection Floor concept, while the World Bank opposed such an approach, preferring to build on the VUP (int. respondent RG6). In addition, UNICEF, the World Bank, and the ILO all paid for government officials to attend training courses advocating their favoured types of social protection.

An initial draft strategy drew on the Social Protection Floor's lifecycle approach, replacing VUP's direct support with categorical cash transfers for children, the elderly, and the disabled. The public works component, meanwhile, would be transformed into an Employment Guarantee Scheme, providing a guaranteed number of workdays to participants. While the foreign consultant drafting the strategy apparently gained the support of the State Minister, it was dismissed in pre-Cabinet discussions for being too expensive and a poor fit for Rwanda. In particular, Protais Musoni, then Minister for Cabinet Affairs with responsibility for reviewing all policy proposals, felt this new strategy threatened to 'distort' and undermine the VUP (int. respondent RG6). The strategy argued that universal grants for vulnerable groups would make them easier and cheaper to administer. However, Cabinet expressed concern that universal grants would foster dependency and undermine fertility policy (int. respondents RG6, RD6). A new consultant was brought in to revise this draft, and a more modest proposal built around the VUP was approved in 2011 (int. respondents RG6, RC1). In contrast to the original VUP proposal, which clearly resonated with core paradigmatic ideas within the ruling coalition, the proposal to transform the programme was rejected because of the inconsistency between categorical transfers and core paradigmatic ideas regarding self-reliance and dependency.

In 2013, the NSPS was revised for consistency with the EDPRS2, which focused on progress towards the revised Vision 2020. As part of the revision, the VUP—previously a flagship programme—has been subsumed within the Rural Development theme, which is dominated by a focus on livelihoods rather than social protection. MINECOFIN's Chief Economist expressed concerns that the VUP had not been able to demonstrate much impact on poverty to that point:

> The EICV3 showed that the VUP did not have much impact... Actually agriculture can be the best social protection programme. If you increase productivity, you can reduce poverty. In the discussion that we had we insisted on putting social protection under rural development since agriculture is an important component. (int. respondent RG10)

While scepticism about the VUP clearly remains within MINECOFIN, this does not necessarily mean a complete loss of commitment. Rather, the EDPRS2 commits to further VUP expansion, alongside a re-focusing of efforts to maximize impact in line with EDPRS2 targets. First, the annual addition of one sector per district was ended and the decision made to target the poorest remaining sectors from 2012/13. Though facilitated by improved data availability in EICV3 (int. respondents RG6, RG7, RD2), this change signifies a shift from previous concerns regarding geographic impartiality to maximizing resources for the poorest parts of the country to achieve Vision 2020. Second, direct support has been fast-tracked and was planned to reach every sector in the country by mid-2016, while the more logistically challenging public works component expands more slowly. Respondents expressed differing opinions as to the origins of these changes, including: discussions in the Social Protection Sector Working Group (int. respondents RG6, RG7, RD2); a request by some MPs (int. respondent RC2); and MINECOFIN demands to ensure resources had the biggest possible impact (int. respondent RG10).

Third, EDPRS2 has a renewed focus on graduation. Although the original programme document envisaged graduation within six months, over time the approach had become more realistic, gradually extending intervals between re-targeting to three years (int. respondent RC2). MINECOFIN pushed MINALOC to commit to specific graduation targets (int. respondents RC2, RD2, RG7) because of the escalating costs of the roll-out and what they considered to be the VUP's minimal impact in its first five years (int. respondent RG10). As the Chief Economist in MINECOFIN argued,

> You cannot have people receiving support for 3–5 years, it is too much . . . a person who is 30–40 years old who is not disabled, they cannot be in a social protection programme for 5 years. A success story is when after three years someone graduates from poverty and we do not need to support them anymore. (int. respondent RG10)

4.4. Elite commitment and the challenges of implementation

Strong elite commitment to the VUP is indicated by its implementation, with government financing a significant proportion of the costs, hiring staff, and institutionalizing the programme. Furthermore, while there have undoubtedly been corruption cases, there is no evidence of widespread use of the VUP for patronage, as is evident in some other countries. Regular audits by the Office of the Auditor-General (OAG 2012), prosecutions of officials who misappropriated funds, and exposés of corruption cases in government-controlled media (Karuhanga 2012; Rugira 2015) suggest intolerance for such activities, in line with paradigmatic ideas regarding the importance of avoiding corruption and clientelism.

This does not mean, however, that implementation has always been effective. Notably, programme participants have consistently received fewer workdays than government targets, while only 54 per cent of eligible households actually participated in public works in 2011/12 (MINALOC 2013: 53). Though poverty reduction was a core concern driving the adoption of the VUP, these implementation failings point to competing priorities within the ruling coalition that undermine the programme's impact on poverty. Although there are no robust, independent evaluations of the programme's impact, interviews, donor-commissioned reviews, and programme statistics highlight three main implementation challenges.

First, the VUP faces significant financial constraints. CDF receives a minimum of 10 per cent of the government budget by law. Social protection funding has grown over time to account for 40 per cent of this statutory funding, the majority of which goes to the VUP (int. respondents RG8, RC2). Nevertheless, low graduation rates and the annual expansion to new sectors have resulted in resource shortages. Although MINALOC has requested an increase of 5 per cent of the budget, this has not been sanctioned by MINECOFIN (int. respondent RG8). The shortage of finance has led the government to reduce staff per district responsible for administering the programme, resulting in capacity constraints (int. respondent RC2). Financial restrictions also present a partial explanation for the shortage of workdays and the low rates of participation.

Second, the question remains as to whether poverty reduction is really the government's top priority and whether the VUP constitutes an effective form of social protection. The VUP's potential to contribute to multiple government objectives was a key feature of the original programme document and, it would seem, one reason for strong elite commitment. However, there has been a recurrent tension within the VUP between the relative importance of poverty reduction and infrastructure development. The key variable in this respect is the labour intensity of public works, which determines the proportion of programme resources transferred to participants.

The VUP has never come close to the target of spending 80 per cent of the public works budget on wages. Indeed, over time the labour intensity of public works has reduced and, in 2013/14, was just 38 per cent. Consequently, one respondent questioned whether VUP public works could be characterized as social protection at all (int. respondent RC7). The VUP was originally located in CDF, which has a mandate to deliver value for money in community infrastructure projects. The original programme coordinator reported that CDF management pushed him to use contractors and capital-intensive production techniques that undermined the programme's protective contribution (int. respondent RG9). These tensions eased when CDF became the Rwandan Local Development Support Fund (RLDSF)[8] in 2011 with a broader mandate, including social protection (int. respondents RG8, RC2). Government respondents argue that from that point the top priority was to support the poor and infrastructure development was a secondary concern.

Whatever central government intentions, the VUP remains subject to competing pressures in local government. While public works projects are supposed to be selected by communities, there has long been evidence that government priorities dominate decision-making (Devereux and Ndejuru 2010). *Imihigo* for local government officials contain a range of targets, including infrastructure development. The inflow of significant VUP resources provides strong incentives for local governments to use these funds to meet infrastructure targets, undermining the VUP's protective role (int. respondents RC2, RC4). This problem has grown in importance as local governments have taken on increasing responsibility for planning projects, in line with the use of the VUP to support decentralization (int. respondents RC3, RC4). This focus on infrastructure development provides a partial explanation for the low and falling labour intensity of public works.

The third major challenge concerns targeting. From the initial design discussions, donors expressed concern about the use of *Ubudehe* wealth classifications to select VUP participants. The World Bank repeatedly advocated a proxy means test, without success (int. respondents RD1, RD4, RC4, RC7). A recent study by Sabates-Wheeler et al. (2015) matched individuals' *Ubudehe* classification with household consumption in EICV3—the quantitative assessment used to assess poverty nationally. The results suggest there is no relationship between the two, with *Ubudehe* categories evenly distributed across consumption quintiles. Not only does this represent a challenge for assessing graduation, but it also raises serious questions about the VUP's poverty targeting: 62 per cent of the poorest quintile in the EICV are excluded from the VUP as they are not in categories 1 or 2 (Sabates-Wheeler et al. 2015: 108). Growing evidence of these problems prompted the 2014 leadership

[8] Re-named the Local Administrative Entities Development Agency (LODA) in 2014.

retreat to demand MINALOC 'expedite revision of Ubudehe categorization' (RoR 2014: 1). MINALOC piloted a new scheme in five districts from late 2014. This revised version reduced the number of categories from six to four and complemented community assessments with a thirteen-question household asset survey intended to add an objective dimension. The new scheme was approved for nationwide use in 2016. Several respondents nonetheless expressed doubts about whether the new questions would provide any basis for identifying the poorest households.

While there is little evidence to date that clientelism and corruption have had a major impact on programme implementation, there remain significant implementation challenges that limit the VUP's effectiveness. These challenges result at least partly from the drivers of commitment to social protection, namely the pressure to use the VUP as a productive investment in rural infrastructure and to build on existing programmes such as *Ubudehe.* While political legitimacy and social cohesion were also vital objectives of the VUP, further research is required to assess whether the programme has succeeded in meeting those goals.

5. Conclusion

Respondents from government, development partners, and consultants were unanimous that the government drove the VUP policy-making process. The original initiative can be linked to core paradigmatic ideas within the RPF and the understanding that poverty and inequality constituted a threat to the political settlement that needed to be addressed. Donors certainly influenced the programme through the policy coalition by suggesting the PSNP as a policy model and strengthening the programme's problem framing regarding social protection. However, the VUP is an example of existing elite commitment in search of a policy idea, rather than donors advocating a policy and trying to generate commitment within government, as in several of the other countries examined in this volume.

While the VUP was a government initiative and significant elite commitment has remained, there are lingering doubts as to quite what the government is committed to. While the original initiative stems from the slow rate of poverty reduction, Cabinet approved the programme based on its potential to contribute to productive objectives in addition to assisting the poorest. These multiple objectives have proven to be a recurrent challenge in implementation, with infrastructure targets, in particular, in tension with those of poverty reduction. As such, while there is some complementarity between the protective and productive objectives of the VUP, this can be over-estimated. While the programme's productive goals may have been essential to securing elite commitment within the context of a dominant coalition settlement, they also present a challenge to the implementation of social protection.

As such, this chapter shows that the adapted political settlements framework provides valuable insights into the Rwandan government's motivations for adopting the VUP. While social protection does not yet constitute an integral feature of the bargains that underpin the political settlement, the political settlement has shaped commitment to and design of the VUP in vital ways. The VUP is an example of an elite-driven, top-down initiative to address a perceived emerging threat to the political settlement and, as such, is inherently intertwined with the political legitimacy of the ruling coalition.

However, the interests of the ruling elite cannot be neatly separated from paradigmatic ideas that shape both the orientation of the political settlement and, as argued here, policy. Core paradigmatic ideas within the political settlement are evident in the government's commitment to economic growth and poverty reduction, the emphasis on self-reliance, and the importance of avoiding regional bias. Although the PSNP design and donor advocacy of social protection were also influential, Rwandan officials assessed these transnational ideas for the degree of ideational fit with underlying paradigmatic ideas and adapted these policy ideas to ensure compatibility. The result was the integration of the VUP into the development strategy—rather than a standalone anti-poverty programme—and the expectation that the programme should have a range of productive impacts, as well as providing protection for the poor.

Acknowledgements

This research greatly benefited from research assistance by Hinda Ruton and comments on earlier drafts by Daniel Béland, Sam Hickey, and three anonymous reviewers. The support of the College of Medicine and Health Sciences of the University of Rwanda (research clearance no. MINEDUC/S&T/300/2015) and the International Labour Organization, particularly Sangheon Lee and Colin Fenwick, in facilitating fieldwork is gratefully acknowledged.

Interviews Conducted

Government officials

RG1, Deputy Director-General for Social Protection, LODA, Kigali, 19 and 21 May 2015

RG2, former Minister of Local Government, Kigali, 28 May 2015

RG3, former Minister of Health, Kigali, 29 May 2015
RG4, Director-General, Community Development and Social Welfare Department, MINALOC, Kigali, 26 May 2015
RG5, Head, Human Settlement Planning and Development Department, MININFRA, Kigali, 21 May 2015
RG6, former Monitoring and Evaluation Specialist, MINALOC, Kigali, 27 May 2015
RG7, VUP Director, LODA, Kigali, 22 May 2015
RG8, Director-General, LODA, Kigali, 22 May 2015
RG9, former VUP Programme Coordinator, CDF, Kigali, 20 May 2015
RG10, Chief Economist, MINECOFIN, Kigali, 20 May 2015
RG11, Vice-Governor, National Bank of Rwanda, Kigali, 7 July 2015

Development partners

RD1, representative of a development partner by Skype, 20 March 2015
RD2, representative of a development partner, Kigali, 27 May 2015
RD3, representative of a development partner by Skype, 1 July 2015
RD4, representative of a development partner by Skype, 24 March 2015
RD5, representative of a development partner, Kigali, 22 May 2015
RD6, representative of a development partner, Kigali, 27 May 2015
RD7, representative of a development partner, Kigali, 27 May 2015
RD8, representative of a development partner, Geneva, 14 May 2015
RD9, representative of a development partner, Kigali, 20 May 2015

Foreign consultants

RC1, consultant on NSPS by Skype, 25 November 2014
RC2, technical assistant to RLDSF/LODA by Skype, 16 April and 25 May 2015
RC3, consultant on VUP design by Skype, 16 March 2015
RC4, technical assistant to RLDSF/LODA by Skype, 18 March 2015
RC5, consultant on VUP design by Skype, 27 April 2015
RC6, consultant on VUP design by Skype, 27 March 2015
RD7, consultant on NSPS by Skype, 2 July 2015

References

Ansoms, A. (2009). Re-engineering rural society: the visions and ambitions of the Rwandan elite. *African Affairs*, 108(431), 289–309.

Behuria, P. (2015). Between party capitalism and market reforms: understanding sector differences in Rwanda. *The Journal of Modern African Studies*, 53(3), 415–50.

Booth, D. and F. Golooba-Mutebi (2011). Developmental patrimonialism? The case of Rwanda. *Africa Power and Politics Working Paper*, 16.

Chemouni, B. (2014). Explaining the design of the Rwandan decentralization: elite vulnerability and the territorial repartition of power. *Journal of Eastern African Studies*, 8(2), 246–62.

Chemouni, B. (2018). The political path to universal health coverage: elite commitment to community-based health insurance in Rwanda. *World Development*, 106, 87–98.

Clark, P. (2014). After genocide: democracy in Rwanda 20 years on. *Juncture*, 20(4), 308–11.

Desrosiers, M.-E. and S. Thomson (2011). Rhetorical legacies of leadership: projections of 'benevolent leadership' in pre- and post-genocide Rwanda. *The Journal of Modern African Studies*, 49(3), 429–53.

Devereux, S. and A. Ndejuru (2010). *Annual Review of DFID Support to the Vision 2020 Umurenge Programme (VUP), Rwanda*. Falmer: IDS.

Doner, R.F., B.K. Ritchie, and D. Slater (2005). Systemic vulnerability and the origins of developmental states: Northeast and Southeast Asia in comparative perspective. *International Organization*, 59(2), 327–61.

Gaynor, N. (2014). 'A nation in a hurry': the costs of local governance reforms in Rwanda. *Review of African Political Economy*, 41(suppl), S49–63.

George, A.L. and A. Bennett (2004). *Case Studies and Theory Development in the Social Sciences*. Cambridge, MA; London: MIT.

Golooba-Mutebi, F. (2008). Collapse, war and reconstruction in Rwanda: an analytical narrative on state-making. *Crisis States Research Centre Working Paper* No. 28.

Golooba-Mutebi, F. and D. Booth (2013). *Bilateral Cooperation and Local Power Dynamics: The Case of Rwanda*. London: Overseas Development Institute.

Government of Rwanda (GoR) (2007). *Vision 2020 Umurenge: An Integrated Local Development Program to Accelerate Poverty Eradication, Rural Growth, and Social Protection*. Kigali: Government of Rwanda.

Hayman, R. (2009). Rwanda: milking the cow. Creating policy space in spite of aid dependence. in L. Whitfield (Ed.), *The Politics of Aid: African Strategies for Dealing with Donors*. Oxford: Oxford University Press, 156–84.

Hilhorst, D. and M.V. Leeuwen (2000). Emergency and development: the case of Imidugudu, villagization in Rwanda. *Journal of Refugee Studies*, 13(3), 264–80.

IMF (2015). *Rwanda: Third Review Under the Policy Support Instrument*. Washington DC: IMF.

Ingelaere, B. (2011). The ruler's drum and the people's shout: accountability and representation on Rwanda's hills. In S. Straus and L. Waldorf (Eds.), *Remaking Rwanda: State Building and Human Rights after Mass Violence*. Madison, WI: University of Wisconsin Press, 67–78.

Jowell, M. (2014). Cohesion through socialization: liberation, tradition and modernity in the forging of the Rwanda Defence Force (RDF). *Journal of Eastern African Studies*, 8(2), 278–93.

Karuhanga, J. (2012). Gakenke ordered to recover embezzled funds, *The New Times*. Available at http://www.newtimes.co.rw/section/article/2012-11-10/59577 [Accessed 6 July 2015].

Khan, M. (2010). *Political Settlements and the Governance of Growth-Enhancing Institutions*. SOAS, London: Mimeo.

Lavers, T. (2019). Social protection in an aspiring 'developmental state': the political drivers of Ethiopia's PSNP. *African Affairs*, Advance access online.

Lavers, T. and S. Hickey (2016). Conceptualising the politics of social protection expansion in low income countries: the intersection of transnational ideas and domestic politics. *International Journal of Social Welfare*, 25(4), 388–98.

Mann, L. and M. Berry (2016). Understanding the political motivations that shape Rwanda's emergent developmental state. *New Political Economy*, 21(1), 119–44.

McCord, A. (2008). Recognising heterogeneity: a proposed typology for public works programmes. *SALDRU Working Paper* 26.

MINALOC (2009). *Vision 2020 Umurenge Programme (VUP): Direct Support Operational Framework and Procedure Manual*. Kigali: Ministry of Local Government (MINALOC).

MINALOC (2013). *EDPRS2: Social Protection Strategy*. Kigali: Ministry of Local Government (MINALOC).

MINECOFIN (2007). *Economic Development and Poverty Reduction Strategy 2008–2012*. Kigali: Ministry of Finance and Economic Planning (MINECOFIN).

MINECOFIN (2013). *Economic Development and Poverty Reduction Strategy 2013–2018: Shaping Our Development*. Kigali: Ministry of Finance and Economic Planning (MINECOFIN).

NISR (2007). *EICV Poverty Analysis for Rwanda's Economic Development and Poverty Reduction Strategy*. Kigali: National Institute of Statistics of Rwanda.

NISR (2015). *Rwanda Poverty Profile Report 2013/14*. Kigali: National Institute of Statistics of Rwanda.

OAG (2012). *Performance Audit Report of Vision 2020 Umurenge Program (VUP) for the Period 2008–2011*. Kigali: Office of the Auditor General.

Pottier, J. (2002). *Re-Imagining Rwanda: Conflict, Survival and Disinformation in the Late Twentieth Century*. Cambridge: Cambridge University Press.

Prunier, G. (1998). The Rwandan Patriotic Front. In C. Clapham (Ed.), *African Guerrillas*. Oxford: James Currey.

Purdeková, A. (2011). 'Even if I am not here, there are so many eyes': surveillance and state reach in Rwanda. *The Journal of Modern African Studies*, 49(3), 475–97.

Reyntjens, F. (2013). *Political Governance in Post-Genocide Rwanda*. Cambridge: Cambridge University Press.

Reyntjens, F. (2015). Lies, damned lies and statistics: poverty reduction Rwandan-style and how the aid community loves it. *African Arguments*. Available at http://africanarguments.org/2015/11/03/lies-damned-lies-and-statistics-poverty-reduction-rwandan-style-and-how-the-aid-community-loves-it [Accessed 13 April 2016].

Reyntjens, F. (2016). (Re-)imagining a reluctant post-genocide society: the Rwandan Patriotic Front's ideology and practice. *Journal of Genocide Research*, 18(1), 61–81.

RoR (2014). *11th Leadership Retreat Resolutions, March 8–10, 2014*. Kigali: Republic of Rwanda.

Rugira, L. (2015). Corruption: the case of the hiccups in Rwanda's scientific state. *The New Times*. Available at http://www.newtimes.co.rw/section/article/2015-03-30/187385 [Accessed 6 July 2015].

Sabates-Wheeler, R., S. Yates, E. Wylde, and J. Gatsinzi (2015). Challenges of measuring graduation in Rwanda. *IDS Bulletin*, 46(2), 103–14.

Straus, S. and L. Waldorf (2011). *Remaking Rwanda: State Building and Human Rights after Mass Violence*. Madison, WI: University of Wisconsin Press.

Uvin, P. (1998). *Aiding Violence: The Development Enterprise in Rwanda*. Sterling, VA: Kumarian Press.

World Bank (2015). *Rwanda Poverty Assessment*. Washington DC: World Bank.

5

Pushing for Policy Innovation

The Framing of Social Protection Policies in Tanzania

Marianne S. Ulriksen

1. Introduction

In the early 2000s, there was low elite commitment to social protection on mainland Tanzania.[1] Being a low-income country, Tanzania has high levels of deprivation and high demand for income security, but limited resources to address these issues. However, while a general lack of financial resources and capacity both within government and civil society were compounding factors, a 'lack of political will [also explains the state's] failure to provide adequate social protection to the poor' (Lerisse et al. 2003; Mchomvu et al. 2002). In fact, as late as 2009, Tanzania only spent 0.29 per cent of GDP on social safety nets, which was much less than any of its neighbouring countries (World Bank 2015).[2] Thus, although fiscal constraints are considerable, Tanzania still spent substantially less than other countries on a similar economic level.

Yet, in 2012, the government approved the implementation of the Productive Social Safety Net (PSSN) programme, which is a nationwide conditional cash transfer (CCT) programme that targets the extreme-poor population. The programme was estimated to cost US$300 million per year and was targeted at reaching over 1.2 million households (nearly five million people) by the end of the initial phase closing 2017 (the programmes extended to 2019).[3]

[1] Tanzania is a union between the Mainland and the Zanzibar islands. This chapter only focuses on social protection policies as they have developed on Mainland Tanzania during the period from the early 2000s to 2015.

[2] Burundi 4.21%, Kenya 2.73%, Rwanda 2.14%, Uganda 1.02% (although note that some of these figures are more recent than 2009) (World Bank 2015).

[3] World Bank websites: http://www.worldbank.org/projects/P124045/tanzania-third-social-action-fund-productive-safety-nets-program-tasaf-iii-psnp?lang=en&tab=overview; and http://www-wds.worldbank.org/external/default/WDSContentServer/WDSP/AFR/2016/01/07/090224b0840378dd/1_0/Rendered/PDF/Tanzania000Tan0Report000Sequence006.pdf; accessed on 28 July 2016.

Marianne S. Ulriksen, *Pushing for Policy Innovation: The Framing of Social Protection Policies in Tanzania*
In: *The Politics of Social Protection in Eastern and Southern Africa*. Edited by: Sam Hickey, Tom Lavers, Miguel Niño-Zarazúa, and Jeremy Seekings, Oxford University Press (2020).
DOI: 10.1093/oso/9780198850342.003.0005

The launch of the PSSN was the outcome of a process of policy innovation and experimentation, which this chapter analyses. The change in elite commitment to social protection can be indicated in monetary terms, where social protection spending increased to 2.3 per cent of GDP around 2015 (UN n.d.).[4]

This study asks: what explains the change in elite commitment to social protection from the early 2000s through to 2015? The argument put forward is that the push for social protection, specifically CCTs, has been driven by multilateral institutions (World Bank) in collaboration with domestic policy-making and -implementing institutions, specifically TASAF (Tanzania Social Action Fund). These institutions have been resourceful and strategic in their approach to promoting their favoured policy solution to social protection through workshops and evidence-based reporting. More importantly, in gaining elite commitment to the PSSN, the institutions have also been able to show how this social protection policy provides a solution to some of Tanzania's main social problems as expressed by the elite.

The chapter follows the theoretical foundation that the incentives and ideas, which shape elite behaviour, depend on the type of political settlement in place and that policy-making is a process of negotiation and bargaining between political and bureaucratic elites. Moreover, in situations where policy areas are of low interest to elites, there is room for transnational institutions (such as the World Bank) to promote specific policy solutions. The chapter's contribution to the social protection literature lies in the focus on policy promotion and negotiation by institutions outside, or 'below', the elite, and by including not only transnational actors but also domestic institutions responsible for policy development and implementation. Hence, it is shown how ideas and strategies of international *and* domestic policy institutions influence the politics of elite commitment to social protection.

The structure is as follows: First, a theoretical framework is provided that builds on Lavers and Hickey's approach to explaining social protection expansion in Africa, which combines political settlement theory and discursive institutionalism (Lavers and Hickey 2015). Second, as the first part of the analysis, the chapter explores how the Tanzanian elite has outlined its overarching goals in order to address the country's main social problems. Third, the main part of the analysis narrates how the PSSN was developed and promoted by transnational and domestic institutions as the policy solution fitting the elite's programmatic responses to the country's social problems.

[4] Note that the estimates of spending/GDP come from two different sources and may therefore not be directly comparable.

Fourth, to critically assess the findings and the strength of the theoretical framework, the promotion of the PSSN is compared to the attempt to introduce a social pension over the same period. The conclusion highlights theoretical and empirical implications of the study.

2. Theoretical Framework: Policy Solutions by Policy Entrepreneurs

Within a given political settlement, defined as the balance or distribution of power between contending social groups in a country, there is room for different policy approaches. Furthermore, in policy domains of less concern to the elite's survival and legitimacy—such as social protection in Tanzania in the early 2000s—there is space for other actors to promote their favoured policy solutions (Lavers and Hickey 2015). Hence, in the case of Tanzania, it is reasonable to explore the role of institutions outside, or on the margins of, the political settlement in promoting specific types of social protection policy designs. Nevertheless, if these institutions want to get the policy implemented, they need to get commitment from the political and bureaucratic elite, and consequently it is important to understand the nature of the political settlement in Tanzania.

The political settlement in Tanzania has been defined as a 'dominant party ruling coalition' (Khan 2010), which is characterized by a strong ruling governing party with a relatively coherent elite group that excludes opposing elite factions at the horizontal level. Vertically, the elite coalition is reliant on lower-level factions (party officials at local levels) to maintain legitimacy and ensure regime survival. In recent years, opposition parties in Tanzania have gained strength and factions within the ruling party (CCM: Chama Cha Mapinduz) have become more pronounced, which might indicate a move towards a 'competitive clientelism' political settlement (Khan 2010). However, thus far, the label as a dominant party ruling coalition seems fitting. There is agreement among political observers that, although internal factions persist, the core of the ruling CCM government controls policy-making in a centralized and top-down manner, which means that the actual and final policy decisions sits with the president, key ministers, and high-level public officials (Booth et al. 2014; Hoffman 2013; Lofchie 2014; Therkildsen and Bourgouin 2012).

According to Lavers and Hickey (2015: 3), 'the success of attempts by transnational actors to promote social protection expansion [. . .] depend on the compatibility of these ideas with existing political settlements, their underlying interests and [...] the ideas of powerful factions therein'. Given the neglect of social protection in Tanzania in the early 2000s and hence social protection's limited interest to elite factions, the role of ideas become particularly prominent in convincing the elite of the need for policy change. Critically, specific policy ideas must fit the elite's general understanding of the complex reality and problems facing the country (Lavers and Hickey 2015; Mehta 2011), as explained in the following.

Ideational approaches to policy analyses typically distinguish between levels of ideas going from the abstract to the more specific (Hall 1993; Lavers and Hickey 2015; Mehta 2011; Von Gliszczynski and Leisering 2016). Hall distinguishes between three levels: 'the overarching goals that guide policy in a particular field, the techniques or policy instruments used to attain those goals, and the precise settings of these instruments' (Hall 1993: 278). The analysis focuses on the first two levels, which are elaborated upon in the following.

The framework of ideas related to the overarching goals is termed *policy paradigm* and is the most abstract level. Policy paradigm provides 'a relatively coherent set of assumptions about the functioning of economic, social and political institutions' (Beland 2005: 8). In Hall's words, policy paradigm 'specifies not only the goals of policy and the kind of instruments that can be used to attain them, but also the very nature of the problems they are meant to be addressing' (Hall 1993: 279). Thus, in the context of Tanzania, problems in need of being addressed—and from which goals arise—can, for instance, relate to poverty reduction, economic development, or vulnerability (Lavers and Hickey 2015). Policy paradigms are quite stable and most likely to only change when overall policy fields fail (Hall 1993; Von Gliszczynski 2015) or if the political settlement is disrupted (Lavers and Hickey 2015).

The second level of ideas are policy instruments (Hall 1993), or *policy solutions*, which refer to the idea of specific policy schemes provided as the means to counter social problems (Lavers and Hickey 2015; Mehta 2011). There may be several policy solutions relevant to addressing the defined problems and meeting the overarching goals. Policy solutions anchored in the higher ideational level of the policy paradigm as defined by the elite will have the greater chance of getting elite commitment (Von Gliszczynski and Leisering 2016). Whereas, according to Hall, changes of policy paradigms are rare and, when they do occur, are driven by politicians and the media, civil servants and policy experts are the primary actors in changing policy instruments.

Regarding the actors involved in policy change, ideational analyses of social protection primarily focus on the role of transnational actors in promoting social protection expansion (Deacon and Stubbs 2013; Foli and Béland 2014; Kaasch 2013; Kpessa and Béland 2012; Kwon et al. 2014). Yet Lavers and Hickey point out that 'successful ideational influence is dependent on the actions of policy entrepreneurs who lead domestic debate, advocate for change and build advocacy coalitions' (Lavers and Hickey 2015: 15), and they propose that such policy entrepreneurs can include donor agencies, domestic and international civil society organizations, as well as individuals within the ruling coalition.

Policy entrepreneurs may thus include a range of international and domestic actors. In order to narrow the concept, I follow Hall who, as mentioned, regards civil servants and policy experts as the primary drivers of policy change at the instrumental level. Hall focuses on England and consequently he does not have an eye for the role of international actors who, however, are relevant in lower-income countries such as Tanzania. *Policy entrepreneurs* therefore refer to international experts and technocrats working for international organizations, and domestic civil servants and national policy experts. Although the initial policy ideas and resources may come from the international partners, civil servants at the lower levels of the bureaucracy are important as they are active in policy formulation (Sabatier 1988); these bureaucrats are not necessarily part of the elite political settlement, but they play central roles in developing and implementing policy. Together these international and domestic policy entrepreneurs are active in promoting policy change.

Policy entrepreneurs need resources, expertise, and moral authority to successfully pursue the development of their favoured policy solutions (Orenstein 2008), but they also need to use these attributes strategically if they want to ensure elite commitment to their policy solution and thereby ensure its political viability. Borrowing from and building on Von Gliszczynski and Leisering's (2016) framework for spreading policy models, I suggest that there are five interrelated strategies, which enable the successful promotion of a favoured policy solution by policy entrepreneurs:

1. Contextualization: the policy solution is framed to fit the higher ideational level of problems and goals as described by the elite.
2. Presentation: details of the policy (technical aspects, labels, etc.) that are seen to have political and social appeal are included.
3. National examples: the policy is shown to have worked well in other countries, although local adaptation and references to earlier practices are also part of securing political acceptability.

4. Empirical knowledge: the policy solution is underpinned by references to empirical evidence provided by experts.
5. Organizational mandate: the policy solution is presented to be within the institution's mandate and the institution presents itself as the natural authority to successfully implement the policy.

To sum up: an ideational approach is applied to analyse what drove the change in elite commitment to social protection. As social protection in the early 2000s was of little interest to the Tanzanian elite, there was room for international and domestic policy entrepreneurs to promote their favoured policy solutions. The policy entrepreneurs can pursue different strategies, which are manifested in their resources, expertise, and moral authority. As policy solutions are more likely to gain elite commitment if they are anchored in more general ideas (policy paradigm) as described by the elite, the following analysis starts with highlighting how the Tanzanian ruling government has described the main goals and the social problems they are meant to address.

The analysis centres on key government documents that describe Tanzania's developmental challenges (social problems) as these documents represent the views of the ruling government. This analysis is furthermore supported by speeches of various presidents and prime ministers. The analyses on the development of the PSSN and social pension are based on interviews,[5] newspaper articles, and the study of government documents, policy analyses, and evaluations, as well as research papers and academic articles.

3. Policy Paradigm: Development Challenges and Goals

The Development Vision 2025 (of 2000) and the Tanzania Five-Year Development Plan (FYDP) 2011/12–2015/16 (of 2011) are the primary documents that lay out the government's approach to development. Both have been driven by the government, not donors (Ulriksen 2016a), and in this way they are fit to illustrate the prevailing policy paradigm in Tanzania, which largely reflects a productivist strategy in 'realising the country's aspirations as stipulated in the Development Vision'.[6]

[5] List of interviews and references to them in the analysis can be found in Ulriksen (2016b), which this chapter builds on.

[6] Prime Minister Hon. MP Pinda, in opening speech at the Annual National Policy Dialogue at Ubungo Plaza, Dar es Salaam, 26 January 2012.

The work on the Development Vision 2025 started under President Mkapa in 1995 and was unveiled in 2000. The Vision was developed through discussions with a wide range of domestic stakeholders,[7] which makes it a truly Tanzanian document. However, in a political settlement described as a dominant party ruling coalition, it reflects more the views of the ruling government than the Tanzanian population in general. The Vision highlights as the first impediment to development the 'Donor-Dependence Syndrome and a Dependent and Defeatist Development Mindset'. As elaborated: 'The mindset of the people of Tanzania and their leaders has succumbed to donor dependency and has resulted in an erosion of initiative and lack of ownership of the development agenda [...] The mindset... has neither been supportive of hard work, ingenuity and creativity' (URT 2000: 8). The Vision suggests the following responses to this state of affairs:

> The effective transformation of the mindset and culture to promote attitudes of *self-development*, *community development*, confidence and commitment to face development challenges and exploit every opportunity for the improvement of the quality of livelihood is of prime importance. The effective ownership of the development agenda coupled with the *spirit of self-reliance*, at all societal levels, are major driving forces for the realization of the Vision. Tanzanians *should learn to appreciate and honour hard work*, creativity, professionalism and entrepreneurship. (URT 2000: 17; my italics)

Responses to development challenges thus lies in ideas around the need to strive for self-development within communities and to cherish self-reliance, responsibility, and hard work. In the analysis of the development of the CCT programmes, these issues feature prominently in how the policy is framed. The political elite's concern with the Tanzanian 'mindset' remains pronounced. Thus, the new President Dr J Magufuli has emphasized the main drawbacks in Tanzania as corruption, poor management, waste of public resources, and 'a culture that encouraged laziness and did not reward hard work'.[8]

In line with the Vision, the FYDP also highlights the need for people to 'move out of the now entrenched dependency mindset'. Instead, 'every Tanzanian has the duty and responsibility to play an active part in the

[7] President BW Mkapa in Foreword to the 2025 Vision (URT 2000).

[8] Speech by President Dr J Magufuli at the inauguration of the eleventh parliament as cited in *The Citizen*, 'Magufuli: My Priorities', 21 November 2015.

development of the motherland' and 'to build a culture and attitude of "we can do"'. The response is to 'enhance[e] entrepreneurship and ... targeted support for disadvantaged and most vulnerable groups in society' (URT 2011: 102).

The objective of the FYDP 'is to unleash Tanzania's latent growth potentials [... by] the targeting of strategic priority interventions to move Tanzania to a higher growth trajectory coupled with a shift from an Agriculture-Based to an Industry-Based economy'.[9] Specific strategies include addressing infrastructural bottlenecks, increasing the pool of skilled labour, improving the business environment, and enhancing productivity in agriculture.[10] Clearly, the focus is on engineering productivity and enabling pro-poor growth. Any strategies aimed at the poor relate to 'attracting investments, particularly in areas where the poor are more involved' (URT 2011: 10). Thus, any growth strategy including the poor 'must involve substantial growth of agricultural productivity and allow most of the rural population to benefit from such growth through selling the increased produce domestic and export markets'; only the most vulnerable may receive some targeted support (ibid.: 17).

The Tanzanian leaders' overall vision to address its development problems prioritizes growth and productivity. Key terms are community development, self-reliance, responsibility, and hard work. Problems of development and poverty are framed within an economic rationale, where social protection policies are regarded as instruments to strengthen the agency of the poor and allow them to participate in markets. In this ideational orientation, one can draw links to both Nyerere's socialist policy, Ujaama, of the 1960s and 1970s and the subsequent decades of economic liberalization. In the Arusha Declaration of 1967, the then president, Julius Nyerere, emphasizes self-reliance and hard work—dedicating a whole section to the 'policy of self-reliance' and dwelling specifically on how 'hard work is the root of development' (Nyerere 1967). These aspects of social idealism continue to feature in Tanzanian politics, but these ideas nowadays co-exist with liberal economic views that underscore the importance of the poor participating in the economic markets in order to escape poverty (Lofchie 2014).

In international aid agencies, productivist approaches to development were dominant in the 1960s and 1970s, but were subsequently discarded for developmentalist approaches focusing on improving human capital, institutional capacity, and increasingly also human rights (Niño-Zarazúa 2016). Hence,

[9] Prime Minister Hon MP Pinda, in opening speech at the Annual National Policy Dialogue at Ubungo Plaza, Dar es Salaam, 26 January 2012.

[10] Keynote speech by President Dr JM Kikwete, at the USAID Forum on Frontiers in Development: Ending Extreme Poverty, 19 September 2014, Washington DC.

another current ideational approach to social protection is related to human rights within which the rationale for social protection is related to the right to social security and adequate standards of living (Von Gliszczynski 2015). Other than the mentioning of rights to land, human rights do not feature in the documents and may thus be perceived by the elite to be an unimportant ideational basis for development. This is not necessarily surprising in a sub-Saharan African context, where political elites often stress production over protection (Hickey and Bracking 2005). This productivist focus of the Tanzanian government also follows the general trend in the region, where industry and infrastructure are now prioritized over social policy (Kjær and Ulriksen 2014). Section 4 explores how policy entrepreneurs use different strategies to present policy solutions fitting the government's ideational approach to development challenges.

4. Social Protection Policy Solution: The Promotion of the PSSN

In 2012, the Tanzanian government launched the nationwide PSSN programme, which is a CCT (including elements of public works and livelihood enhancement) targeting the extreme poor (calculated as 9.7 per cent of the population of 50 million (UN, n.d.)). According to TASAF (2015: 1), 'households benefit from a combination of basic and conditional cash transfers, cash transfers through participation in labor-intensive Public Works, and advice and support concerning savings and investments'. The ambition set in 2012 was to reach at least one million food-insecure households (TASAF 2015). As described in the following, the PSSN was not an entirely new invention but instead has its roots in small community development projects implemented by TASAF in the early 2000s.

The analysis chronologically narrates how the PSSN developed from these early community-based projects aimed at improving livelihoods and lifting people out of poverty (the main events and actors related to the development of the PSSN as well as the old-age pension, which is discussed later, are listed in Table 5.1). The narrative relates the ideational aspect of the policy solutions to the policy paradigm of the elite, and I refer to the use of different strategies by the policy entrepreneurs. The analysis shows, and the discussion in section 5 elaborates on, how the process of developing and promoting the PSSN has been driven by international and domestic policy entrepreneurs with the resources, expertise, and authority to present a policy solution, backed by national examples and empirical evidence, that is fitting to how the elite

Table 5.1 Development of conditional cash transfer and social pension: main events and actors

Year	PSSN		Social pension	
	Events	*Actors*	*Events*	*Actors*
2000	TASAF I starts	TASAF and World Bank		
2003			KwaWazee project starts	HelpAge International, REPSSI
2005	TASAF II starts; Exposure to other cash transfer programmes for TASAF staff begins	TASAF and World Bank; World Bank		
2006	Design of cash transfer programme starts	TASAF, World Bank	Feasibility study	ILO, DFID
2008			Social Protection Expenditure Review Evaluation of KwaWazee project	Ministry of Labour, ILO HelpAge International
2009	CB-CCT pilot starts	TASAF, World Bank		
2010–11	Workshops and publications on the pilot and other evidence	TASAF, World Bank	Feasibility study	Ministry of Labour, HelpAge International
2012	Commitment to PSSN	Government (incl. Ministry of Finance)		
2013–	Search for additional funding	TASAF, government, other donors	Additional studies	Ministry of Labour, SSRA
2014			Government announce introduction of pension	Ministry of Finance

Source: author's compilation.

perceive the main social problems. Community development, self-reliance, responsibility, and hard work were key terms in the early projects and have continued to feature as the advocated policy solution was transformed to the PSSN. This strong productivist notion fits well with the ruling government's overarching goals as outlined in the Vision 2025 and the FYDP above.

4.1. From community development to CCT pilot

In 2000, the government established a programme to 'facilitate improvements in socio-economic infrastructure in rural and peri-urban communities under TASAF' (Lerisse et al. 2003). The programme falls under the President's Office and was formed as 'part of the government of Tanzania's strategy for reducing poverty and improving livelihoods by stimulating economic activity at the community level' (Evans et al. 2014). In wording, the programme falls in line with the government's Vision 2025 in which dissatisfaction with previous attempts at rural development and poverty reduction is expressed, and in which the idea of self-development is promoted to effectuate transformation (URT 2000). At this stage, TASAF was more akin to a community development programme rather than simply a cash transfer programme. The main purpose was to oversee smaller projects, which were decided, managed, and implemented by the communities; such projects included the construction and improvement of community social services and infrastructural assets. Poor and vulnerable households were identified by community leaders together with TASAF officials, and targeted households could become part of public works programmes (receiving income for work on community assets) or other smaller income-generating projects; thus active community involvement was an essential element of the programme (Evans et al. 2014; Lerisse et al. 2003).

TASAF I was followed by TASAF II in 2005, which continued in much the same way with the aim of 'empowering communities to access opportunities so that they can request, implement and monitor subprojects that contribute to improved livelihoods' (TASAF 2008). TASAF II covered 121 local communities in mainland Tanzania and supported the improvement of access to and use of basic social services, and assisted food-insecure households and vulnerable individuals through public works subprojects and income-generating activities (TASAF 2008). According to the UN, TASAF I and II 'achieved impressive results in facilitating community access to social services through infrastructure projects such as schools, health facilities and water points reaching 7.3 million people in TASAF I and 16.1 million in TASAF II' (UN, n.d.).

During TASAF II, the idea of a CCT programme took form. The World Bank has been the primary funder of TASAF since its inception, and from around 2005, the Bank organized international workshops and exchange travels so that TASAF staff and other key stakeholders could learn about social protection interventions and programmes elsewhere. TASAF officials learned from other regional programmes such as in Ethiopia and Kenya, but they also travelled as far as Jamaica to study different programme designs. With the assistance of the World Bank, the TASAF started to design a cash transfer system around 2006–7. The basic elements of the suggested pilot programme are similar to many other World Bank-supported cash transfers in the global South (Hall 2007; Von Gliszczynski 2015). Thus, an initial pilot project should run in a few districts (with already identified control group communities); the project should—as was already the case within the TASAF programmes—target the poorest and most vulnerable groups who should receive a small regular cash transfer based on certain conditions. The pilot also fitted the ruling government's policy paradigm as discussed earlier, which highlights targeted support to only the most vulnerable and emphasizes community development and responsibility. According to TASAF officials, the technical policy aspect of including conditionality was regarded as important politically in a context where the idea of responsibility as a positive behavioural attribute features prominently, whereas it was feared that cash transfer programmes could otherwise be perceived as handouts.

In keeping with the spirit in TASAF I of co-responsibility, active engagement, and relying on earlier practices, the targeting of beneficiaries and the monitoring of the programme were to be done at the community level with a strong influence of the people living within the community. Thus, CB (community-based) was added to the abbreviated name of the proposed project to be CB-CCT. In the proposed design, it was suggested that the CB-CCT pilot programme would work most cost effectively if building on the already existing structures that TASAF had built in the communities that had benefited from previous programmes. In this way, TASAF gave itself the organizational mandate to implement the pilot programme.

With the World Bank as leader, the policy entrepreneurs had sufficient resources and expertise to fund the pilot project, provide opportunities for learning about other examples, set up a project with opportunities for building empirical knowledge, and present a policy solution with features that had political appeal. The policy solution was also made attractive through the local adaptation that cemented the central role of community development, and the domestic policy entrepreneur, TASAF, was able to present itself as the natural authority to successfully implement the policy. The centrality of TASAF was strengthened by its partnership with the resourceful World Bank, but probably also by TASAF's institutional placement within the President's Office, rather than within a line ministry. The government agreed to the project and it was initiated in 2009 with the first cash transfer payments completed in January 2010 (Evans et al. 2014).

4.2. From CCTs to productive social safety nets

The pilot CCT in Tanzania built on community development projects as implemented by TASAF and with the bulk of funding from the World Bank. The projects had a specific focus on poverty reduction and included a strong emphasis on supporting beneficiaries to be capable of helping themselves and escaping the poverty trap. The ideas of productivity and co-responsibility have remained strong elements in developing the policy design as the CB-CCT moved to become a nationwide programme (the PSSN).

As the CB-CCT was a pilot project, monitoring and evaluation were of course essential components. Some documentation includes internal reports developed by or in consultation with TASAF for its own internal use and in sharing with its government counterparts and international development partners. However, there are also publicly available reports and documentation that have been shared more widely. The following describes how the World Bank and TASAF have organized events and disseminated reports in order to gain support for the upscaling of the CCT programme. Already in June 2010, the World Bank and TASAF organized an international conference for participants across the global South to engage in a Public Works Learning Forum. TASAF was to showcase its public works programmes as implemented in TASAF I and II and the forum would engage in sharing knowledge and expertise among World Bank officials and their country-level counterparts, to 'catalyse improved understanding and know-how on the role of public work programs as part [of] national safety net and social protection agendas'.[11]

In 2011, the World Bank published a report on Tanzania with the subtitle *Options for a National Productive Safety Net Program*. The report 'explores the role safety nets and transfers can play in reducing poverty more rapidly in Tanzania' (World Bank 2011: i). It is not an evaluation of the ongoing CB-CCT programme, but instead engages with the question of how a social safety net system is not just a mechanism to reduce poverty and improve human capabilities (as in the CB-CCT), but also a means to increase beneficiaries' productivity so that they can help themselves escape poverty. In advocating for CCTs with a 'productivist' element, the report—not unlike the wording in the FYDP—suggests:

[11] Media Briefing Note circulated by TASAF and the World Bank's Social Protection and Labour Department for the workshop that took place on 14–18 June 2010.

> ...the primary focus of reducing poverty clearly needs to remain on re-engineering growth to reach poor Tanzanians. This means raising the productivity of subsistence agriculture, improving markets and access, investing in education and infrastructure, and encouraging smallholder cash cropping and small business. But judicious transfers to the poor can complement these efforts and hasten reduction of extreme poverty. A central role of safety net transfers is to equip the poor to participate more fully in this growth process, and to bridge 'gaps' that are preventing them from realizing potential income gains. 'Smart' safety nets can increase their productivity (by building human and physical capital); allow the poor to take on higher-risk, higher-return activities (for example using fertilizer); and increase the returns to their labour. (World Bank 2011: 54)

TASAF officials have emphasized that the idea of 'productivity' was important in building political support for an upscaling of the CCT programme, which links well with the political leaders' focus on 'unleashing Tanzania's latent growth potential', as discussed earlier. The reference to productivity raises the question whether there has been policy diffusion from other countries in the region, such as the social protection programmes in Ethiopia and Rwanda, which also refer to the term productivity (see Chapters 3 and 4). TASAF officials maintain that the PSSN largely builds on the experiences stemming from TASAF I and II, but they also acknowledge drawing inspiration from the Productive Safety Net Programme (PSNP) in Ethiopia.

Gathering evidence from the pilot was another important aspect of 'selling' the programme. Although only published in 2014, a World Bank-led evaluation report provided important information about the impact of the CCT pilot, with a mid-term review in 2011, draft versions of the report, and presentations of key findings being available earlier (Evans et al. 2014). The report is extensive and thorough in its assessment of impacts on beneficiary communities, which can be summarized as follows:

> On the whole, the community-based CCT program led to improved outcomes in both health and education. Households used the resources to invest in livestock, in children's shoes, in insurance, and—for the poorest households—in increased savings. This suggests that the households focused on reducing risk and on improving their livelihoods rather than principally on increasing consumption. There is also evidence that the project had positive effects on community cohesion. (Evans et al. 2014: 8)

Based on the experiences of the CB-CCT pilot, the evaluations and reports as exemplified above, as well as lessons learned from other national examples, the government decided in 2012 to design and implement a countrywide PSSN programme (UN, n.d.). The PSSN was argued to be 'fundamentally a conditional cash transfer program, complemented by a seasonal intensive public works labor program' (World Bank 2013: 42), which follows well in line with the CCT pilot and the public works aspects of TASAF I and II. Thus, at this point, the government committed itself to the PSSN as part of its overall strategy to overcome the persistence of extreme poverty in the country. This move was widely championed by the Department of Poverty Eradication within the Ministry of Finance. Incidentally, the permanent secretary of the Ministry of Finance was previously the Director of TASAF. Hence, although the World Bank initially was a strong policy promoter, the role of TASAF staff and their relations with other civil servants higher up in the bureaucracy were also essential in pushing for the introduction of the PSSN.

Even though there was a *decision* to implement the PSSN, the *actual* implementation and upscale of the programme countrywide required additional funding. The World Bank had been the primary funder of TASAF I and II, including the CB-CCT (with some limited government contributions as well), but was now looking to other donors to be co-funders and to the government to turn its initial support into actual budgetary commitment and ownership of the programme. From 2013 to 2015, the World Bank and TASAF worked hard to get funding commitment from the government and other donors, as discussed in the following.

In December 2013, the World Bank launched the report *Tanzanian Economic Update 2013* at an event attended by government officials and donor partners. In the report the World Bank specifically promoted the idea of 'lessening extreme poverty by transferring cash directly to the most vulnerable groups' and advocated that '[t]he scaling up of this program [CCT to PSSN] to achieve national coverage could result in significant reductions in extreme poverty without excessively high expenditure' (World Bank 2013: iii, x–xi). World Bank officials challenged the Tanzanian government 'to seriously invest in social protection if it really aims to combat poverty',[12] and sought to provide good arguments for why the government should 'give money to Tanzania's poor'.[13]

[12] *The Citizen*, 'WB advocates cash handouts poor', 15 December 2013; accessed 23 March 2015.

[13] *The Citizen*, 'Should government give money to Tanzania's poor', by Jacques Morriset, World Bank's lead economist for Tanzania, Burundi, and Uganda, 17 December 2013; accessed 23 March 2015.

Another important event that can be seen as a clear attempt by the Ministry of Finance to get domestic political support for the PSSN was the international conference in Arusha on 15–17 December 2014. The conference was titled Social Protection: Building Effective and Sustainable Systems for Equitable Growth and was facilitated by the Ministry of Finance. A range of ministries related to social protection broadly were represented by their deputy ministers, who were given the tasks of chairing different sessions and, as such, their active participation was ensured. The programme included a wide variety of presentations on experiences of social protection programmes internationally, regionally, and within Tanzania. Most presentations focused on targeted cash transfers and CCTs, including experiences of combining these with public works.

Some donors were not particularly keen on certain aspects of the PSSN, particularly the use of conditionalities. Nevertheless, DFID, USAID, and SIDA (Swedish International Development Cooperation) joined as the primary donors alongside the World Bank. The UN bodies also support the PSSN programme on the fringes with technical assistance and training to strengthen the capacity of TASAF and other implementing institutions. Some of the main rationales put forward by the donors to support PSSN were that this was a programme already in existence and that the government had made it clear that it wanted the PSSN as the main poverty-reducing social protection strategy. The programme furthermore fitted with overall donor strategies of reducing poverty, improving education (especially for girls), and contributing to employment and income security among the poorest.

Already by May 2014, TASAF was confident of the government's commitment to the PSSN, whereas the final commitment from some donors took a little longer to achieve. With the financial requirements of the PSSN estimated at US$300 million per year, the agreement achieved during 2015 was for the government to fund US$100 million per year through domestic revenue finances, US$100 million through credit from the World Bank, and the last US$100 million per year from development partners.

As should be clear by now, the road to the PSSN has been driven by the World Bank together with TASAF. Through the implementation of TASAF I and II and the CB-CCT pilot, the two institutions have built a foundation on which it seemed only natural that TASAF should implement the country-wide programme. The nature of the policy solution, with elements such as co-responsibility (conditionalities) and productive economic activities (public works), fits with the ruling government's ideational approach to the country's development challenges. TASAF officials emphasize that beneficiaries should 'graduate' out of the programme within three years; they regard social pensions as problematic and inefficient as one cannot 'graduate' and because a universal pension will also include non-poor beneficiaries; and they see conditionalities as essential in ensuring that beneficiaries prioritize health and education and in building political support. With the emphasis on productive self-reliance and co-responsibility rather than protective entitlements and rights, they have been able to ensure that the PSSN corresponds with the responses to development challenges as laid out in the FYDP.

4.3. How the policy entrepreneurs achieved elite commitment for the PSSN

Returning to the specific strategies of policy entrepreneurs as discussed in section 2, the analysis of the development of PSSN shows how policy entrepreneurs can build elite commitment to social protection. Initially, in a context where the domestic elite had little interest in social protection, the World Bank (a transnational actor) drove the process, strongly helped by the institution's availability of resources and expertise as well as being seen as an authority that drives productive and pro-poor economic development. However, the World Bank was not the only policy entrepreneur. The analysis makes evident how domestic policy institutions (here TASAF) are important partners in designing, implementing, and, in time, advocating for a policy solution. This alliance of policy entrepreneurs also gained the backing of an important faction within the ruling government, namely the Ministry of Finance, which was also partly enforced by the personnel connections between the Ministry and TASAF.

Specifically, the analysis underlines the following: the PSSN was a policy solution that fitted with the problem definition and programmatic responses as defined by the ruling government, which emphasized a productivist approach to development and featured responses such as community development, responsibility, and self-reliance (*contextualization*). The PSSN included details that were seen as critical to ensure political support. Thus, in *presentation* the policy solution featured targeting of the most vulnerable, conditionality (e.g. co-responsibility), and public works (production and hard work).

In promoting their policy solution, the policy entrepreneurs used examples to show ruling government officials (and other donors) how the policy has worked in other countries such as in Ethiopia—that the PSSN is not a handout, but instead enables poor recipients and their families to become self-reliant and responsible agents that can partake in the economy (*national examples*). The legitimacy of the policy was enhanced by its local adaptation and use of earlier practices by including communities in the identification of beneficiaries and monitoring of the programme. The policy solution was furthermore promoted by presenting empirical evidence by experts in a range of workshops and publications (*empirical knowledge*). Finally, as the policy developed out of TASAF-implemented community projects, TASAF was able to present itself as the national authority to successfully implement the policy solution (*organizational mandate*).

5. Contrasting the PSSN with the Promotion of the Social Pension

Thus far, we have established that in the case of social protection in Tanzania, international and domestic policy entrepreneurs have played a critical role in getting the ruling government to endorse social protection in the form of the PSSN. In order to scrutinize the theoretical framework further, I discuss in this section the concurrent attempt by other policy entrepreneurs to promote an old-age pension, again linking the idea of policy solutions to the policy paradigm of the governing elite.

Initially, during the 2000s, the idea of a non-contributory old-age pension was promoted by international NGOs, the ILO, and some international donors through internationally funded pilot projects, workshops, and reporting that included examples from elsewhere and empirical evidence. According to one study in the early 2000s, 'the elderly are the least supported' with only the international NGO, HelpAge, paying attention to 'the impoverishing forces facing the elderly' (Lerisse et al. 2003: 69). With the assistance of HelpAge International and REPSSI (Regional Psychosocial Support Initiative), the KwaWazee pension fund was started in the Nshamba villages in the Muleba District, north-western Tanzania, at the end of 2003. The project initially started small scale with the intention of learning about the lived realities of elderly people and identifying ways to respond to their needs. However, as more funds became available, KwaWazee developed into a cash transfer programme with the aim of providing poor and vulnerable people over the age of sixty, including those caring for children without parents, with regular cash payments in the form of pensions and child benefits (Hofmann et al. 2008; Kessy 2014).

Although the KwaWazee project has remained rather small scale in reach, the project has played an important role in documenting and evaluating the impact of regular cash transfers for the wellbeing of pensioners and their families. An evaluation of the project was published in 2008 with a strong justification of its value for policy-making: 'There is very little documentation in Tanzania on social pensions or social assistance for older people. Thus, the KwaWazee scheme can be regarded as a step towards the introduction of more such provisions in Tanzania' (Hofmann et al. 2008: xiv). In line with other studies of social cash transfers elsewhere (e.g. UNDP and ILO 2011), the evaluation report documents a range of positive impacts of pensions on older people and recommends the consideration of a universal pension scheme (Hoffman et al. 2008).

The civil society organizations involved with the KwaWazee project have continued to put the importance of an old-age pension on the agenda. Other stakeholders have added their voices too. In 2006, the UK's Department of International Development (DFID) funded an ILO-led feasibility study (Gassmann and Behrendt 2006). The study provided a micro-simulation for Tanzania and Senegal to test different social policy options and their potential impact on poverty at household levels. For Tanzania, it was argued in the report that a combination of universal old-age pension and child benefit 'would achieve a reduction in poverty rates of 35 per cent, with even more substantial effects for individuals living in households with children and elderly (a drop of 46 per cent), which face the highest poverty risk' (Gassmann and Behrendt 2006: vi).

The ILO was also involved when in 2008 the Ministry of Labour, Employment and Youth Development undertook a social protection expenditure performance review. In this study, it was highlighted that the feasibility of a universal non-contributory old-age pension should be investigated as there was a high rate of poverty among households containing older people (ILO 2008). Based on that recommendation, the labour ministry, in collaboration with HelpAge International, and with funding from the German Federal Ministry of Economic Cooperation, embarked on a study to assess the feasibility of introducing a universal old-age pension (Ministry of Labour 2010). The study offered an analysis of the costs, fiscal sustainability, and financing options for an old-age pension and included inputs from a broad range of government, parastatal, non-governmental, and private institutions. A number of scenarios were offered on cost and age eligibility, which estimated that a universal old-age pension could cost the government between 0.26 and 1.28 per cent of GDP (ibid.).

Around the same time, the independent research institution Research on Poverty Alleviation (REPOA) published a report, which analysed the material wellbeing and living arrangements of Tanzanians sixty years of age and older and assessed the affordability of a universal pension. In line with the report from the Ministry of Labour, Employment and Youth Development, this report also argued that an old-age pension would substantially decrease poverty—that it could 'lift over 3 million Tanzanians out of poverty' and that it would be affordable (Mboghoina and Osberg 2010). In the years that followed, HelpAge and its partners in the KwaWazee project continued to lobby for an old-age pension and to provide evidence of its value, for instance with an evaluation report published in 2014 (Heslop and Hofmann 2014). Furthermore, the SSRA (Social Security Regulatory Authority) under the Ministry of Labour was tasked with running additional feasibility studies and designing the programme.

It is evident from the above that the promotion of the old-age pension largely focused on showing the various positive impacts of the pension and estimating its (limited) costs. The policy solution is framed to help achieve poverty reduction and realize Tanzania's development potential but does not otherwise speak to the ruling government's problem definition and programmatic responses in the way that the PSSN does. From one ideational perspective, the promotion of social pensions can be advocated as an instrument to meet basic human rights (Von Gliszczynski 2015). However, most of the reports only refer to human rights in passing and in a recent report there is no rights argument presented to support the case of an old-age pension (Heslop and Hofmann 2014).

Given that the ruling government has not put any emphasis on human rights in its primary development documents, it is perhaps not surprising that policy entrepreneurs have tried to focus on other ideational frames to promote their policy solution. Instead, the potential of the old-age pension to reduce poverty, its wide reach, and its limited costs have been expressed as positive attributes of the policy. However, the proposed pension has also met with criticism that follows the programmatic development approach of the government. Thus, the pension is argued to be ineffective in addressing poverty, as it will also reach the non-poor elderly. Also, unlike the PSSN, which already reaches the elderly in vulnerable households, there are no 'productivist' elements in the policy design that relate to support for asset investment and graduation out of poverty.[14]

[14] Interviews and conversations with TASAF and World Bank officials, May and December 2014.

Despite such misgivings, the finance minister announced in December 2014 that the government was in the initial phases of introducing a pension system for the elderly. While there had been some lobbying for an old-age pension, particularly by HelpAge International, the announcement still came as a surprise to many and, theoretically, this policy solution does not appear as well anchored to the ruling elite's problem definition and programmatic responses. Specifically, the proposal to make the pension universal, rather than means-tested, seems to be at odds with the government's policy orientation of social protection.

Rather than discrediting the role of ideas, however, it is possible that the initial policy space for policy entrepreneurs in social protection has been closed as the ruling government has taken a stronger interest in the role that social protection policies can play in legitimizing their rule. Certainly, it is telling that the pension was announced by the Ministry of Finance, and not its erstwhile promoter—the Ministry of Labour—and that the proposal came within a year of the recent parliamentary and presidential election in October 2015. The political interest in announcing an old-age pension before the elections is quite obvious: the ruling CCM was under pressure from increased competition from opposition parties (Gray 2015) and a pension with its wide reach can be expected to give an electoral 'bonus' to the incumbent government. While the policy announcement supported electoral interests, it is less certain—in the current post-election context—whether the promise will be transformed to actual budgetary commitment by the government. At the time of writing, an actual old-age pension scheme has not come into place. There are nevertheless indications that the speed and scale of implementation of the PSSN accelerated in 2015 (Jacob and Pedersen 2018), which again suggests that once the programme is in place, the government will see its instrumental value in the elections.

By contrasting the promotion of the old-age pension with the PSSN, there are some clear similarities in the types of policy entrepreneurs involved and the strategies used. In both cases, international policy entrepreneurs were the initial and primary promoters of policy solutions. That the World Bank sponsored CCTs and that the ILO and HelpAge International advocated for social pensions is in line with the general global trends (Von Gliszczynski 2015). Policy entrepreneurs also similarly used national examples, pilots, and empirical evidence as strategies to promote their policy. The theoretical framework also endorses the different success rates in the two cases. The ILO and HelpAge International have not had the same resources and ability to fund projects in Tanzania as the World Bank have. In addition, the World

Bank had stronger domestic partners in the TASAF and the finance ministry, whereas HelpAge International have partnered with a smaller NGO (KwaWazee project) and the less centrally placed labour ministry. Importantly, in contextualization and presentation the World Bank and TASAF provided a policy solution that better fitted the elite's problem definition and programmatic responses, which was not entirely the case with the pension policy. That an old-age pension has now been announced suggests the possible theoretical limits of ideational approaches vis-à-vis the role of political interests. Section 6 highlights some theoretical and empirical implications of the study.

6. Conclusion

This chapter took as a starting point that within a given political settlement and in a policy area of little interest to the elite, there is room for policy entrepreneurs to promote their favoured policy solutions. Thus, in this context, ideas take a prominent role in explaining policy development. Yet, it appears that the space for policy entrepreneurs outside or on the margins of the elite to shape policy may be closing as social protection has now got the attention of the ruling government. Consequently, interest as an explanatory factor may again become the primary focus of analyses.

The theoretical framework, based on ideational approaches, proved valuable in explaining how specific types of social protection policies have developed in Tanzania. Of broader relevance, the study showed how not only transnational actors but also domestic institutions at the lower levels of government shape specific policy solutions. The policy entrepreneurs can use different strategies to promote their policy, but it seems particularly important that the policy fits the elite's understanding of the country's challenges and possible responses thereto.

Fitting the ruling government's productivist approach to development, the PSSN programme represents an economic rationale for social protection in which the policy's aim of poverty reduction is achieved by enhancing the agency of the poor to participate in the market. Yet a government committing to a programme promoted by policy entrepreneurs does not alone ensure its long-term sustainability. First, the Tanzanian government has showed limited actual budgetary commitment, so far leaving the bulk of funding to international donors. Second, while policy entrepreneurs promoted ideas of self-reliance, responsibility, and hard work, the PSSN is still largely a cash transfer programme, and if the Tanzanian discourse turns against this because of a predominant perception that cash transfers are 'handouts', the continued existence of the PSSN may be challenged. These are the themes analysed and discussed in a study that follows the developments of the PSSN programme where this chapter ends.[15]

References

Beland, D. (2005). Ideas and social policy: an institutionalist perspective. *Social Policy and Administration*, 39(1), 1–18.

Booth, D., B. Cooksey, F. Golooba-Mutebi, and K. Kanyinga (2014). *East African Prospects: An Update on the Political Economy of Kenya, Rwanda, Tanzania and Uganda*. ODI report. London: Overseas Development Institute.

Deacon, B. and P. Stubbs (2013). Global social policy studies: conceptual and analytical reflections. *Global Social Policy*, 13(1), 5–23.

Evans, D.K., S. Hausladen, K. Kosec, and N. Reese (2014). *Community-Based Conditional Cash Transfers in Tanzania: Results from a Randomized Trial*. Washington DC: World Bank.

Foli, R. and D. Béland, D. (2014). International organizations and ideas about poverty in sub-Saharan Africa. *Poverty & Public Policy*, 6(1), 3–23.

Gassmann, F. and C. Behrendt (2006). *Cash Benefits in Low-Income Countries: Simulating the Effects on Poverty Reduction for Senegal and Tanzania*. Geneva: International Labour Office.

Gray, H. (2015). The political economy of grand corruption in Tanzania. *African Affairs*, 114(456), 382–403.

Hall, A. (2007). Social policies in the World Bank: paradigms and challenges. *Global Social Policy*, 7(2), 151–75.

Hall, P.A. (1993). Policy paradigms, social learning, and the state: the case of economic policy-making in Britain. *Comparative Politics*, 25(3), 275–96.

Heslop, M. and S. Hofmann (2014). *Towards Universal Pensions in Tanzania: Evidence on Opportunities and Challenges from a Remote Area, Ngenge Ward, Kagera*. London: HelpAge International.

Hickey, S. and S. Bracking (2005). Exploring the politics of chronic poverty: from representation to a politics of justice? *World Development*, 33(6), 851–65.

Hoffman, B.D. (2013). *Political Economy of Tanzania*. Georgetown University: Center for Democracy and Civil Society.

[15] http://ps.au.dk/forskning/forskningsprojekter/political-settlements-and-revenue-bargains-in-africa/about-the-project/shifting-financial-responsibility.

Hofmann, S., M. Heslop, G. Clacherty, and F. Kessy (2008). *Salt, Soap and Shoes for School: Evaluation Report: The Impact of Pensions on the Lives of Older People and Grandchildren in the KwaWazee Project in Tanzania's Kagera Region*. London: HelpAge International.

ILO (2008). *Tanzania Mainland, Social Protection Expenditure and Performance Review and Social Budget*. Geneva: International Labour Office.

Jacob, T. and R. Hundsbæk Pedersen (2018). Social protection in an electorally competitive environment (1): The politics of Productive Social Safety Nets (PSSN) in Tanzania. ESID Working Paper No. 109. Manchester: University of Manchester. Available at www.effective-states.org.

Kaasch, A. (2013). Contesting contestation: global social policy prescriptions on pensions and health systems. *Global Social Policy*, 13(1), 45–65.

Kessy, F.L. (2014). Assessing the potential of development grants as a promotive social protection measure. REPOA Special Paper 14/1. Dar es Salaam: REPOA.

Khan, M.H. (2010). Political settlements and the governance of growth-enhancing institutions. Unpublished manuscript.

Kjær, A.M. and M.S. Ulriksen (2014). From consensus to contention: changing revenue and policy dynamics in Uganda. UNRISD Working Paper 2014–21. Geneva: UNRISD.

Kpessa, M. and D. Béland (2012). Transnational actors and the politics of pension reform in Sub-Saharan Africa. *Review of International Political Economy*, 19(2), 267–91.

Kwon, H.J., S. Cook, and Y. Kim (2014). Shaping the national social protection strategy in Cambodia: global influence and national ownership. *Global Social Policy*. doi:10.1177/1468018114543310.

Lavers, T. and S. Hickey (2015). Investigating the political economy of social protection expansion in Africa: at the intersection of transnational ideas and domestic politics. ESID Working Paper No. 47. Manchester: Effective States and Inclusive Development Research Centre, University of Manchester, Manchester.

Lerisse, F., D. Mmari, and M. Baruani (2003). *Vulnerability and Social Protection Programmes in Tanzania*. Dar es Salaam: Research and Analysis Working Group.

Lofchie, M.F. (2014). *The Political Economy of Tanzania: Decline and Recovery*. Philadelphia, PA: University of Pennsylvania Press.

Mboghoina, T. and L. Osberg (2010). Social protection of the elderly in Tanzania: current status and future possibilities. Special paper, Research on Poverty Alleviation. Dar es Salaam: REPOA.

Mchomvu, A., F.S. Tungaraza, and S. Maghimbi (2002). Social security systems in Tanzania: Phase I: Overview of social security in Tanzania. *Journal of Social Development in Africa*, 17(2), 11–27.

Mehta, J. (2011). The varied roles of ideas in politics: from 'whether' to 'how'. In D. Beland and R.H. Cox (Eds.), *Ideas and Politics in Social Science Research*. Oxford: Oxford University Press, 23–46.

Ministry of Labour (2010). *Achieving Income Security in Old Age for All Tanzanians: A Study into the Feasibility of a Universal Social Pension*. Dar es Salaam: The Ministry of Labour, Employment and Youth Development in collaboration with HelpAge International.

Niño-Zarazúa, M. (2016). Aid, education policy, and development. *International Journal of Educational Development*, 48, 1–8.

Nyerere, Julius. (1967). The Arusha Declaration. Available at https://www.marxists.org/subject/africa/nyerere/1967/arusha-declaration.htm.

Orenstein, M.A. (2008). *Privatizing Pensions: The Transnational Campaign for Social Security Reform*. Princeton, NJ: Princeton University Press.

Sabatier, Paul A. (1988). An advocacy coalition framework of policy change and the role of policy-oriented learning therein. *Policy Sciences*, 21(2/3), 129–68.

Therkildsen, O. and F. Bourgouin (2012). Continuity and change in Tanzania's ruling coalition: legacies, crises and weak productive capacity. DIIS Working Paper 2012: 06. Copenhagen: Danish Institute for International Studies, DIIS.

Ulriksen, M.S. (2016a). The development of social protection policies in Tanzania, 2000–2015. UCT CSSR Working Paper No. 377. Cape Town: University of Cape Town.

Ulriksen, M.S. (2016b). Ideational and institutional drivers of social protection in Tanzania. WIDER Working Paper No. 2016/142.

UN (United Nations) (n.d.). *Social Protection in Tanzania: Establishing a National System Through Consolidation, Coordination and Reform of Existing Measures*. Dar es Salaam: United Nations Tanzania.

UNDP and ILO (2011). *Sharing Innovative Experiences: Successful Social Protection Floor Experiences. Special Unit for South-South Cooperation*. New York: United Nations Development Programme.

URT (United Republic of Tanzania) (2000). *The Tanzania Development Vision 2025*. Dar es Salaam: President's Office: Planning Commission.

URT (United Republic of Tanzania) (2011). *The Tanzania Five Year Development Plan 2011/12–2015/16: Unleashing Tanzania's Latent Growth Potential*. Dar es Salaam: President's Office, Planning Commission.

Von Gliszczynski, M. (2015). *Cash Transfers and Basic Social Protection: Towards a Development Revolution?* Basingstoke: Palgrave Macmillan.

Von Gliszczynski, M. and L. Leisering (2016). Constructing new global models of social security: how international organizations defined the field of social cash transfers in the 2000s. *Journal of Social Policy*, 45(2), 325–43.

World Bank (2011). *Tanzania: Poverty, Growth, and Public Transfers—Options for a National Productive Safety Net Program*. No. 64620-TZ. Human Development Department, Social Protection Unit, Africa Region.

World Bank (2013). *Tanzania Economic Update: Raising the Game: Can Tanzania Eradiate Extreme Poverty?* Issue 4. African Region, Poverty Reduction and Economic Management, The World Bank Group.

World Bank (2015). *The State of Social Safety Nets 2015*. Washington DC: The World Bank.

6

Policy Diffusion, Domestic Politics, and Social Assistance in Lesotho, 1998–2012

Maria Granvik Saminathen

1. Introduction

In the 2000s interest in the use of cash transfer programmes grew across much of sub-Saharan Africa (Garcia and Moore 2012; Niño-Zarazúa et al. 2012), and unconditional cash transfers began to replace food aid as the central form of social transfers in many African countries (Devereux 2012). Hanlon, Barrientos, and Hulme (2010) have described this as a paradigmatic shift in thinking about development towards a 'welfarist' approach.

Policies are often replicated and adapted from one country to another. In a review about policy diffusion, Obinger et al. (2013: 112) concluded that 'nation-states do not act independently of each other' and that 'interdependencies exist between countries which, in conjunction with domestic factors, account for policy outcomes'. The conventional wisdom about reforms in sub-Saharan Africa is that there have been two models of policy diffusion: a 'Southern African' or 'middle-income country' model (present in South Africa, Namibia, Botswana, Lesotho, Swaziland, Mauritius, and the Seychelles) and a 'Middle Africa' or 'low-income country' model (present in, for example, Zambia and Kenya) (Garcia and Moore 2012; Niño-Zarazúa et al. 2012). Yet, unlike the 'donor-driven' middle African/low-income countries, in the southern African/middle-income countries, the diffusion of South African policies (e.g. social pensions) to its neighbours has been said to play a critical role in welfare reform (Niño-Zarazúa et al. 2012).

Diffusion often takes place through policy makers such as international agencies (for instance, UNICEF, ILO, World Bank) and donor organizations such as the UK's Department for International Development, DFID (see, for example, Hickey et al. 2009). The global literature on policy diffusion emphasizes, however, that external ideas rarely resonate in the absence of favourable

Maria Granvik Saminathen, *Policy Diffusion, Domestic Politics, and Social Assistance in Lesotho, 1998–2012* In: *The Politics of Social Protection in Eastern and Southern Africa.* Edited by: Sam Hickey, Tom Lavers, Miguel Niño-Zarazúa, and Jeremy Seekings, Oxford University Press (2020).
DOI: 10.1093/oso/9780198850342.003.0006

local conditions (including possibly political incentives for local policy makers). For instance, donor pressure on the Zambian government in the 2000s failed to convince the latter that the donor-driven pilot programmes should be rolled out nationally (Kabandula and Seekings 2014). In Uganda, a donor-driven social assistance initiative also ran aground in the 2000s (Grebe and Mubiru 2014).

Lesotho, a small lower-middle-income country characterized by poverty and extreme vulnerability, appears to be a strong candidate for this narrative of policy diffusion. Similar to its neighbour South Africa, the elderly and children have been the foci for social assistance in Lesotho, and the introduction of Lesotho's old-age pension (OAP) programme is widely seen as part of a general diffusion of the South African model to its neighbour. Although existing studies (Barrientos 2009; Devereux 2013; Pelham 2007) emphasize that the introduction of the OAP was a response to domestic factors as well as an example of policy diffusion, there is a lack of clear evidence on the importance of domestic factors.

In order to investigate to what extent Lesotho is indeed an example of such a 'diffusion narrative', this study re-examines two of the country's cash transfer programmes, the OAP and the child grant programme (CGP), by means of novel primary data. This chapter argues that there is no evidence of any direct 'diffusion' effects from South Africa (although the absence of evidence is not evidence of absence, especially with regard to a weak regional demonstration effect). Rather, in line with Lavers and Hickey (2016) who have analysed social protection in the light of political settlement frameworks, the Lesotho case seems to confirm that the implementation of social assistance programmes in developing countries is in some cases more strongly shaped by political settlement dynamics than donor pressure or policy diffusion. A society's political settlement presents a foundation for development, solving the problem of violence, and entails both formal and informal processes, agreements, and practices that help consolidate politics (Kelsall 2016). Thus, the instigation and implementation of social protection programmes are linked with the dynamics of a country's political settlement (Lavers and Hickey 2016). Accordingly, this study suggests that the introduction of the OAP in Lesotho was facilitated by a political shift that brought about a rare period of stability, with a relatively dominant government led by Prime Minister Mosisili[1] who

[1] Mosisili became prime minister after the elections in 1998, and won two further elections in 2002 and 2007, but was unseated by a coalition of opposition parties after elections in 2012. Mosisili was once again appointed as prime minister in 2015, a few months after the second round of fieldwork for this case study took place. Yet, in the (early) 2017 elections he was defeated by Thomas Thabane and the All Basotho Convention.

was in favour of a dormestic response to socioeconomic change and the rampant HIV/AIDS epidemic. Yet, the OAP was not part of a strategic distributional regime. In contrast, the case of the CGP involved donors who laid the foundation for a social cash transfer policy coalition in Lesotho. This donor-initiated programme faced initial government scepticism, although the Lesotho government quickly took control (and assumed financial responsibility). This programme has since become an important element of recent progress towards a systemic and inclusive social protection system (Pellerano et al. 2016).

2. Methodology

This case study is based on semi-structured interviews with sixteen key informants conducted in Maseru, the capital of Lesotho (as well as written correspondence with two key informants who were unavailable during fieldwork), in April and August 2014.[2] Key informants were recruited through phone calls and e-mails to various relevant organizations as well as informal visits, for example to the Department of Pensions. Finally, the study relied heavily on snowball sampling, as it was particularly difficult to reach more senior informants without a referral. All interviewees were briefed about the study, and each informant signed a consent form before the interview.

3. Politics, Poverty, and Social Protection in Lesotho in the Late 1990s

Lesotho is a 'parliamentary representative democratic constitutional monarchy', with the king as formal head of state and an elected prime minister as head of government. Since Lesotho's independence, a number of post-election crises have arisen, primarily due to the inadequacy of the 'first-past-the post' system to reflect the number of popular votes secured by political parties in the allocation of parliamentary seats. Through support from the Commonwealth, the South African Development Community (SADC), and other partners, the country went through electoral reform in 2002, introducing a 'mixed member proportional' (MMP) electoral model to

[2] See Granvik (2016) for a more detailed account of the study's methodology as well as a list of key informants.

limit post-electoral contestations and make parliament more inclusive (Commonwealth Secretariat 2012).

By the early 2000s it had become evident that Lesotho had not succeeded at turning economic growth into improvements in the wellbeing of the poor (May et al. 2002: 6). Lesotho has been a beneficiary of international food aid since the 1930s, a trend that has persisted because of environmental factors such as droughts (Makenete et al. 1998). The World Food Programme (WFP) has supported the country in the form of disaster risk reduction and provision for Lesotho's school-feeding programme (World Food Programme 2016). Further, there have been a number of food-for-work programmes in the more recent past that were used to distribute food aid, mostly financed by the WFP (World Bank 2013). Lesotho has also implemented public works programmes, for instance in the context of the Integrated Watershed Management Project, but there has not been an integrated system of such programmes (Olivier 2013b). Increasingly, cash transfers have become major tools of social assistance in Lesotho (Olivier 2013a). Lesotho's first cash transfer, the Public Assistance Grant, was introduced in the 1970s to support the 'destitute', although with very limited coverage and benefit levels.

4. The Old-Age Pension—Another 'Mosisili'?

Considering the rather precarious socioeconomic conditions and fiscal ability, Lesotho has made substantial progress towards developing initiatives to provide minimum levels of protection, introducing social assistance measures such as the OAP and the CGP to target the impoverished and vulnerable (Olivier 2013a). Lesotho's 'National Vision 2020' (Government of Lesotho 2004) presented the foundation of development in the country, and several Poverty Reduction Strategy Papers and National Strategic Development Plans have subsequently been released. Mosisili, who had become prime minister after the 1998 elections, came to play a leading role in the poverty-reduction strategies that were introduced in the Vision 2020.

As a result of the strong positive impacts of social protection initiatives, the provision of so-called 'social pensions' has become an encouraged social protection strategy in southern Africa (ILO 2014; Sepúlveda and Nyst 2012). Lesotho's influential neighbour South Africa had implemented a social pension in the 1920s (although with benefits based on 'race' until the end of apartheid) and Namibia started such a programme in the 1970s. However, the Lesotho pension was a one-off reform at the time, and not part of a coherent social agenda (Pelham 2007). Further, the age threshold of the Lesotho pension was set higher than the South African one (seventy years, compared to sixty-five for men and sixty for women in South Africa at the time), and the benefit levels were significantly lower (M150/US$20 per month), distinguishing this programme from its South African predecessor.

The proportion of elderly is higher in Lesotho than in other sub-Saharan African countries, reflecting the outmigration of young people and the beginning of a demographic transition towards an older society. Today, approximately 83,000 citizens over the age of seventy years receive the OAP, which currently consists of M500 (US$37) per month (Pension Watch Database 2018). The programme is administered by the Pension Division of the powerful Ministry of Finance, and benefits are paid in cash on a monthly basis. Today, Lesotho spends approximately M436 million (US$37.1 million) on the OAP annually, which represents around 3 per cent of total public expenditure, approximately 1.3 per cent of GDP (Pension Watch Database 2018).

4.1. The role of the HIV/AIDS crisis

Lesotho's generalized HIV/AIDS epidemic has affected every sector of society and the combined effects of poverty and inequality underscore the reality of the social and economic impact of HIV and AIDS in Lesotho (Owusu-Ampomah et al. 2009; Mugomeri et al. 2017). Based on the literature and interviews with key informants, the demographic impact of HIV/AIDS appears to have been a critical incentive for the government to (re-) consider a cash transfer scheme for the elderly.

During the time that the OAP was implemented, Lesotho was confronted with an HIV prevalence rate of 31 per cent. In 1999 it was estimated that 80 per cent of those affected by HIV/AIDS were between twenty and thirty-nine years (UNAIDS 2004), which resulted in a heavy burden on the older generation, who needed to care for orphaned children (Casey and McKinnon 2009). The Department of Pensions[3] highlighted that the fact that the elderly are increasingly 'forced to take care of their grandchildren' was a 'point that was raised throughout the conversation [in 2004]'. Similarly, the former Principal Secretary of Public Service[4] explained that 'the original thought behind the pension was to reward the elderly', but as the AIDS epidemic

[3] Interview, bureaucrat, Department of Pensions, Maseru, April 2014.
[4] Interview, former principal secretary, Public Service, Maseru, August 2014.

became more acute, 'the government itself felt that it was important to provide an income for grannies who were taking care of orphans'. The significance of the OVC (orphans and vulnerable children) crisis was also confirmed by Mosisili:[5] 'The epidemic played a pivotal role in influencing the decision [in 2004]. We were generally looking at vulnerable groups, and the OAP was combining the two [the elderly and OVC]'.

The HIV/AIDS crisis undoubtedly warranted an urgent national reaction. Thus, a social pension could have offered a meaningful policy response during this time. However, ostensibly, it was only after a political shift enabled by the 2002 electoral reform that the circumstances were stable enough for the Mosisili government to act on such a social assistance programme.

4.2. A political shift

Scholars (Barrientos 2009; Pelham 2007) seem to agree that the prime minister at the time was the driving force behind the OAP, although the pension scheme was not assessed as having presented a critical election issue. According to Pelham (2007), a social pension had appeared on the manifesto of the ruling Basutoland Congress Party (BCP) as early as 1993, but the literature is inconclusive regarding why the pension was only finalized eleven years later, and what eventually prompted its very sudden introduction (Barrientos 2009; Devereux and Cipryk 2009; Niño-Zarazúa et al. 2012; Pelham 2007). Further, authors such as Pelham (2007: 11), Barrientos (2009: 4), and Niño-Zarazúa et al. (2012: 20) have all suggest that the existence of a social pension in South Africa played a significant role in the formation of a universal pension in Lesotho through policy diffusion in the region. While the South African pension may have served as inspiration, the Lesotho's OAP does appear to be 'home-grown' in many respects. It was eventually enabled by a period of political stability under a dominant prime minister, as section 4.3 will discuss with the support of new primary data.

Lesotho's political history has been shaped by conflicts, despite the absence of significant ethnic, religious, and ideological differences among contesting parties (Rosenberg and Weisfelder 2013). Considering the political instability that shaped the 1990s in Lesotho, the long delay of the pension is essentially not very unexpected, and several key informants referred to the political

[5] Interview, former prime minister, Maseru, August 2014.

challenges that the incumbent government(s) were faced with between 1993 and 2002. For example, Dr Thahane,[6] the finance minister at the time, recalled that 'the budget moved to security matters. We had to think about survival first!' While the idea of a pension still appeared to be 'on the table' in the late 1990s, a 1998 government-commissioned consultancy study[7] had determined that granting a social pension in Lesotho would be too costly (Hagen 2008).

In 2002, multi-party competition and democratic stability seemed to have emerged in Lesotho after the new electoral system had been instigated (Rich et al. 2013), and Mosisili led the Lesotho Congress for Democracy (LCD) to a substantial and peaceful victory (Rosenberg and Weisfelder 2013; Weisfelder 2015). Finally, Lesotho thus found itself politically stable and free of post-election conflicts—the opposition parties had been given some representation and visibility, but failed to attain a strong opposition towards the dominant LCD. Applying Khan's (2010) political settlement typology (2010) as employed by Lavers and Hickey (2016), Lesotho's political setting after the 2002 elections could thus be classified as 'dominant'. Accordingly, the leading position enjoyed by Mosisili and the LCD is likely to have facilitated the swift introduction of a social pension.

4.3. Emergence of a policy

As mentioned above, a certain interest in a social policy to support the elderly had already been established in the early 1990s. Prior to the 2002 elections, a plan for a pension had reappeared on some political programmes, most clearly on the manifesto of the winning LCD (Hagen 2008: 13). Mosisili's LCD had thus promised a pension, but with the condition that the financial resources of the government were sufficient to implement a universal scheme. The Department of Pensions[8] explained that during the first two years following the 2002 elections, 'the budget could not sustain a pension due to the aftermath of the 1998 turbulence'. However, according to Mosisili,[9] a pension was on the agenda of the new government at this time: 'It had to be implemented! In 2002, for the first time, there was post-election peace. Now we could focus on

[6] Interview, former finance minister, Maseru, August 2014.

[7] This study has been mentioned by Hagen (2008) and was also confirmed by David Croome during an August 2014 meeting, but no further evidence regarding the timing of this study (i.e. whether it took place before or after the 1998 elections) has been identified.

[8] Interview, bureaucrat, Department of Pensions, Maseru, April 2014.

[9] Interview, B.P. Mosisili, Prime Minister, Maseru, August 2014.

development, not just extinguishing fires'. The former principal secretary of finance[10] recalled that 'he [Mosisili] chaired a Cabinet meeting in 2004 that directed that we test the affordability and sustainability again . . . when government's fiscal position seemed quite strong. Playing around with unit pay-out and age produced several options from which an affordable and sustainable one was found, presented to Cabinet and approved within two days'. A long-term bureaucrat in the pensions department[11] recalls that 'Mosisili sold the idea [of a pension] to parliament'. Finally, in his 2004/5 budget speech, Lesotho's finance minister (Thahane) announced the introduction of a universal social pension for all citizens aged seventy and older. Parliamentary debates on the pension were held shortly before registration began. As the former Commissioner of Pensions[12] underlined, 'it was implemented purely on the budget statement, without any policy document as a foundation'. Following a month-long registration process, the first pensions were delivered in November 2004 without a (customary) pilot phase.

There had been some media publicity about the pension prior to the registration process, but there was no public consultation or community involvement. Apart from the advocacy of the Maseru Women's Senior Citizens Association (MWSCA), there was no widespread campaigning for the implementation of a social pension (Pelham 2007). During an interview for this case study, the founder of the MWSCA[13] described how the MWSCA tried to push for the pension to finally be implemented by writing letters and even meeting with the prime minister himself. Mosisili[14] admits that this advocacy 'was useful, but they were preaching to the converted'. Thus, while this lobbying may not have been decisive per se, it may have accelerated the process. However, a bureaucrat in the Department of Pensions[15] explained that 'unlike South Africans', who had been 'promised services' by the African National Congress (ANC), there had been no 'demand' from the Basotho for a pension. According to the former principal secretary of finance,[16] 'the announcement [of the OAP] was welcomed, in as much as it was a surprise to many. After many years of non-fulfilment there had not been any expectations'.

[10] Written correspondence, former principal secretary, Ministry of Finance, August 2014.
[11] Interview, bureaucrat, Department of Pensions, Maseru, April 2014.
[12] Interview, former commissioner of pensions, Maseru, August 2014.
[13] Interview, founder MWSCA, Maseru, April 2014.
[14] Interview, former prime minister, Maseru, August 2014.
[15] Interview, bureaucrat, Department of Pensions, Maseru, April 2014.
[16] Written correspondence, former principal secretary, Ministry of Finance, August 2014.

Hence, based on the evidence from the literature and testimonies from key stakeholders, the political instability in the 1990s appears to have been a major obstacle to the realization of the promised pension. However, the former finance minister[17] suggested that the initial proposal of a pension in 1993 had also been poorly thought through. 'Political manifestos outline what parties would like to have. It [a pension] is easy to conceive, but difficult to finance and administer. That is where it got stuck'. It is possible that Mosisili's appointment of the very experienced economist Thahane as finance minister provided for strong teamwork with Mosisili and thus enabled a professional and credible assessment of a pension to be carried out. Also, the capacity of Thabo Thulo, the Commissioner of Pensions at the time, may have played a role. Thulo undeniably succeeded in the demanding task of swiftly designing a pension scheme, registering beneficiaries, and ensuring that the first payments were made only eight months after the pension had been announced. Thulo himself[18] admitted that he was caught off guard by the announcement of the OAP in 2004: 'I was surprised! I thought, "my office will have to oversee it"'. It is likely that the confidence of both the Lesotho parliament and the Ministry of Finance in Thulo's ability to administer a universal pension may thus have contributed to the relatively straightforward policy process behind the pension, and its prompt completion.

As previously mentioned, existing literature indicates that Mosisili was the main driver and thus 'the champion' of the OAP (Pelham 2007; Devereux and White 2008; Barrientos 2009; Olivier 2013). Undeniably, political elites tend to hold certain 'policy space' to implement their own ideas and policies (Lavers and Hickey 2016). With regards to countries that present with a dominant type of political settlement such as Lesotho in the early 2000s, Lavers and Hickey (2016) suggest that the top-level leadership tends to determine a policy. Typically, there is no subsequent debate or attempts to undermine the policy. Correspondingly, Pelham (2007: 12) indicates that Mosisili's 'personal style of government' may have 'afforded him the ability to make decisions and have them acted upon without the political turbulence or lengthy administrative procedures that may hinder other democracies'. Mosisili's 'personal style' is certainly evident in the unremitting association of social welfare with his name. Children who have attended Lesotho's free

[17] Interview, former finance minister, Maseru, August 2014.
[18] Interview, former commissioner of pensions, Maseru, August 2014.

primary schools are called 'bana ba Mosisili' ('Mosisili's children') and the elderly who receive the OAP are said to 'collect their Mosisili'. Consequently, while the initial proposal of a social pension may not have directly affected the outcome of the 1993 election (Matlosa 1997), and the introduction of the OAP may not have been a desperate attempt to remain in power, Mosisili's strong association with the social policies mentioned implies that the implementation of the OAP ultimately benefited the incumbent government's position.

4.4. Politicization of the OAP

Lavers and Hickey (2016) propose that political feedback and popular pressures matter once social policies have actually been implemented—this is a phenomenon that has been observed by the authors in the context of social protection initiatives in countries such as Kenya, Uganda, and Zambia. This was also the case in Lesotho during the 2007 elections—once the OAP had finally been introduced, the programme did come to present an election issue (Devereux and White 2008). The opposition party All Basotho Convention's (ABC's) pledge to raise the monthly pension payment if they were elected prompted Mosisili's governing party (LCD) to promise a reconsideration of the pension payment level if they were re-elected. After the LCD's victory in coalition with the National Independence Party (NIP), the finance minister announced a 33 per cent increase in the monthly pension in the first budget speech after the elections, adhering to the LCD's election promise. Lesotho's OAP thus exemplifies the idea of 'positive politicization' (Devereux and White 2008), as the popularity of this programme forced the government to respond positively to opposition campaign pledges to raise the payment level. Further, the introduction of the OAP, and, to a lesser extent, the decision to make primary education free were the overwhelming reasons given for voting for the governing party in 2007 (Croome et al. 2007; Devereux and Cipryk 2009).

While these circumstances alone do not substantiate to what extent the intentions behind the OAP were in fact political, it is likely that the LCD's decision to 'thank' the elderly through a universal pension may have benefited Mosisili and his party, at least in the short term, based on the broad approval of the OAP in Lesotho. The prime minister may have been aware of the potential 'reciprocity' effect (Baez et al. 2012) of introducing a cash transfer to a vulnerable population group, thus the OAP could, at least to some extent, have been part of a political strategy.

4.5. The financing of the OAP

While the decision to provide a pension was clearly politically unopposed in Lesotho, the capacity to finance the pension was nonetheless not self-evident. Financing social pensions can present a significant challenge for low-income countries. As the case of Zambia has shown (Kabandula and Seekings 2014), the judgement of the Ministry of Finance may ultimately decide whether social protection programmes such as cash transfers are ultimately prioritized or not. In this case, a donor-driven attempt to provide cash transfers to poor households failed to become 'owned' by government (Kabandula and Seekings 2014).

In Lesotho, on the other hand, the Ministry of Finance did not present an obstacle to the OAP (or, later, the CGP). The fact that Thahane was recruited by Mosisili himself, and was said to have worked closely together with the prime minister, may have shaped his attitude towards social policies such as the OAP, and thus motivated him to cooperate with Mosisili's plans. The views that Thahane[19] expressed towards 'welfare' during his interview corresponded with Mosisili's and the LCD's: 'Welfare can keep you alive, so that you can do something sustainable. We felt that the elderly are a legitimate target'. The former principal secretary of the finance ministry[20] highlighted that Thahane's financial management experience encouraged trust in the Ministry of Finance: 'Cabinet tended to accept the lead of the professionals in the Finance Ministry'.

The period after the change of the electoral system in 2002 brought unprecedented GDP growth (Maleleka 2009), creating a favourable time for investing in a social programme such as the OAP. Fiscal reprioritization finally enabled the government to shoulder the burden of expenditure. The OAP has largely been funded through Southern African Customs Union (SACU) revenues received by Lesotho, which indicates the government's willingness to find and increase fiscal space (Hagen 2008), even during times of global economic crisis.

Ultimately, it seems clear that the Lesotho OAP is largely financially feasible because the benefits are comparatively small and the age for entitlement is relatively high. Although the monthly value increased from M150 (US$23) to M500 (US$47) over ten years, the practical extent of this increase is rather limited. Taking inflation into account, M500 in 2014 would have been

[19] Interview, former finance minister, Maseru, August 2014.

[20] Written correspondence, former principal secretary, Ministry of Finance, August 2014.

equivalent to merely M273 in 2004. In 2018, the monthly benefit still consisted of M500. By comparison, the age threshold of the South African social pension is sixty years and the current monthly-level benefit payment is ZAR1,420 (US$107) (Pension Watch 2018). As time passed, the former Commissioner of Pensions[21] explained that 'the government had to consider whether to lower the qualifying age, or to increase the benefit rates. Also, increasing the benefits will benefit children. It is better to give more to fewer people'. Mosisili[22] explained that 'we were careful not to bite more than we could chew... We will grow it with time'. This decision to 'give more to fewer people' (although many elderly citizens below seventy years of age may be just as destitute as those who currently do receive the OAP) is noteworthy, as it may have implications for the 'developmental' objectives behind the pension. Further, the Lesotho OAP is not targeted based on socioeconomic position, unlike the South African 'older persons' grant' that is subject to a means test that excludes the wealthy elderly. Thus, higher benefits make the transfer more effective for the beneficiaries, but at the same time the exclusion of the elderly below seventy years and the lack of a means test does not correspond with a 'classic' poverty-reduction strategy.

4.6. Absence of transnational encouragement

Another striking aspect of the Lesotho pension is the absence of the international arena, which also stands in contrast to the origins of the child grant, which will be discussed in section 5. The process behind the OAP in Lesotho has certainly gone against Bonnerje's (2003: 29) prediction that 'in the initial stages of setting up such arrangements [social pensions] in other countries of the region [sub-Saharan Africa], major international donors would have to play a lead role'.

According to Mosisili,[23] the government purposely did not involve foreign donors: 'We were very clear that this was an initiative that we were coming up with as government... We will start this on our own, with limited resources... We will not make it a foreign aid-driven initiative'. He also acknowledged international donors' scepticism: 'The IMF and the World Bank appreciated the problem that we were grappling with, but they were

[21] Interview, former Commissioner of Pensions, Maseru, August 2014.
[22] Interview, former prime minister, Maseru, August 2014.
[23] Interview, former prime minister, Maseru, August 2014.

worried about sustainability'. Of course, it may have been a potential refusal by the World Bank to support the government's endeavour of installing a universal pension that ignited the government's later emphasis on donor independence, but there is no indication that the government had actively pursued external funding for the OAP. According to Pelham (2007), donor agencies generally expressed interest and overwhelming support for the pension, but they had very little knowledge about it. Regardless, the absence of external assistance contributes to the uniqueness of the policy process behind the OAP, which further supports the argument that this initiative was mostly 'home-grown'.

4.7. Back to the roots

A remaining question mark surrounding the pension concerns the *roots* of the idea for a universal cash transfer for the elderly. Mosisili[24] insisted that 'the idea for an OAP stemmed from the BCP's ideology, it was very people-oriented. It was clear that people in the private sector[25] and subsistence farmers were vulnerable once they reached old age. The majority of people can no longer fend for themselves... they are dependent on their children. With time, it became clear that we can no longer rely on that'. Yet, where did the BCP look for inspiration for such a policy, even if it had not yet been very well 'conceived' in 1993? Barrientos (2009: 79) has asserted that the presence of social pension schemes as the dominant form of welfare provision in neighbouring countries exerted an influence on Lesotho. Similarly, Pelham (2007: 11) suggests that the introduction of a social pension in Lesotho in 2004 was 'a product of regional geopolitics and a concern for equity' in order to provide the elderly in Lesotho with an equivalent to the social pension in neighbouring South Africa. Yet, Pelham's (2007) study also acknowledges the lack of advocacy for a social pension from civil society, and the absence of a public reaction to the introduction of the OAP.

The low level of anticipation among the elderly was highlighted by a bureaucrat at the Department of Pensions[26] who has been involved with the OAP since its commencement: 'they [the government] had been saying it over and over again [that there would be a pension]'. Upon registration, many

[24] Interview, former prime minister, Maseru, August 2014.

[25] Mosisili used the word 'private sector' here to highlight that before the OAP was introduced, only former civil servants received a government pension (thus anyone who was not in the 'public sector' did not receive any government pension).

[26] Interview, bureaucrat, Department of Pensions, Maseru, April 2014.

elderly 'did not believe' that a pension would actually be paid—apparently there was even some 'resistance' at first, as some people assumed that it was a 'trick for the next elections'. Once the first round of pensions had been distributed, this disbelief was overcome and the elderly Basotho increasingly began to register for the pension. This response was confirmed by Mosisili:[27] 'We had talked about introducing a pension since 1993, but nothing had happened. So when we announced it in 2004, there was a lot of doubt as to whether we would really carry it through'. This evidence could possibly indicate that the Basotho did not *expect* their government to provide such a grant for the elderly, which weakens Pelham's argument that the Basotho felt that universal pensions were a 'right' of the elderly based on the *South African* example, prior to the introduced of the social pension in Lesotho.

4.8. A diffusion effect?

Barrientos (2009) concludes that even if the OAP in Lesotho was indeed an effect of regional 'diffusion', 'it is hard to see the example of Lesotho [...] as indicative of more general trends [...] in low-income countries' (Barrientos 2009: 79). Consequently, while the pension is likely to have been prompted by the South African (and possibly other countries') welfare model(s) to some extent, Lesotho seems to have created its own version of a social pension, possibly with a somewhat different objective in mind. Undoubtedly, the small benefit, the high age of qualification, and its universal nature make the Lesotho pension considerably different from the South African social pension.

Perhaps not too unexpectedly, none of the key stakeholders interviewed affirmed any 'connection' between the Lesotho OAP and the South African social pension. Some appeared rather surprised by this suggestion, such as the former Principal Secretary of Public Service.[28] Correspondingly, Mosisili[29] very firmly stated that 'I would not attribute it to the example of South Africa in any way'. Thahane[30] reacted rather strongly to the question regarding a possible diffusion effect. 'They think we have no brains! The pension is home-grown, like the free primary education. It's like saying that Sweden invented Volvo only because there were cars in other countries'. For a small, poverty-stricken country like Lesotho that is highly dependent on South Africa,

[27] Interview, former prime minister, Maseru, August 2014.
[28] Interview, former PS of Public Service, Maseru, August 2014.
[29] Interview, former prime minister, Maseru, August 2014.
[30] Interview, former finance minister, Maseru, August 2014.

programmes such as the OAP may thus be highly symbolic of the country's increasing ability to 'help itself'. Evidently, Lesotho did not discover the *concept* of a 'social pension', but the insinuation that Lesotho may have simply 'copied' the pension from South Africa could still be perceived as offensive by its implementers, who consider their pension scheme 'unique'.

4.9. The right to a pension

While the OAP is unquestionably a legal entitlement based on the 2005 Old-Age Pension Act (Government of Lesotho 2005), the common reference to OAP as a 'right' (Pelham 2007)—as opposed to merely 'support' or 'welfare'—may point to a potentially unique incentive behind the pension, since far from all social protection programmes are framed in this manner. The Minister of Finance at the time, Dr Tim Thahane,[31] recounted: 'We felt that the elderly are a legitimate target. We wouldn't be where we are if it hadn't been for them. The pension gives them dignity'. The rights-argument was also strongly emphasized by Prime Minister Mosisili,[32] who explained that 'a pension is something that one qualifies for on the basis of age. Anybody can get a grant. Also, a pension is something one deserves. We are not doing them a favour'. Yet, it is unclear if Mosisili expanded on a policy discourse that had already been created by the BCP in 1993, or if Mosisili *himself* decided to present the pension as 'a right' of the people of Lesotho. It is also intriguing that the social pension in Lesotho is in fact called a 'pension', although it is non-contributory. This choice of word may reflect the idea that the Lesotho OAP was truly a gesture of appreciation and respect towards the elderly from the Lesotho government, and less a simple 'imitation' of the existing South African set-up. As the former finance minister[33] highlighted, 'The pension is an entitlement. You deserve something, you have worked for the country. A *grant* you can stop at any time'.

Yet, as Pelham (2007) and Croome et al. (2007) have asserted, the small amount of the pension is insufficient to sustain an entire household. Further, considering that almost two-thirds of the OAP went to non-poor households in 2013 (World Bank 2013), the introduction of the pension cannot be understood as a strategic developmental response to extreme poverty, per se

[31] Interview, former finance minister, Maseru, August 2014.
[32] Interview, former prime minister, Maseru, August 2014.
[33] Interview, former finance minister, Maseru, August 2014.

(Casey and McKinnon 2009: 97). This does not essentially discredit the potentially developmental purpose of the pension, but it is questionable whether it is able to make a substantial difference to the livelihood of an impoverished elderly citizen who is caring for orphaned grandchildren. Thus, perhaps the pension should indeed be understood as a 'token of thanks' to the elderly, whose purpose may be more complementary and symbolic than effectively 'developmental'. Nonetheless, it appears that the domestic process that prompted the OAP may have been the first step towards developing a 'social contract' (Pelham 2007). The alleged positive impact of the OAP (Croome et al. 2007) and the programme's popularity among the Basotho may have shaped the Lesotho government's affirming attitude towards cash grants for vulnerable population groups. The positive responses triggered through the OAP process may further have 'opened a window of opportunity for donor influence' in the field of social assistance (Lavers and Hickey 2016) and thus paved the way for the subsequent rather smooth introduction of the child grant only a few years later.

5. The Child Grant—An African Success Story?

The Lesotho CGP was the second major social assistance reform under Mosisili's LCD government. However, unlike the OAP, this cash transfer is an example of a social assistance programme that is based on transnational ideas about social protection for vulnerable populations promoted by donors (Lavers and Hickey 2016). The CGP took off as a donor-funded 'pilot' cash transfer programme that gradually expanded and became 'government-owned' (Davis et al. 2015). In 2013 this means-tested programme provided a quarterly transfer of between M360 and M750 (US$36–US$74) to poor households with children. According to the World Bank (2013), the CGP is 'one of the few programmes [in Lesotho] that make a systematic effort to identify the most vulnerable'. Unlike the OAP, the CGP purposely attempts to target the *poorest* households. Initially it was financed by the European Union (EU), with the technical support of UNICEF, and was originally implemented by the former Department of Social Welfare. Today the programme is run by the Ministry of Social Development, which was established in 2012.[34] Since

[34] After the 2012 elections, Thomas Thabane (not to be confused with former finance minister, Tim Thahane) succeeded Mosisili as prime minister with his ABC party by building a coalition government with the support of two opposition parties.

October 2013, all the benefit costs of the grant have been funded by the government. In the year 2017, 27,000 households with about 80,000 children benefited from the CGP (UNICEF 2017).[35]

5.1. A donor-driven policy coalition

The CGP has followed a very different policy process compared to the OAP, although it was initiated only three years later and under the same government. However, by 2006, the LCD hegemony had begun to decline (Likoti 2009). In order to win the 2007 elections, Mosisili's LCD had to enter an alliance with the NIP, and from this point on, coalitions started dominating Lesotho politics (Booysen 2015). With regards to the development of a distributional regime, building on existing programmes such as the OAP, this changing power balance may have undermined Mosisili's opportunities to pursue his preferred policies (if he had any such plans). Further, the years after the 2007 elections were shaped by political turmoil. Hence, grievances regarding access to power and succession to party leadership (Weisfelder 2015) may further have distracted the LCD from policy-making, creating a fresh space for transnational actors to step in, particularly as Lesotho found itself in a fragile economic period.

The CGP is part of the EU project, 'Support to Lesotho HIV and AIDS Response: Empowerment of Orphans and Vulnerable Children' that was initiated in 2006 as a reaction to the absence of an effective support system for OVC in the HIV/AIDS context (Thomson and Kardan 2012). The aim of the programme was to enhance the living standards of OVC by reducing malnutrition, improving health status, and increasing school enrolment. A second objective of the programme was to eventually strengthen the capacity of the government to deliver cash grants to households with children (Blank 2008). As the National OVC Strategy highlights, the traditional practice in the rural communities vis-à-vis orphaned children was based on community involvement; yet, predictably, these mechanisms had become overstretched.[36] Since there are many 'non-poor' orphans and many other children who are not orphans but are nonetheless living in extreme poverty and vulnerability in Lesotho, the CGP targets 'orphans *and* vulnerable

[35] Table showing the progression of the CGP available in Granvik (2016).

[36] Another transfer programme that specifically targets OVC is the OVC Bursary Scheme that provides bursaries to OVC in secondary school, yet prior to the CGP there was no initiative that supported the general needs of OVC and their families.

children'. The programme defines OVC as orphans (having lost one or both parents), or those children who are HIV positive, or those living without adequate adult support (World Bank 2013).

As the former Department of Social Welfare lacked the capacity to administer a complex means-tested social assistance programme, UNICEF was selected to take on the role of delivering technical assistance to the government in order to build its competency to independently run the CGP (World Bank 2013). A community-based targeting system was developed and studies on appropriate delivery mechanisms were commissioned. First payments were made to households in one pilot district in April 2009 and by January 2010 the programme had reached 1,000 households, caring for over 2,700 OVC with quarterly payments of M360 (Thomson and Kardan 2012). By early 2010, the CGP pilot was expanded to an additional three community councils. An external consultancy company that specializes in cash transfer programmes, Ayala Consulting, was brought in to complete the technical design and to develop technical guidelines and computer models. Further, a National Information System for Social Assistance (NISSA) was created to register information on all households, to be used for the selection of the CGP beneficiaries.

5.2. The role of the Lesotho government

The information provided by the EU Delegation to Lesotho and by Thomson and Kardan (2012) indicates that the EU was the main driver of the CGP. By the early 2000s, assistance to children in Lesotho had been primarily delivered through a WFP school-feeding programme or through small programmes by nonprofit organizations (NPOs) (e.g. World Vision). Some efforts that specifically acknowledged children's vulnerability had previously taken place in the context of temporary international emergency relief, for instance during several natural disasters during the 2000s, such as the 2002 drought. According to a World Vision Lesotho employee,[37] voices regarding the need for targeted assistance to OVC were first raised through government social workers. Similarly, the Ministry of Social Development[38] stated that 'the government went looking for funding' after concerns regarding OVC had been identified. According to the former principal secretary of the former

[37] Interview, manager, World Vision, Maseru, April 2014.
[38] Interview, manager, Ministry of Social Development, Maseru, April 2014.

Department of Social Welfare,[39] the child grant was 'the government's idea in the context of HIV. There was a need for the Department of Social Welfare to come up with a programme to assist OVC'.

Mosisili[40] expressed uncertainty regarding the roots of the CGP: 'I cannot quite say whose idea it was'. However, he emphasized that 'it was something we saw the need for'. Mosisili explained the involvement of external stakeholders as follows: 'We didn't have the resources... We were being assisted'. Further, he disclosed that 'the availability of funding came at a time when we were still grappling with teething problems with the OAP'. Thus, challenges faced with the OAP may have discouraged the government from attempting to initiate another (much more advanced) social assistance programme. According to key stakeholders,[41] such challenges included general issues with fraud and corruption, the difficulty of the overlap with the pension for civil servants, and the lack of capacity to deliver cash to remote areas. Overall, Mosisili's personal vision[42] of the state as a provider of social protection appeared affirmative: 'It [state support to vulnerable groups] makes sense, it is the right thing to do, to make sure that children have a chance. The more we invest in our people, the better chance we have to break the cycle [of poverty]. The government will have to make provision for it'. Based on his statements, Mosisili appears to perceive social assistance as a necessary 'stepping stone' to economic and social development. Yet, it must be kept in mind that it is not very surprising that a former (and, with hindsight, aspiring) prime minister would want to take 'credit' for the poverty-reduction programmes that his government implemented.

Elite commitment to social protection is essential (Lavers and Hickey 2016), and it is possible that Mosisili's views regarding the assistance of vulnerable groups shaped the government's willingness to adopt and implement programmes such as the CGP, even if accompanied with imminent financial obligations for the government. Conversely, Mosisili does not appear to have been as closely associated with the CGP as he was with the free primary school education and the OAP that were implemented a few years earlier. It is likely that the much more limited and 'targeted' coverage of the CGP had limited the general population's level of awareness about this cash transfer. Also, the fact that the grant was initiated and initially funded by a foreign donor may have

[39] Written correspondence, former PS, Ministry of Finance, August 2014.

[40] Interview, former prime minister, Maseru, August 2014.

[41] Interviews with bureaucrat in the Department of Pensions, April 2014; project manager at Ayala Consulting, August 2014; and former commissioner of pensions, Ministry of Finance, August 2014.

[42] Interview, former prime minister, Maseru, August 2014.

prevented Mosisili and other politicians from 'personalizing' this programme for political gains.

Nonetheless, according to the EU Delegation to Lesotho,[43] 'the Lesotho child grant is distinctive in as much that it has been directly implemented by the government, with strong technical support from UNICEF. The Ministry of Health and Social Welfare has had a strong involvement from the beginning and this has certainly facilitated the transition from a fully donor-funded project to a national programme, a unique success story of this magnitude in the sub-Saharan continent'. Mosisili[44] recounted: 'The understanding has always been there that the government would take over'. The effective cooperation between the funder and the government is confirmed by the EU:[45] 'The Government of Lesotho has been praised for the commitment shown up to now and for having allocated the required financial resources for the Child Grant Programme in its 2013/2014 and 2014/2015 budgets'.

5.3. Convincing the sceptics

The ultimate willingness of the government and the rather powerful Ministry of Finance, led by Dr Thahane, to agree to take on the CGP during an economically insecure time is noteworthy, especially considering the earlier reluctance to involve foreign donors with the OAP. According to the key informants, including Mosisili, the finance ministry did not stand in the way of this programme. However, Pellerano et al. (2016: 269) report 'criticism from key stakeholders' such as the finance ministry in the early stages of the CGP, 'grounded in the lack of evidence that the CGP was an affordable and beneficial intervention that the government could integrate into its budget'. The authors also mention that donors faced 'ideological resistance to cash transfers' (Pellerano et al. 2016: 268).

Certainly, during the interview, Dr Thahane[46] expressed more caution about the child grant than when discussing the OAP: 'The Ministry of Finance reacted cautiously. We had not yet built up a model that would support it. Money was needed for such an investment—can we sustain it? Also, how do you administer it?' Further, the scepticism about donor

[43] Written correspondence, programme manager, EU Delegation to Lesotho, August 2014.
[44] Interview, former prime minister, Maseru, August 2014.
[45] Written correspondence, programme manager, EU Delegation to Lesotho, August 2014.
[46] Interview, former finance minister, Maseru, August 2014.

involvement that Thahane[47] had revealed regarding the implementation of the OAP was evident in the CGP context as well: 'UNICEF, FAO [Food and Agriculture Organization], and the World Bank, they do their separate thing. We need investments that lead to long-term results, and that will increase the tax-base. The finance ministry looks at the total needs of the country'. The former principal secretary of the finance ministry[48] who worked with Thahane at the time also implied that the ministry felt somewhat 'run over' by donors: 'Assuming the responsibility for the child grant was inevitable and known in advance. Donors tend to catalyse policies that would otherwise not receive attention based on single year fiscal considerations. On the other hand, they can elevate donor priorities to be assumed into the budget without much fiscal analysis'. According to Pellerano et al. (2016), the EU and UNICEF addressed government scepticism by providing rigorous evidence through evaluations, and study tours to other countries operating cash transfer systems at a large scale. This was confirmed by the EU representative.[49]

As conveyed by Pellerano et al. (2016: 268), 'the broader political dimension mattered', and the government's commitment to contribute to the CGP was primarily achieved through an agreement with IMF 'for bridging funds and support to its budget'. This circumstance suggests that the Government of Lesotho (GoL) was to some extent pressured to commit domestic resources to this cash transfer programme, regardless of the government's initial concerns about dependency (Pellerano et al. 2016: 268), for instance. Further, the administrative difficulties associated with the OAP and the weakness of the Department of Social Welfare may have contributed to the realization that external technical support was indispensable, even if it would require the involvement of transnational actors.

Consequently, it may have been a combination of the increasingly acute situation created by the HIV/AIDS epidemic in the country, the ability of the EU and UNICEF to 'sell' the programme to the government, as well as pressure by the IMF that enabled the relatively straightforward conception and expansion of the CGP. Mosisili's self-reported favourable views towards the protection of the vulnerable may also have played a role, but they are unlikely to have been decisive. Thus, while the popularity of Mosisili's OAP may have facilitated the gradual acceptance of a cash transfer benefiting OVC,

[47] Interview, former finance minister, Maseru, August 2014.
[48] Written correspondence, former principal secretary of finance ministry, August 2014.
[49] Written correspondence, programme manager, EU Delegation to Lesotho, August 2014.

this programme has followed a very different trajectory than the social pension. Nevertheless, although the CGP initiative was undoubtedly primarily donor-driven, both with regards to ideas and technical expertise, its success would have been unlikely without governmental commitment to the long-term provision for such an initiative.

6. Discussion and Conclusion

While the Lesotho OAP and the CGP certainly differ in terms of their origins and perhaps also in their purpose, both cash transfers provide assistance to destitute groups and have become significant elements of Lesotho's social protection landscape. It can be concluded that both programmes have emerged and grown as the result of an explicit political will to invest in social protection programmes, highlighting the significance of a country's political settlement dynamics as advocated by Lavers and Hickey (2016).

This study suggests that it was the political shift in the early 2000s that facilitated the implementation of a social pension in Lesotho. While interviews with key informants were not able to *unambiguously* provide an explanation for why the OAP was not put into practice until 2004, or uncover why a social pension was added to the political agenda in Lesotho in the first place, the regime change in the early 2000s appears to have been significant. Firstly, Mosisili was an ideological leader holding strong electoral legitimacy. Faced with the HIV/AIDS crisis and its socioeconomic consequences, he appears to have been dedicated to finally initiating the long-promised social pension, having appointed a capable Minister of Finance to support him. Further, there was no debate prior to implementation or attempts to undermine this policy (Lavers and Hickey 2016), corresponding with Khan's 'dominant coalition' type.

Ultimately, the commitment to the OAP does not appear to have been triggered by threats to regime stability but rather by the shift in the power balance from ongoing political conflict to relative stability. Further, this shift and the elite cohesion within the Mosisili government is likely to have improved state capacity to effectively implement social protection programmes, similar to the case studies presented by Lavers and Hickey (2016). Further, the insistence on defining the pension as a right of the elderly and something that one 'deserves' signals that the Lesotho social pension is not simply perceived as a typical 'social welfare' or poverty-reduction initiative. Thus, the strong association of the OAP with former prime minister Mosisili completes the image of a consciously home-grown initiative, particularly since the process behind it deviates significantly from the subsequent donor-driven initiation of the CGP, which lacks such political 'champions'.

The CGP was certainly driven by transnational actors and the GoL may have had to 'give in' to donor pressure to commit domestic funding to the programme. This circumstance strengthens the argument that the CGP developed primarily through a transnational process. Yet, as examples from other African countries show, even donor-driven programmes such as cash grants for OVC require political commitment from the national government in order to succeed long-term. Pellerano et al.'s (2016) account of the extensive efforts required to consolidate the CGP in the government agenda reveal that it was not self-evident that the government would see the value of a CGP and eventually take over the programme. Once again, Lesotho's political stability and rather dominant government may have worked to the advantage of the donors involved in promoting this social protection initiative.

In conclusion, the case of Lesotho indicates a broader preference of some African governments to focus on social assistance for the elderly, as opposed to allocating state funds to similar programmes that are more poverty-focused and specifically target vulnerable groups such as OVC. Firstly, many governments may not have the administrative and technical capacity that is required to carry out complex means testing, so that universal programmes are considered more feasible. Further, the elderly tend to be a rather small group in most sub-Saharan African countries, thus limiting the costs of such programmes. It is also worth bearing in mind that universal (or near-universal) programmes such as the OAP are likely to arouse more enthusiasm among the general population than poverty-targeted ones. Accordingly, as Peyre Dutrey (2007) has suggested, targeted poverty alleviation programmes (as opposed to providing universal support) can even undermine political backing, as the population receiving benefits becomes smaller and less powerful, which may not result in any significant 'political benefits'.

Examples such as Lesotho may thus provide valuable guidelines for foreign donors attempting to collaborate with sub-Saharan African governments when initiating social protection programmes. Kelsall (2016: 3), for instance, proposes that a political settlement analysis can be valuable when distinguishing between country contexts and identifying priority areas in which to work and with whom to partner. Unless supporters of social protection manage to 'get the politics right' in a particular country, as Niño-Zarazúa et al. (2012: 32) have emphasized, it is doubtful whether a proposed social cash transfer programme will obtain government ownership and thus become sustainable, regardless of the target group.

In 2015, after a few years in opposition, Pakalitha Mosisili was once again declared prime minister (as the head of a coalition) after early elections that followed an attempted military coup that had once again triggered a political crisis (The Commonwealth 2016). Thus, Lesotho again found itself in a fragile democracy, while also facing economic hardship (Weisfelder 2015; World Bank 2016a, 2016b). In light of the country's political and financial challenges, the sustainability of the current social cash transfer programmes and the feasibility of their expansion are unclear. Not only has the development budget decreased, partly because of the unstable political situation (UNICEF 2017), but both the OAP and the CGP are still battling with a lack of efficiency, which undermines the impact of these programmes. For instance, 56 per cent of OAP beneficiaries are believed to be 'ghost' pensioners (UNICEF 2017), and Lesotho social assistance transfers have yet to be adjusted for inflation, eroding the practical value of the transfer for its vulnerable recipients (UNICEF 2017). The future of social assistance in Lesotho will most likely continue to depend on political commitment to creating fiscal space for such programmes and their development. Yet, as long as initiatives that aim to relieve poverty and create a foundation for long-term development are overshadowed by inter-party conflicts (and potential donor withdrawal), the odds of the prioritization of such initiatives seem ominous.

Acknowledgements

I would like to express my gratitude to Jeremy Seekings as well as Liz Welsh, Nondumiso Hlwele, and Marius Coqui from the Centre for Social Science Research, University of Cape Town, for their academic, administrative, and practical support. I would also like to thank Miguel Niño-Zarazúa from UNU-WIDER who generously provided me with comments and suggestions on an earlier version of this chapter. Further, this case study would not have been realizable without the valuable time and efforts of the key informants. Your contribution is much appreciated! Finally, a special thank you to Litsoanelo Mapulane Phohleli Tsikoane who very kindly connected me with former Prime Minister Mosisili.

References

Baez, J.E., A. Camacho, E. Conover, and R.A. Zarate (2012). Conditional cash transfers, political participation, and voting behavior. Poverty Reduction and Economic Management Network, Policy Research Working Paper 6215.

Washington DC: World Bank. Available at http://ftp.iza.org/dp6870.pdf [Accessed 15 March 2014].

Barrientos, A. (2009). *Social Pensions in Low-Income Countries*. Manchester: Brooks World Poverty Institute, University of Manchester.

Blank, L. (2008). *Lesotho Child Grant Pilot Operations Manual* (accessed through UNICEF Lesotho in Maseru, May 2014).

Bonnerje, A. (2003). *Pensions in Sub-Saharan Africa: The Urgent Need to Act*. Washington DC: HDNSP, World Bank.

Booysen, S. (2015). The 2015 parliamentary elections in Lesotho. *Electoral Studies*, 40, 430–47.

Casey, B.H. and R. McKinnon (2009). Social pensions and policy learning: the case of Southern Africa. *International Social Security Review*, 62(4), 81–102.

The Commonwealth (2016). Lesotho: constitution and politics. Available at http://thecommonwealth.org/our-member-countries/lesotho/constitution-politics [Accessed 25 May 2016].

Commonwealth Secretariat (2012). *Lesotho Parliamentary Elections*. Report of the Commonwealth Observer Group. Available at http://thecommonwealth.org/sites/default/files/news-items/documents/120529.pdf [Accessed 20 June 2016].

Croome, D., A. Nyanguru, and M. Molisana (2007). *The Impact of the Old-Age Pension on Hunger Vulnerability: A Case-Study from the Mountain Zone of Lesotho*. Prepared for the Regional Hunger Vulnerability Programme. Lesotho: Institute of Southern African Studies, National University of Lesotho.

Davis, B., S. Daldone, and J. Dewbre (2015). *The Impacts of the Child Grants Programme in Lesotho*. The International Policy Centre for Inclusive Growth (IPC-IG). Available at http://www.ipc-undp.org/pub/eng/OP281_The_Impacts_of_the_Child_Grants_Programme_in_Lesotho.pdf [Accessed 25 October 2016].

Devereux, S. (2012). Social protection for enhanced food security in sub-Saharan Africa. UNDP Working Paper 2012-010. United Nations Development Programme, Regional Bureau for Africa.

Devereux, S. (2013). *Social Protection in Swaziland: What Role for the UN?* Centre for Social Protection. Brighton: IDS.

Devereux, S. and P. White (2008). *Social Protection in Africa: Can Evidence, Rights and Politics Converge?* Paper prepared for the conference 'Social Protection for the Poorest in Africa– Learning from Experience'. Entebbe, Uganda.

Devereux, S. and R. Cipryk (2009). *Social Protection in Sub-Saharan Africa*. Brighton: IDS.

Garcia, M. and C.M.T. Moore (2012). *The Cash Dividend. The Rise of Cash Transfer Programs in Sub-Saharan Africa*. Washington DC: World Bank, Directions in Development.

Government of Lesotho (2004). *National Vision 2020*. Maseru: Government of Lesotho.

Government of Lesotho (2005). *Old-Age Pensions Act*. Maseru: Government of Lesotho. Available at http://ilo.org/dyn/natlex/natlex4.detail?p_lang=en&p_isn=93021&p_count=97611 [Accessed 28 May 2016].

Granvik, M. (2016). Policy diffusion, domestic politics and social assistance in Lesotho, 1998–2012. WIDER working paper 2016/146. Helsinki: UNU-WIDER.

Grebe, E. and J.B. Mubiru (2014). Development and social policy reform in Uganda: the slow emergence of a social protection agenda (1986–2014). CSSR Working Paper 353. Cape Town: University of Cape Town.

Hagen, K. (2008). *The Old-Age Pension in Lesotho: An Examination of the Institutional Impact*. Amsterdam: World Granny, University of Utrecht.

Hanlon, J., J. Barrientos, and D. Hulme (2010). *Just Give Money to the Poor: The Development Revolution from the Global South*. Sterling, VA: Kumarian Press.

Hickey, S., R. Sabates-Wheeler, B. Guenther, and I Macaulsan (2009). Promoting social transfers: DFID and the politics of influencing. DFID Working Paper 32. London: DFID.

International Labour Office (ILO) (2014). *Pensions and Other Social Protection Benefits for Older Persons: Insights from the ILO World Social Protection Report 2014/15*. Geneva: ILO.

Kabandula, A. and J. Seekings (2014). *The Limits of Donor Influence and Scaling up Cash Transfer Programmes in Zambia (2003–2013)*. Workshop on Social Protection in Africa. University of Cape Town.

Kelsall, T. (2016). *Thinking and Working with Political Settlements*, ODI Briefing. London: Overseas Development Institute.

Lavers, T. and S. Hickey (2016). Conceptualising the politics of social protection in low income countries: the intersection of transnational ideas and domestic politics. *International Journal of Social Welfare*, 25(4), 388–98.

Likoti, F.J. (2009). The 2007 general election in Lesotho: the application and the challenges of the electoral system. *African Studies Quarterly*, 10(4), 57–69.

Makenete, A., G. Ortmann, and M. Darroch (1998). Food-aid dependency in Lesotho: issues and policy implications. *Development Southern Africa*, 15(2), 251–65.

Maleleka, D. (2009). *The Impact of Democracy in Lesotho: Assessing Political, Social and Economic Developments Since the Dawn of Democracy*. Johannesburg: Centre for Policy Studies.

Matlosa, K. (1997). The 1993 elections in Lesotho and the nature of the BCP victory. *African Journal of Political Science*, 2(1), 140–51.

May, J., B. Roberts, G. Moqasa, and I. Woolard (2002). Poverty and inequality in Lesotho. Working Paper 36. KwaZulu-Natal: Centre for Civil Society, University of KwaZulu-Natal.

Mugomeri, E., B.S. Bekele, M. Mafaesa, C. Maibvise, C. Tarirai, and S.E. Aiyuk (2017). A 30-year bibliometric analysis of research coverage on HIV and AIDS in Lesotho. *Health Research Policy and Systems*, 15(1), 21.

Niño-Zarazúa M., A. Barrientos, D. Hulme, and S. Hickey (2012). Social protection in sub-Saharan Africa: getting the politics right. *World Development*, 40(1), 163–76.

Obinger, H., C. Schmitt, and P. Starke (2013). Policy diffusion and policy transfer in comparative welfare state research. *Social Policy & Administration*, 47(1), 111–29.

Olivier, M. (2013a). Social protection in Lesotho: innovations and reform challenges. *Development Southern Africa*, 30(1), 98–110.

Olivier, M. (2013b). *Study on Social Protection in Sub-Saharan Africa.* Lesotho Case Study: Report. Available at http://www.saspen.org/DocumentsThirdParty/EC_Report-Lesotho-Social-Protection_2013-Olivier.pdf [Accessed 5 June 2017].

Owusu-Ampomah, K., S. Naysmith, and C. Rubincam (2009). *Reviewing 'Emergencies' in HIV and AIDS-Affected Countries in Southern Africa: Shifting the Paradigm in Lesotho.* National AIDS Commission, Lesotho and Health Economics and HIV/AIDS Research Division (HEARD), University of KwaZulu-Natal.

Pelham, L. (2007). The politics behind the non-contributory old age social pensions in Lesotho, Namibia and South Africa. CPRC Working Paper 83. Manchester: Chronic Poverty Research Centre, Institute for Development Policy and Management, School of Environment and Development, University of Manchester.

Pellerano, L., S. Daidone, B. Davis, M. Farooq, M. Homayoun, A. Kardan, M. Masasa, O. Niang, B. Ramirez, and N. Safi (2016). Does evidence matter? Role of the evaluation of the child grants programme in the consolidation of the social protection sector in Lesotho. In B. Davis, S. Handa, N. Hypher, N. Winder Rossi, P. Winters, and J. Yablonski (Eds.), *From Evidence to Action.* Oxford: Oxford University Press.

Pension Watch (2018). HelpAge International Pension Watch Database. March 2018. Available at http://www.pension-watch.net/social-pensions-database/social-pensions-database—[Accessed 15 December 2018].

Peyre Dutrey, A. (2007). Successful targeting? Reporting efficiency and costs in targeted poverty alleviation programmes. United Nations Research Institute for Social Development, Social Policy and Development Programme Paper 35. Available at http://www.unrisd.org/80256B3C005BCCF9/(httpAuxPages)/

0B87C67449C938EDC12573D10049830B/$file/Peyrepap.pdf [Accessed 28 October 2016].

Rich, T.S., V. Banerjee, and S. Recker (2013). Identifying the institutional effects of mixed systems in new democracies: the case of Lesotho. *Journal of Asian and African Studies*, 12, 1–17.

Rosenberg, S. and R.F. Weisfelder (2013). *Historical Dictionary of Lesotho*. Plymouth: Scarecrow Press.

Sepúlveda, M. and C. Nyst (2012). *Human Rights Approach to Social Protection*. Ministry of Foreign Affairs, Finland. Helsinki: MFA Finland. Available at http://www.ohchr.org/Documents/Issues/EPoverty/HumanRightsApproachToSocialProtection.pdf [Accessed 5 November 2016].

Thomson, A. and A. Kardan (2012). *Support to Lesotho HIV and AIDS Response: Empowerment of Orphans and Other Vulnerable Children*. Final Evaluation. Oxford: Oxford Policy Management.

UNAIDS (2004). Lesotho: epidemiological fact sheets on HIV/AIDS and sexually transmitted infections. Available at http://data.unaids.org/publications/fact-sheets01/lesotho_en.pdf [Accessed 30 October 2016].

UNICEF (2017). Lesotho social assistance budget brief. Available at https://www.unicef.org/esaro/UNICEF-Lesotho-2017-Social-Assistance-Budget-Brief.pdf.

Weisfelder, R.F. (2015). Free elections and political instability in Lesotho. *Journal of African Elections*, 2, 50–80.

World Bank (2013). *Lesotho, a Safety Net to End Extreme Poverty*. Report 77767-LS. Washington DC: World Bank.

World Bank (2016a). Lesotho. Washington DC: World Bank. Available at http://www.worldbank.org/en/country/lesotho/overview [Accessed 1 November 2016].

World Bank (2016b). *Macro Poverty Outlook for Lesotho*. Available at http://www-wds.worldbank.org/external/default/WDSContentServer/WDSP/IB/2016/04/14/090224b084298a56/1_0/Rendered/PDF/Macro0poverty0outlook0for0Lesotho.pdf [Accessed 1 November 2016].

World Food Programme (2016). Lesotho. Available at https://www.wfp.org/countries/lesotho [Accessed 22 October 2016].

7

The Politics of Promoting Social Cash Transfers in Zambia

Kate Pruce and Sam Hickey

1. Introduction

In 2013, Zambia's then Minister of Finance announced that there would be a 700 per cent increase in the budget for what was then a pilot social cash transfer programme. The move took everyone by surprise, including the coalition of international donors, government officials, and civil society actors who had been responsible for promoting the pilot programme and who had been calling for its scale-up, amidst support for a broader social protection agenda in Zambia for nearly a decade. Over roughly the same period, barely any progress had been made on other elements of this agenda. By mid-2016, the social cash transfer scheme had received another boost, with the 2015 budget being further increased by two thirds, from 180 million kwacha to just over 300 million kwacha, enabling a scale-up from fifty to seventy-eight districts by the end of the year.

In seeking to account for the shifting politics of commitment to social protection in Zambia, this chapter goes beyond the focus on elections and institutions within mainstream accounts of how social protection is likely to emerge in Africa, and draws attention instead to the underlying dynamics of politics and power that shape elite commitment. This chapter focuses on social cash transfers (SCTs) as the most rapidly expanding aspect of Zambia's National Social Protection Strategy, and argues that their rise reflects the interplay of transnational advocacy with the shifting dynamics of Zambia's 'political settlement', as primarily shaped by the incentives and ideas of ruling elites. These insights emerge from our employment of a new conceptual approach to understand the political economy of social protection in Africa (Lavers and Hickey 2016). This approach incorporates insights from the literature on welfare state development and social protection in both industrialized countries

Kate Pruce and Sam Hickey, *The Politics of Promoting Social Cash Transfers in Zambia* In: *The Politics of Social Protection in Eastern and Southern Africa*. Edited by: Sam Hickey, Tom Lavers, Miguel Niño-Zarazúa, and Jeremy Seekings, Oxford University Press (2020).
DOI: 10.1093/oso/9780198850342.003.0007

and the global South (Huber and Stephens 2012; Kpessa and Béland 2013; also Barrientos and Pellissery 2012; Hickey 2007; Niño-Zarazúa et al. 2012); the politics of development, with a focus on power relations (DiJohn and Putzel 2009; Khan 2010); the role of ideas in shaping political behaviour and institutional change (Hay 2011; Schmidt 2008); and the role of transnational actors, including global policy networks (Stone 2008). The framework is explained further in Lavers and Hickey (2016) and also in Chapter 1 of this book.

The policy case examined here helps illustrate the potential of this new approach for understanding how welfare regimes may be emerging in Africa. We demonstrate that struggles to promote social protection in Zambia have occurred both within and between the policy coalition promoting SCTs and the national ruling coalition. This is taking place in a transnationalized context in which global actors and flows of both resources and ideas are embedded within these coalition-building processes. For example, the efforts of a transnational policy coalition to promote SCTs over the 2000s had been heavily contested by officials and politicians, particularly the Minister of Finance who stated that poverty did not exist and that SCTs encouraged laziness (Hickey et al. 2009; Kabandula and Seekings 2016), reflecting a view that the main policy priority should be growth (Barrientos et al. 2005). By 2012, advocates had made some inroads into this opposition, producing a wealth of evidence in support of cash transfers and undertaking extensive informal lobbying. In 2011 a new political party came to power with a mandate to distribute resources to poorer groups. However, our analysis shows that the actual decision to scale up government support in 2013 came about not from these enabling factors per se but from the shifting dynamics of Zambia's political settlement, and in particular a perceived crisis within existing means of distributing resources to rural areas.

This narrative, which we set out in more detail below, emerges from our adoption of a process-tracing methodology that seeks to identify the causal mechanisms leading to specific observed outcomes, through a theoretically based historical explanation of a sequence of events (George and Bennett 2005). In this study, the observed outcome is the political decision to scale up SCTs in Zambia. This investigation involved documentary analysis and over thirty semi-structured key informant interviews with the main stakeholders involved in the process, including government representatives, both politicians and technocrats; Zambian organizations ranging from civil social organizations to think tanks and consultancies; representatives of co-operating partners, mainly the multilateral and bilateral donors engaged in the process; as well as key individuals who are currently unaffiliated. The interviews were conducted during fieldwork undertaken in Zambia in April to May 2015.

The chapter proceeds by outlining the shifting political settlement in Zambia from independence to the present day. It then sets out the process through which the transnational policy coalition sought to promote SCTs from the early 2000s, before providing an analytical discussion through the lens of our political settlements framework, and finally a conclusion.

2. The Political Settlement in Zambia

Zambia's political settlement, understood here as 'the balance of power between contending social groups on which any state is based' (Di John and Putzel 2009: 4), has undergone a series of shifts in the decades since independence. Strongly informed by the legacy of colonial rule, under which projects of state formation and governmentality took shape around the construction of ethno-linguistic groups, the efforts of successive ruling coalitions to enforce a stable set of institutions capable of delivering an acceptable distribution of rents have been influenced by this balance of power (Khan 2010). Colonial rule saw the country divided into five ethno-linguistic groupings: Bemba (43 per cent of the population), Nyanja (18 per cent), Tonga (including Ila and Lenje, 19 per cent), Lozi (8 per cent), and the north-west region (12 per cent) (Scarritt 2006). As Scarritt (2006: 239) notes, 'these linguistic groups were constructed before they were politicised through conflicts within the nationalist movement and post-independence parties' with the north-west region, where none of the four major languages predominate, 'constructed ... in response to the politicisation of the other groups' (ibid.). With no single group able to dominate alone, the politics of forming ruling coalitions in post-colonial Zambia has been shaped by efforts to form coalitions across these groups, with a tendency to seek 'inclusive or oversized rather than minimum winning coalitions' (Scarritt 2006: 234).

Following Khan (2010), forming such coalitions involves navigating the balance of power both in horizontal terms, regarding relations between elite factions, and also vertically, regarding the relationship between elites and wider social groups. We now set out the historical character of the political settlement in Zambia since independence until the current moment, with a focus on the shifting balance of power along these dimensions and the dominant incentives and ideas that have prevailed within different ruling coalitions over this time period. Although this history includes the shift from the single-party tendencies of Kenneth Kaunda's United National Independence Party (UNIP) to the return of multi-party politics in 1991, our focus on the underlying logics of how ruling coalitions are formed enables the analysis to move beyond the limits of formal institutional analysis in examining the deeper politics of development in Zambia.

2.1. Inter-elite relations and coalition-building in post-colonial Zambia

In the early independence period, the strategy of building inclusive ruling coalitions, the related discourse of 'One Zambia, One Nation', and modernist narratives of development as part of the nationalist, state-building project led by Kaunda (Larmer et al. 2014) all helped underpin an often progressive period of economic and social development. Boosted by high copper prices, the initial political and development strategy had positive pay-offs in terms of generating stability, a sense of nationhood, and a degree of human development (Noyoo 2010). However, the centralization of power within the presidency and the emergence of a system of neopatrimonialism, both to satisfy the demands of factions and for personal gain, undermined bureaucratic capacity and autonomy, and reduced public sector efficiency (Erdmann and Simutanyi 2003). The inclusive strategy also proved costly, including through the establishment of numerous ministerial positions and the nationalization of several economic enterprises in the late 1960s, primarily as a means of allocating rents between dominant groups (Lindemann 2011: 1852). The falling prices of copper during the 1970s threw this politics of development into sharp relief: drastic reductions were made to expenditure on social services, the greater proportion of which was spent on personal emoluments, such as salaries and expenses for staff, with only 2.3 per cent being spent on programmes in 1980 (Dixon 1987).

This mode of governance would also have political ramifications for Zambia's first ruling coalition, in part because it failed to align itself fully with the country's resource-based political economy. The centrality of the Copperbelt to the extractive strategies of the colonial administration led to widespread in-migration into the area and the formation of socio-political identities along class rather than ethnic lines. As a result, 'the multi-ethnic Copperbelt gave rise to a broad-based nationalist movement' (Lindemann 2011: 1848), generating urban and unionized factions that closely shaped the politics of independence in Zambia but which gained very little from Kaunda's use of ethno-linguistic ties as the basis for political inclusion. Importantly, it was these groups, along with businessmen, churches, and intellectuals, which would eventually depose Kaunda through the Movement for Multiparty Democracy (MMD) in 1991 (Erdmann and Simutanyi 2003).

The reintroduction of multi-party politics at this time changed but did not fully transform how politics works in Zambia. Once in power, successive governments would seek to cement inclusive coalitions, deploying a strategy of ethno-regional balance in the allocation of key positions within the executive, administration, military, and parastatal sector (Lindemann 2011). Although successful in terms of maintaining stability, the rapid growth of ministries and the civil service that this strategy entailed would once again undermine the country's development prospects. As Lindemann (2011: 1864) notes, 'while the civil service as an important bastion of the elite bargain was protected, expenditure cuts were implemented in public investment and social spending, with obvious implications for economic development' (ibid.: 1864). This mode of elite incorporation, with appointments given on the basis of identity rather than expertise, helped feed expectations amongst citizens that the primary role of their representatives in power was to secure their support through the vertical distribution of rents, particularly through public sector employment and agricultural food subsidies (see section 2.2).

The incentive to forge an inclusive coalition inevitably directs a great deal of energy inwards to managing competing factions within the ruling coalition, thus reducing the level of elite cohesion and focus on development (Levy 2014). There was also an important ideational element to this apparent reluctance to redistribute resources in a systematic way. A survey of Zambia's elite in the first decade of independence found that they tended to emphasize equality of opportunity rather than equality of outcome, a tendency that seems likely to have reduced their preference for redistributive policies (Scarritt 2006). More recent findings (Scarritt 2010) reveal that Zambia's political elites tend to prioritize the acquisition of status over concerns with equality. This helps to explain their emphasis on maintaining status through centralized processes of capturing rents and inter-elite bargaining regarding the horizontal balance of power amongst elites, rather than putting in place effective mechanisms of rent distribution to manage the vertical dimensions of power within Zambia's political settlement.

The extension of political space offered by the return of multi-party politics has arguably intensified this tendency by creating a clearer exit option for elites dissatisfied with their status within the ruling coalition. The incentives for dissatisfied elites to leave and form their own challenger parties are further raised by the presidentialist character of the political system in Zambia, whereby the president holds significant personal powers concerning appointments and rents. This centralization of power has created numerous problems in Zambia, including deficits in political accountability and a weak parliament that struggles to make meaningful policy changes without executive turnovers (Evans 2018). Importantly, it creates a strong incentive for internal squabbles over party leadership and succession issues (Scarritt 2006: 240), and raises the attractiveness for elites of leaving and forming their own party as a basis for running for office. This occurred during Frederick Chiluba's push for a third term (Lindemann 2011: 1860), which saw MMD Minister Michael Sata leave and form his own party, the Patriotic Front (PF) (Scarritt 2006: 249).[1]

2.2. The increased importance of vertical power relations under multi-party politics in Zambia

The broad-based coalition of economic and social interest groups that brought the MMD to power soon splintered. This was partly due to Chiluba's brand of presidentialism and partly because ongoing processes of economic and political liberalization were undermining the productive and organizational basis of key socioeconomic groupings in ways that limited their role in governance (Rakner 2003). Increasingly closely fought elections further increased the vulnerability of the MMD ruling coalition over the 2000s. With the political loyalties of lower-level factions now up for grabs within the new political marketplace, certain forms of clientelism intensified, particularly in the form of agricultural subsidies, mainly fertilizer and maize seed (Mason et al. 2013).

The MMD's distribution of agricultural subsidies during the 1990s and 2000s was highly politicized. Universal subsidies were replaced by more targeted approaches, ostensibly on cost-cutting grounds but in ways that enabled government to target them politically. According to Mason et al. (2013: 2) 'the scale of the programs . . . has increased dramatically over the last decade, e.g. from 48,000 metric tons (MT) of fertilizer in 2002 to 184,000 MT in 2012', with households in constituencies won by MMD in the last presidential election receiving an average of between 16.2kg and 23.2kg more subsidized fertilizer compared to households in areas that MMD lost. Just before the September 2011 elections, 'Banda dramatically scaled up Farmer Input

[1] Which, contrary to earlier history (Scarritt 2006), proved to be an electorally successful strategy in the end, perhaps as Sata worked out how to mobilize a different kind of coalition based on urban support, as MMD did when they gained power in 1991.

Support Programme from 100,000 MT in 2009/10 to 178,000 MT in 2010/11. The move proved insufficient to secure a victory, however, and Michael Sata (Patriotic Front) defeated him by nearly seven percentage points' (ibid.: 4).

Politics took on a more populist character in Zambia over this time period (Cheeseman and Hinfelaar 2010), not least in the pursuit of the urban vote which has become increasingly crucial to the electoral turnovers (Rakner and Helle 2012) that help define Zambia's competitive clientelism. When MMD took power in 1991 they gained 95 per cent of seats in urban areas, and urban voters would again be critical in bringing the PF to power in 2011. Under Michael Sata's leadership the PF would promote a distinctive brand of 'ethno-populism', aimed at wooing urban voters and challenging the sense that the party was over-reliant on support from Bemba voters (Cheeseman and Larmer 2015; Larmer and Fraser 2007). A focus on generating support amongst urban working classes and the intelligentsia led to a leftist policy agenda focused on the labour market: minimum wages, labour relations, and being tough on businesses (Rakner and Helle 2012: 11). Sata's strategy also included messages on social inclusion and anti-elitism to attract the urban poor (Resnick 2014). Its appeal to rural voters was also populist in tone, with broad claims to be 'pro-poor' and promises to 'put more money in people's pockets'. In electoral terms, this strategy helped enable the PF go from gaining 3 per cent of the vote in 2001 to winning the 2011 election (Cheeseman and Larmer 2015), and brought into power a ruling coalition more directly oriented towards subordinate groups than its predecessors.

Meanwhile, the formal institutional aspects of democratization in Zambia seemed to be stalling. The vibrant independent media and civil society that initially flourished in the transition to multi-party politics struggled to become institutionalized. Although civil society recorded an historic victory in preventing President Chiluba from amending the constitution in order to allow him to stand for a third term (Gould 2006), later campaigns around the constitution in 2007 and democracy in 2012 largely failed. Given the defining influence of clientelism over state–society relationships, observers noted that the influence of the citizen voice over the delivery of public goods and services tended to flounder (Harland 2014; Kuss 2015).

3. The Rise of Social Cash Transfers in Zambia

Efforts by external actors to promote a government-owned social protection agenda in Zambia from the early 2000s encountered a challenging environment, not only in terms of the political settlement dynamics at the time but also with regards to the country's institutional and ideational context. From 1975 onwards, reform and structural adjustment programmes had promoted the role of market, rather than state, as the mechanism for allocating resources in Zambia (Mhone 2004). Along with declining civil service performance, this led to a wide range of non-state actors, including NGOs and church organizations, playing an increased role in delivering services (Duncan et al. 2003). The influential role of international agencies over social policy at this time further underlined the growing 'externalisation of social provision' within Zambia's 'welfare regime' (Larmer et al. 2014).

Despite Zambia experiencing a significant decline in living standards over this period, the 'social protection agenda' was virtually non-existent beyond a residual Public Welfare Assistance Scheme (PWAS) (Harland 2014). Established in the 1950s, PWAS is an unconditional in-kind transfer with the aim of meeting the basic needs of people unable to support themselves, which was redesigned and relaunched in the late 1990s in response to the country's experience of one of Africa's worst HIV/AIDS pandemics. While PWAS and the first SCT pilot both aimed to mitigate the effects of HIV/AIDS on households with limited labour capacity and high dependency ratios, this factor did not emerge as being central to the strategy to influence government to adopt social protection in this case. Importantly, the pandemic did not lead to the crisis of governance that some predicted at the time (de Waal 2003), and therefore had relatively little impact on the functioning and character of the political settlement in Zambia.

More broadly, Zambia's high levels of indebtedness had led it to sign up to the Poverty Reduction Strategy Paper experiment in 2001. Although this would provide a window through which donors could start promoting social protection, there was strong opposition from within government to pursuing a redistributive agenda which was at odds with both the then government's 'growth-first' approach and longer-standing elite ideas around deservingness and equality, such that: 'the prevailing political discourse in Zambia tends to favour the "productive" segment of the population' (Hickey et al. 2009: 77). This was reflected in programmes being targeted at 'vulnerable but viable' farmers and the productivist, infrastructure-oriented character of Zambia's Fifth National Development Plan that replaced the Poverty Reduction Strategy Papers in 2006.

Towards the end of the 2000s, however, it was increasingly clear that Zambia's impressive rates of growth of 5–6 per cent had not translated into poverty reduction. The number of people falling below the poverty line remained stubbornly high at 60.5 per cent in 2010, with the number in extreme poverty standing at 42 per cent (Central Statistical Office 2011). This convergence between questions being raised over the growth-first strategy and the ascent to power of the PF in 2011 on a pro-poor agenda raised hopes that Zambia's national development planning would become more focused on poverty reduction, including social protection.

By the time of this promising convergence, international development agencies had spent nearly a decade trying to promote social protection in Zambia. This effort unfolded through three main phases: the first involved the introduction by the German Development Agency (GTZ) of a pilot cash transfer scheme in 2003 which catalysed a concerted effort by donors to promote social protection through building a broader constituency of support behind this new policy agenda. Once a scaled-up SCT programme was agreed with the Zambian government in 2010, the next phase involved donors building the capacity of the government to deliver SCTs alongside a continued advocacy campaign. Finally, the current phase of expansion and roll-out began in 2013 with the announcement of a 700 per cent increase for SCTs in the national budget and adoption of a national social protection strategy.[2] This increased financial commitment from the government, from a base of 17.4 million kwacha to 150 million kwacha, meant that the government displaced donors as the main financier of cash transfers and would enable a further expansion to fifty districts by the end of 2014. Section 3 describes how these phases unfolded before section 4 analyses the political drivers of these shifts through the political settlements framework introduced earlier.

3.1. Promoting social protection and cash transfers in Zambia

In 2003, GTZ approached the Ministry of Community Development with the suggestion of a pilot cash transfer scheme. The GTZ model was designed to respond to high levels of food poverty and labour constrained households, exacerbated by the burden of HIV (Schubert 2005). Despite requests from relevant officials that the pilot scheme be integrated within the scaled-up

[2] In June 2014 the Zambian government published a National Social Protection Policy that encompassed a range of instruments, including the scaled-up SCT programme, a new social health insurance scheme, and proposed reforms to public sector pensions. This umbrella approach was proposed by a Cabinet sub-committee chaired by the Cabinet Secretary and the various stakeholders had little choice but to support it, despite some disagreements between the Ministries of Community Development and Health, and their respective co-operating partners, regarding which of their preferred policy instruments should be pursued as a priority.

PWAS, which the then finance minister supported (ZK1), the project was designed as a separate entity, with GTZ focusing its assistance only on the structures and capacity needed for implementation in a small part of Kalomo district (Harland 2014). This scheme would go on to generate what one respondent referred to as 'Kalomo mania' (ZK1), forming a key reference point in the wider transnational effort to establish social protection as a global policy agenda (Hickey and Seekings 2017). Meanwhile, the resources and attention directed to the new national PWAS dwindled (Harland 2014).

In late 2003, social development advisors from the UK Department for International Development (DFID) and the World Bank proposed to the government that they establish a Sector Advisory Group on Social Protection. This would be chaired by the Ministry of Community Development and directly inform the Poverty Reduction Strategy Paper review process. The two agencies were not always in accord: they strongly disagreed about the use of conditionality in low-income African countries (Schubert and Slater 2006), and the Bank promoted its 'social risk management' approach whilst DFID chose a consultant associated with an alternative perspective on social protection as transformation to write the strategy paper for the new sector (Hickey et al. 2009). A chapter on social protection nonetheless formed part of what became the Fifth National Development Plan, and although the numerous programmes listed there received little funding or political attention, social protection had been established on the policy, if not the political, agenda.

By 2007, variants of the Kalomo scheme were operating in parts of five districts, reaching some 12,000 beneficiary households, with funding from DFID (Harland 2014). Delivery was undertaken by the Ministry of Community Development with assistance from GTZ (Schubert 2005), CARE International, and HelpAge International. Meanwhile, the shifting dynamics of aid enabled DFID to take a lead on policy advocacy and development. Zambia's adoption of the Joint Assistance Strategy in 2007, informed by Paris Declaration principles concerning harmonization, led both GTZ and the Bank to leave the social protection sector, clearing the way for DFID to take a lead alongside like-minded donors such as UNICEF and Irish Aid.

DFID's efforts to promote social protection in partnership with the Ministry of Community Development enabled it to strongly influence policy development and build a cadre of committed civil servants. An account of this process in Zambia drawing on insights from practitioners attests to the strengthening of Zambian technical assistants vis-à-vis their international counterparts between 2005 and 2010 (Quarles van Ufford et al. 2016). However, this did not lead to increased government ownership of the agenda, given the ministry's marginal role within the Zambian government and strong opposition from more powerful ministries (Hickey et al. 2009), particularly the finance ministry (ZG9). From 2005 onwards, DFID Zambia started to adopt a more politically informed approach to building a constituency for social protection, informed in part by their commissioning of a 'drivers of change' study (Barrientos et al. 2005). This strategy had both technical and political elements, from building the evidence base for social protection through to study tours (including to Kalomo, South Africa, Lesotho, Brazil, and Chile) and informal meetings, increasingly targeted at powerful players within the finance ministry and the political elite.

3.2. Strengthening and scaling up

By 2009, DFID had been joined by UNICEF as co-leads of the social protection co-operating partners group and succeeded in gaining government support for the Social Protection Expansion Programme. This included a gradual expansion of SCTs targeting the poorest and most vulnerable households made up of the elderly above the age of sixty, children under the age of five, and adults who are chronically ill, affected by HIV/AIDS, or living with disabilities, to be increasingly funded by GRZ. At the meeting scheduled for signing this agreement, the Minister of Finance (Dr Situmbeko Musokotwane) was 'very nervous' that DFID were proposing a programme of £32 million over only seven years, after which the responsibility for its continuation would fall to the government. He therefore requested that DFID commit for ten years, which it duly did to the tune of £38 million (ZC2). This marked a significant shift regarding the ministry's erstwhile opposition to social protection. The previous finance minister, N'gandu Magande (2003–8), opposed SCTs, with objections that were 'rooted in his own personal narrative of hard work and determination' (Kabandula and Seekings 2016: 23) but which were also characteristic of the political elite in Zambia (Scarritt 2006). Committed to the trickle-down model of growth, Magande believed that SCTs would encourage dependency (ZG1, ZG9), rather than upwards mobility (ZC2), and had declared that 'poverty did not exist in Zambia'; rather, the problem was 'laziness' (Barrientos et al. 2005).

Like Kabandula and Seekings (2016), we identify Magande as a significant barrier to the expansion of SCTs because of his ideological resistance to the programme and critical role in the policy process as Minister of Finance. When President Mwanawasa passed away in office in 2008 and Rupiah

Banda was elected as his replacement in the presidential by-election, the resulting Cabinet reshuffle led to Magande's replacement by a finance minister less ideologically opposed to cash transfers. It was under this new minister that the DFID agreement was signed. However, where they use this case to demonstrate the limits of donor power and suggest the failure of the political advocacy undertaken by the pro-social protection policy coalition (Kabandula and Seekings 2016), we note that this coalition was successful in attracting meaningful support from lower-level officials within the finance ministry that would later prove beneficial. In particular, and in line with the 'best-placing' logic of the thinking-and-working politically approach (Booth and Unsworth 2014), coalition members worked hard to identify and persuade fast-rising finance ministry officials of the economic benefits and moral case for cash transfers. When the political window opened in 2013, it was these officials, now operating at more senior levels within the ministry, who were able and willing to draw the president's attention to the SCT pilot programme as a mechanism for achieving certain campaign promises.

From 2010 onwards, there was a concerted effort by the policy coalition to build a stronger evidence base in support of SCTs. This went beyond the initial evaluations of the Kalomo pilot (MCDSS and GTZ 2007; Wietler 2007), which lacked a control group, and focused on randomized controlled trial (RCT) evaluations carried out by independent consultancy firms (ZG1). This approach was considered more politically persuasive: 'they certainly like evidence, ministers love it, they're all doctors so they love RCTs' (ZC2). Nonetheless, the process of getting the evidence in front of senior government figures required a significant, and largely informal, backstage effort by a senior Zambian consultant who had been hired by DFID to deploy his long-established elite-level networks to generate awareness of and support for social protection in Zambia. This 'broker' managed to convene a high-level workshop in 2012 during which the results of both the RCT studies and a recent World Bank assessment of SCTs were delivered and discussed with senior civil servants from all key ministries, including finance, and with the Cabinet secretary chairing.

The impact evaluations refuted the belief that recipients of cash transfers would work less, and offered clear evidence that the transfers could reduce poverty and contribute to the economy (ZG1). Importantly, the World Bank report revealed how badly other interventions, including agricultural subsidies, were faring in comparison to SCTs, both in terms of their cost-effectiveness and success in reaching poor people. This evidence base was particularly critical to gaining support within the finance ministry.

3.3. Government budget increase for SCTs

When the PF gained power in 2011 on a pro-poor ticket, including a manifesto commitment to rolling out 'social transfers', this raised hopes that social protection would now become a political priority. Nonetheless, the Minister of Finance's announcement on 11 October 2013 that the 2014 budget would increase government financing for SCTs by 700 per cent and that a national social protection policy would be prioritized (Chikwanda 2013) came 'out of the blue' (ZC2) to proponents of the programme. The commitment exceeded both the co-financing agreement within the Social Protection Expansion Programme and the budget request from the Ministry of Community Development for that year, which was only 53 million kwacha (ZG2).

This announcement flowed directly from a scandal that broke in 2013 concerning massive overspending on the budget lines for the Farmer Input Support Programme (FISP) and the Food Reserve Agency (FRA) (ZC6, ZK2). This crisis led to a public announcement by Sata that resources would be channelled to 'the very poor citizens of our society'[3] with some funds redirected from agricultural subsidies to the SCT programme. The amount allocated to the SCT programme at this point was still tiny compared to such subsidies.[4] Programmes such as FISP and FRA continue to pull significant resources away from other forms of social protection, with budgeted amounts for FISP actually increasing in 2014–15. When the SCT budget failed to increase as expected in 2015 there were fears that the scale-up would stall, not least as President Sata, apparent champion of cash transfers, passed away in 2014. These fears seemed to be confirmed when the Medium-Term Expenditure Framework (MTEF) for 2015–17 indicated that the budget for SCTs would remain at 150 million kwacha per year until 2016/17 (Ministry of Finance 2014). These concerns have since been allayed by renewed government promises to progressively increase the SCT budget allocation, supported by the new MTEF for 2016–18 in which the domestically financed contribution to SCTs would be increased to 350 million kwacha by 2018 (Ministry of Finance 2015).

[3] https://www.lusakatimes.com/2013/05/15/president-michael-sata-defends-the-removal-of-maize-subsidies.

[4] In the 2015 budget, 1.3 billion kwacha is included for social protection, which is 2.7 per cent of the total budget, but the majority is for the Public Service Pension Fund. The amount allocated to SCTs, 180 million kwacha, is only 0.4 per cent of the total budget (Chikwanda 2014). A further 1.1 billion kwacha (2.3 per cent of the total budget) has been allocated to FISP.

4. Transnational Policy Coalitions, the Political Settlement, and the Role of Ideas

Our investigation suggests that elite commitment to social protection in Zambia has been shaped by the interplay of a transnational effort to form a policy coalition in favour of the agenda, political settlement dynamics, and the cross-cutting role of ideas. This section analyses the relative progress of the SCT policy reform in relation to these key elements of the conceptual framework outlined in Lavers and Hickey (2016).

4.1. Transnational policy coalitions and local wars of position

The formation of policy coalitions has become increasingly deployed as a strategy for achieving policy reform in developing countries (Leftwich 2012), perhaps reflecting the reduced capacity of donors to directly influence policymaking in fast-developing countries.[5] In Zambia, this involved international donors trying to shift the balance of power between the 'civil society tendency' (involving social sector ministries, certain donors, and civil society organizations) and the finance ministry tendency, with its often paradigmatically opposed ideas about development (Kanbur 2001), a divide that reflected the global level 'wars of position' being fought over social protection at this point (Deacon 2007).

Informed by a political economy analysis of the policy process in Zambia, donors deployed a mixture of technical and political strategies within this struggle. This went beyond producing and disseminating evidence and offering technical assistance for programme design, to directly targeting rising stars within the finance ministry (two of whom would become Permanent Secretary and Director of Planning) and ensuring that the Ministry of Community Development had a desk officer in the Ministry of Finance. The use of a 'broker' with high-level political and bureaucratic connections and the skills to facilitate discussions across competing tendencies assisted this process.

This politically attuned strategy was further enabled by the nature of the development advisors and agencies involved. Two of the key proponents

[5] Assistance to the budget from traditional donors has declined in recent years from around 60 per cent in the early 1990s to less than 30 per cent in 2009, with official development assistance down to 11.2 per cent of Gross National Income (GNI) in 2009 (BTI 2012). This reflects debt relief and economic growth and the growing role of new donors such as China and private foundations (Faust et al. 2012).

working for DFID and UNICEF were strongly rooted in the Zambian context and remained in their posts much longer than is normal within the development industry's usual three-year posting cycle. This, and their close working relationship, helped to further improve the level of donor co-ordination after the departure of the World Bank and GTZ in 2007.[6] Strong support from the country leads and headquarters of each agency was also important here.

The relative power of the government protagonists in this struggle was also significant. For most of the 2000s the Ministry of Community Development and Social Services was 'not seen by more powerful ministries as a particularly convincing policy champion in the field of poverty reduction' (Barrientos et al. 2005: 10). Under the PF government, the ministry was renamed the Ministry of Community Development and Mother and Child Health (MCDMCH). With its new remit over a significant proportion of the health budget and health sector personnel, the ministry became the second biggest-spending ministry after education, and was seen as a more credible home for new policy initiatives and increased budgetary allocations (ZG2, ZK1).[7] The Ministry of Finance also underwent important shifts, most notably in terms of ministerial appointments and a growing appreciation of the limits of its neoliberal growth-first strategy.

4.2. Political settlement dynamics in Zambia: the deepening of competitive clientelism and enduring importance of rent distribution

Whilst the efforts of the transnational policy coalition helped turn SCTs into a credible policy instrument, the dramatic funding increase in 2013 directly reflected the wider workings of Zambia's competitive clientelist political settlement, particularly in terms of the shifting nature of the ruling coalition and a crisis of rent distribution to rural areas. In their account of the 2013 SCT scale-up, Quarles van Ufford et al. (2016) argue that there was a combination

[6] The re-entry of the World Bank into the social protection sector in 2012 has raised concerns that earlier disagreements will resurface and undermine the coherence of the policy coalition. However, the critical 2013 workshop revealed the benefits of having the convening power of this 'knowledge broker' onside, not least as the Bank has so far been the only agency brave enough to tackle the Zambian government concerning its use of agricultural subsidies (ZC2).

[7] However, this realignment has now been reversed with responsibility for maternal and child health moved back to the Ministry of Health; it remains to be seen whether the increased status and capacity brought about by the larger mandate are retained.

of influential factors, with no single factor sufficient to trigger the decision.[8] We have shown above that the increase in funding for SCTs was directly informed by a public scandal in 2013 concerning massive overspending on the FISP and the FRA (ZC6, ZK2). Elected on a pro-poor policy platform, this led the PF president to actively search out alternative policy instruments which could help him to fulfil this pledge,[9] whereupon finance ministry officials with access to the evidence on SCTs cited above advised that funds currently going towards FISP should be moved to the SCT programme (ZG18).

Despite a commitment to 'social transfers' appearing in the PF's 2011 Manifesto, the president had taken no steps to meet this promise. More directly concerned with urban and formal sector workers, one senior insider reports that Sata had actually used red ink to strike out any mention of cash transfers from the first draft of the Manifesto (ZG19). It was later reinserted by another senior member of the PF Cabinet who was closely connected to a leading player within the transnational policy coalition. Siachiwena (2016) argues that there was a programmatic shift in policy under PF, influenced by a 'social democratic' faction within the party. While he rightly points out the close links between the PF and the policy coalition promoting social protection, the fact that this centred on one leading figure in the party whose partner was a key player in the policy coalition seems to underline the personalized rather than programmatic tendencies of policy-making in Zambia. The inclusion of cash transfers in the PF manifesto without Sata's approval, acknowledged by Siachiwena in his paper, and the lack of fit between SCTs and the main constituency-building strategies adopted by the PF at the 2011 elections (as discussed in section 2.2), further question the existence of a programmatic faction in support of SCTs.

The timing of the budgetary boost to SCTs in relation to the FISP scandal suggests that it was an opportunistic reaction to the crisis of how to keep social goods flowing to rural areas to maintain the broader political settlement, rather than a programmatic commitment to poverty reduction. This reflects the wider sense in which the PF has focused strategically on the unmet demands of distinct social groups rather than a particular ideology (Larmer and Fraser 2007). Resnick (2014) highlights Sata's populist strategies leading up to the 2011 elections, including programmatic messaging around social

[8] They identify these factors as momentum on the political agenda; a context of sustained criticism of Zambia's subsidy programmes for fertilizer, maize, and fuel; the consultation process on the National Social Protection Policy; and the timely release of the impact evaluation reports, accompanied by advocacy and networking activity (Quarles van Ufford et al. 2016).

[9] https://www.daily-mail.co.zm/?p=10654.

inclusion. However, while there is no doubt that Sata employed a 'pro-poor brand' (Siachiwena 2016), this does not adequately explain the increased investment in SCTs under the PF government. Firstly, Sata specifically targeted the urban poor (Resnick 2014), while the SCT programme is predominantly targeted at rural areas. The expansion of SCTs to some urban districts that are not among the poorest only highlights the continuation of patronage seen under previous governments (Siachiwena 2016). Secondly, the SCT programme existed before the PF government came to power and only gained Sata's attention when it proved useful, as outlined in section 3.3. In addition, the government's expenditure priorities in the first two years after gaining power were tilted towards delivering highly visible public infrastructure that the PF deemed would be electorally popular, particularly roads and new universities, rather than redistributive measures to enhance livelihoods.

Nor did the increased budgetary emphasis on SCTs reflect a strong commitment to tackle political clientelism in favour of more effective and rules-based distributive mechanisms. Although Sata publicly condemned the profligacy of the agencies responsible for FISP and food relief, he lacked the capacity to challenge the interests vested in these programmes at multiple levels of governance and spending levels for these programmes were soon re-established.

Programmes such as FISP and FRA still pull significant resources away from other forms of social protection, with budgeted amounts for FISP actually increasing in 2014–15. Despite compelling evidence that these subsidies, especially FISP, are not a cost-effective way of reducing poverty among the poorest as those who benefit are mostly larger, non-poor farmers (Tesliuc 2013), 'social protection' in Zambia, as a form of state-subsidized support to rural areas, remains conceived of primarily in terms of agricultural and food subsidies. This is underpinned by the configuration of power within Zambia's political settlement, whereby these subsidies are protected by powerful vested interests. They constitute 'an animal on its own, too big to challenge, very much a political programme' (ZC2), with SCTs not yet politically popular enough to displace them (ZC7, ZO4). The so-called 'maize mafia', which controls and benefits from the distribution of fertilizer and collection of maize in rural areas, includes national-level companies and a widespread network of local bureaucrats, security officials, and politicians (ZC2, ZK2). Studies show that agricultural subsidies in Zambia are used primarily to reward loyalty amongst the ruling party's voter base, particularly among wealthier households, although interestingly they do not have an impact on the share of votes won by the incumbent (Mason and Ricker-Gilbert 2013;

Mason et al. 2013).[10] This form of political clientelism reflects the kind of decentralized rent-seeking that is characteristic of competitive clientelist settings and which is particularly difficult to rein in or render developmental (Kelsall 2013).

This underlines the importance of framing social protection interventions in relation to their role in sustaining a particular distribution of power, rather than as a development intervention per se (Lavers and Hickey 2016). Growing support for the SCT programme amongst parliamentarians—according to one former member of the current government, 'The rural MPs loved the idea, it was largesse without any bullshit, you just give money away' (ZG19)—may herald a longer-term shift here, although it is notable that there is as yet little evidence of strong demands for SCTs from voters. In terms of the distributional regime required to maintain ruling coalitions in power in Zambia, the SCT initiative has struggled to gain pre-eminence vis-à-vis other redistributive policies that have already secured a political constituency of support and which play a role in sustaining the current political settlement.

4.3. The role of ideas

Although political settlement dynamics and the interests of powerful actors within the ruling coalition are clearly a determining factor in the uptake of social protection, ideas have also played a role here. This includes issues of 'fit' between the normative policy ideas of dominant players in the ruling coalition and the role played by more cognitive forms of evidence concerning problems of poverty with the potential of social protection to act as a solution (Schmidt 2008). As illustrated in section 3.2, the capacity of the policy coalition to mobilize both normative ideas and a credible evidence base directly shaped the progress and the form of social protection, at least as a policy agenda. This was particularly evident at the level of problem-framing (e.g. the rise of poverty rates in the mid-2000s) and policy solutions (e.g. evidence that SCTs could work in Zambia).

The initial design of SCTs in Zambia was directly influenced by the German development consultant Bernd Schubert and his '10% model' which, with its focus on targeting 'incapacitated' households, was directly aligned with elite

[10] In the same paper Mason et al. (2013) also demonstrate that poverty reduction gains more votes than agricultural subsidies and on this basis recommend that the government invests in programmes that reduce poverty and inequality.

concerns over creating dependency amongst able-bodied people. Other donor-influenced models, including a UNICEF-backed child grant, were also piloted but later resisted. Although the results of the evaluation for the child grant programme were particularly strong, a separate targeting assessment conducted by external consultants in 2013 found that this model was unpopular in communities as it is not in line with perceptions of poverty based on labour constraints (Beazley and Carrero 2013). On this point we concur with Quarles van Ufford et al. (2016) that the impact evaluations have helped promote the merits of SCTs in general, but have been less influential over the design process, which has been shaped more directly by elite and popular perceptions of which groups deserve to receive transfers.

More broadly, however, there is little sign that social protection has traction within the normative, paradigmatic views of political elites in Zambia. The SCT programme was not a significant issue during the 2014 presidential by-election campaigns, and when questioned directly on their policy agenda around social protection during a pre-election radio debate, presidential candidates revealed either a lack of awareness or outright hostility (ZO2). Our own interviews with opposition leaders suggest that members of the political elite see SCTs as a 'foreign-grown programme' and as a form of dependency on the state (ZG7), with one leader stating, 'I hate that stuff' (ZS1). The evidence we present in section 4.2 regarding the 'programmatic' nature of Sata's apparent commitment to cash transfers suggests that his pro-poor messaging may have been used as legitimation for a decision that was actually triggered by the agricultural subsidy crisis. Framing SCTs as a more effective and pro-poor alternative to subsidies then may have been a form of 'communicative discourse' to persuade other stakeholders and the public (Schmidt 2002), particularly as it is a predominantly rural programme unlikely to appeal to the PF's urban constituency.

Some close observers have argued that there is scope to link social protection in Zambia to longer-standing notions of welfare, particularly the 'humanism' that emerged under Kaunda. Harland (2014) argues that this still resonates in Zambia, particularly through the continued use of the 'One Zambia, One Nation' rhetoric, and could offer the basis on which a future welfare state might be built. However, our respondents contrast these former attitudes with young professionals and decision makers who today are 'nonchalantly happy to denounce poor people' for their poverty (ZC3). This echoes earlier analyses of negative attitudes towards the poor amongst Zambia's political elite, and runs counter to the kinds of ideas that have historically been aligned with stronger elite support for social protection, particularly the notion that structural forces rather than the poor themselves are to blame for persistent poverty (Hickey 2012).

Moreover, the most pervasive developmental paradigm in Zambia has been less concerned with social welfare than with 'modernity', which is where Zambia, with its high rate of urbanization and processes of class formation, seemed to be heading in the 1970s (Ferguson 1999). This still prevails today: 'Zambians have not stopped thinking about the potential for both national development and personal transformation in decidedly modernist ways' (Larmer et al. 2014: 899). Neither the humanism nor the Christian ideals played on by certain leaders have gained the same degree of social and political salience as this discourse. As such, one of the reasons why social protection has yet to become more fully established in Zambia may flow from the sense in which the discourse on social protection has not tapped into the deeper paradigmatic ideas (Schmidt 2008) that underpin the political settlement in Zambia, or fundamentally challenged elite ideas about dependency and deservingness.[11]

5. Conclusion

Our argument that elite commitment to social protection in Zambia needs to be understood in relation to the interplay of political settlement dynamics and transnational advocacy represents a challenge to mainstream accounts of how welfare states are likely to emerge in developing countries. The formation of a transnational policy coalition was critical to developing and promoting social protection as a credible policy agenda, but the agenda only gained political traction when there was a shift in political settlement dynamics which led social protection to become more aligned with the interests and ideas of a new ruling coalition. The key dynamic here was not the ascent to power of a programmatic political party per se, but rather an opportunistic response to a crisis within the existing system of rent allocation.

While the pro-poor, urban-based PF has to some extent played to lower-level factions through its populist approach, the horizontal distribution of power between elite factions in Zambia has ensured that it remains more clearly focused on maintaining the settlement through a 'maximum coalition'. This practice heralds a continuation of existing political and developmental

[11] See Lavers and Hickey (2016) for a fuller elaboration of Schmidt's (2008) schema of ideas and how this relates to the interaction of policy coalitions and political settlements.

strategies, rather than a significant rupture in the way in which power is held and legitimized, including through processes of resource allocation. The shift towards a pro-poor agenda marked a shift in ideational rhetoric that provided some space for the social protection agenda to gain ground, but only to a certain degree, and without having the power to displace more deeply embedded interests, policies, and rent-allocation practices. Neither have proponents of social protection as yet managed to either align the agenda fully with the paradigmatic ideas that prevail in Zambia or to challenge these ideas.

How the politics of social protection plays out in the future remains to be seen. There are some signs that tensions are growing concerning the always fused technical and political aspects of this kind of programme, with parliamentarians increasingly perceiving the political benefits of the programme. If SCTs start to generate higher levels of localized support amongst voters, it is difficult to see them being removed. What remains to be seen is whether they may start to challenge the clientelistic basis of resource distribution within Zambia's current political settlement, in line with the broader claims that the National Social Protection Policy heralds a paradigm shift that will 'enhance access to justice for the poor' (Ministry of Community Development, Mother and Child Health 2014). As things stand, the conditions do not yet exist for social protection to be institutionalized as part of a new social contract in Zambia, with government and recipients alike both seeming to perceive cash transfers through the idiom of a gift rather than a right.

Interviews Conducted

Government representatives

ZG1, SCT Unit, MCDMCH, Lusaka, 13 April 2015
ZG2, Director, MCDMCH, Lusaka, 14 April 2015
ZG3, Accountant, MCDMCH, Lusaka, 14 April 2015
ZG7, Opposition party leader, Lusaka, 15 April 2015
ZG8, Senior Officer, MCDMCH, Choma, 27 April 2015
ZG9, Provincial Officer, MCDMCH, Choma, 27 April 2015
ZG10, District Officer, MCDMCH, Monze, 28 April 2015
ZG11, Member of Parliament UPND, Lusaka, 29 April 2015
ZG12, Member of Parliament UPND, Lusaka, 30 April 2015
ZG13, Member of Parliament PF, Lusaka, 30 April 2015
ZG14, Member of Parliament MMD, Lusaka, 30 April 2015
ZG15, Member of Parliament PF, Lusaka, 30 April 2015
ZG16, Senior official, MCDMCH, Lusaka, 6 May 2015

ZG17, Director, MCDMCH, Lusaka, 7 May 2015
ZG18, Desk Officer, Ministry of Finance, Lusaka, 7 May 2015
ZG19, Politician, Lusaka, 17 and 30 April 2015

Zambian organizations (CSOs, think tanks, consultancies)

ZO1, CSO representative, Lusaka, 13 April 2015
ZO2, CSO representative, Lusaka, 13 April 2015
ZO3, Consultant, Lusaka, 13 April 2015
ZO4, Consultant, Lusaka, 14 April 2015

Co-operating partners

ZC1, representative of co-operating partner involved in SCT, Lusaka, 13 April 2015
ZC2, representative of co-operating partner involved in SCT, Lusaka, 14 April 2015
ZC3, representative of co-operating partner involved in SCT, Lusaka, 14 April 2015
ZC4, representative of co-operating partner involved in SCT, Lusaka, 15 April 2015
ZC5, representative of co-operating partner involved in SCT, Lusaka, 15 April 2015
ZC6, representative of co-operating partner involved in SCT, Lusaka, 16 April 2015
ZC7, representative of co-operating partner involved in SP, Lusaka, 20 April 2015
ZC8, representative of co-operating partner involved in SCT, Lusaka, 21 April 2015

Key individuals

ZK1, Consultant and former co-operating partner representative, 17 April and 8 May 2015
ZK2, Consultant, Lusaka, 13–17 April 2015

Public speeches

ZS1, Hakainde Hichilema, Cape Town, 5 June 2015

References

Barrientos, A. and S. Pellissery (2012). Delivering effective social assistance: does politics matter? ESID Working Paper No. 9. Manchester: Effective States and Inclusive Development.

Barrientos, A., S. Hickey, N. Simutanyi, and D. Wood (2005). *Final Report of Study on Drivers of Change for a National Social Protection Scheme in Zambia.* Lusaka: DFID Zambia. Available at http://www.ids.ac.uk/publication/final-report-of-study-on-drivers-of-change-for-a-national-social-protection-scheme-in-zambia [Accessed 2 February 2015].

Beazley, R. and L. Carraro (2013). *Assessment of the Zambia Social Protection Expansion Programme Targeting Mechanisms.* Oxford: Oxford Policy Management.

Bertelsmann Stiftung (BTI) (2012). *Zambia Country Report.* Gütersloh: Bertelsmann Stiftung.

Booth, D. and S. Unsworth (2014). *Politically Smart, Locally Led Development*. ODI Discussion Paper. London: Overseas Development Institute.

Central Statistical Office (2011). *Living Conditions Monitoring Survey Report 2006 and 2010*. Lusaka: Central Statistical Office.

Cheeseman, N. and M. Hinfelaar (2010). Parties, platforms, and political mobilization: the Zambian presidential election of 2008. *African Affairs*, 109(434), 51–76.

Cheeseman, N. and M. Larmer (2015). Ethnopopulism in Africa: opposition mobilisation in diverse and unequal societies. *Democratization*, 22(1), 22–50.

Chikwanda, A. (2013). 2014 budget address by Hon. Alexander B. Chikwanda M.P., Minister of Finance. Delivered to the National Assembly on 11 October 2013.

Chikwanda, A. (2014). 2015 budget address by Hon. Alexander B. Chikwanda M.P., Minister of Finance. Delivered to the National Assembly on 10 October 2014.

Deacon, B. (2007). *Global Social Policy and Governance*. London: SAGE Publications.

Di John, J. and J. Putzel (2009). Political settlements: issues paper. Governance and Social Development Resource Centre, University of Birmingham.

Dixon, J. (Ed.) (1987). *Social Welfare in Africa*. London: Croom Helm.

Duncan, A., H. Macmillan, and N. Simutanyi (2003). *Zambia—Drivers of Pro-Poor Change: An Overview*. Oxford: Oxford Policy Management.

Erdmann, G. and N. Simutanyi (2003). *Transition in Zambia: The Hybridisation of the Third Republic*. Lilongwe: Konrad Adenauer Foundation.

Evans, A. (2018). Amplifying accountability by benchmarking results. *Development Policy Review*, 36(2), 221–40.

Faust, J., S. Leiderer, and J. Schmitt (2012). Financing poverty alleviation vs. promoting democracy? Multi-donor budget support in Zambia. *Democratization*, 19(3), 438–64.

Ferguson, J. (1999). *Expectations of Modernity: Myths and Meanings of Urban Life on the Zambian Copperbelt*. Berkeley, CA: University of California Press.

George, A.L. and A. Bennett (2005). *Case Studies and Theory Development in the Social Sciences*. Cambridge, MA; London: MIT.

Gould, J. (2006). Strong bar, weak state? Lawyers, liberalism and state formation in Zambia. *Development and Change*, 37(4), 921–41.

Harland, C. (2014). Can the expansion of social protection bring about social transformation in African countries? The case of Zambia. *European Journal of Development Research*, 26(3), 370–86.

Hay, C. (2011). Ideas and the construction of interests. In D. Béland and R.H. Cox (Eds.), *Ideas and Politics in Social Science Research*. Oxford: Oxford University Press.

Hickey, S. (2007). Conceptualising the politics of social protection in Africa. In A. Barrientos and D. Hulme (Eds.), *Social Protection for the Poor and Poorest*. Basingstoke and New York: Palgrave Macmillan.

Hickey, S. (2012). Turning governance thinking upside-down? Insights from 'the politics of what works'. *Third World Quarterly*, 33(7), 1231–47.

Hickey, S. and J. Seekings (2017). The global politics of social protection. UNU-WIDER Working Paper 2017/115. Helsinki: UNU-WIDER.

Hickey, S., R. Sabates-Wheeler, G. Guenther, and I. Macauslan (2009). Promoting social transfers: DFID and the politics of influencing. Evaluation Working Paper/ Evaluation Report A2. London: Department for International Development.

Huber, E. and J.D. Stephens (2012). *Democracy and the Left: Social Policy and Inequality in Latin America*. Chicago, IL: University of Chicago Press.

Kabandula, A. and J. Seekings (2016). Donor influence, the Minister of Finance and welfare policy reform in Zambia, 2003–2011. CSSR Working Paper No. 395. Cape Town: Centre for Social Science Research, UCT.

Kanbur, R. (2001). Economic policy, distribution and poverty: the nature of disagreements. *World Development*, 29(6), 1083–94.

Kelsall, T. (2013). *Business, Politics and the State in Africa: Challenging the Orthodoxies on Growth and Transformation*. London: ZED Books.

Khan, M. (2010). *Political Settlements and the Governance of Growth-Enhancing Institutions*. London: School of Oriental and African Studies (mimeo). Available at http://eprints.soas.ac.uk/9968. [Accessed 16 December 2014].

Kpessa, M.W. and D. Béland (2013). Mapping social policy development in sub-Saharan Africa. *Policy Studies*, 34(3), 326–41.

Kuss, M. (2015). The prospects and politics of social protection reform in Zambia. IDS Working Paper No. 453/CSP Working Paper No. 011. Brighton: Institute of Development Studies.

Larmer, M. and A. Fraser (2007). Of cabbages and King Cobra: populist politics and Zambia's 2006 election. *African Affairs*, 106(425), 611–37.

Larmer, M., M. Hinfelaar, B.J. Phiri, L. Schumaker, and M. Szeftel (2014). Introduction: narratives of nationhood. *Journal of Southern African Studies*, 40(5), 895–905.

Lavers, T. and S. Hickey (2016). Conceptualising the politics of social protection expansion in low income countries: the intersection of transnational ideas and domestic politics. *International Journal of Social Welfare*, 25(4), 388–98.

Leftwich, A. (2012). Coalitions in the politics of development. Research and Policy Workshop Report. Sydney: Developmental Leadership Program.

Levy, B. (2014). *Working with the Grain: Integrating Governance and Growth in Development Strategies*. Oxford: Oxford University Press.

Lindemann, S. (2011). Inclusive elite bargains and the dilemma of unproductive peace: a Zambian case study. *Third World Quarterly*, 32(10), 1843–69.

Mason, N. and J. Ricker-Gilbert (2013). Disrupting demand for commercial seed: input subsidies in Malawi and Zambia. *World Development*, 45, 75–91.

Mason, N., T.S. Jayne, and N. van de Walle (2013). Fertilizer subsidies and voting patterns: political economy dimensions of input subsidy programs. Selected Paper prepared for Presentation at the Agricultural & Applied Economics Association's 2013 AAEA & CAES Joint Annual Meeting, Washington DC, 4–6 August.

MCDSS and GTZ (2007). *Final Evaluation Report—Kalomo Social Cash Transfer Scheme.* Lusaka: MCDSS and GTZ.

Mhone, G. (2004). Historical trajectories of social policy in post-colonial Africa: the case of Zambia. In T. Mkandawire (Ed.), *Social Policy in a Development Context.* Geneva: UNRISD.

Ministry of Community Development, Mother and Child Health (2014). *National Social Protection Policy: Reducing Poverty, Inequality and Vulnerability.* Lusaka: Ministry of Community Development, Mother and Child Health.

Ministry of Finance (2014). *The Proposed 2015–2017 Medium Term Expenditure Framework and Policies for the 2015 Budget.* Lusaka: Ministry of Finance.

Ministry of Finance (2015). *The Proposed 2016–2018 Medium Term Expenditure Framework and the 2016 Budget.* Lusaka: Ministry of Finance.

Niño-Zarazúa, M., A. Barrientos, S. Hickey, and D. Hulme (2012). Social protection in sub-Saharan Africa: getting the politics right. *World Development*, 40, 163–76.

Noyoo, N. (2010). *Social Policy and Human Development in Zambia.* London: Adonis & Abbey Publishers Ltd.

Quarles van Ufford, P., Harland, C., Michelo, S., Tembo, G., Toole, K., and Wood, D. (2016). The role of impact evaluation in the evolution of Zambia's cash transfer programme. In B. Davis, S. Handa, N. Hypher, N. Winder Rossi, P. Winters, and J. Yablonski (Eds.), *From Evidence to Action: The Story of Cash Transfers and Impact Evaluation in Sub-Saharan Africa.* Oxford: Oxford University Press.

Rakner, L. (2003). *Political and Economic Liberalisation in Zambia 1991–2001.* Uppsala: Nordic Africa Institute.

Rakner, L. and S.-E. Helle (2012). The interplay between poverty and electoral authoritarianism: Poverty and political mobilization in Zambia and Uganda. CMI Working Paper 2012:3. Bergen: Chr. Michelsen Institute.

Resnick, D. (2014). *Urban Poverty and Party Populism in African Democracies.* Cambridge: Cambridge University Press.

Scarritt, J. (2006). The strategic choice of multiethnic parties in Zambia's dominant and personalist party system. *Commonwealth & Comparative Politics*, 44(2), 234–56.

Scarritt, J. (2010). 'One Zambia, one nation', many groups. In A. Lecours and L. Moreno (Eds.), *Nationalism and Democracy: Dichotomies, Complementarities, Oppositions.* Oxon and New York: Routledge.

Schmidt, V.A. (2002). Does discourse matter in the politics of welfare state adjustment? *Comparative Political Studies*, 35(2), 168–93.

Schmidt, V.A. (2008). Discursive institutionalism: the explanatory power of ideas and discourse. *Annual Review of Political Science*, 11(1), 303–26.

Schubert, B. (2005). *The Pilot Social Cash Transfer Scheme Kalomo District—Zambia.* SSRN Scholarly Paper ID 1753690. Rochester, NY: Social Science Research Network.

Schubert, B. and Slater, R. (2006). Social cash transfers in low-income African countries: conditional or unconditional? *Development Policy Review*, 24(5), 571–8.

Siachiwena, H. (2016). Social protection policy reform in Zambia during the Sata presidency, 2011–2014. CSSR Working Paper No. 380. Cape Town: Centre for Social Science Research, UCT.

Stone, D. (2008). Global public policy, transnational policy communities, and their networks. *Policy Studies Journal*, 36(1), 19–38.

Tesliuc, C.M. (2013). *Using Social Safety Nets to Accelerate Poverty Reduction and Share Prosperity in Zambia.* Washington DC: World Bank.

Waal, A. de (2003). How will HIV/AIDS transform African governance? *African Affairs*, 102(406), 1–23.

Wietler, K. (2007). *The Impact of Social Cash Transfers on Informal Safety Nets in Kalomo District Zambia.* Lusaka: MCDSS/GTZ.

8

The Politics of Promoting Social Protection in Uganda

A Comparative Analysis of Social Cash Transfers and Social Health Insurance

Badru Bukenya and Sam Hickey

1. Introduction: Researching the Politics of Social Protection in Uganda

This volume seeks to explain the uneven progress of the social protection agenda across different countries within sub-Saharan Africa, particularly those in its eastern and southern regions. This chapter contributes to this effort by exploring the extent of elite commitment to social protection in the case of Uganda. However, it goes further by asking why certain parts of the social protection agenda have spread further than others *within* the same country. To date, most efforts to understand how this phenomenon has played out within sub-Saharan African countries have focused solely on the spread of cash transfers (e.g. Cherrier 2014; Lavers 2019a). The smaller number of studies into the spread of social health insurance in Africa, including within Ethiopia (Lavers 2019b) and Rwanda (Chemouni 2018), tend not to adopt a comparative focus with regards to focusing on more than one policy instrument within the same context.[1] Our comparative approach can offer a more rigorous test of frameworks designed to understand how far social protection policies are taken up by low-income countries, including those deployed within this volume. By holding both the timeframe and the country context constant, our comparative study of how two different policy initiatives in

[1] The working paper by Pruce and Hickey (2017) on Zambia is an exception here.

Badru Bukenya and Sam Hickey, *The Politics of Promoting Social Protection in Uganda: A Comparative Analysis of Social Cash Transfers and Social Health Insurance* In: *The Politics of Social Protection in Eastern and Southern Africa*. Edited by: Sam Hickey, Tom Lavers, Miguel Niño-Zarazúa, and Jeremy Seekings, Oxford University Press (2020).
DOI: 10.1093/oso/9780198850342.003.0008

Uganda have fared helps to specify the key factors that explain the variable progress of different social protection initiatives.

Specifically, we examine whether the focus on transnational policy coalitions and political settlement dynamics can help explain why some policy ideas on social protection take root in some parts of sub-Saharan Africa whereas others don't. The conceptual framework, which was introduced in Chapter 1 and elaborated fully in Lavers and Hickey (2016), is inspired by three bodies of literature that focus on the politics of development, of building welfare regimes in the global South (Huber and Stephens 2012) and of global policy transfer (e.g. Stone 2012). The approach helps to go beyond the current literature which has tended to either underplay the role of politics by emphasizing the influence of donors (Cherrier 2014) and income levels (Niño-Zarazúa et al. 2012) or by focusing only on formal aspects of politics, such as democracy and good governance. Such approaches tend to obscure the significance of informal relationships between elites and between elites and their followers, and how these interact with transnational processes of policy transfer. Of particular importance here is the 'political settlement', defined as 'the balance or distribution of power between contending social groups and social classes, on which any state is based' (Di John and Putzel 2009: 4). A political settlement analysis seeks to identify the underlying drivers of elite commitment to development by examining how changes in the distribution of power amongst elites, and between elites and their followers, can (re)shape incentives around particular policy agendas (Whitfield et al. 2015). To capture the influence of transnational actors, we focus on how they seek to render new policy ideas legible within particular contexts through forming policy coalitions with domestic actors (Peck and Theodore 2015; Hickey and Seekings, this volume).

The questions we seek to explain through this framework are, first: to what extent has political commitment to social protection emerged in Uganda? Second, why have some social protection initiatives gained greater traction in Uganda than others? Specifically, we explore why efforts to promote social cash transfers have been relatively more successful than efforts to promote social health insurance. Although efforts to promote each instrument in Uganda have been active since the early 2000s, the government has moved more swiftly and extensively to provide social cash transfers (SCTs) for old-age pensioners. The national roll-out of the senior citizens' grant that the President called for in 2013 is now being implemented, whilst as of late 2018 the national health insurance scheme (NHIS) remained unfunded and subject to continued debate. We do not argue that the government of Uganda has made a significant investment in SCTs: it certainly trails behind other countries discussed in this volume in terms of the extent of coverage and budgetary allocations to social assistance. However, it has moved notably further with this than with social health insurance. We argue here that the limited level of commitment to social protection in Uganda, and the variation that exists within this policy domain, can be explained by the interaction between transnational policy coalitions and the domestic political settlement.

The chapter draws on primary research conducted over March to May 2014, May to July 2015, and January 2016 in Kampala. This involved over fifty key informant interviews with representatives from all of the major stakeholders that have played a role in promoting and resisting our two policy initiatives, including government officials, donor agency staff, parliamentarians, private sector employer associations, insurance companies, donor agencies, labour unions, and wider civil society actors. Our methodological approach involved identifying key moments within each policy process, and then systematically tracing these back to their drivers followed by comparative analysis across the two policy cases (George and Bennet 2004). The chapter proceeds by briefly introducing the nature of Uganda's transnationalized political settlement and how this shapes the politics of development. It then discusses the process through which each policy has been promoted in Uganda from the early 2000s until 2016 before analysing this through the conceptual framework identified above and concluding with reflections on the future politics of social protection in Uganda.

2. The Politics of Development in Uganda

The National Resistance Movement (NRM) regime that took power in Uganda in 1986, and which under President Yoweri Museveni has led the country ever since, initially demonstrated a clear commitment to development through a mixture of presidential patronage and programmatically informed policy reforms. Following a successful guerrilla struggle during the early 1980s, the NRM forged a ruling coalition that was sufficiently inclusive, and powerful in military terms, to impose political stability on the majority of the country (Lindemann 2011). This 'dominant-developmental' political settlement,[2] within which opposition was muted through the abolishment of multi-party elections, introduced a series of policy reforms that had largely

[2] For further details on the nature of the political settlement in Uganda see Golooba-Mutebi and Hickey (2013, 2016), Kjær (2015), and Whitfield et al. (2015).

progressive outcomes, particularly for the NRM's key constituency of the rural poor. Pro-poor policies were introduced after successive presidential elections in 1996 (universal primary education) and 2001, most notably the abolishment of health user fees, which some have framed as an initial foray into the social protection agenda (Yates et al. 2006). Certain donors were highly influential during this period, particularly the international financial institutions and some European agencies, although there was a strong sense that the main impetus behind the reforms came from domestic rather than external sources (Kutesa et al. 2010; Hickey 2005).

From the early 2000s onwards, the ruling coalition became increasingly vulnerable to pressure from excluded elite factions that were seeking political power, and from lower-level factions seeking to ensure the extension of patronage (Whitfield et al. 2015). The re-introduction of multi-party politics in 2006 helped deepen an increasingly populist and personalized approach to development policy, with the President undertaking 'poverty tours' through which hand-outs and promises of investment in local projects were made in a highly personalized and populist manner. Social sector ministries that had previously benefited from technocratic leadership, such as Health, were handed to party big-men to be used as avenues for rent-seeking and building patronage networks as opposed to promoting service delivery (Bukenya and Golooba-Mutebi 2019). The ruling coalition's need to fund closely fought election campaigns and to underwrite Uganda's particular mode of 'inflationary patronage' further reduced the fiscal space for addressing development priorities (Barkan 2011; Golooba-Mutebi and Hickey 2016). Importantly, the global political economy context for development in Uganda also underwent a series of shifts from around 2005–6, with Uganda graduating from the Highly Indebted Poor Countries Initiative, discovering commercial quantities of oil, and signing the Sino-Africa Agreement (Hickey 2013). These shifts reduced the power of western donors and encouraged a major spending focus on infrastructure and energy projects at the expense of social sectors. The programmatic focus on poverty reduction became displaced by the agenda of 'Prosperity for All' and structural transformation, reflecting a prevailing political discourse that tended to favour the 'economically active' segment of the population (Hickey 2005).

It was into this generally unpromising context that the social protection agenda started to be promoted by international development organizations during the early 2000s, in line with a broader shift within the emerging post-Washington Consensus (see Hickey and Seekings, this volume). Early movers here included the World Bank, the United Kingdom's Department for

International Development (DFID), and various United Nations agencies. On paper, they encountered a favourable legislative and policy context: the 1995 Constitution has an explicit focus on provisions that protect the rights of the poor and vulnerable groups in society, which is in turn supported by legislation that includes Acts for Children (1997), Workers (2000), and Persons with Disabilities (2006). A wide range of policies have flowed from these acts, including the National Orphans and Other Vulnerable Children Policy (2004); the National Policy for Older Persons (2009); the Uganda Gender Policy (2007); and the National Policy on Disability 2006. However, international development agencies, working in particular with bureaucrats in the Ministry of Gender, Labour and Social Development (MGLSD), were keen to ensure that the government of Uganda adopted a specific national policy on social protection. This was eventually achieved in 2015 when the government approved a new Uganda National Social Protection Policy, after over five years of research, consultations, benchmarking, and drafting. The policy identifies six policy priorities: extending social security coverage to the informal sector; expanding access to direct income support for vulnerable groups in need; strengthening family and community capacity to provide and care for vulnerable groups and individuals; reforming the Public Service Pension scheme; expanding coverage of formal social security including affordable health insurance; and enhancing the institutional capacity for provision of comprehensive social protection services (GoU 2015). However, whilst Uganda is renowned for being an early adopter of developmental policies, its record of implementation is considerably weaker (Andrews and Bategeka 2013; Bukenya and Muhumuza 2017). There has been a great deal of variation with regards to which elements of this social protection agenda have actually been adopted and implemented in Uganda. This chapter examines the politics behind how two of these priorities—namely, social health insurance (SHI) and direct income support via SCTs—have been promoted, and compares their relative fortunes in relation to the ideas, incentives, and actors that predominate within Uganda's transnationalized political settlement.

3. Social Health Insurance in Uganda

There is some evidence of elite-level commitment to adopting a national health insurance scheme in Uganda, in rhetorical terms at least. The policy formed part of the ruling party's manifestoes for the 2006, 2011, and 2016 elections, albeit with a decreasing emphasis in the latter, and the second

National Development Plan (2015/16–2019/20), promised that the government would 'fast-track the implementation of the National Health Insurance Scheme' (GoU 2015: 217). However, as of late 2018, the National Social Health Insurance Bill in Uganda remains stalled; despite the Ministry of Finance finally agreeing to fund the scheme in 2017, subsequent budgets have failed to include any allocation for the scheme. Here we set out the process through which the scheme has been promoted and contested over the past two decades.

3.1. The contested process of promoting social health insurance in Uganda

The first proposition of a NHIS in Uganda came in the 1987 Health Policy Review Commission report. Formed to advise government on reconstructing the country's collapsed health system after two decades of political instability and conflict, the Commission suggested cost-sharing and social health insurance as funding alternatives. Both proposals were initially unpopular among the political elites, with cost-sharing rejected by parliament in 1990 after legislators argued that 'the population was already paying for their health through taxes and therefore there was no need for extra payment for the health services' (Kivumbi and Kintu 2002: 65). In 1993 the Ministry of Health (MoH) nonetheless introduced cost-sharing via a loophole in the Local Government Act that gave district authorities revenue-raising powers. The policy lasted until 2001 when it was abolished by a presidential decree in an electoral commitment to 'free' healthcare.

This move triggered a small group of MoH officials to promote a NHIS as an alternative means of meeting the huge gap in financing. Most of the officials had undergone World Bank training about health financing options during the structural adjustment era of the late 1980s, and were sceptical about the President's free healthcare policy from the outset (interviews with a senior MoH official and WHO official, 12 May 2015). MoH officials were further encouraged by assurances from the Bank that it would fund the initial costs for setting up and operationalizing the scheme (Talemwa 2009), and its funding of study tours to learn from existing health insurance schemes in Thailand, Vietnam, and China. Armed with evidence from these trips and two feasibility studies done in 1996 and 2001, the latter by academics from Harvard with World Bank support, the MoH argued that the systematic fall in poverty rates during the 1990s meant that many people could afford to pay premiums. In 2006, Cabinet encouraged MoH to devise a health insurance scheme, which they embarked on via the creation of a National Health Insurance Scheme Secretariat within MoH, albeit with funds for only two staff members.

The bill was drafted and presented to Cabinet in 2007. Recognizing the need to secure presidential support for the bill, officials from MoH sought an audience with the President. He declined and instead met with private sector representatives who were strongly opposed to the scheme, claiming that it would gravely hurt their businesses and that they had not been consulted (interview with MoH official, 7 May 2015). In a frustrated tone, one MoH official recounted that,

> ...the Uganda Manufacturers Association, which was not totally in agreement with our proposals, met the President and complained about the potential increase to the cost of production. The President listened to them and wrote to us to halt the process. He asked us to make more consultations.
> (Interview, 7 May 2015)

Cabinet advised the Ministry to undertake a more participatory process for drafting a revised insurance bill that would be agreeable to all parties. In 2009 the MoH established a multi-sectoral National Task Force, which included representatives from trade unions, employers' organizations (e.g. the Federation of Ugandan Employers, the Private Sector Foundation, the Uganda Manufacturers Association, the Uganda Insurance Commission and Insurers Association), and both the WHO and the World Bank. The Task Force developed a number of detailed documents, including the draft NHI Bill, proposals for the organizational aspects of a NHIS and its provider payment, and accreditation systems for providers. However, our interviews with members of the Task Force reveal that these documents were highly contested amongst members.

In parallel, the President shared the draft NHI Bill and implementation plans with the Medicines and Health Services Delivery Monitoring Unit (MHSDMU). This then powerful Unit reported back that the parlous state of the country's health infrastructure meant that the NHIS would only be viable within Kampala and bigger towns, where health facilities could feasibly qualify for accreditation. The President was warned that launching a health insurance scheme before addressing infrastructural and human resource gaps in the public health system would mean that his core rural constituents would suffer (interview with former MHSDMU staff, May 2015). Perhaps coincidentally, the Minister of Health from 2011 to 2013 instructed MHSDMU to investigate the NHIS Secretariat for alleged corruption. According to one ex-member of the Secretariat, 'the Medicines Monitoring Unit descended on us. We lost morale. The few staff we had, after being cleared by CID [Criminal Investigations Department of the Uganda Police], just resigned' (MoH official, 7 May 2015). Out of the team of five technical staff at the Secretariat, the investigations left only Dr Runumi in charge; they also lost the Director for Planning and immediate supervisor of the Secretariat to retirement, Dr Lawrence Kaggwa, who had both the technical and political connections required to push the scheme forward. The new Minister for Health, a leading figure in the NRM with close links to the President, failed to submit a single memo to Cabinet on the scheme (former NHIS Secretariat staff, 14 May 2015), claiming that his approach was 'deliberately slow to allow for wider consultations and learning' (MoH 2014).

The process was also stymied by the Ministry of Finance, Planning and Economic Development's (MFPED's) refusal to provide the necessary financial support, which was critical given the absence of donors willing to fund the scheme. The NHIS was expected to start in the 2012/13 financial year. In 2013 MoH submitted the application to MFPED for a certificate of financial implications, which MFPED kept until April 2014 before requesting that MoH reformat the document following new MFPED guidelines. MoH resubmitted in November 2014, and MFPED again stalled the process until the following April (2015), when they wrote to MoH saying that the submission had been declined because the costs were too high: 'They advised that we should start small. Once this is done it will be resubmitted' (male MoH KI, 7 May 2015). MFPED officials were particularly concerned with the capital required to establish a semi-autonomous agency to administer the scheme, which would amount to 50 per cent of the current government annual allocation to the health sector (Munabi 2015: 35).

The finance ministry was also concerned with the proposed design of the scheme. The health ministry had proposed to introduce the scheme to different population groups in a phased manner. This approach reflected the need to move slowly to allow expertise in managing the scheme to develop (Nabyonga and Zikusooka 2010), but also the hierarchical ordering of citizenship in Uganda. The scheme would enrol public servants initially during the first three years, then formal private sector workers over a second period of three years, with enrolment of the informal sector and indigents poised to start in year seven; universal coverage would be achieved within fifteen years (Basaza et al. 2013). The premium of the poorest of the poor or indigents, estimated at 25 per cent of the population, would be paid for using a proportion of contributions by formal sector workers (public and private) as well as

Table 8.1 Comparison of national health insurance scheme provisions before and after the 2017 revisions

Contributor category	Old monthly contribution	Revised monthly contribution
GoU	4%	1%
Public servants	4%	4%
Private employers	4%	1%
Private employees	4%	4%
Pensioners	Not catered for	1%
Self-employed individuals	Not catered for	UGX 100,000 per annum
Indigents	0	0

Source: Authors' construction.

subsidies from government and/or donors. For people in formal employment the scheme required a total contribution equivalent of 8 per cent of the employee salary, with employee and employer contributing 4 per cent each. The proposed benefits to members included virtually all inpatient and outpatient care provided within Uganda.

This approach was opposed both by MFPED as unaffordable and also by private sector actors who lobbied hard against their proposed 4 per cent contribution. In 2016/17 MoH eventually revised the plan to placate these two powerful opponents (see Table 8.1). A major change was the shift from a single scheme to three sub-schemes running concurrently, namely: Social Health Insurance for formal sector workers, Community-Based Health Insurance (CBHI) for informal sector workers, and Private Commercial Health Insurance for private citizens. The level of contribution required from both government and private sector employers was reduced from 4 per cent to 1 per cent, with the government not making any contribution towards subsidizing premiums for indigents and informal sector workers (indigents would instead benefit from SHI and CBHI contributions). Although these revisions were enough to persuade MFPED to issue MoH with a certificate of financial implications in 2017, there remains no official budgetary allocation for national health insurance in Uganda.

3.2. Stakeholder analysis of the struggle over social health insurance

> ...there is nowhere in the world where health insurance has been welcomed by vested interests. It is always a firm decision from the political class to say that we have to move.
>
> (Trade Union Representative, 12 May 2015)

> ... fundamentally there is no political champion. It has to be a political issue for it to move. If you take Tanzania, Ghana, and Rwanda, their presidents really see this as the way to go. In Uganda I don't think the government is supportive, they are sitting on the fence... The NRM just [stops at] making this on paper, but they are not championing it. NHIS is a MoH thing, not government.
>
> (World Bank official, 28 May 2015)

Any major policy initiative in Uganda requires the personal support of the President, who has dominated the political and policy agenda since coming to power in 1986. However, President Museveni has been reluctant to offer public support for national health insurance, preferring instead to champion the case for the 'free' healthcare policy he introduced in 2001. This lack of executive commitment to social health insurance has undermined the possibility of any sustained support for it from within the government, including the key ministries of finance and even health itself. Technocratic leaders of the health ministry, who had supported the Secretariat to promote the scheme, including Alex Kamugisha and Richard Nduhura, had their tenures cut short in the 2011 and 2013 Cabinet reshuffles, respectively. As noted above, subsequent ministers actively frustrated the process.

Support from donors has clearly played an important role here. However, the level and type of support have been limited in nature, with only the Bank and WHO playing a significant role (the largest provider of finance to Uganda's health sector, USAID, has been a notable absentee). The approach to policy advocacy followed a standard pattern. From 2007, a mixture of donor and government funds were used by MoH to send officials, and in some cases members of the parliamentary health committee, on fourteen foreign trips to visit countries such as Ghana, Nigeria, Thailand, Israel, Rwanda, Tanzania, Vietnam, Germany, and China, and also the International Labour Organization (ILO) in Switzerland. WHO provided support for a combined team from the ministries of health and finance to develop robust estimates for NHIS revenue and expenditure (Basaza et al. 2013), with further studies undertaken with the support of the Providing for Health (P4H) alliance.[3] However, donors were unwilling to fund a pilot scheme, with one key official noting that most of the donors are on the fence, waiting to see what the government will do (former NHIS Secretariat staff, 14 May 2015). They were also reluctant to

[3] P4H includes four European governments (Germany, Switzerland, Spain, and France), two multilateral organizations (World Bank, African Development Bank), and two United Nations agencies (the ILO and WHO).

engage in a wider effort to build political support for health insurance, with one donor official noting that whilst 'adopting health insurance is a political as opposed to a technical issue' for some, 'for us we look at the technical side' (interview with World Bank official, 28 May 2015).

Civil society actors have opposed the scheme, albeit from different perspectives. Those claiming to represent the poorest criticize the phased approach, whereby 'it is those most in need of this health insurance who will benefit from it last' (Barthelemy 2015: 14). Others raised more practical concerns, noting that since salaries in the public sector are low, then collections during the first phase will be too low to support a benefit package of reasonable quality (Nabyonga and Zikusooka 2010: 5). The two workers' unions in Uganda represented on the NHIS taskforce were supportive of the scheme, but argued that contributions should come from employers rather than workers directly (civil society representative, 5 June 2015). Associations with a stronger middle-class base have also lodged their opposition on the basis that formal sector workers are already paying taxes for services and should not be overburdened with further payments (Insurers Association official, 11 May 2015).

However, the main opposition for the introduction of NHIS in Uganda (beyond MFPED) emanated from the private sector, particularly from private-for-profit health providers, health insurance providers, employers' associations, and manufacturers' associations. Whereas most of the private sector representatives we interviewed for this research agree in principle that all employers should be mandated to provide medical insurance to their employees, they argue that the original proposal to levy a 4 per cent equivalent of each employee's gross salary would increase their costs of doing business in an unsustainable manner. Noting that they already contribute 10 per cent on every employee's salary to the retirement fund in the National Social Security Fund (NSSF), they argued that funding for health insurance should come from this source (Employers' Association official, 12 May 2015), something the powerful leaders of NSSF successfully opposed. The President's response is understandable given the role of the private sector within Uganda's political settlement. Private sector firms provide some of the electoral financing required by the NRM and are central to the neoliberal vision of development the government has largely pursued since the early 1990s. Consulted regularly, private sector actors were able to convince the President that NHIS might negatively impact on the environment of doing business in Uganda. Their opposition stopped the scheme in its tracks in the late 2000s and then forced major revisions whereby the latest plan reduces the contribution to be made by employers from 4 per cent to 1 per cent (see Table 8.1).

There remains a pressing need to reform the health sector in Uganda. However, it is not clear that national health insurance enjoys popular support despite the crisis that is currently afflicting the existing model of financing the health system. The largest proportion of health expenditure is borne by individuals: Uganda's out-of-pocket expenditure is 41 per cent of total health care expenditure (MoH 2018), way above the 15 per cent recommended by WHO. A significant proportion of households suffer from catastrophic expenditure as they often resort to distressed sale of productive assets to pay for health services, thereby driving their members deeper into poverty. The system is unable to provide adequate coverage. Uganda's core health professionals only numbered 1.85 per 1,000 people, well below the minimum WHO target of 2.5/1,000 and the 4.5/1,000 required to attain universal health coverage (MoH 2018: 57). These problems damage the case for a NHIS, eroding public trust in the health system and reducing the possibility of persuading citizens to invest their money or entrust their healthcare to it.

4. Social Cash Transfers in Uganda

4.1. Getting cash transfers on the policy agenda

Advocacy for social assistance started somewhat later than it did for social health insurance in Uganda, and was driven more directly by donors than domestic actors.[4] The first mover was the World Bank in 2002, which at this point was promoting the notion of 'social risk management' via training programmes with government officials in a range of low- and middle-income countries. A DFID Social Development advisor attended the training sessions, which were targeted primarily at officials within the MGLSD, and decided that DFID should both get behind the agenda and seek to extend the focus beyond 'risk' towards a more holistic agenda (interviews with donor officials in Kampala, October 2005). Academics with expertise on social protection in Africa were hired to help encourage different sectors to adopt social protection as part of their strategic approach, which would in turn feed into the next national Poverty Eradication Action Plan (2005–8). Some efforts were also

[4] The more detailed story of how SCTs rose to the policy and political agenda in Uganda can be found in Hickey and Bukenya (2016).

made to undertake a wider advocacy campaign through some civil society organizations (CSOs) and the media. Various social protection measures did indeed figure within the next Plan, but none attracted significant funding or became priorities thereafter (Hickey et al. 2009).

Encouraged by DFID adopting a stronger strategic focus on social cash transfers in the mid-2000s (see Hickey and Seekings, this volume), DFID officials in Uganda stepped up their promotional activities. The concurrent move towards donor harmonization under the Paris Declaration principles helped generate a more coordinated and coherent policy coalition: with the World Bank taking up leadership responsibilities in other sectors, DFID was able to lead the campaign alongside more like-minded donors such as UNICEF. Moreover, DFID started to approach the promotion of social protection as a fundamentally political challenge rather than as a more technocratic process of policy transfer (Stone 2012).

During 2006–7, DFID commissioned a political economy analysis of social protection in Uganda, to try and identify the key sources of support and opposition for the agenda. This then informed a more targeted and politicized campaign that included sending senior officials and politicians on study tours, lobbying ministers over breakfast meetings, and encouraging sympathetic politicians to deliver briefings on social protection at ruling party conventions and Cabinet retreats (interview with development agency officials, March 2014). Efforts to secure the support of civil and political society were extended, with the formation of the Uganda Social Protection Platform in 2008 and the subsequent establishment of a parliamentary forum on social protection. A technocratic focus remained: research papers and evaluations were produced to persuade officials and politicians of the effectiveness of social protection and fiduciary risk assessments undertaken to offset concerns around corruption. However, this was now directed in a more politically informed direction, with a particular focus on senior figures within the finance ministry, especially on the technocratic side, which constituted the primary locus of opposition. At this stage, the President and Cabinet more broadly shared MFPED's opposition to SCTs, seeing them as an unaffordable handout that would create dependency (interviews with MFPED and MGLSD officials, March 2014).

Nonetheless, towards the end of the 2000s the pressure was starting to tell. Donors had secured a Memorandum of Understanding to undertake the piloting of cash transfer schemes in 2006 and then gained agreement from the government to move into the design phase in 2007. MFPED initially blocked attempts by donors to transfer funds for the pilots, but by 2009 it had agreed to the scheme and in June 2010 Cabinet approved the establishment of the Expanding Social Protection (ESP) programme, a new secretariat within MGLSD with responsibility for rolling out SCTs. The move was informed in part by the decision by international donors to focus mainly on an old-age pension, which helped alleviate ruling elite concerns over the 'deservingness' (interview with ESP official, 12 March 2014). However, the breakthrough owed as much to serendipity as to strategy: the new finance minister who signed off on the agreements, and who was appointed in 2008, had been gender minister and was both knowledgeable of and sympathetic towards the social protection agenda.

4.2. From the policy to the political agenda within Uganda's shifting political settlement

Once established, the ESP Secretariat moved swiftly to capitalize on the initial sign of political support. Pilot projects involving two social assistance programmes—a senior citizen's grant (SCG) worth roughly US$10 per month for all aged over sixty-five and a livelihood support programme for vulnerable households—were established in fourteen districts. From the start the ESP Secretariat operated not only as a project delivery unit but also as the strategic centre of an ongoing advocacy effort. According to one donor official involved in the process, 'The ESP programme has been extremely strong in both areas: implementation has been really strong. And then they've twinned that with the focus on the politics and really building political support' (interview with authors, 18 February 2014). A particular focus was on ensuring that influential politicians and bureaucrats were taken to see how the pilot projects were actually operating on the ground in Uganda. However, the next and major breakthrough came through an unforeseen route, whereby community members from Yumbe in northern Uganda, a district that bordered one of the pilot districts, decided to lobby the President directly to be included in the social pension scheme. In August 2013, after the group had visited the President at his rural retreat, Museveni wrote a letter to the gender minister stating that Yumbe would be the next district to receive the social pension and that she should prepare to roll the programme out nationally (interviews with various stakeholders, March to April 2014).

Even with the President now on board, the policy coalition involved in promoting SCTs still faced opposition. Senior officials in MFPED, supported by their new Minister of State, actively sought to limit the pace of any further roll-out of the project by drawing attention to the significant costs involved and the constrained nature of the budgetary envelop (interviews with MFPED officials, March 2014). This worked until the 2015–16 Budget when, with an election looming in February 2016, the policy coalition launched a comprehensive advocacy campaign demanding that the government honour its commitments to co-financing the roll-out. Donors directly lobbied the President and his wife, threatened to withdraw their support for the SCG, encouraged MPs to put pressure on parliament, and funded a highly visible media campaign. The campaign eventually worked, with MFPED increasing their budgetary allocation from two to nine billion Uganda Schillings and announcing year-on-year increases to help roll out the SCG to forty new districts by 2020 (interviews with leading MFPED and donor officials, January 2016).

4.3. A comparative analysis of the politics of cash transfers and health insurance in Uganda

Elite commitment to social protection in Uganda remains both limited and uneven. To date, more progress has been made in institutionalizing social cash transfers than any other form of social protection, including social health insurance, despite both being promoted within Uganda over roughly the same period.[5] Here we argue that the different levels of progress made by these policy agendas have been directly shaped by two main factors: the capabilities of the transnational policy coalitions that have formed around each agenda and (in particular) their ability to secure an alignment between their respective policy agendas and the dominant ideas and incentives within Uganda's political settlement. The analysis is summarized in Table 8.2.

4.3.1. Transnational policy coalitions and the power of ideas

It is now well understood that policy ideas are not free-floating entities but instead have to be actively created and sustained by particular actors in alliance with each other (Mosse 2005). Processes of policy learning and transfer involve particularly important roles for epistemic communities of academics and policy entrepreneurs who have the capacity to make the scientific case for adopting a new approach, as well as actors with the financial and organizational resources to support them (Peck and Theodore 2015; Stone 2012). In relation to

[5] The main research for this chapter was undertaken over 2014–16. By 2017, there seemed to have been some shift in the President's position on NHIS; for example, in his 2017 State of the National Address, the President included the NHIS Bill as being amongst those to be tackled by government and parliament in the 2017/18 financial year.

Table 8.2 The politics of social cash transfers and social health insurance in Uganda compared

Drivers/obstacles	Social cash transfers	Social health insurance
Policy coalition	Organizationally strongPolitical and technical strategyBureaucratic champions protected through donor supportPilot helps generate evidence and political momentum	Organizationally weakLacked a political strategyBureaucratic champions undermined by political dynamicsNo pilot project
Key actors within Uganda's political settlement	President: eventually supports under pressure from donors and grassroots actorsMFPED: oppositional, some internal champions MPs: broad support base CSOs: supportive Middle-class: support not required Rural poor: supportive	President: largely opposes under pressure from private sector actorsMFPED: oppositional, no internal championsMPs: narrow support base CSOs: mixed Middle-class: opposed Rural poor: sceptical
Political settlement dynamics	Increased competitive pressures catalyse inflationary patronage/ populism that SCTs can be aligned with	Increased competitive pressures catalyse inflationary patronage/ populism that undermines systemic responses
Ideas: paradigmatic	Alignment with patronage and 'dignity' eventually trumps concerns with dependency and deservingness	Poorly aligned with culture of patronage and presidential commitment to 'free' healthcare
Ideas: policy solution	Simple ideaGrowing global consensus on effectiveness and mode of delivery	Complex ideaNo consensus on ideal form or mode of delivery

Source: Authors' construction. MFPED: Ministry of Finance, Planning and Economic Development; CSOs: civil society organizations; SCTs: social cash transfers.

the promotion of social protection in Uganda, similar types of coalitions formed around both SCTs and SHI, in that they were composed above all of government bureaucrats and international development agencies, which then drew in and helped nurture a wider 'epistemic community', before trying to enrol further support from within local civil and political society.

However, in every respect, the transnational policy coalition that formed around SCTs in Uganda, and the strategies that it devised and deployed to promote SCTs, outweighed and outperformed the coalition that formed around SHI. A stark illustration of this can be found in a comparison of the ESP Secretariat, which acted as both a policy advocacy and project delivery unit for SCTs within the Ministry of Gender, with that of the NHIS Secretariat within the Ministry of Health. Whereas the latter consisted of between two and five officials located within a small part of the main ministry building, ESP has over twelve senior staff based in the central office with a further team of regional coordinators. ESP's office occupied its own plot in a prime part of Kampala and is very well equipped with computers and a fleet of vehicles. These differences directly reflect the uneven prioritization given to the two policy initiatives amongst donors. DFID and the World Bank are amongst the most powerful development agencies in Uganda, and were also promoting cash transfers more broadly as part of a new global policy agenda that their organizations were playing a central role in establishing during the mid-2000s (Hickey and Seekings, this volume). DFID in particular proved able to form a sustained coalition of agencies around social protection. In comparison, the World Bank has not been as active in promoting health insurance in Uganda (or elsewhere); sustained support for social health insurance in Uganda came from WHO alone.

The coalition in support of SCTs proved much more adept at navigating the politics of social protection in Uganda. Whilst the NHIS Secretariat gained the support of key actors on the health committee of parliament, little effort was made to broaden this nucleus into a wider forum of support within parliament (as happened with cash transfers) or to include oppositional figures in higher-profile events such as international study tours, as occurred around cash transfers. Strongly informed by political economy analysis, the SCT coalition engaged in a campaign that was persistent, well resourced, clearly targeted, and both creative and flexible in nature. The SHI policy coalition was further hampered by the fact that its advocacy efforts generated opposition from players with significant holding power and close connections to the President, namely the Private Sector Working Group, that formed a coalition against a NHIS. This did not occur with the SCT case, where opposition was centred around some influential actors within MFPED who could be targeted more easily.

Importantly, the SCT policy coalition was able to draw on a relatively simple policy idea that was gaining global traction at the time, whereas social health insurance remains a more complex and technical agenda that lacks the wider appeal of 'just giving money to the poor' (Hanlon et al. 2010). In contrast to the growing consensus about the value of cash transfers and growing experience of how they could be implemented from pilot schemes, there remains no wider consensus on the best way of constructing and delivering health insurance schemes in low-income contexts (Lagomarsino et al. 2012: 933).

4.3.2. Political settlement dynamics: elite ideas, incentives, and holding power

Ideas clearly mattered here, from the nature of the policy solutions through to the fit between these and paradigmatic ideas within Uganda's political settlement (Schmidt 2008). Unlike the SCT coalition, advocates of SHI lacked a pilot scheme that could generate evidence and help persuade powerful players that a new policy idea could work effectively within Uganda. At a higher level, shifting the focus to 'vulnerable groups' rather than 'the poorest' per se allowed SCT advocates to overcome elite concerns around dependency and deservingness and tap into a belief that older people deserved help to secure their dignity. The trope of just giving money to the poor also aligned well with the increasing tendency of the President to do just that through the 'poverty tours' that were being used to shore up declining political support in rural areas and undermine opposition support in the north.[6] In contrast, the notion of SHI directly contradicted an earlier electoral promise of free healthcare, something that—as with universal primary education (Kjær and Muwanga 2016)—the President was unwilling to row back on within the context of the shifting dynamics of Uganda's political settlement from the early 2000s onwards, which had rendered him more vulnerable to pressures from both the political opposition and grassroots actors.

Whereas the increasingly personalized and populist approach to governance that the President adopted during this period was relatively easy to align with the logic of cash transfers, it was inimical to the more institutionalized and systematic approach required to deliver both a higher-performing health sector and a complex new scheme for financing it. The leadership crisis that has characterized the health ministry since the mid-2000s is symptomatic of these wider shifts within Uganda's political settlement, in which increased levels of political competition and internal factionalism within the NRM have forced the President to view appointments in such ministries as an avenue for building patronage networks and securing elite support as opposed to promoting service delivery (Bukenya and Golooba-Mutebi 2019). These shifts, and the damage they did to the possibility of bureaucrats performing their roles in a technocratic and effective manner, directly undermined the progress

[6] As discussed in more depth in Hickey and Bukenya (2016), it was not accidental that the north featured heavily in the initial roll-out of the pilot, or that Yumbe, which the President ordered would become the fifteenth district to benefit, is based in the region. The SCG was seen as part of a wider charm offensive that was undertaken by the NRM within the north after peace had largely been established after 2006, and which was aimed at both offering a post-conflict dividend and turning an historically oppositional region into supporters of the NRM.

of the NHIS, both in terms of the Ministry's capacity and commitment to deliver reforms effectively and with regards to the poor quality of provision undermining popular support for a scheme that would render them more dependent on a failing system, and having to pay more for the privilege.

The logic of exchange that characterizes the notion of health insurance also runs counter to the reciprocal logic of the patron–client relationships that continue to predominate in Uganda. Rather, they invoke the terms of a new 'social contract' that involves the government delivering higher-quality services in exchange for tax-payers' money, and also a sense of social solidarity amongst citizens, whereby a pooled financial risk mechanism for healthcare access is created within which the rich can subsidize the poor, the single can subsidize those with families, the healthy can subsidize the unhealthy, and the young can subsidize the old. Writing with reference to 'free' basic primary education, but with obvious parallels to the abolishment of fees in the health sector, Tripp notes that free social policies make it difficult to develop productive relationships between citizens and the state 'built on mutual obligation, for example, paying taxes in exchange for the provision of public goods' (Tripp 2010: 188). At the local level, the abolition of citizens' contributions towards services they consume is associated with an apparent disconnect between service delivery institutions such as hospitals and schools, on one hand, and their communities on the other (Dauda 2004).

5. Conclusion

The fact that Uganda has made more progress with social cash transfers than social health insurance, despite each having been promoted over roughly the same period, reflects the differing nature of the two policy agendas, the ways in which they have been promoted and by whom, and the level of 'fit' with domestic political economy factors. In both cases, the critical factors have been the extent to which a transnational policy agenda has been persuasively promoted by a policy coalition in ways that rendered it legible to the dominant interests, actors, and ideas within Uganda's shifting political settlement (Lavers and Hickey 2016). Comparative insights on the politics of health insurance in sub-Saharan Africa suggest that progress requires not only high levels of elite commitment but also a high degree of capacity when it comes to enforcement, as in the cases of Ethiopia (Lavers 2019b) and Rwanda (Chemouni 2018). Although the 'dominant-developmental' nature of Uganda's political settlement might have been up to this challenge during the initial period of NRM rule, since then its commitment to poverty reduction and its capacity to deliver institutionalized responses to it have both waned. A key issue here is that each policy invokes different types of state–society relationship, whereby the logics of SCTs largely go with the grain of Uganda's political settlement, whilst social health insurance requires a move against this grain in pursuit of a new social contract between government and citizen. Unfortunately for Uganda's significant population of vulnerable citizens, there are few signs at present that such a contract is in the process of emerging.

References

Andrews, M. and L. Bategeka (2013). Overcoming the limits of institutional reform in Uganda. ESID Working Paper No. 27. Manchester: ESID.

Barkan, J. (2011). *Uganda: Assessing Risks to Stability*. Washington, DC: Centre for Strategic and International Studies.

Barrientos, A. (2013). *Social Assistance in Developing Countries*. Cambridge: Cambridge University Press.

Barthelemy, L. (2015). *Is the National Health Insurance Scheme Ill-Conceived?* ESRA Brief April 2015, 14–17.

Basaza, R.K., T.S. O'Connell, and I. Chapčáková (2013). Players and processes behind the national health insurance scheme: a case study of Uganda. *BMC Health Services Research*, 13(357), 1–13.

Bukenya, B. and F. Golooba-Mutebi (2019). Political settlements and the delivery of maternal health services in rural Uganda. ESID Working Paper No. 113. Manchester, UK: The University of Manchester. Available at http://www.effective-states.org/wp-content/uploads/working_papers/final-pdfs/esid_wp_113_bukenya_golooba-mutebi.pdf.

Bukenya, B. and W. Muhumuza (2017). The politics of core public sector reform in Uganda: behind the façade. ESID Working Paper No. 85. Manchester, UK: The University of Manchester. Available at http://www.effective-states.org/wp-content/uploads/working_papers/final-pdfs/esid_wp_85_bukenya_muhumuza.pdf.

Chemouni, B. (2018). The political path to universal health coverage: power, ideas and community-based health insurance in Rwanda. *World Development*, 106, 87–98.

Cherrier, C. (2014). The politics of revenue mobilisation for social transfers in sub-Saharan Africa. Paper presented at the 14th EADI General Conference on Responsible Development in a Polycentric World. Bonn.

Dauda, C.L. (2004). The importance of de facto decentralization in primary education in Sub-Saharan Africa PTAs and local accountability in Uganda. *Journal of Planning Education and Research*, 24(1), 28–40.

Di John, J. and J. Putzel (2009). Political settlements: issues paper. Governance and Social Development Resource Centre, University of Birmingham, June.

George, A.L. and A. Bennett (2004). *Case Studies and Theory Development in the Social Sciences*. Cambridge, MA: MIT Press.

Golooba-Mutebi, F. and S. Hickey (2013). Investigating the links between political settlements and inclusive development in Uganda: towards a research agenda. ESID Working Paper 20. Manchester: ESID.

Golooba-Mutebi, F. and S. Hickey (2016). The master of institutional multiplicity? The shifting politics of regime survival, state-building and democratisation in Museveni's Uganda. *Journal of Eastern African Studies*, 10(4), 601–18.

Government of Uganda (GoU) (2015). *Uganda National Development Plan II*. Kampala: National Planning Authority.

Hanlon, J., A. Barrientos, and D. Hulme (2010). *Just Give Money to the Poor*. London: Kumarian Press.

Hickey, S. (2005). The politics of staying poor: exploring the political space for poverty reduction in Uganda. *World Development*, 33(6), 995–1009.

Hickey, S. (2013). Beyond the poverty agenda? Insights from the new politics of development in Uganda. *World Development*, 43, 194–206.

Hickey, S. and B. Bukenya (2016). The politics of promoting social cash transfers in Uganda. ESID Working Paper No. 69. Manchester, UK: The University of Manchester. Available at http://www.effective-states.org/wp-content/uploads/working_papers/final-pdfs/esid_wp_69_hickey_bukenya.pdf.

Hickey, S., R. Sabates-Wheeler, G. Guenther, and I. Macauslan (2009). Promoting social protection and social transfers: the politics of influencing. DFID internal report.

Huber, E. and J.D. Stephens (2012). *Democracy and the Left: Social Policy and Inequality in Latin America*. Chicago, IL: University of Chicago Press.

Kivumbi, G.W. and F. Kintu (2002). Exemptions and waivers from cost sharing: ineffective safety nets in decentralized districts in Uganda. *Health Policy and Planning*, 17(Suppl 1), 64–71.

Kjær, A.M. (2015). Political settlements and productive sector policies: understanding sector differences in Uganda. *World Development*, 68, 230–41.

Kjær, A.M. and N.K. Muwanga (2016). Inclusion as political mobilisation: the political economy of quality education initiatives in Uganda. ESID Working Paper No. 65. Manchester, UK: The University of Manchester. Available at http://www.effective-states.org/wp-content/uploads/working_papers/final-pdfs/esid_wp_65_kjaer_muwanga.pdf.

Kuteesa, F., E. Tumusiime-Mutebile, A. Whitworth, and T. Williamson (Eds.) (2010). *Uganda's Economic Reforms: Insider Accounts*. Oxford: Oxford University Press.

Lagomarsino, G., A. Garabrant, A. Adyas, R. Muga, and N. Otoo (2012). 'Moving towards universal health coverage: health insurance reforms in nine developing countries in Africa and Asia. *The Lancet*, 380(9845), 933–43.

Lavers, T. (2019a). Social cash transfers in Ethiopia. *African Affairs*, Advance access online.

Lavers, T. (2019b). Towards universal health coverage in Ethiopia's 'developmental state'? The political drivers of health insurance. *Social Science & Medicine*, https://doi.org/10.1016/j.socscimed.2019.03.007.

Lavers, T. and S. Hickey (2016). Conceptualising the politics of social protection in low income countries: the intersection of transnational ideas and domestic politics. *International Journal of Social Welfare*, 25(4), 388–98.

Lindemann, S. (2011). Just another change of guard? Broad-based politics and civil war in Museveni's Uganda. *African Affairs*, 110(440), 387–416.

Ministry of Health (MoH) (2014). National symposium on universal health coverage in Uganda. Imperial Royale Hotel, Kampala, 25–6 June 2014.

Ministry of Health (MoH) (2018). Health sector strategic plan mid-term review report. Kampala: Ministry of Health.

Munabi, A.W. (2015). Fundamentals for achieving universal health insurance in Uganda. *ESRA Brief*, 35–6.

Nabyonga, J. and C.M. Zikusooka (2010). Health financing reform in Uganda: how equitable is the proposed National Health Insurance scheme?' *International Journal for Equity in Health*, 9(1), 23.

Niño-Zarazúa, M., A. Barrientos, S. Hickey, and D. Hulme (2012). Social protection in sub-Saharan Africa: getting the politics right. *World Development*, 40, 163–76.

Peck, J. and N. Theodore (2015). *Fast Policy: Experimental Statecraft at the Thresholds of Neoliberalism*. Minneapolis, MN: University of Minnesota Press.

Pruce, K. and S. Hickey (2017). The politics of promoting social protection in Zambia. ESID Working Paper No. 75. Manchester, UK: The University of Manchester. Available at http://www.effective-states.org/wp-content/uploads/working_papers/final-pdfs/esid_wp_75_pruce_hickey.pdf.

Schmidt, V.A. (2008). Discursive institutionalism: the explanatory power of ideas and discourse. *Annual Review of Political Science*, 11(1), 303–26.

Stone, D. (2012). Transfer and translation of policy. *Policy Studies*, 33(6), 483–99.

Talemwa, M. (2009). World Bank refuses to fund health insurance. *The Observer*. Available at http://www.observer.ug/news-headlines/3368-world-bank-refuses-to-fund-health-insurance.

Tripp, A.M. (2010). *Museveni's Uganda: Paradoxes of Power in a Hybrid Regime*. London: Rienner.

Whitfield, L., O. Therkildsen, L. Buur, and A.M. Kjær (2015). *The Politics of African Industrial Policy: A Comparative Perspective*. Cambridge: Cambridge University Press.

Yates, J., R. Cooper, and J. Holland (2006). Social protection and health: experiences in Uganda. *Development Policy Review*, 24(3), 339–56.

9

Social Assistance, Electoral Competition, and Political Branding in Malawi

Sam Hamer and Jeremy Seekings

1. Introduction

The proliferation of social assistance programmes across Africa has coincided with redemocratization, i.e. the return of multi-party systems with regular, competitive elections in place of one-party states and military regimes. Elections replaced coups as the primary mechanism for leadership change. Studies of other areas of public policy, including health and education, suggest that democracy sometimes prompts public policy reforms (e.g. Harding and Stasavage 2013; Carbone and Pellegata 2017) and has almost always prevented death through famine (Devereux and Tiba 2007). To date, however, there has been little analysis of whether and how democratization matters for social assistance in Africa, or of whether and how social assistance informs electoral and partisan politics.

The standard explanation of why elections matter focuses on the representation of poorer citizens. Opposition parties may oust incumbents whom poor voters consider insufficiently responsive to their needs. Even when opposition parties fail to win an election, they sometimes pose a sufficiently serious challenge that incumbent parties are pushed into reforms intended to bolster their support. Democratic freedoms also allow the media and civil society to monitor more effectively governments' performance and to draw attention to governments' failings.

The experience of the advanced capitalist countries suggests that democratic competition shapes both the extent and form of welfare state-building. Indeed, Huber and Stephens argue that 'partisan politics was the *single most important factor* that shaped the development of welfare states through time' (2001: 1, emphasis added). The form of welfare state-building in the advanced capitalist countries after the Second World War was largely determined by whether their governments were dominated by a social democratic party, a Christian

Sam Hamer and Jeremy Seekings, *Social Assistance, Electoral Competition, and Political Branding in Malawi*
In: *The Politics of Social Protection in Eastern and Southern Africa*. Edited by: Sam Hickey, Tom Lavers, Miguel Niño-Zarazúa, and Jeremy Seekings, Oxford University Press (2020).
DOI: 10.1093/oso/9780198850342.003.0009

democratic party, or parties in the 'secular centre and right' (Esping-Andersen 1990; Huber and Stephens 2001). In Latin America and South and East Asia, social assistance reforms have generally been pioneered by politicians or parties on the left or centre-left (Seekings 2012), although some right-wing candidates have subsequently embraced and even extended these reforms (Fairfield and Garay 2017).

In Africa, few parties line up neatly on the left–right political continuum associated with industrialized societies. Many presidents and parties have regional or even ethnic support bases and vague ideological positions. Populist leaders and parties have emerged, but their populism tends to be rather nebulous. Politicians, and even presidents, move from one party to another (Rakner et al. 2007; Resnick 2012). Voters expect their parliamentary representatives to deliver patronage to their constituents rather than legislate programmatic reforms (Cheeseman 2016) and vote at least in part along ethnic lines (e.g. Norris and Mattes 2013; Hoffman and Long 2013). Election campaigns tend to focus on valence issues, with competing candidates claiming to be more efficient (and less corrupt) (Bleck and Van de Walle 2013).

Nonetheless, recent studies suggest that electoral competition in Africa has contributed to social assistance policy reforms. Changes of government were consequential in Zambia (Siachiwena 2016, Pruce and Hickey, Chapter 7 of this volume), Zimbabwe (Chinyoka and Seekings 2016), and perhaps also Ghana (Grebe 2015). The vulnerability of incumbent parties drove reform in Botswana (Hamer 2015; Seekings, Chapter 2 of this volume) and Zanzibar (Seekings 2016). In most of these cases, social assistance has been a valence issue, in that the competing parties have not staked out starkly contrasting positions. In any particular country, parties generally concurred on the direction of reform, i.e. they were usually either uniformly supportive (at least rhetorically, claiming pro-poor credentials) or uniformly opposed (sharing concerns over both the affordability of and 'dependency' on government 'handouts'). Elections may have sometimes provided a mechanism through which voters have held governments to account, but they have rarely been decided on the basis of distinct policy platforms. In office, however, parties have differed in their approaches to social protection, shaping the *form* of welfare state-building. In Botswana, for example, the Botswana Democratic Party built a welfare state with conservative characteristics (see Seekings, Chapter 2 of this volume).

Malawi has been a significant exception to some of these more general patterns. Until the mid-2000s, Malawian parties were largely indistinguishable, voters did not form blocks defined by their common interests, and elections were therefore not mechanisms for the representation of voters with well-defined interests (Rakner et al 2007; Svåsand 2013). Since 2005, however, the fluidity in partisan politics provided a powerful incentive to individual presidential candidates to develop strong, clear, and national 'brands'. The dominant 'brand'—developed by Bingu wa Mutharika (president from 2004 until 2012) and then inherited by his brother Peter Mutharika (who was elected president in 2014)—focused on generous support for small farmers to expand agricultural production. When Joyce Banda succeeded the older Mutharika as president in 2012, she chose to brand herself as the champion of social assistance. Despite widespread ambivalence within the Malawian elite and the absence of any organized domestic constituency in favour of social assistance reforms, the issue was raised high up the national policy agenda. Starkly contrasting positions on social assistance reform featured prominently in the 2014 elections.

This chapter contributes to the growing literature on the political conditions leading to social assistance policy reform in Africa. We argue that competitive elections in Africa *can* provide an incentive to reform by pushing presidential candidates and parties to brand themselves, often in populist ways. The chapter also points to the limits of this electoral impetus to reform. Joyce Banda was defeated heavily in the 2014 election. Although the scale of her defeat reflected other factors also, the case of Malawi does not support the contention by Hanlon, Barrientos, and Hulme (2010) that social assistance is uniformly popular. Voters might prefer alternative forms of public expenditure and might also doubt the deservingness of at least some categories of grant beneficiaries. Competition can push candidates to brand themselves with social assistance reform, but this may not be a sufficiently popular brand to win an election. Indeed, if it was clearly a popular issue, the other parties might be expected also to express at least rhetorical support for reform.

2. The Economy, Politics, and Policy Under Bingu wa Mutharika

Malawi has long been one of the poorest countries in southern Africa, suffering from slow economic growth, chronic food insecurity, widespread poverty, and dependence on foreign aid. The overwhelming majority of the population remained dependent on peasant agriculture, supplemented with migrant remittances. Malawi's first president, Hastings Kamuzu Banda, imagined that agricultural estates would be the primary engine of economic growth.

At the same time, he sought to encourage smallholder maize production, through price support and subsidized inputs. In the 1980s, economic crisis and pressure from the World Bank led to the liberalization of farm input and maize markets. Peasant cash crop production expanded, but maize production faltered (Harrigan 2003, 2005). Banda suppressed any discussion of poverty, but the country's first household survey, conducted in 1997–8 after Banda had been ousted from office, showed that almost two thirds of the population lived in poverty (Ellis, Kutengule, and Nyasulu 2003).

In 1993, after a devastating drought, deepening domestic opposition, and growing international criticism, Banda acceded to a referendum on the restoration of multi-party democracy. Banda lost the referendum, and the following year he and his Malawi Congress Party (MCP) were defeated in multi-party elections by the United Democratic Front (UDF), led by former MCP secretary-general Bakili Muluzi. Both the MCP and UDF had regional support bases, in the central and southern parts of the country, respectively. A third party—the Alliance for Democracy (AFORD)—was based in the north. All three parties tried but failed to project themselves as supra-regional (van Donge 1995). The parties did not have distinctive political platforms, and their leaders readily switched loyalties in shifting coalitions, changing their colours in a 'democracy of chameleons' (Englund 2002: 17). This regional distribution of support was largely repeated in 1999 (when Muluzi was re-elected) and 2004 (when his chosen successor Mutharika was elected). Voters seem to have been swayed by their perceptions of regional favouritism in patronage by successive governments (Ferree and Horowitz 2010).

The Muluzi governments acknowledged the scale of poverty in Malawi, in contrast to the previous regime, and focused on smallholder production. In 1998, one year prior to elections, the government launched a Starter Pack Programme to encourage maize production. Initially funded in large part by donors (primarily the UK's Department for International Development, DFID, and the World Bank), the Starter Pack Programme provided free seeds and other inputs to almost 3 million households in 1999/2000. Donors became increasingly sceptical, however, preferring to address poverty through targeted public works programmes[1] and other measures. Donor pressure

[1] The World Bank supported successive phases of the Malawi Social Action Fund (MASAF): MASAF I (1996–2001), MASAF II (1998–2003), MASAF III (in three stages from 2002), and, much later, MASAF IV (from 2013). Most of these phases included a public works component, although most of the funds seem to have been allocated to the provision of building materials. Communities were expected to provide free labour; little MASAF funding was spent on paying for labour. We are grateful to one of the reviewers for clarifying this point.

resulted in subsidized inputs being targeted more narrowly on the poor, as a safety net rather than a production-oriented intervention (Harrigan 2005; Potter 2005). Nonetheless, and despite drought and food crisis in 2001–3 (during which one third of the population needed food aid—Devereux and Tiba 2007), real GDP per capita rose and poverty declined (albeit slowly).

The political landscape changed dramatically in 2005. One year after his election, President Mutharika resigned from the UDF and founded a new party, the Democratic Progressive Party (DPP). Mutharika chose to brand himself by launching what he presented as a historic crusade against famine and food insecurity. His flagship programme—the Agricultural Input Subsidy Programme (AISP), later renamed the Farm Input Subsidy Programme (FISP)—massively expanded the provision of subsidized fertilizer and seed to smallholder farmers. The programme was launched in the 2005/6 season, following a drought, raised maize prices, and food shortages (Chinsinga and Poulton 2014). The programme helped to stimulate rapid growth in maize yield and restored national food security (Denning et al. 2009). This in turn contributed to a sharp rise in real GDP per capita.

The AISP was not only the government's flagship programme; it was also what defined the DPP, which adopted a logo featuring four maize cobs. Mutharika himself took over the portfolio of Minister of Agriculture and Food Security. AISP subsidies were symbolically important as well as materially valuable to small farmers. Subsidized or free farm inputs appealed to strongly held values. Because 'a good and respectable life in the village means growing one's own food', programmes such as the Starter Pack Programme and AISP helped 'to restore self-respect' (Van Donge, 2005: 125). In addition, Mutharika could tap into nationalist sentiment in a populist but positive way. When the international development community insisted that the government accept more food aid instead of offering subsidies, Mutharika famously declared: 'Enough is enough; I am not going to go on my knees to beg for food; let us grow the food ourselves'.[2] In the 2009 election, Mutharika used the AISP to present himself as a 'food security president'. Mutharika even boasted that the programme's success showed that 'it is possible for Africa to become the food basket of the world'.[3] In the run-up to the election, Mutharika's

[2] 'Unravelling the "Miracle" of Malawi's Green Revolution', GRAIN, 14 January 2010 (http://www.grain.org/article/entries/4075-unravelling-the-miracle-of-malawi-s-green-revolution, accessed 19 April 2017).

[3] Molalet Tsedeke, '"It Is Possible for Africa to Become the Food Basket of the World", Says Mutharika', *Nepad.org*, 28 October 2010 (http://www.nepad.org/news/it-possible-africa-become-food-basket-world-says-mutharika, accessed 3 June 2019).

government scaled up subsidies massively, to almost US$300 million, i.e. one sixth of all government expenditure and about 6.5 per cent of GDP.

Malawi's citizens rewarded Mutharika and the DPP with their votes. Mutharika himself won 66 per cent of the presidential vote, with clear majorities in all three regions. No previous candidate had won even a plurality outside his home region. The DPP won 114 of the 193 seats in the National Assembly. Mutharika's defiance of international aid donors in implementing the AISP and boosting maize production underpinned his supra-regional appeal and hence his electoral victory (Ferree and Horowitz 2010).

The AISP reached a large number of voters across the country. A panel study of three districts (one in each region) found that three quarters of rural households benefited. The programme did not target the poorest (or most food-insecure) households; indeed, female-headed households were less likely to receive benefits.[4] The study found no evidence of either partisan or ethnic targeting, but there were partisan consequences. Households that received a subsidy in 2009/10 were more likely to become DPP partisans than households that did not receive the subsidy, and this effect remained significant even when controlling for a range of other variables (Dionne and Horowitz 2016; see also Brazys et al. 2015).

Mutharika showed little interest in social assistance, despite evidence that farmer support programmes were missing many poor households. In 2006, a report co-authored by German consultant Bernd Schubert suggested that one in ten households in Malawi was poor because it had no one able or available to work and was thus unable to benefit from farm input subsidies. It was estimated that a targeted cash transfer programme costing approximately 1 per cent of GDP would reduce the ultra-poverty rate from 22 to 12 per cent. In 2006, a pilot Social Cash Transfer Programme was initiated in Mchinji District, with backing from UNICEF. Only 'labour-constrained' households below the ultra-poverty line were eligible for the modest benefits (which averaged just over US$11/month/household). The programme's advocates envisaged that coverage would be gradually extended, reaching about 140,000 households by the end of 2012. Even though the programme was almost entirely funded by donors, and a preliminary impact evaluation showed positive effects, the Mutharika government was not enthusiastic. By 2012, the programme reached only 30,000 households in total, and the roll-out

[4] The 2010/11 Integrated Household Survey found no difference between male- and female-headed households, but did find that access was higher among non-poor than among poor households (World Bank 2013: 117).

was yet to begin in nineteen of the country's twenty-eight districts (Angeles et al. 2016: 282–305). A draft National Social Support Policy was not approved by the government. Many poor households did benefit from school feeding programmes, and some from other programmes, but less than 1 per cent of households received cash transfers (Malawi 2012: 173–4, 177–8). In contrast, about one half of all rural households received FISP subsidies. FISP, almost entirely funded by the government, cost five times as much as *all* social protection programmes (including feeding and public employment programmes), almost entirely funded by donors (World Bank 2013: 111).

The slow expansion of cash transfer programmes in Malawi reflected ambivalence or even hostility towards cash transfers not only within the DPP but also within the Malawian elite more generally. In 2008, Kalebe-Nyamongo interviewed ministers and MPs, senior government officials, and prominent people in the media, academia, and NGOs. She found that Malawi's elites tended to view poverty as 'normal' (at least in rural areas) such that it could not be eliminated in the short-term. Whilst elites attributed poverty to insufficient economic development and political will, and poor education, they also blamed poor people for not trying hard enough to escape poverty. Social assistance programmes were said to encourage laziness and 'dependency' on 'handouts'. The elites preferred policies that assisted the poor to work their way out of poverty (Kalebe-Nyamongo and Marquette 2014). Our interviews with Malawian government officials and other members of Malawi's elite broadly corroborated this assessment.[5]

3. Joyce Banda, Social Assistance, and Political Branding

Mutharika pushed for his brother Peter to succeed him as DPP leader. When the elected vice-president, Joyce Banda, declined to step aside, Mutharika expelled her from the DPP, but was unable to depose her as vice-president of the country. In April 2012, Mutharika suffered a heart attack and died. Banda—who had established her own party, the People's Party (PP), four months earlier—became president.

Her expulsion from the DPP and then unexpected ascent to the presidency presented Banda with the challenge of constructing a distinctive national and moral image. She chose to brand herself and her party as pro-poor. Whereas,

[5] Sam Hamer interviewed sixteen political leaders, officials in government and NGOs, and academics, in mid-2014.

she claimed, Mutharika and his DPP had been pro-growth without concern for the poor, she and the PP were both pro-growth and pro-poor. Social assistance programmes played a central part in her branding exercise, distinguishing both her and her party from Mutharika and the DPP's embrace of farmer input subsidies.

Banda thus staked out a public brand not only outside the mainstream of the elite, but in defiance of it. 'The Joyce Banda I have come to know', commented blogger Kondwani Munthali, 'is the mother who speaks on empowering the poor [...] who removed all the trappings of the Vice Presidency and went to sit down on a mat in [the peri-urban township of] Ndirande to console a [...] victim of police brutality'.[6] Indeed, Mutharika had reportedly chosen Banda as his running mate in 2009 precisely because of her pro-women and pro-poor image.[7] Banda's own story was one of success in the face of the difficulties facing many women in Malawi. She completed secondary school at the age of twenty-five, having had three children. She left an abusive marriage, remarried, and opened a textile manufacturing company that grew to employ more than a hundred people. She made it her 'mission in life to assist women and youth to gain social and political empowerment', she claimed, just as she herself had experienced empowerment through education and business. In the 1980s, she co-founded the National Association of Business Women, which grew into the country's largest network of rural women, with more than 50,000 members. She co-founded the Young Women Leaders Network and the Hunger Project. The Joyce Banda Foundation provided meals and care for thousands of orphans and vulnerable children, earning Banda a Goodwill Ambassadorship for Safe Motherhood from the African Union. In interviews, Banda explained her decision to enter politics as following on from her work as an activist and philanthropist: 'For me, the motivation [...] was to be involved in influencing laws that have a big impact on women and children'.[8]

Reality did not entirely match this carefully constructed image. Banda's second husband was the Chief Justice, and the two of them were considered to

[6] Kondwali Munthali, 'The Joyce Banda I Know and Trust', 26 April 2012, http://www.munthali.com/2012/04/joyce-banda-i-know-and-trust.html.

[7] 'Malawi Leader Chooses Foreign Minister as Running Mate', *Reuters*, 6 February 2009, (http://www.reuters.com/article/ozatp-malawi-election-idAFJOE5150KO20090206, accessed 19 April 2017).

[8] Joyce Banda, 'Why We Care', not dated (http://www.universalaccessproject.org/global-leaders/joyce-banda, accessed 7 March 2017); 'President Joyce Banda on Women's Health and Empowerment in Malawi', January 2013 (https://www.youtube.com/watch?v=EzcoHYNR0yA), 'The Journey of Dr Joyce Hilda Banda, the President of Malawi', November 2013 (https://wethewomenourjourneys.wordpress.com/2013/11/28/dr-joyce-hilda-bandathe-president-of-malawi, accessed 16 March 2015).

be core members of the powerful 'Zomba mafia' within the political parties that governed Malawi for twenty years. The National Association of Business Women celebrated successes that were far removed from the lives of poor women. Whatever the reality, however, Banda was energetic in promoting her new brand.

Banda refused to resign as vice-president after she was expelled from the DPP because, she declared, she had a constitutional responsibility and mandate to fight for the well-being of the 'ordinary Malawian'.[9] As leader of a new opposition party, and then as president, Banda developed her brand as a champion of women and the poor, whom (she claimed) Mutharika had neglected. Distancing herself from her more elitist and male peers, Banda professed to understand the challenges facing women and the poor. At a rally in the north, Banda—herself from Zomba in southern Malawi—explained:

> I know the kind of suffering that women are going through in this country. Their suffering does not need any introduction to me. I am the best advocate of the poor because I know what poverty is. I have fought against this, and will continue to fight.[10]

Mutharika's widow mocked Banda for supposing that someone who had distributed a 'little money here and there for village women to sell fritters or doughnuts' could become president.[11] Banda turned this around, responding: 'she is right, because I've spent thirty years of my life empowering rural women; if I am aligned with the majority of women who struggle every day [...] that's fine, that's my mission'.[12] Banda used her first State of the Nation Address, in May 2012, to distance her government from her predecessor's. In addition to 'transforming the structure of the economy in order to achieve economic growth', her government would protect 'the vulnerable and the excluded'. She staked out a distinctive populist position: 'As a Malawian woman who knows the humiliation of Malawian women; as a Malawian who has championed the plight of rural poor', she would champion

[9] 'Malawi: Vice President Joyce Banda Launches New Party', *Vibe Ghana*, 8 September 2011 (http://vibeghana.com/2011/09/08/malawi-president-joyce-banda-launches-new-party, accessed 3 June 2015).

[10] 'JB Attacks Poverty: "I Know Malawians Are Suffering"', *Nyasa Times*, 22 July 2013 (https://www.nyasatimes.com/jb-attacks-poverty-i-know-malawians-are-suffering, accessed 9 June 2015).

[11] 'Malawi's First Lady Weighs in on Sacked VP Vilification Campaign', *Afrique en ligne*, 19 December 2012 (https://web.archive.org/web/20101220022458/http://www.afriquejet.com/news/africa-news/malawi-first-lady-weighs-in-on-sacked-vp-vilification-campaign-2010121864612.html, accessed 7 March 2017).

[12] 'Madam President: Meeting Malawi's Joyce Banda', *Guardian*, 20 December 2012 (https://www.youtube.com/watch?v=qBmaeOM1omY&feature=youtube_gdata_player).

the causes of people who had fallen through the cracks as a result of Mutharika's growth-focused policies.[13]

In practice, Banda's government's first priority was to stabilize the economy, which had slid into crisis under Mutharika's second government. She sought a rapprochement with international aid donors, agreed an aid package from the IMF and World Bank in exchange for devaluing the currency, and reversed several Mutharika-era laws curtailing political freedoms. Banda became the darling of the international community. She ordered the government to shed its fleet of Mercedes-Benz automobiles, sold the presidential jet, and reduced her own salary by one third.[14] 'I had to look at the situation of my fellow Malawians', Banda said; 'if we are going to ask Malawians to make sacrifices, I must be the first to do it'. Her government's austerity measures did indeed require sacrifices by many Malawians, through inflation and food shortages. In response, the government sought social programmes that could 'cushion' the poor.[15]

In July 2012, the new government approved the long-dormant National Social Support Policy. The value of the social cash transfer (SCT) was increased and an ambitious implementation programme was developed. The SCT Scheme Pilot was renamed the SCT Programme. Whilst no new programmes were introduced (as DPP MPs pointed out[16]), the new government proposed a rapid, countrywide roll-out of the SCT Programme as well as the expansion of public employment and school feeding programmes, with the cost to be shared between donors and the government of Malawi. SCTs would be rolled out to the poorest 10 per cent of the population, i.e. about 300,000 households, at a total cost of more than 1 per cent of GDP, of which the government would pay 40 per cent (Angeles et al 2016; Juergens and Pellerano 2016). The World Bank was broadly supportive, recommending that FISP focus on 'viable' peasant farmers, i.e. farmers with the capacity to expand production significantly, so that funds could be freed up for SCTs targeted more precisely on the poor (World Bank 2013).

[13] State of the Nation Address, May 2012.

[14] 'Malawi Sells Presidential Jet to Feed Poor', *Sydney Morning Herald*, 6 September 2013 (http://www.smh.com.au/world/malawi-sells-presidential-jet-to-feed-poor-20130906-2t944.html, accessed 18 March 2015).

[15] Interview with Joyce Banda, *Talk Africa*, 28 August 2013 (https://www.youtube.com/watch?v=yS0FR2XDDSU, accessed 7 March 2017); 'Malawi Leader Defends China Links, Tells the West: "Don't Tell Us What to Do"', *Nyasa Times*, 22 March 2013 (http://www.nyasatimes.com/2013/03/22, accessed April 2017).

[16] George Chaponda, Response to the State of the Nation Address, *Hansard*, 20 May 2013. There does not appear to have been any significant discussion of an old-age pension. It was only in 2015/16 that the ILO and HelpAge International began to work with Malawi government officials in developing new plans for a more comprehensive social protection 'floor', including social pensions.

Banda herself was said to be 'euphoric on how the social protection programme has [. . .] acted as a cushion against devaluation'.[17] In practice, however, programmes expanded much more slowly than envisaged. Service delivery failed to match the ambitious rhetoric. Only modest additional funding was provided for public works programmes by either the government or the World Bank (Juergens and Pellerano 2016).[18] Whilst there are no available data on the coverage and cost of SCT programmes at the end of Banda's government in mid-2014, data for late 2015 show that even then SCTs reached only 160,000 households (in eighteen of the country's twenty-eight districts), at a cost of just under 0.6 per cent of GDP. Both coverage and expense were just over one half of the targets set in 2012/13. Moreover, the government was paying for only 11 per cent of the cost (less than 0.1 per cent of GDP), compared with the target of 40 per cent (or just under 0.5 per cent of GDP). School feeding programmes had expanded slowly, but only to reach 25 per cent of all primary school children. The government contribution to the costs of the school feeding and public works programmes had remained low, at between 10 and 20 per cent (Juergens and Pellerano 2016).

Faced with slow progress in the roll-out of these programmes, and the imminence of elections in May 2014, Banda resorted to the longstanding practice of high-profile handouts, packaged as new presidential programmes, implemented through her office and run by her own appointees. The Presidential Initiative on Poverty and Hunger Reduction (PIPaHR) targeted rural women,[19] including through the provision of seeds and a 'Cow-a-Family' programme that (borrowing from a similar programme in Rwanda) provided poor families with a cow. Banda herself regularly and personally distributed cows to beneficiaries. Although the Cow-a-Family programme had distributed only 756 dairy cows by the end of April 2014, it was given massive publicity. Banda announced her intention for the programme to benefit 1.5 million people over the following five years, if she was re-elected as president. The government also distributed 8,680 goats and sheep through a parallel Small Stock Project.[20] The *Mudzi* (Village) Transformation Trust (MTT) was

[17] Chaponda, *Hansard*, 20 May 2013.

[18] 'Malawi President Launches K10bn Public Works Programme: Economic Recovery', *Nyasa Times*, 9 December 2012 (https://www.nyasatimes.com/malawi-president-launches-k10bn-public-works-programme-economic-recovery, accessed June 2015).

[19] 'Presidential Initiative on Hunger Reduction to Realize K7 Billion', *Banthu Times*, 12 December 2013 (http://banthutimes.com/presidential-initiative-on-hunger-reduction-to-realize-k7-billion, accessed 18 March 2015).

[20] 'JB Launches "a Cow a Family" Initiative: Pledges Houses for Malawi Flood Victims', *Nyasa Times*, 28 February 2013 (https://www.nyasatimes.com/jb-launches-a-cow-a-family-initiative-pledges-houses-for-malawi-flood-victims, accessed 8 June 2015); Henry Nyaka, 'Malawi: One Cow a Family

another hallmark programme on Banda's 'people-centred development agenda'. 'As a mother', Banda explained, 'it is my sincere wish that Malawians must have decent, adequate and affordable accommodation'. By building houses for poor households, the MTT would ensure that development was inclusive and prosperity was shared. Banda herself presented 'Mudzi houses' to beneficiaries, with much publicity—although only 500 houses had been built by the end of 2013.[21]

Banda's new programmes were widely criticized as entailing self-promotion more than poverty reduction: 'The president is just trying to popularise herself'.[22] Opposition MPs claimed that the president's travel to deliver cows cost many times the value of the cows themselves.[23] But even critics acknowledged that these programmes were politically popular.[24] Giving cows to poor women was reported to be 'effective with female voters especially'.[25] In her campaign for re-election in 2014, Banda emphasized both the cow and house programmes as symbols of her dedication to the poor. 'It is a known fact that

Initiative Goes to Rumphi', *Malawi News Agency*, 16 July 2013 (https://allafrica.com/stories/201307170205.html, accessed 7 March 2017); 'JB Says "One Cow per Family" to Benefit 1m Families in Malawi', *Nyasa Times*, 5 April 2013 (https://www.nyasatimes.com/jb-says-one-cow-per-family-to-benefit-1m-families-in-malawi, accessed 8 June 2015); Memory Kutengule, '756 Cows Distributed to Vulnerable Farm Families', *Malawi Voice*, 29 April 2014 (http://joycebanda2014.org/?p=518, accessed 19 April 2017).

---

[21] 'Malawi Leader Lays Foundation Stone for 7,500 Houses', *Nyasa Times*, 2 July 2013 (https://www.nyasatimes.com/malawi-leader-lay-foundation-stone-for-7500-houses-chinese-company-to-build, accessed 7 June 2015); 'Malawi President Banda Leaves for US for UN General Assembly', *Nyasa Times*, 16 September 2013 (https://www.nyasatimes.com/malawi-president-banda-leaves-for-us-for-un-general-assembly, accessed 7 June 2015); 'Mzimba Chiefs Happy with Mudzi Trust', *Nyasa Times*, 22 September 2013 (https://www.nyasatimes.com/mzimba-chiefs-happy-with-mudzi-trust, accessed 7 June 2015); 'JB Hands Over Mudzi House to Gogo Nyasoko of Kasungu', *Nyasa Times*, 3 December 2013 (https://www.nyasatimes.com/jb-hands-over-mudzi-house-to-gogo-nyasoko-of-kasungu, accessed 7 June 2015); Memory Kutengule, 'Malawi: Almost K1 Billion Spent On Mudzi Transformation Trust Project', *Malawi News Agency*, 25 November 2013 (https://allafrica.com/stories/201311260092.html, accessed 19 April 2017); 'JB Storms Ndirande, Assures Better Life for Malawi Citizens', *Malawi Nyasa*, 9 December 2013 (http://www.nyasatimes.com/2013/12/09/jb-storms-ndirande-assures-better-life-for-malawi-citizens, accessed June 2015); 'Mudzi Transformation Trust to Continue', *Malawi24*, 7 July 2014 (http://malawi24.com/2014/07/07/mudzi-transformation-trust-to-continue-pp, accessed 12 June 2015).

[22] 'Queries Over Joyce Banda Maize', *Face of Malawi*, 3 November 2012 (http://www.faceofmalawi.com/2012/11/queries-over-joyce-banda-maize, accessed 23 March 2015).

[23] Chaponda, *Hansard*, 20 May 2013; 'JB Takes Food Distribution Exercise to Mangochi', *Nyasa Times*, 9 November 2012 (https://www.nyasatimes.com/jb-takes-food-distribution-exercise-to-mangochi, accessed 26 May 2015).

[24] 'CSOs Thrash JB on Mudzi Transformation Trust, One Family One Cow', *Malawi Voice*, 20 June 2013 (http://malawivoice.com/2013/06/20/csos-thrash-jb-on-mudzi-transformationtrust-one-family-one-cow-we-need-decisions-that-transcend-political-considerations-81875, accessed 18 March 2015).

[25] McGroarty, Patrick, 'Malawi President Looks to Ride Free Cows to New Term', *Wall Street Journal*, 20 May 2014 (http://www.wsj.com/articles/SB10001424052702304908304579565453088446512, accessed 19 April 2017).

anyone who will come after me will not continue these projects', she beseeched voters at one rally in early 2014; 'so for the continuation, vote for me'.[26]

Banda herself embraced the discourse of 'handouts', using a word that was usually anathema to elites not only in Malawi but also across much of Africa. 'Even in Western countries', she said, 'there are ultra-poor people who survive on handouts'. If re-elected, she would 'continue to give help to those in need'.[27] 'I want all of you to know', she proclaimed at a November 2012 food distribution event, 'that I will continue distributing maize to the needy people of this country. There is no way I can stand by and drink tea when people are suffering'. Moreover, she emphasized that these were her initiatives, rather than government programmes: 'I will not tire, myself and various members of the People's Party will continue to distribute maize where it is needed most'.[28] Images of Banda personally delivering bags of maize, dancing with rural women, and sitting with elderly villagers appeared in the media during the weeks leading up to the election.[29] The PP's logo was adorned with PIPaHR maize bags (which were also stamped 'Joyce Banda') and Mudzi houses.[30] Whilst the distribution of cash and even houses during elections was a well-established practice in Malawi, Banda differed from her predecessors in that she formalized 'handouts' as programmes and explicitly incorporated these into the core of her political brand.

As the election approached, Banda attempted to keep the public's attention on her ambitions to reduce poverty. The PP manifesto, 'Transforming Malawi Together', trumpeted Banda's successes in 'modernizing rural areas and fighting poverty' through the MTT. In her preface, Banda wrote that she remained 'committed to continue to champion the cause of the rural and urban poor' (PP 2014). Banda toured the country, touting her record on poverty alleviation and distributing maize, livestock, and houses at 'development rallies', reinforcing the notion that she was the champion of the poor

[26] 'JB Vows to Continue Pro-Poor Initiative: Seeks Her Own Mandate', *Nyasa Times*, 11 May 2014 (https://www.nyasatimes.com/jb-vows-to-continue-pro-poor-initiative-seeks-her-own-mandate, accessed 26 May 2014).

[27] 'JB Vows to Continue Pro-Poor Initiative: Seeks Her Own Mandate', *Nyasa Times*, 11 May 2014 (http://www.nyasatimes.com/2014/05/11/jb-vows-to-continue-pro-poor-initiative-seeks-her-own-mandate, accessed 26 May 2014).

[28] Chaponda, *Hansard*, 20 May 2013; 'JB Takes Food Distribution Exercise to Mangochi', *Nyasa Times*, 9 November 2012 (https://www.nyasatimes.com/jb-takes-food-distribution-exercise-to-mangochi, accessed 26 May 2015).

[29] 'Malawi's First Lady Weighs in on Sacked VP Vilification Campaign', *Afrique en ligne*, 19 December 2012 (https://web.archive.org/web/20101220022458/http://www.afriquejet.com/news/africa-news/malawi-first-lady-weighs-in-on-sacked-vp-vilification-campaign-2010121864612.html, accessed 7 March 2017).

[30] 'A Long Way to Go', *Economist*, 19 March 2013 (http://www.economist.com/blogs/baobab/2013/03/malawi, accessed 19 April 2017). See also Gabay (2014).

(Dulani and Dionne 2014: 219). 'If you want the programmes we have been doing for the people of Malawi [. . .] to continue, vote for me'.[31] 'The president loves handouts', noted one observer; 'she says she's a charitable president and would like to give to people to alleviate their poverty'.[32]

4. The 2014 Election and the Limits to the Social Protection Brand

Banda approached the election in 2014 with a clear brand but a party in disarray. After forming a party in 2011, and especially after assuming the presidency in 2012, Banda had achieved considerable success in building up her party, recruiting seventy-seven MPs (out of 193) from other parties by February 2013. In September 2013, however, the 'Cashgate' corruption scandal broke. It was revealed that civil servants and senior ministers in the Banda government had stolen about US$30 million from government coffers, prompting donors to withhold about US$150 million in budgetary support. Corruption had long been a concern to voters (Zimmerman 2015), but Cashgate served to link this firmly to Banda's government specifically. The prospects for Banda and the PP began to look bleak, and many of her party's MPs defected. Lacking an established grassroots network or a reliable bureaucracy that could implement a large-scale poverty-alleviation programme, Banda had little choice but to emphasize her brand on the basis of her 'handout' initiatives.

Both major opposition parties were outspoken in their condemnation of Banda's initiatives. They denounced 'handouts' and insisted that economic growth was the only way to alleviate poverty. The president's fiercest critic was the MCP's presidential candidate Lazarus Chakwera, a minister in the Assemblies of God church and a newcomer to national politics. In his preface to the MCP's election manifesto, Chakwera wrote of the 'dependency syndrome', which was 'being exploited by the leaders to gain political popularity through handouts'. The manifesto itself emphasized the importance of economic growth and did not specify any poverty-alleviation programmes (MCP 2014). In his stump speech, Chakwera attacked Banda's programmes on the basis that they actually increased poverty: 'Malawians are poor not just

[31] 'JB Increasingly Upbeat to Win Malawi Elections', *Nyasa Times*, 11 May 2014 (https://www.nyasatimes.com/jb-increasingly-upbeat-to-win-malawi-elections, accessed 18 March 2015).

[32] Interview with Henry Chingaipe, Director, Institute for Policy Research & Social Empowerment, by Sam Hamer, 19 May 2014.

because of God's will but [. . .] due to the spirit of hand-outs which has grown roots among Malawians', Chakwera declared; 'no country in the world can develop through the spirit of giving its citizens Cows, Houses and any other Materials'; development required 'teaching people to work hard'.[33] On Election Day, Chakwera urged voters to vote for him 'not because I am giving you handouts in this campaign but because you desire to see change of things in a Malawi to come [sic]'.[34]

Peter Mutharika—the DPP leader and presidential candidate—simply promised to 'continue from where my brother left off'.[35] The DPP added pictures of Bingu wa Mutharika to their party regalia alongside the maize cob motif. It promised to abolish the Banda government's reforms of FISP and to 'make subsidized fertilizer available for every maize subsistence farmer that needs it'. Malawi would be transformed 'from being a predominantly importing and consuming country to a predominantly producing and exporting country; and a food-sufficient country where hunger is eliminated' (DPP 2014). Subsidies were still needed, Mutharika explained, 'so that every Malawian can afford the means to produce food while earning the dignity of labouring to feed [themselves]'.[36] Whereas Banda and the PP simply handed out houses, the DPP would subsidize cement so that Malawians could 'build what they want by themselves'.[37] The DPP also promised to pass a 'Law on Handouts', without providing any detail (DPP 2014: 11).

The three major parties thus campaigned with three distinct brands with respect to poverty alleviation and hence to the moral imagery required of political leaders in order to build supra-regional coalitions (as van Donge had argued in 1995). Banda branded herself unapologetically as the champion of 'handouts' to the poor, including especially her own initiatives. Chakwera branded himself (and the MCP) as the pro-growth party, and denounced 'handouts'. Mutharika and the DPP rebranded themselves as the party of

[33] 'Southern Region Shuns MCP Once More, as Chakwera Scorns JB's One Cow per Family Initiative', *Malawi Voice*, 8 May 2014 (http://malawivoice.com/2014/05/08/southern-region-shuns-mcp-chakwera-scorns-jbs-one-cow-per-family-initiative, accessed 23 March 2015); 'Chakwera Attacks JB on Hand-Outs in Zomba', *Nyasa Times*, 8 May 2014 (https://www.nyasatimes.com/chakwera-attacks-jb-on-hand-outs-in-zomba, accessed 23 March 2015).

[34] 'Chakwera Bemoans Handouts', *Afriem.org*, 12 May 2014 (http://www.afriem.org/2014/05/chakwera-bemoans-handouts-2, accessed 23 March 2015).

[35] 'The Spirit of Bingu and a Leadership Without an Agenda: Z Allan Ntata', *Maravi Post*, 11 May 2014 (http://www.maravipost.com/the-spirit-of-bingu-and-a-leadership-without-an-agenda-z-allan-ntata, accessed 22 June 2015).

[36] 'Mutharika Wants Feedback on Proposals to Tackle Malawi "Intellectual Crisis"', *Nyasa Times*, 19 April 2014 (https://www.nyasatimes.com/mutharika-wants-feedback-on-proposals-to-tackle-malawi-intellectual-crisis, accessed 24 March 2015).

[37] 'Goodall Mocks JB's Mudzi Transformation Trust', *Malawi Oracle Times*, 7 April 2014 (http://www.orakonews.com/goodall-mocks-jbs-mudzi-transformation-trust, accessed 11 June 2015).

farm input subsidies. Both Chakwera and Mutharika lauded hard work, but Mutharika and the DPP were happier for the state to play a large role in fostering agricultural growth.

The three parties articulated the three dominant approaches to poverty reduction across east and southern Africa. Chakwera's position resembled that of political leaders such as Peter Ng'andu Magande, the Finance Minister of Zambia in the mid-2000s, who had blocked donor-backed social protection programmes (Kabandula and Seekings 2016). The Mutharika/DPP position was the classic 'agrarian' route to poverty alleviation that had been more common in the first decades after independence (see Lavers on Ethiopia, Chapter 3 of this volume). Banda's position was an unequivocal defence of social assistance for the poor, especially those poor people who were unable to take advantage of farming subsidies. In contrast to most advocates of social assistance, however, Banda chose not to defend it on developmental grounds—as, for example, the World Bank did, including in Malawi (World Bank 2013)—but on the basis of need. This was a discourse employed more often by foreign and local NGOs, and only rarely by political leaders.

In the run-up to the election, these differences were overshadowed by other issues. In addition to the Cashgate scandal, the government's perceived competence was undermined by another drought, which left almost 10 per cent of the population (or 1.5 million people) dependent on food aid. Amidst the swirling scandal and a stuttering economy, Banda won only 20 per cent of the vote, behind both Chakwera (with 28 per cent) and Mutharika (with 36 per cent). Banda won pluralities in every northern district, and majorities in southern districts where her co-ethnic Lomwes predominated. Chakwera and the MCP won all of the central districts. Atupele Muluzi, son of the former president, earned pluralities for the UDF in south-eastern districts where co-ethnic Yaos predominated. The DPP dominated the rest of the south. The PP won only twenty-six parliamentary seats, behind the DPP (fifty-one seats) and MCP (forty-eight seats).

The election outcome seemed to mark a return to the regional patterns characteristic of Malawi prior to 2009. There were, however, two significant shifts between the pre-2009 and 2014 elections. First, although he did not win a majority of the votes in any northern or central district, Mutharika nonetheless came second in both of those regions, suggesting that there may have been some residual support there for the Mutharika/DPP food security brand (Patel and Wahman 2014). Second, Banda did win one in five votes—rather more in the north—after she was endorsed by important northern politicians. Banda's result suggests also that her pro-poor brand did not preclude all support.

In early 2014, prior to the election, Afrobarometer asked Malawian citizens to identify the most important difference between the incumbent and opposition parties. The largest proportion (40 per cent) indicated 'economic and development policies', with much smaller proportions opting for the honesty or integrity of leaders, ethnic or regional loyalties, or the leaders' personalities. The Afrobarometer data suggest, however, that Malawian voters prioritized food security over the alleviation of poverty per se. When they were asked to identify the most important problem facing the country that the government should address, the most commonly cited problem in every Afrobarometer poll between 2003 and 2014 was 'food shortage and famine'. The proportion of respondents citing this peaked at almost 50 per cent in the 2005 survey, declined in the 2008 and 2012 surveys, but then rose somewhat in the 2014 survey, to 27 per cent. By comparison, 'poverty and destitution' were cited by between 4 and 7 per cent across these surveys. In both 2012 and 2014, the second most frequently cited 'most important problem' was the 'management of the economy'. All of this suggests that there remained a strong constituency for programmes to support small farmers, and this constituency grew during periods of drought. The Banda 'brand' was probably not a substantial vote-winner. Dorward et al. (2009: 9–10) report research that suggested that poor farmers preferred programmes that helped them to produce more food themselves than food- or cash-for-work programmes (as suggested earlier by van Donge 2005). Several of our interviewees suggest that Banda may have been misguided in her belief that a focus on direct transfers ('handouts') would endear her to poor voters.[38]

Afrobarometer polls in June 2012 and March/April 2014 show that Banda's branding did not prevent a rapid decline in popular approval of her performance, from more than 65 per cent to less than 40 per cent. Approval of the government's economic management also declined dramatically. The proportion of voters saying that they would vote for the PP, if elections were held tomorrow, fell from 46 per cent in 2012, when the PP was ahead of both the DPP and MCP, to only 19 per cent in 2014, behind both the DPP and MCP (which was almost exactly the outcome of the election). By 2014, the DPP was identified by most voters as the party most likely to solve every one of a set of challenges, including not only fighting corruption, managing the economy, and ensuring food security, but also reducing poverty.

Whilst Banda's brand did not prevent a decline in support, had the election been fought in 2012 (or early 2013) then—the data suggest—she would have

[38] Interviews by Sam Hamer, 16 May 2014.

performed strongly. The 2012 Afrobarometer survey found strong evidence of enthusiasm for Joyce Banda, presumably in part because she was seen to be strong on the valence issues of economic management and fighting corruption. At that time, her distinctively pro-'handout' stance did not seem to have been a political liability, although it was yet to be subjected to the intense criticism of an actual election campaign. The sharp decline in support for Banda and the PP between 2012 and 2014 suggests that a strong pro-poor or, more specifically, pro-'handout' brand is likely to succeed only if the candidate is expected to deliver also on basic economic management and action against corruption. Put another way, if the economy is growing or expected to grow, voters may feel more indulgent towards the poor, but at times of economic difficulty and widespread corruption, voters veer towards more conservative candidates with their discourse of hard work and responsibility.

5. The Conditions for Social Assistance Branding

The presidential election in Malawi in 2014 was unusual, at least within Africa, in that the candidates held strong and contrasting positions on poverty-reduction strategy. Social assistance was, unusually, *not* a valence issue. In post-apartheid South Africa, the major parties have broadly concurred over the importance of extensive social protection. In Botswana, the opposition parties have accused the governing party of not doing enough, but they share a general commitment to both the principle of state responsibility for the poor and specific social protection programmes. In Kenya, rival coalitions share both a rhetorical commitment to social protection and a reticence to implement reforms when in office. In Zimbabwe, the entry of the opposition Movement for Democratic Change into a Government of National Unity in 2009 did lead to reforms, but these were not because the MDC itself had any clear commitment to social protection. In Zambia, the then opposition Patriotic Front did include a commitment to expanded social protection in its 2011 election manifesto, but it was not a prominent element in its campaign. The 2014 Malawi election was perhaps the first election in which contrasting positions on 'handouts' featured prominently in the rhetoric of the competing candidates and parties.

Why, then, did Banda seize on social assistance when branding herself and her new party? Conditions specific to Malawi in the 2000s may have favoured the emergence of social assistance on the electoral agenda despite elite ambivalence and uncertainty as to how voters would respond. Most obviously, political parties in Malawi were unusually weakly institutionalized. Malawian parties have long been weak on the ground, MPs often switch allegiance from one party to another, and even opposition party leaders defect to join the government (Rakner et al. 2007; Svåsand 2013). Moreover, the parties of both presidents Mutharika (DPP) and Banda (PP) broke away from existing parties. Given that, 'as a new party' in 2005, Mutharika's DPP had 'lacked even minimal infrastructure and was poorly suited to monitor clientelist exchanges at the local level' (Dionne and Horowitz 2016: 217; see also Dulani and Dionne 2014), bold branding was the obvious strategy—and, as it turned out, a very successful one. Banda's expulsion from the DPP in 2011 placed her in a similar position. If she formed a new party rather than joining one of the existing opposition parties, bold branding was the obvious strategy.

Immediately after the 1994 election, van Donge (1995) argued that the regional and ethnic demographics of Malawi led presidential candidates to search for a moral brand that could underpin and justify a supra-regional (and supra-ethnic) coalition. For ten years, political leaders failed to develop a successful brand (see also Rakner et al. 2007). In 2009, it seemed that Bingu wa Mutharika had found a winning formula: his support for small farmers (at a time of sustained economic growth) enabled him to win the election by an unprecedented margin and with unprecedentedly broad support. Although support for Mutharika and the DPP declined thereafter, their 'capture' of the pro-farmer brand pushed rivals into alternative positions that they might otherwise not have chosen. The MCP was pushed into a stark neoliberal position, advocating growth and the state's retreat from statist interventions ('handouts', whether for farmers or the poor). This left little space for Banda and the PP other than to adopt an interventionist, pro-poor position, distinguished from the DPP by its support for the poor rather than farmers, i.e. social assistance rather than farm input subsidies.

Neither Banda/PP nor the Mutharikas/DPP adopted the kind of populist strategy discussed by Resnick, with particular reference to the experience of Michael Sata (and his Patriotic Front) in Zambia. Sata's populism was characterized by 'an anti-elitist discourse, a policy message oriented around social inclusion, and a charismatic leader who professes an affinity with the underclass' (Resnick 2012: 1352; see also Pruce and Hickey, Chapter 7 of this volume and Siachiwena 2016). Sata adopted a populist stance in opposition to the broadly pro-market incumbent Movement for Multiparty Democracy (MMD), appealing to poor urban voters not through clientelism (or vote-buying), or through ethnic appeals, but rather through a populist promise to incorporate them into the political arena. Resnick shows that this populism made particular sense in Zambia, with its unusually large, urbanized populations in Lusaka and the Copperbelt. In Malawi, in contrast to Zambia, the urbanized population was small, and elections were fought and won in rural areas. Both Mutharika and Banda therefore developed brands that were in their own way populist but were quite different from that of Sata and the PF, appealing to rural voters. Moreover, Banda could not brand herself as a critic of the poverty generated by free market policies given that the DPP was already championing massive (and expensive) state support for farmers.

One other southern African leader who sought to develop a personal 'social protection' brand was Ian Khama in Botswana. Khama became president in 2008, largely on the basis that he was the son of founding president Seretse Khama and, like his father, had been chief of the BaNgwato. His party—the Botswana Democratic Party—had been in power since independence in 1966, but its support had fallen to only just over one half of the vote. Ian Khama needed a distinctive brand that would carry him through the election in 2009 by allowing him to claim his father's mantle at the same time as emphasizing novelty and distancing himself from his immediate predecessors. Like Banda, Ian Khama seized on social protection as the basis of his brand, but his chosen focus was a public employment programme. He had the advantages of being able to dust off a public employment programme associated with his father—and appealing to conservatives concerned with the work ethic—whilst presenting this as an innovative reform that would address problems of urban as well as rural unemployment. He succeeded in sustaining the BDP's share of the vote in the 2009 election. In 2014, he held onto enough votes to be re-elected, despite not winning a majority (Hamer 2015; see also Seekings, Chapter 2 of this volume).

The case of Malawi in the 2010s contributes not only to a rethinking of the factors underlying electoral success in contemporary Africa but also to a fuller understanding of the emerging politics of social assistance. In the 2009 and 2014 elections in Malawi, presidential candidates offered clearly distinctive brands to the voters, even if their parties' manifestos did not demonstrate meaningful or obvious ideological or policy differences (as noted by Dulani and Dionne 2014: 220). In 2014, the three major candidates offered brands corresponding to the key developmental and political choice facing governments across much of Africa: liberalized markets (Chakwera), statist interventions to sustain small and medium farmers (Mutharika), or pro-poor interventions (Banda). In practice, even Mutharika's subsidies—costing about 5 per cent of GDP—mitigated rather than ended poverty. They helped poor households 'to "hang in" but not "step up" or "step out"' from poverty (Dorward et al. 2013: 103). Banda's 'handouts' were even more modest, although they were more precisely targeted at the poor. Under Banda, the roll-out of cash transfer and workfare programmes was accelerated but failed to achieve the targets. Even statist interventions were constrained by a general conservatism. Pro-poor rhetoric was not matched by service delivery on the scale required to reduce poverty significantly. Nonetheless, social assistance had been placed on the agenda, and 'handouts' loudly championed by an incumbent president. Critics of 'handouts' will be expected to deliver on their promises. If they do not, then electoral pressure for social assistance programmes is likely to intensify.

References

Angeles, G., S. Abdoulayi, C. Barrington, S. Handa, E. Kainja, P. Mvula, H. Mwamlima, M. Tsoka, and T. Spadafora (2016). The social cash transfer programme of Malawi: the role of evaluation from the pilot to the expansion. In B. Davis, S. Handa, N. Hypher, N. Winder Rossi, P. Winters, and J. Yablonski (Eds.), *From Evidence to Action: The Story of Cash Transfers and Impact Evaluation in Sub-Saharan Africa*. Oxford: Oxford University Press.

Bleck, Jaimie and Nicolas Van de Walle (2013). Valence issues in African elections: navigating uncertainty and the weight of the past. *Comparative Political Studies*, 46(11), 1394–421.

Brazys, S., P. Heaney, and P.P. Walsh (2015). Fertilizer and votes: does strategic economic policy explain the 2009 Malawi election? *Electoral Studies*, 39, 39–55.

Carbone, Giovanni and Alessandro Pellegata (2017). To elect or not to elect: leaders, alternation in power and social welfare in sub-Saharan Africa. *Journal of Development Studies*, DOI: 10.1080/00220388.2017.1279733.

Cheeseman, N. (2016). Patrons, parties, political linkage, and the birth of competitive-authoritarianism in Africa. *African Studies Review*, 59(3), 181–200.

Chinsinga, B. and C. Poulton (2014). Beyond technocratic debates: the significance and transience of political incentives in the Malawi Farm Input Subsidy Programme (FISP). *Development Policy Review*, 32(2), 123–50.

Chinyoka, I. and J. Seekings (2016). Social policy reform under the Government of National Unity in Zimbabwe, 2009–13. CSSR Working Paper 373. Cape Town: Centre for Social Science Research, University of Cape Town.

Denning, G., P. Kabambe, A. Sanchez, et al. (2009). Input subsidies to improve smallholder maize productivity in Malawi: toward an African green revolution. *PLoS Biology*, 7(1), xx.

Devereux, Stephen and Z. Tiba (2007). Malawi's first famine, 2001–2002. In S. Devereux (Ed.), *The New Famines: Why Famines Persist in an Era of Globalization*. Abingdon: Routledge, 143–77.

Dionne, K.Y. and J. Horowitz (2016). The political effects of agricultural subsidies in Africa: evidence from Malawi. *World Development*, 87, 215–26.

Dorward, A., B. Guenther, and R. Sabates-Wheeler (2009). Agriculture and social protection in Malawi. Future Agricultures Working Paper 7. Brighton: University of Sussex.

Dorward, A., E. Chirwa, M. Matita, W. Mhango, P. Mvula, E. Taylor, and K. Thorne (2013). Evaluation of the 2012/13 Farm Input Subsidy Programme, Malawi. Report prepared for the Ministry of Agriculture and Food Security, Lilongwe.

DPP (2014). Towards a people-centred government. Democratic Progressive Party 2014 Election Manifesto.

Dulani, B. and K.Y. Dionne (2014). Presidential, parliamentary, and local government elections in Malawi, May 2014. *Electoral Studies*, 36, 218–25.

Ellis, Frank, Milton Kutengule, and Alfred Nyasulu (2003). Livelihoods and rural poverty reduction in Malawi. *World Development*, 31(9), 1495–510.

Englund, H. (2002). The culture of chameleon politics. In H. Englund (Ed.), *A Democracy of Chameleons: Politics and Culture in Malawi*. Uppsala: Nordic Africa Institute, 11–24.

Esping-Andersen, G. (1990). *The Three Worlds of Welfare Capitalism*. Oxford: Oxford University Press.

Fairfield, Tasha and Candelaria Garay (2017). Redistribution under the right in Latin America: electoral competition and organized actors in policymaking. *Comparative Political Studies*. doi: 0010414017695331.

Ferree, K. and J. Horowitz (2010). Ties that bind? The rise and decline of ethno-regional partisanship in Malawi, 1994–2009. *Democratization*, 17(3), 534–63.

Gabay, C. (2014). 'Two transitions': the political economy of Joyce Banda's rise to power and the related role of civil society organisations in Malawi. *Review of African Political Economy*, 41(141), 374–88.

Grebe, E. (2015). The politics of social protection in a competitive African democracy: explaining social protection policy reform in Ghana (2000–2014). CSSR Working Paper 361. Cape Town: Centre for Social Science Research, University of Cape Town.

Hamer, S.F. (2015). 'Our father's programmes': political branding around social protection in Botswana, 2008–2014. CSSR Working Paper 370. Cape Town: Centre for Social Science Research, University of Cape Town.

Hanlon, Joseph, Armando Barrientos, and David Hulme (2010). *Just Give Money to the Poor: The Development Revolution from the Global South*. Sterling, VA: Kumarian Press.

Harding, Robin and David Stasavage (2013). What democracy does (and doesn't do) for basic services: school fees, school inputs, and African elections. *Journal of Politics*, 76(1), 229–45.

Harrigan, Jane (2003). U-turns and full circles: two decades of agricultural reform in Malawi 1981–2000. *World Development*, 31(5), 847–63.

Harrigan, J. (2005). Food security policies and starter pack: a challenge for donors? In Sarah Levy (Ed.), *Starter Packs: A Strategy to Fight Hunger in Developing Countries? Lessons from the Malawi Experience 1998–2003*. Wallingford: CABI, 229–46.

Hoffman, Barak D. and James D. Long (2013). Parties, ethnicity, and voting in African elections. *Comparative Politics*, 45(2), 127–46.

Huber, E. and J. Stephens (2001). *Development and Crisis of the Welfare State: Parties and Policies in Global Markets*. Chicago, IL: University of Chicago Press.

Juergens, F. and L. Pellerano (2016). *Review of the National Social Support Programme*. Lilongwe: Ministry of Finance, Economic Planning and Development, Poverty Reduction and Social Protection Division.

Kabandula, A. and J. Seekings (2016). Donor influence, the Minister of Finance and Welfare policy reform in Zambia, 2003–11. CSSR Working Paper 395. Cape Town: Centre for Social Science Research, University of Cape Town.

Kalebe-Nyamongo, C. and H. Marquette (2014). Elite attitudes towards cash transfers and the poor in Malawi. DLP Research Paper 30. Birmingham: Developmental Leadership Programme, University of Birmingham.

Malawi (2012). *Integrated Household Survey, 2010/11: Household Socio-Economic Characteristics Report*. Zomba: National Statistical Office.

MCP (2014). Nothing for us without us. Malawi Congress Party 2014 Election Manifesto.

Norris, Pippa and Robert B. Mattes (2013). Does ethnicity determine support for the governing party? In Michael Bratton (Ed.), *Voting and Democratic Citizenship in Africa* (Boulder, CO: Lynn Rienner), 41–60.

Patel, N. and M. Wahman (2014). The presidential, parliamentary and local elections in Malawi, May 2014. *Afrika Spectrum*, 50(1), 79–92.

Potter, Harry (2005). The players and the policy issues. In Sarah Levy (Ed.), *Starter Packs: A Strategy to Fight Hunger in Developing Countries? Lessons from the Malawi Experience 1998–2003*. Wallingford: CABI, 29–40.

PP (2014). It is possible (Nzotheka). People's Party 2014 Election Manifesto.

Rakner, L., L. Svåsand, and N.S. Khembo (2007). Fissions and fusions, foes and friends: party system restructuring in Malawi in the 2004 general elections. *Comparative Political Studies*, 40(9), 1112–37.

Resnick, D. (2012). Opposition parties and the urban poor in African democracies. *Comparative Political Studies*, 45(11), 1351–78.

Seekings, J. (2012). Pathways to redistribution: the emerging politics of social assistance across the global 'South'. *Journal für Entwicklungspolitik (Austrian Journal of Development Studies)*, 28(1), 14–34.

Seekings, J. (2016). The introduction of old age pensions in Zanzibar. CSSR Working Paper 393. Cape Town: Centre for Social Science Research, University of Cape Town.

Siachiwena, H. (2016). Social protection policy reform in Zambia in Zambia during the Sata presidency, 2011–2014. CSSR Working Paper 377. Cape Town: Centre for Social Science Research, University of Cape Town.

Svåsand, L. (2013). The concept of opposition and the structure of opposition in Malawi. *Commonwealth & Comparative Politics*, 51(3), 306–25.

Ulriksen, M.S. (2016). The development of social protection policies in Tanzania, 2000–2015. CSSR Working Paper 380. Cape Town: Centre for Social Science Research, University of Cape Town.

van Donge, J.K. (1995). Kamuzu's legacy: the democratization of Malawi—or searching for the rules of the game in African politics. *African Affairs*, 94(375), 227–57.

van Donge, J.K. (2005). The farmer's perspective: values, incentives and constraints. In Sarah Levy (Ed.), *Starter Packs: A Strategy to Fight Hunger in Developing Countries? Lessons from the Malawi Experience 1998–2003*. Wallingford: CABI, 117–28.

World Bank (2013). Malawi public expenditure review. World Bank Report 79865-MW. Washington DC: World Bank.

Zimmerman, Brigitte (2015). Voter response to scandal: Cashgate. In Nandini Patel and Michael Wahman (Eds.), *The Malawi Tripartite 2014 Elections: Is Democracy Maturing?* Lilongwe: The National Initiative for Civic Education, 215–35.

10

Who Should Get What, How, and Why?

DFID and the Transnational Politics of Social Cash Transfers in Sub-Saharan Africa

Sam Hickey and Jeremy Seekings

1. Introduction

Social cash transfers (SCTs) proliferated across much of sub-Saharan Africa (SSA) from the early 2000s (Garcia and Moore 2012; Bastiagli et al. 2016). 'Social protection', which was variously defined but always included SCTs, was endorsed by one after another of the international agencies and bilateral aid donors. The early frontrunner was the World Bank, whose enthusiasm for SCTs deepened, shifting in part from 'social safety nets' to 'conditional cash transfers' (CCTs). Towards the end of the 2000s, the International Labour Organization (ILO) assumed a leading role in global debate. Its need to reach out beyond formally employed workers led it to champion the expansion of coverage through 'social protection floors'. HelpAge International and UNICEF identified SCTs as crucial to the well-being of the elderly and children, respectively. The World Food Programme (WFP) sought to channel more of its relief through cash-for-work programmes, which served similar functions as SCTs; the Food and Agriculture Organization (FAO) also adopted a social protection strategy. Various European national donor aid agencies identified social protection as central to their poverty-reduction strategies and, by 2012, even the International Monetary Fund (IMF) acknowledged that social protection was necessary if development was to be inclusive. Whereas in 2000 there had been no place for social protection in the Millennium Development Goals, by 2015 SCTs were widely regarded as crucial to the new Sustainable Development Goals. SCTs had become a truly 'global social policy'.

Agreement over the importance of SCTs, and social protection more generally, did not mean that these diverse international and national agencies shared the same view of SCTs. They differed in their views not only of who

Sam Hickey and Jeremy Seekings, *Who Should Get What, How, and Why? DFID and the Transnational Politics of Social Cash Transfers in Sub-Saharan Africa* In: *The Politics of Social Protection in Eastern and Southern Africa.* Edited by: Sam Hickey, Tom Lavers, Miguel Niño-Zarazúa, and Jeremy Seekings, Oxford University Press (2020).

DOI: 10.1093/oso/9780198850342.003.0010

should get what (and, to a lesser extent, how) but also of the overall purpose or role of SCTs. Gramscian wars of position were fought within and between agencies as individuals and groups sought to define the policy agenda. In an early analysis of this contestation, Deacon (2007) contrasts the 'neoliberal' position of the US-based World Bank and the supposedly 'social democratic' position of the ILO and other Europe-based organizations. Hanlon, Barrientos, and Hulme (2010) boldly represent the rise of SCTs as a ('quiet') revolution from the global South, pointing to innovative programmes developed in Mexico, Brazil, South Africa, India, and elsewhere. Deacon (2013) provides an exemplary analysis of the struggles within the ILO, and then between it and other agencies, over the social protection floor initiative. Peck and Theodore (2015) focus on the role of the World Bank in promoting the Mexican model of a CCT, whilst downplaying the alternative Brazilian CCT model. Von Gliszczynski and Leisering (2016) (and Von Gliszczynski 2015) identify the World Bank, HelpAge, and UNICEF as the champions of alternative approaches to SCTs. National aid agencies also promoted their specific approaches to social protection. Across east and southern Africa, the most influential of the national aid agencies was the UK's Department for International Development (DFID).

It is evident from national case studies—in this volume and elsewhere—that there has been a wide array of international actors marching to and fro over the battlefields of agenda-setting and policy-making around SCTs (and other forms of social protection) in SSA. Table 10.1 summarizes our assessment of the lead players in SCT reforms in east and southern African countries. We offer this assessment with trepidation: the relative importance of different agencies has not only changed over time and varied by type of programme (and government department), but it is also often far from clear (especially to participants themselves) who had more or less influence. Despite these caveats, several things seem clear. First, we have not identified 'southern' actors as being directly influential in this process (beyond the single case of Brazil in Ghana; Grebe 2015): 'southern' governments might have developed innovative models, as Hanlon et al. (2010) asserted, but the organizations that promoted their diffusion elsewhere were all based in North America or Europe. Second, the World Bank enjoyed considerable influence but was far from hegemonic. Third, despite its role in promoting the concept of the social protection floor, and thus shaping the nature of social protection as a global policy agenda, the ILO has not proved to be a major actor in the spread at the national level in SSA of social protection or SCTs in particular. Fourth, DFID was a prominent actor in a number of countries. In Anglophone Africa, DFID

Table 10.1 Agencies promoting SCTs and related programmes in eastern and southern Africa[1]

Country	Programme	Lead agency/ies	Support agency/ies
Ethiopia	Productive Safety Net Programme (PSNP)	WB	DFID, USAID, WFP, EU, Irish Aid, CIDA, UNICEF
Kenya	Cash Transfers for Orphans and Vulnerable Children	UNICEF, then DFID, WB	HelpAge
Lesotho	Social pensionsChild Grant Programme	n/aUNICEF	
Malawi	SCT Programme and Public Works Programme	UNICEF and WB	DFID
Rwanda	Vision 2020 Umerenge Programme (VUP)	DFID, with WB	UNICEF, SIDA
Tanzania	Tanzania Social Action Fund (TASAF)	WB	UNICEF, DFID
Uganda	Social Assistance Grants for Empowerment (SAGE)	DFID	Irish Aid, UNICEF, HelpAge, and WB on overall strategy
Zambia	Social Cash Transfer (SCT)	GTZ, then DFID, with UNICEF	FAO
Zanzibar	Universal old-age pension	HelpAge	UNICEF

was certainly the most influential of the government aid agencies from the global North.

In the 2000s, DFID developed a distinctive approach to SCTs. For DFID, SCTs came to be seen in terms of the goal of reducing poverty, not the goal of managing risk (to facilitate development, as the World Bank emphasized) or the goal of securing otherwise corporatist social insurance programmes (as the ILO hoped). Given that the elderly and children were often disproportionately poor, DFID shared many of the concerns of HelpAge and UNICEF. DFID was

[1] This reflects which agencies played leading and supporting roles in ensuring that specific social assistance programmes were adopted and in shaping the form they took. Focus here is on the largest social assistance programme/s in each case. Whilst these 'rankings' are not based on quantified measures, we took into account advocacy, technical assistance, and direct funding. We drew on interviews with staff in the agencies themselves and our country case studies, including: Lavers (Chapter 3 of this volume, Ethiopia), Grebe (2015a, 2015b, Ghana), Granvik and Seekings (2016) and Wanyama and McCord (2017) (Kenya), Granvik Saminathen (Chapter 6 of this volume, Lesotho), Hamer and Seekings (Chapter 9 of this volume, Malawi), Lavers (Chapter 4 of this volume, Rwanda), Ulriksen (Chapter 5 of this volume, Tanzania), Bukenya and Hickey (Chapter 8 of this volume), Grebe and Mubiru (2014), and Grebe (2015) (Uganda), Pruce and Hickey (Chapter 7 of this volume), Kabandula and Seekings (2016), and Siachiwena (2016) (Zambia), and Seekings (2016, Zanzibar).

less enamoured by either World Bank-style conditionalities or large-scale workfare, and had some sympathy for the rights-based approach favoured strongly by some other donor agencies, especially from Nordic countries such as Finland. At the same time, DFID favoured targeting tax-financed benefits on the deserving poor, applying an approach that had long characterized much British social policy-making, without the conditions favoured by either the World Bank (through workfare and CCTs) or the ILO (through contributions). Its approach was, in general, more pragmatic than doctrinaire, but DFID's pragmatism was shaped by specifically British policy traditions, traditions that had influenced the initial adoption of social assistance in SSA in countries such as Mauritius and South Africa (Seekings 2007, 2011). Von Gliszczynski and Leisering (2016) identify 'general household assistance' as one of their models of SCTs, but underestimate the role of DFID in promoting this model. DFID was also unusual in recognizing the limits of a purely technical approach to policy reform. DFID paid close attention to the politics of reform at the national level, working hard to build political constituencies for SCTs in SSA countries and even imagining that SCTs might perform 'transformative' political roles in poor countries.

DFID has been overlooked in the existing literature on international organizations and social protection, despite its prominent role across much of SSA. In this chapter we examine how a distinctive position evolved within DFID, how it compared and contrasted with the approaches of other international organizations, and how its character both underpinned and limited its efficacy on the ground, in national processes of policy-making. Our focus on DFID enables us to fill an important gap in the current literature on how social assistance has been promoted, to locate recent reforms in a more historicized view of the longue duree of policy transfer, and to examine how and why policy ideas 'travel'.

Our approach draws critically on Li's (2007) analysis of how development ideas have travelled and taken root across the global South. Li (2007) first drew on Marx to understand how accumulation, exploitation, and exclusion created the conditions for new policy ideas to be articulated. Li then drew on Gramsci to understand how ideological contests over different forms of development are fought and play out. Finally, she drew on Foucault to understand the ways in which poverty is rendered as a technical problem, prompting specific modes of governmentality. We find Li's use of Gramsci and Foucault particularly useful when tracking the rise of SCTs and their promotion within SSA. It is less clear how far DFID's approach can be explained in terms of a crisis of capitalism rather than the deepening of post-colonial responsibility for poverty that persisted despite global economic growth during the 2000s. We also borrow from Mosse (2005), who called for careful analysis of the internal workings of the 'aidworld'. As Peck and Theodore (2010, 2015) note, even apparently technocratic policies are socially produced. We draw on interviews with key actors within DFID and other international agencies to explore this 'social' construction and promotion of global public policies, following Mosse's entreaty to deepen a Gramscian view of how actors fight on the 'terrain of contestation' through understanding better the ideas and incentives at play *within* organizations. This involved recognizing 'the complexity of policy as institutional practice... the social life of projects, organisations and professionals... the perspectives of actors themselves and... the diversity of interests behind policy models' (Mosse 2005: 6). Our approach thus builds on but also goes beyond current analyses of how social protection has become a global policy agenda, none of which have so far discussed the role played by DFID in this process or actually tracked the process through which SCTs became transferred from a global policy agenda to becoming facts on the ground in SSA.

Paying attention to the role played by DFID also serves to locate the post-2000 proliferation of SCTs in an historical context that is more complex than is generally recognized. SCTs may be substantially novel but they are not entirely unprecedented. When the World Bank, Hanlon et al., and others lauded CCTs in Latin America, they were acknowledging reforms that were innovative across most of that region. In those parts of the world that had been settled or colonized by Britain, however, there was a longer history of SCTs. Imperial Britain exported not only its Poor Laws to some of its 'dominions' and colonies, in the late nineteenth century, but also the social pensions and other SCTs that represented the modernization of poor relief in the early and mid-twentieth century. In SSA, social pensions were first introduced in South Africa in the late 1920s (Seekings 2007). The British government generally tried to dampen any further interest in social pensions, preferring to promote development (and contributory programmes for select groups of workers in formal employment) (Seekings 2013), but social pensions were introduced in Mauritius in 1950 (Seekings 2011) and were debated much more widely across east and southern Africa between the early 1940s and early 1960s. Britain's history of unconditional SCTs represented an alternative to both the CCTs initiated in Latin America (and backed by the World Bank) and the contributory social insurance programmes long championed by the ILO. The design of drought relief from the 1960s reflected British colonial ideas about who deserved what. When SCTs resurfaced on the policy agenda in the 2000s, it is striking that DFID seemed to draw on deep-rooted British traditions in identifying poor households and especially the elderly poor as the primary target for their programmes.

In the post-2000s period, as in earlier periods of policy reform in SSA, reforms have resulted from the interaction between SSA governments and transnational ideas and international actors. SSA governments have variously resisted and embraced, adopted and adapted models from elsewhere, and in so doing created new models. Having emphasized the significant roles played by political actors from within east and southern African countries throughout this volume, this chapter focuses specifically on the transnational dimension of this process.

2. Why Did SCTs Rise Up the Global Policy Agenda?

The process through which global public policies are constructed and transferred can be viewed most clearly from the type of critical constructivist perspective adopted by Li.[2] This approach recognizes that such processes are 'deeply structured by enduring power relations and shifting ideological alignments' (Peck and Theodore 2010: 169) whilst acknowledging the potential for social interaction to reshape the policy models being advocated (Stone 2012; Mosse 2005). Ideas about the welfare state gained traction in western Europe in the middle of the twentieth century, as Polanyi (1944) first observed, as a 'counter-movement' generated by the contradictory forces of industrial capitalism, and specifically by the urge to mitigate the damaging effects of commodification (see also Esping-Andersen 1990). Materialist analysis also helps us to understand how ideas about 'development' have been generated by the need for imminent policy solutions to deal with problems of exploitation and dispossession that arise from immanent processes of economic growth and change (Cowen and Shenton 1996).

SCTs first appeared on the global policy agenda in the 1990s, with the World Bank's largely rhetorical concern to address the social costs of structural adjustment through 'safety nets' (World Bank 1990), and, perhaps more substantively, 'social action funds' (de Haan 2014). Safety nets may have been

[2] See Stone (2012) for the distinction between 'rational-institutionalist' and 'constructivist' positions, and Hickey and Seekings (2017) for a discussion of their relative merits. In brief, we find that rational-institutionalist approaches pay insufficient attention to the role of politics and conflict in how policy ideas travel, and that critical constructivist approaches are more closely attuned to the highly contested and polycentric character of policy transfer today.

very modest, but they marked an important break from the emphasis on contributory programmes that had dominated the global social protection agenda for more than fifty years. It took a larger rupture within the global capitalist economy, however, for mainstream development ideology to shift significantly enough to offer an ideological environment within which social protection could flourish. The East Asian crisis in the late 1990s provided an influential shock, prompting the World Bank to emphasize the role of social protection, particularly safety nets, in managing 'risks', in its 2000/1 *World Development Report.* It served almost as a manifesto for the new 'post-Washington Consensus' (Hayami 2003), based on a partial recognition of the negative consequences of unfettered market capitalism, and of the need to try and re-embed processes of commodification within a social logic (Craig and Porter 2006). The Bank's focus on social protection became institutionalized during this period. It published a 'Social Protection and Labour Strategy' in 2001, established a Social Protection and Labour Unit, and allocated funds to experimental CCT programmes.

In knowledge-broker mode, the Bank made major investments during this period to evaluate the effects of cash transfer programmes in Latin America, and to start sharing learning around such schemes. Peck and Theodore (2015) document the World Bank's infatuation with the Mexican *Progresa* CCT programme (later renamed *Oportunidades*, and later still *Prospera*). In 2002, the World Bank hosted a conference on CCTs in Mexico, and took participants on a 'pilgrimage' to *Oportunidades* facilities. This was the first 'rallying point for the true believers, founding fathers of what would become the CCT *movement*' (Peck and Theodore 2015: 86, emphasis in original). The World Bank promoted SCTs through workshops, conferences, publications, technical assistance, and generous funding. It sought to persuade national governments that they could and should contribute more. The World Bank produced one of the first two estimates of the costs of social protection programmes in SSA in 2005 (Kakwani and Subbarao 2005).

The global financial crisis of 2008/9 provided further impetus to the World Bank's interest in SCTs. In Peck and Theodore's assessment, 'the economic and political dislocations prompted by the global finance crisis . . . widened the ideological bandwidth on a host of issues in the long-neglected field of social security' (2015: 123). In 2012, the World Bank restated forcefully the case for social protection in a new strategy document for 2012–22 (World Bank 2012a). It also published a dedicated 'Social Protection Strategy for Africa' (World Bank 2012b) and an enthusiastic assessment of SCTs in SSA (Garcia and Moore 2012), i.e. in a region where the Bank had hitherto seen SCTs as impractical. As the authors of the latter report wrote, 'the question is not *whether* cash transfers can be used in the region, but *how* they should be used, and how they can be adapted and developed to meet social protection and development goals' (2012: 9, emphasis in original). In 2014, the World Bank produced its first *State of Social Safety Nets Report* (World Bank 2014).

In her analysis of ideas about 'development', Li (2007) also focuses on the World Bank. Given the sensitivity of the Bank (and the international financial institutions (IFIs) in general) to the perceived health of global capitalism, and the Bank's prominence in (re)constructing the idea of development, it is not surprising that Li drew a link between global capitalism and ideas about development. The rise of SCTs up the policy agenda was not due to the World Bank alone, however. Other international organizations besides the Bank took up the issue of social protection, and began to lobby for SCTs, for a variety of reasons less directly related to the health of global capitalism or the 'harm done by the free market' (Hanlon et al. 2010: 167). As Peck (2011: 168) writes, policy transfer in the 2000s has been 'a multi-site, multi-actor process'; 'policy models' need not follow a linear trajectory, or radiate outward, from a singular place of 'invention'; social policy-making has been 'globalizing', but it has been uneven, shaped by the interactions between different international organizations and 'translocal networks'.

The ILO played an especially important role in this at the global level. The ILO had, since the 1920s, been the leading proponent of contributory, insurance-based forms of social protection. The ILO slowly sought a way of broadening its approach to social protection beyond its concern with the privileges enjoyed by workers in formal employment, especially in advanced industrialized economies (Seekings 2010). In the early 2000s the ILO began to prioritize the goal of extending 'coverage' to 'all'. Contestation within the ILO led to the emergence of the 'social protection floor', including tax-financed SCTs and public health care, as the favoured strategy (Deacon 2013). In 2005, at the same time as the World Bank, the ILO published its first study of the cost of SCTs in SSA, attesting to their 'affordability' (Pal et al. 2005). The ILO's efforts were also propelled forward by the global financial crisis (Deacon 2013). When the UN called on its disparate agencies to co-ordinate their responses to the global crisis, the ILO persuaded the other agencies to launch a social protection floor initiative, co-chaired by the ILO and World Health Organization. An Advisory Group—chaired by former Chilean president, Michelle Bachalet—was established to examine proposals. This eventually led to the adoption by the International Labour Conference in 2012 of Recommendation #202 on Social Protection Floors, which its champion

Michel Cichon described as 'a "Magna Carta" of social protection' (Cichon 2013: 37). The ILO also joined with the IMF in arguing for increased expenditure on social protection (ILO and IMF 2012). In 2014, the ILO published a *World Social Protection Report* (ILO 2014), which can be read as an effort to rebrand itself and to reclaim the mainstream terrain of international social protection policy from the World Bank.[3]

Several other agencies took up the issue of social protection not so much in response to the vicissitudes of the global economy but rather to the persistence of poverty. The persistence of both episodic famine and chronic poverty in SSA and elsewhere posed challenges to European aid agencies. Global poverty here was framed as a humanitarian problem more than one flowing from the underlying political economy. Poverty and famine were overwhelmingly concentrated in rural areas, not among industrial or urban populations. They were not so much the products of 'development' (or the harm caused by the free market, as Hanlon et al. put it) as the consequences of the absence of development and the limits to economic growth. Whereas the impetus behind welfare state-building in the global North in the twentieth century had been the counter-movement against commodification through industrialization, the impetus to social protection in Africa was deagrarianization, whether short-term (through drought) or longer-term (through population growth that exceeded both the availability of land and productivity rises). Poverty was also exacerbated in east and southern Africa by AIDS, which (initially) killed working-age adults, resulting in households without anyone available to work. Regardless of the extent to which famine and rural poverty were the consequence of capitalist development under and after colonialism, the agencies themselves understood their roles as primarily humanitarian.

An important early initiative in the formulation of social protection as a global policy agenda developed under the auspices of the Development Assistance Committee (DAC) of the Organisation for Economic Co-operation and Development (OECD). The DAC serves as a thinktank for the governments of industrialized countries on issues around development. In 1999, the DAC established a Network on Poverty Reduction (POVNET), which formed three 'task teams' on agriculture, infrastructure, and private sector development. Pushed by SCT advocates including Timo Voipio (from Finland), Stephen Kidd (from the UK), and Rudiger Krech (from the German GTZ), POVNET appointed in 2004 a fourth Task Team on Risk, Vulnerability, and Social

[3] We are grateful to Tom Lavers for this insight.

Protection (later renamed Social Protection and Social Policy) (Voipio 2007). This brought together a large team of social development and social protection experts from several OECD countries (including Finland, Germany, Sweden, and the UK), international agencies (including the World Bank, ILO, and UNICEF), large international civil society organizations (including HelpAge International), and members from organizations in the global South such as the Commission of the African Union. It became the main forum for consensus-seeking inter-agency dialogue on the social protection agenda and how it could gain a foothold in the broader development agenda. An OECD-POVNET Guidance document on social protection was published in 2009.

The UK's DFID had prioritized poverty reduction since its establishment as a standalone government department in 1997 (Hulme 2010). DFID participated energetically in POVNET, and approached the issue of social protection primarily from a poverty-reduction perspective rather than as a means of addressing risks or promoting rights. DFID—and the other aid agencies working in Africa and South Asia—was influenced by developments on the ground, including the threats to food security posed by drought and AIDS. In an echo of the role played by colonial officials based in Africa during the 1940s and 1950s in calling for more generous welfarist responses to various crises, DFID staff based in countries like Ethiopia and Kenya drew the attention of London-based officials to the role that SCTs might play as a more institutionalized response to pressing social problems on the ground.

There was nothing inevitable about the rise of social protection as a commitment within DFID. In 2002, DFID established a policy team entitled Reaching the Very Poorest (RtVP) within its Policy Division. The RtVP team became the locus for exploring and promoting an institutional-level focus on social protection, especially following the appointment in late 2004 of Stephen Kidd as team leader. It commissioned a series of papers, including the 2005 'practice paper' on Social Transfers and Chronic Poverty (DFID 2005), that helped persuade senior staff within DFID of the need to champion social protection. Buoyed by this initial success, the team leader changed the name of the RtVP policy team to 'Social Protection' and successfully lobbied for a commitment to social protection to be included in DFID's 2006 White Paper. Perversely, this nearly led to the RtVP team being disbanded, on the grounds that it had achieved its objective. After informal back-channelling to UK government ministers, the team was retained through a merger into a broader team on equity and rights (also under Kidd's leadership). For the newly promoted team leader, this meant having a larger budget of £2m with

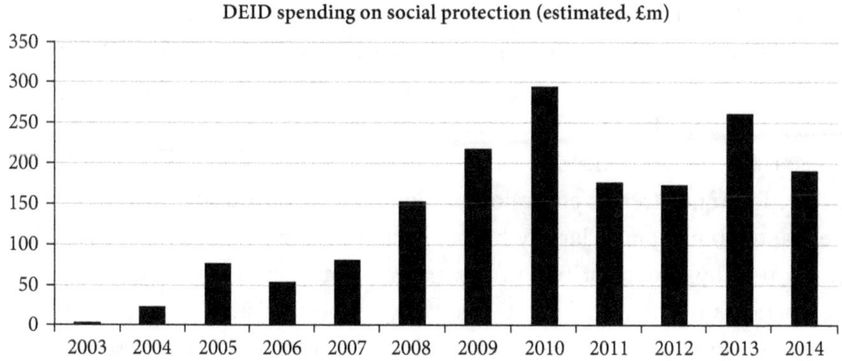

Fig. 10.1. DFID expenditure on social protection, 2003–14.
Source: www.devtracker.dfid.gov.uk.

'complete authority over how spending could be done... that helped us fund all these events, get these things out and going' at the country level in Africa and elsewhere.[4]

From the mid-2000s onwards, DFID worked with other international agencies and domestic policy actors to establish pilot SCT projects and national-level social protection policy processes in several countries. DFID's spending on social protection rose steadily, peaking at almost £300m in 2010 in direct response to the global financial crisis (see Figure 10.1). Expenditures declined after 2010, when a new coalition government comprising the Conservative and Liberal Democrat parties replaced the previous Labour Party government. DFID also helped to fund other initiatives that promoted SCTs. The London-based non-government network HelpAge International was an early convert to SCTs, advocating universal social pensions as a way to protect the rights of older people. With financial support from DFID, HelpAge played a leading role in steering the African Union to recognize social protection as an integral element in social policy through a conference in Livingstone (Zambia) in 2006 and further consultative meetings in different African cities over the following two years (Leutelt 2012). DFID helped to fund further work by the ILO on the costs of SCTs in Zambia and Tanzania, and also helped to establish the African Platform for Social Protection as a network of civil society organizations to advocate for this new policy agenda within and across African countries.

The World Bank, ILO, DFID, and many other international organizations all embraced SCTs as a central element in social protection, tentatively in the

[4] This paragraph is based on interviews with DFID staff in June 2015.

early 2000s, then more forcefully in the aftermath of the 2008/9 global financial and economic crisis, in line with Li's suggestion that shifts in the global political economy can play significant roles in the rise of new global policy agendas. These different organizations had diverse motivations and objectives, extending beyond the stabilization of the global economy to the protection (and strengthening) of existing policies (favouring organized business and labour) and a largely humanitarian concern with poverty reduction (informed by the priorities of tax-paying voters and civil society in the democracies of the global North, as well as problems such as persistent food insecurity in eastern Africa). The common interest in SCTs and social protection was reflected in the apparent consensus eventually achieved over (for example) the ILO-led social protection floor initiative. But international organizations saw SCTs in diverse ways. There was little agreement between them over who should benefit (the poor, the destitute, older people, mothers or families with children, formally employed workers, informally employed workers, peasant farmers, or everyone), by how much (i.e. how generous should benefits be?), and with what (if any) conditions attached. The result was that the international organizations engaged in Gramscian wars of position (Li 2007), not only with respect to the national governments whose policies they hoped to shape, but also with respect to the other international organizations (Deacon 2007) and, as suggested by Mosse (2005), to other interests and ideas within their own organizations.

3. Wars of Position Over Global Social Policy

Almost all of the international organizations published documents, convened workshops and conferences, took national politicians and officials on study tours, and provided or paid for technical assistance. Some of them helped to fund, or funded entirely, approved SCT programmes. These were mechanisms through which international organizations promoted their own vision of SCTs, and sometimes criticized alternative visions. In her work on how ideas about development travelled, Li (2007) employed a Gramscian approach to contestations over ideas and the role of discourse. 'Policy transfer' flows through relations of power not only between the global actors and national governments but also between global actors themselves. International policy spaces are thus 'terrains of contestation' within which advocates play out 'wars of position' over ideas and policies (Deacon 2007). These ideas and discursive struggles took place across three distinct levels: 'paradigmatic' ideas at the level of worldviews, 'problem-framing' ideas which serve to identify and define the 'problems', and specific 'policy solutions' (Schmidt 2008; see also Hall 1993). International organizations differed on all three levels. Workshops, study tours, documents, and the other mechanisms of advocacy were weapons in these wars of position over SCTs.

Writing in 2007, Deacon assessed that the global social policy landscape was contested by three main ideological camps: 'USA-influenced desire for global neoliberal policies'; 'European-influenced desire for global social democratic policies'; and 'Southern-centred debates about getting out from under any northern-imposed agenda for global economic and social policy' (2007: 22). With hindsight, it is clear that this typology was only half valid. Labelling the World Bank approach as neoliberal understates its new-found enthusiasm for large-scale, tax-financed SCTs, within the broad ideological shift towards the '*inclusive* neoliberalism' of the 'post-Washington Consensus' (Craig and Porter 2006), as well as its later willingness to drop conditions in many settings. Viewing the changing in thinking about SCTs as a 'southern' revolution (as Hanlon et al. put it in 2010) was accurate with regard to the geographic *location* of some of the original models (Mexico, Brazil, South Africa, India) but underestimates the importance of international organizations based and rooted in the global North as the *brokers* or agents of subsequent diffusion. Whilst regional organizations (such as the African Union) have adopted policies on social protection, and some governments (notably Brazil) have actively promoted their model,[5] there is little evidence that these have had much effect relative to the influence of northern-based and rooted organizations.[6] Viewing European approaches as broadly social democratic was correct insofar as they proposed a more extensive role for the state than the World Bank, but the label masked deep differences over the form of state intervention between (for example) the ILO, the Nordic countries, and DFID. Whilst the ILO did embrace SCTs, it also rejected proposals from within the ILO for more universal SCT programmes (Deacon 2013). In practice the ILO continued to favour employment-related programmes, viewing tax-financed programmes as residual, for groups of people without any employment. The Nordic social democratic approach—which was especially

[5] The Africa–Brazil Programme on Social Development, financed by DFID, brought together delegations from Brazil and six African countries to discuss SCTs. This seems to have influenced the design of the LEAP programme in Ghana (see Leite et al. 2015: 1454; Grebe 2015).

[6] The diffusion of social pensions to Botswana, Lesotho, and Swaziland seems to be an example of south–south diffusion, from South Africa. But there is no evidence of any active agency by the South African government or any other organization (see Chapters 6 and 2 by Granvik Saminathen and Seekings, this volume).

influential within OECD-POVNET—entailed a rights-based approach and favoured universal programmes over programmes targeted on the poor. A focus on the 'social dimension of development'—as opposed to employment or poverty—was 'characteristic of our Nordic approach to development cooperation', wrote the Finnish chair of the OECD-POVNET Task Team on Social Protection (Voipio 2007: 45). DFID, in contrast, reproduced a distinctively British tradition, which tended to favour the market as the engine of development and residual state programmes targeted at the poor, although more generously and with a broader sense of deservingness than the World Bank.

Each of these organizations sought to promote its models, its definition of the problems to be solved, and even its worldview. The World Bank was especially energetic in this from 2002, hosting major conferences to promote CCTs in Puebla (Mexico, 2002), Sao Paulo (Brazil, 2004), and Istanbul (Turkey, 2006). The Bank promoted CCTs first in Latin America, working with the Inter-American Development Bank, and then in middle-income countries elsewhere (Holzmann 2008; Sugiyama 2011; Peck and Theodore 2015; von Gliszczynski 2015). In 'knowledge-broker' mode, the Bank provided an electronic platform to help establish a Latin American 'community of practice' on social protection and a series of international conferences aimed at facilitating policy learning; starting with the Istanbul conference in 2006, this became institutionalized as a series of 'South–South Learning Forums'.[7]

The World Bank was not initially persuaded that governments in SSA had the capacity or level of social service provision required to adopt CCTs. Presentations at its 2006 CCT conference covered small programmes in Angola and Sierra Leone, but the Bank ignored unconditional SCT programmes in southern Africa and continued to prioritize instead community-driven development initiatives and public works schemes, especially in arid, drought-ravaged areas. By this time DFID had mostly withdrawn from Latin America, and had little direct contact with either Mexico or Brazil. But DFID had personnel all over SSA, and saw the continent as very much its terrain. DFID thus sought to fill the regional gap left by the Bank. Hitherto, DFID's initial forays into the ongoing construction of social protection as a global policy agenda had been timid. DFID staff recall attending World Bank meetings on social protection in Washington DC during 2003–4: 'We saw ourselves as largely falling in with the Bank, we were sent to the Bank to listen and learn, not to challenge'.[8] By 2006, DFID felt able to directly contradict the Bank's

[7] Interview with senior World Bank official, 7 December 2015.

[8] Interview, 12 June 2015.

assumptions that SCTs were only feasible in middle-income countries and its preference for conditional programmes.[9]

This policy-level 'war of position' (Deacon 2007; Li 2007) played out at the third of the World Bank's conferences promoting CCTs, in Istanbul in 2006. Keen to challenge the Bank's hegemony over social protection debates, DFID's Social Protection Team helped co-finance the conference, and brought in some of its favoured consultants, including Dr Michael Samson of the Economic Policy Research Institute (EPRI) in Cape Town, an organization which DFID amongst others helped to finance. At the conference, Samson clashed with the World Bank's Norbert Schady over the evidence in support of conditionality.[10] Although the Bank did not change its position at this stage, DFID secured an agreement for further research to be undertaken, the results of which revealed that conditionality played a partial role at best in securing the developmental impacts associated with cash transfers (Fizbein and Schady 2009). A similar confrontation took place at a workshop on child protection in Kenya, where DFID funded a consultant to challenge the Bank's favoured consultant (Francisco Ayala) on the role that conditions had played in cash transfer programmes in Latin America. This led to a further agreement to test conditional against unconditional grants, and also hard against soft versions of conditionality. According to a DFID team member, the evidence for conditions fell apart when tested through SCTs for orphans in Kenya.[11] When the World Bank later broadened its support for SCTs from workfare to child and family grants, from about 2012, it did not push for conditionality. In the meantime, DFID and other agencies had taken on leading roles in promoting SCTs in SSA, something further enabled by the 'harmonization' dimension of the Paris Declaration, which in some contexts saw the Bank relinquish leadership to DFID in this policy domain (e.g. in Zambia; see Chapter 7 of this volume).

DFID now saw itself as promoting an alternative to the World Bank. As one DFID official put it, the Bank was at the time concerned only with 'risk, they weren't talking about chronic poverty, so we saw a gap' and framed 'ourselves in a way to create a niche for ourselves'.[12] DFID's approach was more European than the World Bank's, but it was not rooted in the strong commitment to rights and universalism that characterized the Nordic agencies.

[9] Interview with World Bank policy expert on social protection, 7 December 2015.

[10] These issues arose at the previous conference, in 2004, when Brazilian scholars challenged the hard conditionality and inattention to rights in the Mexican model (Peck and Theodore 2015), but the Brazilian critics did not have the institutional backing of an international organization.

[11] Interview, 20 June 2015.

[12] Interview, 3 June 2015.

DFID officials saw themselves as pragmatic, approaching things 'in contextual terms, what works and is required in different contexts',[13] a pragmatism typical of British policy and ideological traditions.

DFID sought to displace the indirect influence that the Bank exerted in SSA countries, deploying consultants who favoured bolder SCT programmes (Devereux and Sabates-Wheeler 2004), funding annual training programmes in Mombasa and elsewhere, and seeking a leading role for its own or like-minded personnel on the social protection sector working or advisory groups formed by international organizations to 'harmonize' their approaches and 'advise' national governments. DFID's approach to promoting social protection in SSA would be strongly informed by its institutional practices and the 'zeal' of the Social Protection Team Leader, as well as its wider ideological positionality. Faced with an often sceptical response from government officials, DFID advisors were able to respond rapidly to requests for financial and technical assistance in considering and developing social protection policies (e.g. fiduciary risk assessments, pilot evaluations), proving more nimble than the World Bank, with its more cumbersome internal workings (Hickey et al. 2009).

4. The Governmentality of Social Protection: From 'Rendering Technical' to 'Working Politically'

Despite the contestation within and especially between international organizations over the purpose and form of SCTs, most of the international organizations utilized a discourse that rendered the adoption of SCTs as a purely *technical* process. In their interactions with national governments in SSA, international organizations generally presented arguments in favour of SCTs as technically efficient ways of achieving technical goals such as poverty reduction, downplaying the political choices that had to be made. In the third dimension of her approach, Li draws on Foucauldian studies of governmentality to understand 'the ways in which rule is actually accomplished'. This involves examining the way that powerful transnational actors 'render technical' the intractable challenges of poverty and inequality in order to sustain a particular world order. As Li writes: 'To render a set of processes technical and improvable an arena of intervention must be bounded, mapped, characterised and documented; the relevant forces and relations must be identified; and a

[13] Ibid.

narrative must be devised connecting the proposed intervention with the problem it will solve' (Li 2007: 126).

The technical approach to SCTs is evident for most international organizations. For the ILO: 'The lack of access to social protection constitutes a major obstacle to economic and social development. Inadequate or absent social protection coverage is associated with high and persistent levels of poverty and economic insecurity, growing levels of inequality, insufficient investments in human capital and human capabilities, and weak aggregate demand in a time of recession and slow growth' (ILO 2014: xix). For the World Bank, the 'gold standard experimental design' of the Mexican CCT model served to validate it, and to 'bullet proof' it from 'political interference'; 'what often are inescapably political decisions about the design and financing of antipoverty interventions' were elevated into 'the heady heights of scientific progress' (Peck and Theodore 2015: 93–5). Peck and Theodore note that 'a deepening reliance on technocratic forms of policy development and delivery is a widely observed feature of late-neoliberalism' (ibid.: 172), but with respect to SCTs even many of the Bank's critics couched their counter-arguments in technical terms. Hanlon et al., for example, chose to conclude that SCTs were affordable, that recipients did not 'waste' the money, that SCTs were 'an efficient way to directly reduce poverty, and they have the potential to prevent future poverty by facilitating economic growth and promoting human development' (2010: 2). HelpAge International emphasized strongly the rights of elderly people on its website and in general strategic documents (e.g. HelpAge 2011), but when it promoted SCTs within SSA it emphasized their efficiency in terms of mitigating poverty among the elderly, with hardly a reference to rights (see, e.g., Knox-Vydmanov and Galvani 2016, on Malawi).

Crucial to their projects of specifying and solving 'problems' was the deployment of 'expertise' and the construction of 'epistemic communities'. 'Knowledge networks and epistemic communities give discursive, intellectual, and scientific structure to the global agora', argues Stone (2008: 32); 'they provide scholarly argumentation and scientific justification for "evidence-based" policy formulation'. An important role is played here by 'policy entrepreneurs' who 'use their intellectual authority or market expertise to reinforce and legitimate certain forms of policy or normative standards as "best practice"' (Stone 2012: 494). Policy entrepreneurs and international organizations generally did not invent challenges: poverty, drought, AIDS-mortality, and so on were real. But they did serve to shape how these challenges were packaged as problems, and more specifically as problems that needed to be prioritized, and this prepared the ground for the advocacy of specific suggestions.

In terms of problem-framing, the World Bank funded a series of national-level risk and vulnerability assessments from the early 2000s, in part to help provide a diagnostic basis for its risk-based approach to social protection (Kozel, Fallavier, and Badiani 2008). UNICEF helped to specify the problem of 'orphans and vulnerable children' (OVC), which included those 'single-orphans' who had only lost one parent, regardless of the presence of other kin (Green 2011: 33–58). In SSA, the first SCT policy entrepreneur was probably German development consultant Bernd Schubert, whose experience with a small SCT in Mozambique in the early 1990s was followed by pioneering work in crafting the Kalomo SCT pilot project in Zambia and then further initiatives in Malawi and elsewhere (von Gliszczynski 2015: 28–30). Schubert was deployed variously by GTZ, DFID, and UNICEF. Other agencies deployed their own 'experts'. The World Bank used extensively an ex-staffer from Ecuador, Francisco Ayala, who established his own consulting firm to provide technical assistance on the design and implementation of SCT programmes, with a particular focus on CCTs. DFID (and other agencies such as UNICEF) later countered through using Michael Samson, based in Cape Town, who emphasized a more rights-based and welfarist approach to social protection.[14] Employed by different development agencies to design and help implement schemes that reflected their ideological and programmatic preferences, these and other policy entrepreneurs played important roles in determining the specific form that SCTs actually took on the ground in SSA.

Ferguson (2015) argues strongly that SCTs were fundamentally subversive of the development agenda, by shifting attention from issues of production (and, especially, work) to issues of distribution. Ferguson's point is important because many of the actors in struggles over SCTs did *not* acknowledge this in the discourses they employed to specify and solve problems. In employing developmentalist discourses, international organizations tended to reinforce technical rather than political understandings of the problem. It is not clear that this was politically effective in the SSA countries where they were promoting SCTs. As the country case studies in this volume show, political elites

[14] Interview with ex-DFID policy leader on social protection, 30 June 2015. We discuss these particular policy entrepreneurs not to suggest that they were the only ones who played important roles in shaping which policy ideas travelled to SSA, but to illustrate and extend the broader point that certain individuals were crucial not only to the wars of position within and between international organizations (Deacon (2013), but also to the process of rendering political choices as technical ones at the country level.

in SSA tended to view SCTs through conservative lenses. For political elites across much of SSA, poverty was a moral issue, rooted in the irresponsibility of individual poor people, not primarily a *social* issue. As almost all international organizations recognized, framing SCTs in terms of rights was especially likely to stiffen opposition.[15]

DFID was the first international organization to recognize that the promotion of SCTs was a political challenge and to adapt its strategy accordingly. DFID's initial approach to promoting social protection and SCTs in SSA involved largely standard forms of technical and financial assistance, including a concerted effort to develop a stronger evidence base around social protection and pilot different modes of operationalizing cash transfers. However, where elite resistance was encountered, DFID adapted its approach to incorporate the new 'thinking and working politically' agenda (Dasandi et al. 2016). DFID had been an early adopter of this new approach, and by the mid-2000s had moved from using country-level political economy analysis to inform programming and policy engagement to commissioning studies of particular policy sectors (DFID 2009). This included at least three studies of the political barriers and opportunities associated with promoting social protection in SSA (including Barrientos et al. 2005, on Zambia, a confidential study on Uganda, and a multi-country analysis by Hickey et al. 2009). This led DFID staff to work on building broader 'coalitions' in support of SCTs (see Bukenya and Hickey on Uganda (Chapter 8) and Pruce and Hickey on Zambia (Chapter 7); also Kabandula and Seekings 2016; Siachiwena 2016). Tens of millions of pounds were spent on 'policy engagement projects' aimed at influencing African governments to adopt social protection.[16] Senior bureaucrats and politicians were sent on study tours to witness the benefits of successful cash transfer projects in a range of Latin American and African countries. Pilot projects that were launched to help generate country-specific evidence on the effectiveness of cash transfers started to generate their own political dynamics, leading citizens and MPs to lobby their governments to extend cash transfer programmes. DFID money has also funded media campaigns to help spread awareness of cash transfers and their effectiveness, and has been increasingly willing to do so during key political moments. For example, whereas

[15] National governments (and especially ministers of finance) were also concerned with the costs of social protection programmes (see Seekings 2017b). DFID sponsored some research into the affordability of programmes, including in Tanzania and Zambia.

[16] One example is the Expanding Social Protection programme in Uganda, which spent over £54 million between 2009 and 2015 to try to increase the level of political commitment to social protection in Uganda and the capacity of the Ugandan government to deliver a coherent social protection strategy (https://devtracker.dfid.gov.uk/projects/GB-1-204861).

DFID staff in Zambia sought to hold back the roll-out of a pilot programme for fear of it being used as a form of vote-buying in relation to the 2011 elections, their counterparts in Uganda used the build-up to the 2016 elections to politicize further the case for cash transfers in order to secure further financial support from government for SCTs (see Bukenya and Hickey, Chapter 8 of this volume).

This contrasted markedly with the World Bank's country-level approach to policy engagement; as one World Bank policy expert on social protection noted, when it comes to 'influencing, we don't do the DFID thing' (Interview, 7 December 2015). The approach also created some disquiet within DFID, in part as there was a sense that the advocacy effort was running ahead of the evidence base regarding the effectiveness and affordability of cash transfers in SSA. As one DFID team member admits, 'We were in advocacy mode, we over-egged the growth aspect if we're honest' (Interview, 3 June 2015). Another was concerned that: 'We were handing very difficult problems to our partners, with missionary zeal, and it wasn't very savvy. That is an NGO's job not a donor's job, not really for the UK to throw its weight around in other countries in that way' (Interview with Social Protection Team member, 15 June 2015). This raises important concerns regarding issues of sovereignty and who controls the policy agenda in SSA, despite donor rhetoric around 'ownership' (Whitfield 2009).

DFID tended to understand national-level political dynamics in terms of political disagreements between the 'finance ministry' and 'civil society' tendencies identified by Kanbur (2001).[17] In countries such as Zambia and Uganda in the mid-2000s, one group of government officials was more closely aligned with the policy preferences of the World Bank and other IFIs, whilst a separate group shared many of the preferences of European and UN development agencies. As we have seen above, however, the IFIs were not opposed to SCTs, and at least in the 2010s advocated increased expenditures on them, but they preferred expenditure on children and workfare over other forms of SCT. Also, as we have seen above, the European and UN development agencies did not share exactly the same approaches to SCTs. The result was that each agency sought to mobilize and strengthen its own allies at the national level. The ILO, for example, had much stronger links with ministries

[17] The finance ministry tendency includes not only ministries of finance, but also of trade and business, central banks, many officials within IFIs, and certain civil society organizations, including think tanks. The civil society tendency, meanwhile, is usually constructed of social sector ministries, UN and European aid agencies, and civil society organizations (Kanbur 2001).

of labour (and a specific set of NGOs) than with ministries responsible for 'social development' (and NGOs concerned with this). In relation to struggles over social protection from the early 2000s, DFID generally sought to strengthen specific 'civil society' tendencies at the national level in SSA. Wars of position at the national level were thus shaped by the wars of position at the international level.

The political dynamics over SCTs within SSA countries could not be reduced, however, to disagreements between officials aligned to either the World Bank or one or other of the European and UN agencies. In some countries, political elites were sceptical of SCTs in part on the conservative grounds that SCTs undermined patriarchal family relations and social relationships within communities, eroded the work ethic, and created 'dependency' on the state. By providing 'something for nothing', SCTs violated conservative norms of who deserved what, how, and why (Kalebe-Nyamongo and Marquette 2014; Ferguson 2015; Seekings 2017a). DFID and other agencies sought to challenge these beliefs on largely technical grounds, commissioning studies to demonstrate that SCTs had productive (or developmental) as well as protective benefits. This kind of evidence made sense in a war of position against neoliberal critics, but was largely tangential to more conservative anxieties. DFID and other agencies were generally aware that it was not a good idea to refer to individual social and economic rights in their interactions with national policy-makers, but they lacked a good understanding of how to engage with conservative policy-makers. This helps to explain the narrow and parsimonious form that SCTs have so far taken across much of the continent.

5. Conclusion

The rise of SCTs as a global public policy since the turn of the millennium, and their subsequent (slow) roll-out in SSA, has been shaped by the convergence of different aspects of political economy, ideas, and governmentality, as worked through the aid world and the role of aid agencies in promoting development as specific forms of 'institutional practice'.[18] At both the international and national levels, international agencies fought wars of position with rivals and sceptics. They tended to employ technocratic discourses, but

[18] Note that the slow rate of progress in most countries also needs to be understood in relation to the contraction of fiscal space that most low- and middle-income countries faced as a result of the global financial crisis of 2007 (ILO 2014).

the politics was never far below the surface; 'Global poverty management' is not as technocratic and depoliticized a process as some critics tend to suggest (e.g. Li 2007; Peck 2011). Cash transfers have certainly been presented as the 'practically feasible solution' to an 'ideologically framed consensus' regarding poverty alleviation, but what we found striking with the case of DFID is rather the highly and deliberately politicized approach that this has sometimes involved.

The process through which the global SCT agenda has been created by international organizations with specific interests, practices, and ideas has led to the production of 'a fragmented and incomplete universalism' (Von Gliszczynski and Leisering 2016: 325) on the ground in SSA. This incompleteness includes the absence of a focus on forms of social protection that go beyond the ameliorative to embrace more transformative forms of social protection (e.g. Devereux and Sabates-Wheeler 2004). In one sense, this fits with the critique that global policy transfer today involves promoting technical and ameliorative responses to the highly political challenges of poverty and inequality in order to sustain a particular world order (Li 2007; Peck 2011). The result is a strategy for promoting poverty reduction that responds to failures in market access and poor governance rather than an entirely new, southern-based model of welfare capitalism (as Hanlon et al. (2010) suggest).

However, if one takes more seriously the role of domestic elites and their ideas in transnational processes of policy transfer, as we do within this volume, there is little evidence to suggest that a more radical approach would have been welcomed by political or bureaucratic elites on the continent, whose ideological perspectives are arguably more closely attuned to liberal and conservative forms of social protection, involving minimal transfers to labour-incapacitated or otherwise highly deserving individuals (Seekings 2017a), than to more radical forms of social protection (Hickey 2014). African elites have for around a century been receptive to certain liberal ideas around social assistance, but generally to a parsimonious extent. A 'pauperist' model of welfare reform took hold in some parts of SSA in the mid-twentieth century, and expanded (evolving into a more citizenship-based model) in the (unevenly) democratized polities of late twentieth- and early twenty-first-century SSA. This was because some of the relevant ideas and models articulated or promoted by outsiders resonated with local colonial and post-colonial elites in the face of changing social and economic conditions, which are of crucial importance. Foreign models were therefore only embraced and adapted where they were aligned with the underlying normative worldview of local elites (Seekings 2016)—and, as we show elsewhere in this collection, their political interests. The strongest examples of elite commitment to social protection have little to do with an alignment with either the World Bank's residualist position or the welfarist rights-based approach of the UN (and Nordic agencies) or DFID's poverty agenda, but reflect rather the productivist ideology that has become widespread across SSA, particularly amongst governments with more developmentalist ambitions (see Lavers on Ethiopia and Rwanda, Chapters 3 and 4 of this volume).[19]

However, there has arguably been more space for promoting an approach that reflects the wider lessons from the redistributive benefits of progressive fiscal policy in Latin America (Melo et al. 2014) rather than the narrow version cherry-picked by the World Bank (Peck and Theodore 2015). Cast within the broader goal of securing a stronger fiscal contract between states and citizens (Teichman 2008), this would have involved adopting a more joined-up approach to promoting improved levels of revenue generation and more progressive forms of taxation and government capacity-building, alongside a more ambitious focus on employment as well as social transfers. Promoting a narrow and limited focus on cash transfers risks problems of convergence in the realm of politics as well as undermining developmental progress, whereby, 'in the absence of a redistributive societal compromise involving both increased taxation and social spending, progress on the social policy front (particularly increased financial commitment) raises the spectre of a descent into populism unless increased financial resources are forthcoming' (Teichman 2008: 455).

This scenario already seems to be unfolding in countries such as Uganda and Zambia, where cash transfers are converging with clientelistic and populist forms of politics. This latest phase of transnational–national negotiations over the form that social protection should take in SSA remains a work in progress, and different socio-political implications may emerge from the move to adopt social cash transfers if they start to become a more institutionalized part of state–society relations (Ferguson 2015). For now, however, the narrowness of the instruments being used, the parsimonious level of transfers involved, and the ideational convergence around a thinly redistributive form of liberalism all suggest that any broader gains for citizenship and the social contract in SSA may be a long time coming.

[19] In many cases, national elites have shared the concerns of the World Bank over possible 'dependency' on 'handouts'.

References

Barrientos, A., S. Hickey, N. Simutanyi, and D. Wood (2005). *Final Report of Study on Drivers of Change for a National Social Protection Scheme in Zambia*. Brighton: IDS.

Bastiagli, F. et al. (2016). *Cash Transfers: What Does the Evidence Say?* ODI: London.

Cichon, M. (2013). The social protection floors recommendation, 2012 (No. 202): can a six-page document change the course of social history? *International Social Security Review*, 66(3–4), 21–43.

Cowen, M. and R. Shenton (1996). *Doctrines of Development*. London: Routledge.

Craig, D. and D. Porter (2006). *Development Beyond Neoliberalism?* London: Routledge.

Dasandi, N., H. Marquette, and M. Robinson (2016). Thinking and working politically. Research Paper No. 37. Birmingham: DLP.

Deacon, B. (2007). *Global Social Policy and Governance*. London; Thousand Oaks, CA; and New Delhi: SAGE.

Deacon, B. (2013). *Global Social Policy in the Making*. Bristol: Policy Press.

de Haan, Arjan (2014). The rise of social protection in development. *European Journal of Development Research*, 26, 311–21.

Devereux, S. and R. Sabates-Wheeler (2004). Transformative social protection. IDS Working Paper 232. Brighton: Institute of Development Studies.

DFID (2005). Social transfers and chronic poverty. A DFID Practice Paper. London: DFID.

DFID. (2009). How to note: lessons learned—planning and undertaking a Drivers of Change study. A DFID practice paper. London: DFID.

Esping-Andersen, G. (1990). *The Three Worlds of Welfare Capitalism*. Cambridge: Polity Press.

Ferguson, J. (2015). *Give a Man a Fish: Reflections on the New Politics of Distribution*. Raleigh, NC: Duke University Press.

Fiszbein, A. and N. Schady (2009). *Conditional Cash Transfers: Reducing Present and Future Poverty*, Policy Research Report. Washington DC: World Bank.

Garcia, M. and C.M.T. Moore (2012). *The Cash Dividend*. Washington DC: World Bank.

Grebe, E. (2015). The evolution of social protection policy in Ghana's Fourth Republic. CSSR Working Paper 360. Cape Town: University of Cape Town.

Grebe, E. and J.B. Mubiru (2014). The politics of welfare policy-making and cash transfers in Uganda. CSSR Working Paper 353. Cape Town: Centre for Social Science Research, University of Cape Town.

Green, M. (2011). Calculating compassion. In D. Mosse (Ed.), *Adventures in Aidland*. London: Berghahn.

Hall, P.A. (1993). Policy paradigms, social learning, and the state: the case of economic policy-making in Britain. *Comparative Politics*, 25(3), 275–96.

Hanlon, J., A. Barrientos, and D. Hulme (2010). *Just Give Money to the Poor*. Sterling, VA: Kumarian.

Hayami, Y. (2003). From the Washington Consensus to the post-Washington Consensus: Retrospect and prospect. *Asian Development Review*, 20(2), 40–65.

HelpAge (2011). The right to social security in old age. Briefing. London: HelpAge International.

Hickey, S. (2014). Relocating social protection within a radical project of social justice. *European Journal of Development Research*, 26(3), 322–37.

Hickey, S. and J. Seekings (2017). The global politics of social protection. UNU-WIDER Working Paper 2017/115. Helsinki: UNU-WIDER.

Hickey, S., with R. Sabates Wheeler, G. Guenther, and I. Macauslan (2009). Promoting SP & ST: DFID and the politics of influencing. DFID Working Paper no 32. London: DFID.

Holzmann, R. (Ed.) (2008). *Social Protection and Labour at the World Bank, 2000–2008*. Washington DC: World Bank.

Hulme, D. (2010). *Global Poverty*. London: Routledge.

ILO (2014). *World Social Protection Report 2014/15*. Geneva: ILO.

ILO and IMF (2012). Towards effective and fiscally sustainable Social Protection Floors. Preliminary report prepared for the meeting of the G20 Labour and Employment Ministers in Guadalajara, Mexico, 17–18 May. Geneva and Washington DC: ILO and IMF.

Kabandula, A. and J. Seekings (2016). Donor influence, the Minister of Finance and welfare policy reform in Zambia, 2003–11. CSSR Working Paper 395. Cape Town: Centre for Social Science Research, University of Cape Town.

Kakwani, Nanak and Kalanidhi Subbarao (2005). *Aging and Poverty in Africa and the Role of Social Pensions*. Washington DC: World Bank.

Kalebe-Nyamongo, Chipiliro and Heather Marquette (2014). Elite attitudes towards cash transfers and the poor in Malawi. DLP Research Paper 30. Birmingham: Developmental Leadership Programme, University of Birmingham.

Kanbur, R. (2001). Economic policy, distribution and poverty. *World Development*, 29(6), 1083–94.

Knox-Vydmanov, C. and F. Galvani (2016). *Realising Income Security in Old Age*. Lilongwe: Ministry of Gender, Children, Disability and Social Welfare; and London: Help Age International.

Kozel, V., P. Fallavier, and R. Badiani (2008). Risk and vulnerability analysis in World Bank Analytic Work FY2000-FY2007. Social Protection Discussion Paper Series No. 0812. Washington DC: World Bank.

Leite, I.C., M. Pomeroy, and B. Suyama (2015). 'Brazilian south–south development cooperation. *Journal of International Development*, 27(8), 1446–61.

Leutelt, M. (2012). HelpAge's involvement in spreading social pensions in the global South: slow and steady wins the race? FLOOR Working Paper No. 16. Bielefeld: University of Bielefeld.

Li, T.M. (2007). *The Will to Improve: Governmentality, Development and the Practice of Politics*. Durham, NC and London: Duke University Press.

Melo, M.A., A. Barrientos, and A.C. Coelho (2014). Taxation, redistribution and the social contract in Brazil. IRIBA Working Paper No.11. Manchester: IRIBA.

Mosse, D. (2005). *Cultivating Development*. Chicago, IL: University of Chicago Press.

Pal, K., C. Behrendt, F. Leger, M. Cichon, and K. Hagemejer (2005). Can low-income countries afford basic social security? Issues in Social Protection Discussion Paper 13. Geneva: ILO.

Peck, J. (2011). Global policy models. *Globalizing Poverty Management Geography Compass*, 5(4), 165–81.

Peck, J. and N. Theodore (2010). Mobilizing policy: models, methods, and mutations. *Geoforum*, 41, 169–74.

Peck, J. and N. Theodore (2015). *Fast Policy: Experimental Statecraft at the Thresholds of Neoliberalism*. Minneapolis, MN: University of Minnesota Press.

Polanyi, K. (1944). *The Great Transformation*. New York: Farrar & Rinehart.

Schmidt, V.A. (2008). Discursive institutionalism: the explanatory power of ideas and discourse. *Annual Review of Political Science*, 11(1), 303–26.

Seekings, J. (2007). 'Not a single white person should be allowed to go under': Swartgevaar and the origins of South Africa's welfare state, 1924–1929. *Journal of African History*, 48(3), 375–94.

Seekings, J. (2011). British colonial policy, local politics and the origins of the Mauritian welfare state, 1936–1950. *Journal of African History*, 52, 157–77.

Seekings, J. (2013). The Beveridge Report, the Colonial Office and welfare reform in British colonies. Unpublished paper.

Seekings, J. (2016). Policy diffusion and the enduring distinctiveness of African welfare regimes. Paper presented at UNU-WIDER Symposium Economics and Politics of Taxation and Social Protection, Mexico City, February.

Seekings, J. (2017a). Ideologies of welfare in Africa. Paper presented at RC21 conference Dimensions of Inequality: Causes, Consequences, and Policy Responses, University of North Carolina, Chapel Hill, 22–5 June.

Seekings, J. (2017b). Affordability and the political economy of social protection in contemporary Africa. *UNU-WIDER Working Paper* 2017/43. Helsinki: UNU-WIDER.

Siachiwena, H. (2016). Social protection policy reform in Zambia during the Sata presidency, 2011–2014. CSSR Working Paper 377. Cape Town: Centre for Social Science Research, University of Cape Town.

Stone, D. (2012). Transfer and translation of policy. *Policy Studies*, 33(6), 483–99.

Sugiyama, N.B. (2011). The diffusion of Conditional Cash Transfer programs in the Americas. *Global Social Policy*, 11(2–3), 250–78.

Teichman, J. (2008). Redistributive conflict and social policy in Latin America. *World Development*, 36(3), 446–60.

Voipio, T. (2007). Social protection for poverty reduction: the OECD/DAC/POVNET view. *IDS-Bulletin*, 38(3).

Von Gliszczynski, M. (2015). *Cash Transfers and Basic Social Protection: Towards a Development Revolution?* Basingstoke and New York: Palgrave Macmillan.

Von Gliszczynski, M. and L. Leisering (2016). Constructing new global models of social security. *Journal of Social Policy*, 45(2), 325–43.

Wanyama, F. and A. McCord (2017). The politics of scaling up social protection in Kenya. UNU-WIDER Working Paper 2017/114. Helsinki: UNU-WIDER.

Whitfield, L. (2009). *The Politics of Aid: African Strategies for Dealing with Donors.* Oxford: Oxford University Press.

World Bank (1990). *World Development Report 1990.* Washington DC: World Bank.

World Bank (2012a). *World Bank Social Protection and Labor Strategy 2012–2022.* Washington DC: World Bank.

World Bank (2012b). *Managing Risk, Promoting Growth: Developing Systems for Social Protection in Africa: World Bank's Africa Social Protection Strategy 2012–2022.* Washington DC: World Bank.

World Bank (2014). *State of Social Safety Nets 2014.* Washington DC: World Bank.

Index

For the benefit of digital users, indexed terms that span two pages (e.g., 52–53) may, on occasion, appear on only one of those pages.

The manufacturer's authorised representative in the EU for product safety is Oxford University Press España S.A. of el Parque Empresarial San Fernando de Henares, Avenida de Castilla, 2 – 28830 Madrid (www.oup.es/en or product.safety@oup.com). OUP España S.A. also acts as importer into Spain of products made by the manufacturer.

www.ingramcontent.com/pod-product-compliance
Lightning Source LLC
LaVergne TN
LVHW011916200926
848484LV00002B/638

9780198850342